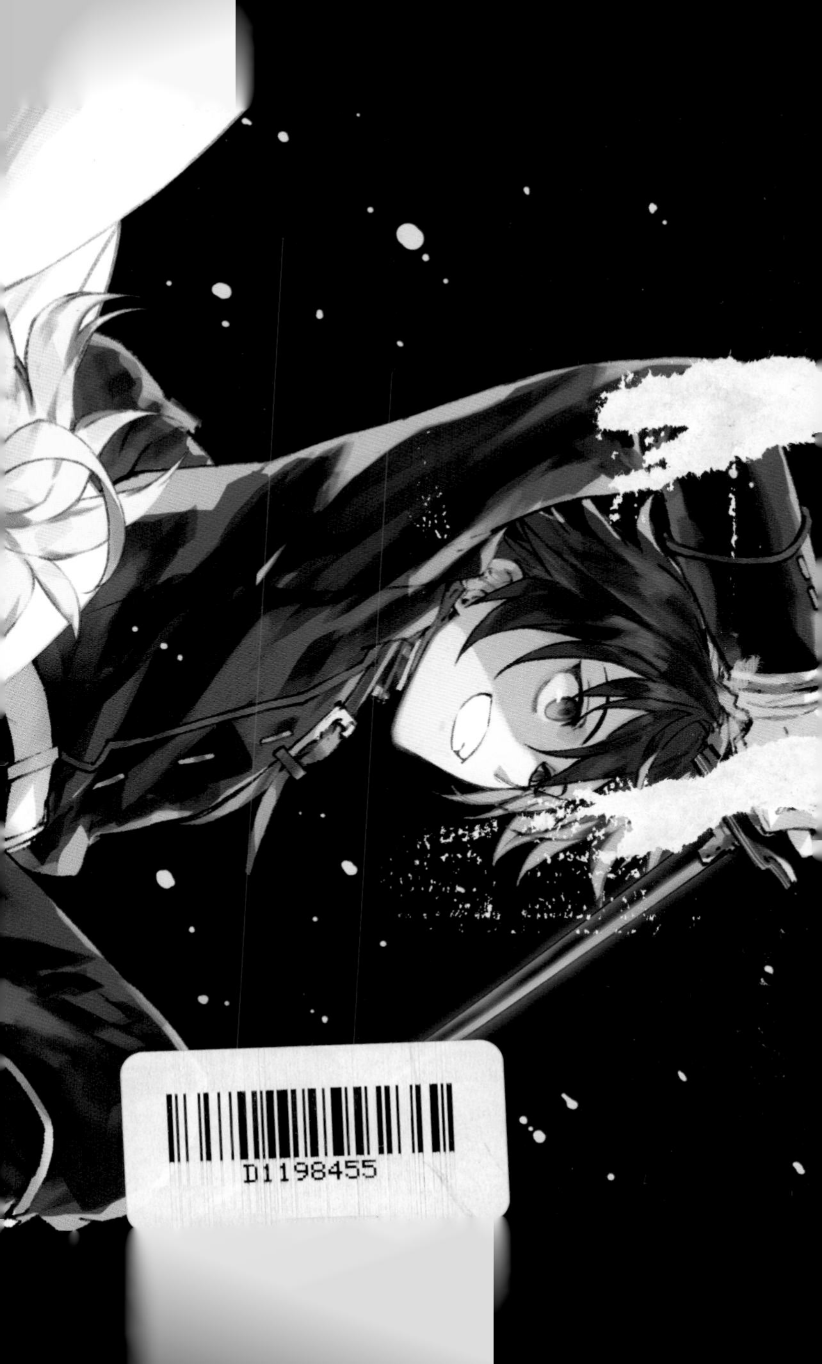

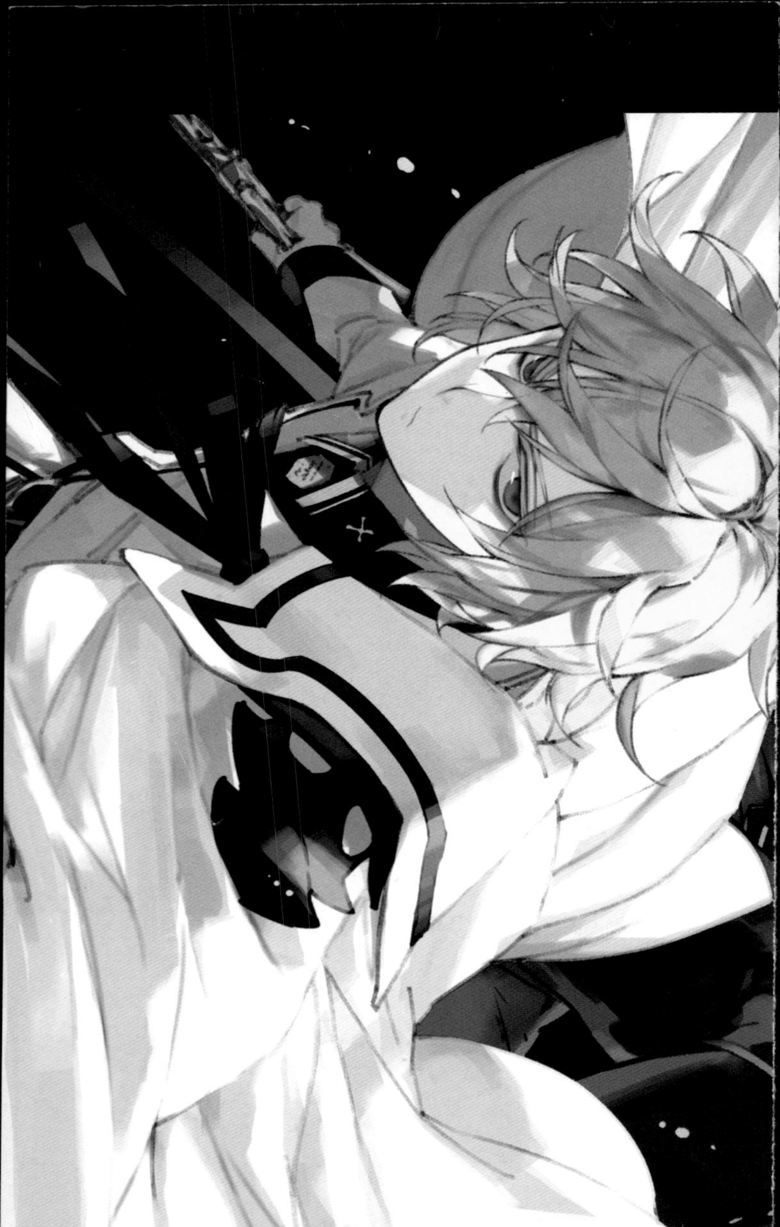

Seraph of the End

VAMPIRE REIGN

19

STORY BY **Takaya Kagami**

ART BY **Yamato Yamamoto**

STORYBOARDS BY **Daisuke Furuya**

CHARACTERS

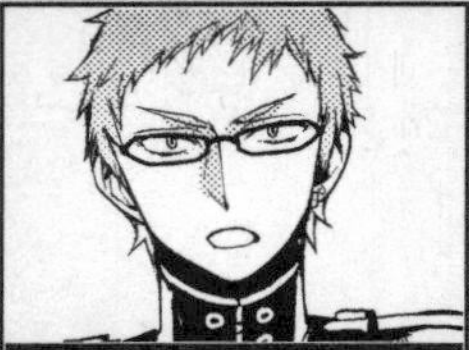

SHIHO KIMIZUKI

Yuichiro's friend. Smart but abrasive. His Cursed Gear is Kiseki-o, twin blades.

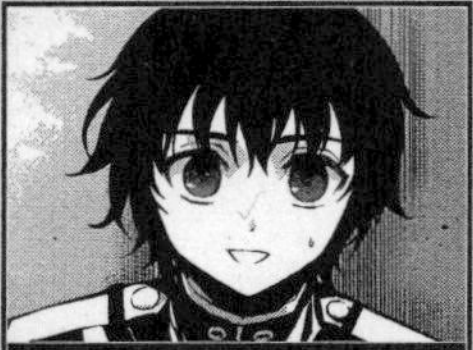

YOICHI SAOTOME

Yuichiro's friend. His sister was killed by a vampire. His Cursed Gear is Gekkouin, a bow.

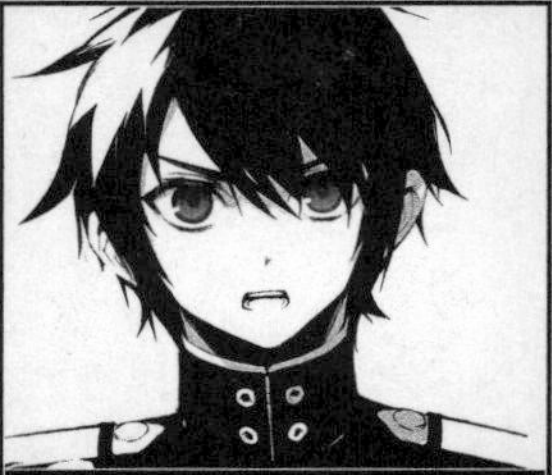

YUICHIRO HYAKUYA

A boy who escaped from the vampire capital, he has both great kindness and a great desire for revenge. Lone wolf. His Cursed Gear is Asuramaru, a katana.

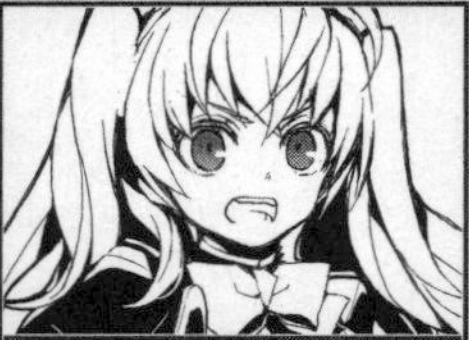

MITSUBA SANGU

An elite soldier who has been part of the Moon Demon Company since age 13. Bossy. Her Cursed Gear is Tenjiryu, a giant axe.

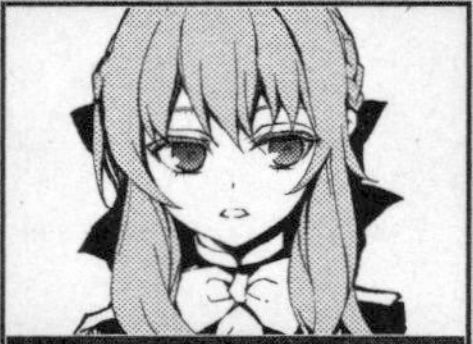

SHINOA HIRAGI

Guren's subordinate and Yuichiro's surveillance officer. Member of the illustrious Hiragi family. Her Cursed Gear is Shikama Doji, a scythe.

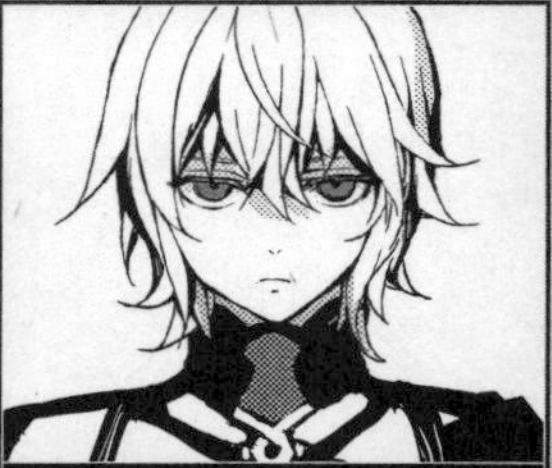

MIKAELA HYAKUYA

Yuichiro's best friend. He was supposedly killed but has come back to life as a vampire. Currently working with Shinoa Squad.

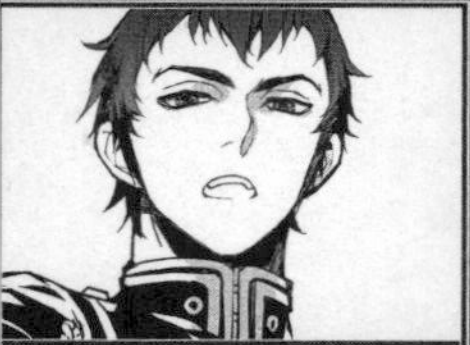

KURETO HIRAGI

A Lieutenant General in the Demon Army. Heir apparent to the Hiragi family, he is cold, cruel and ruthless.

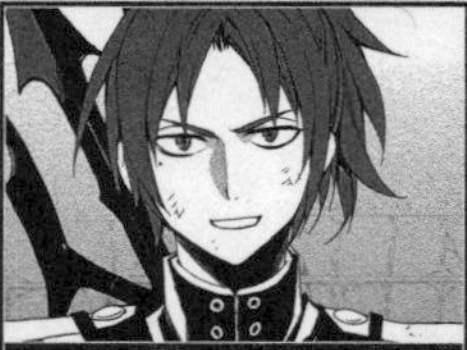

MAKOTO NARUMI

Former leader of Narumi Squad. After his entire squad died during the battle of Nagoya, he deserted the Demon Army with Shinoa Squad.

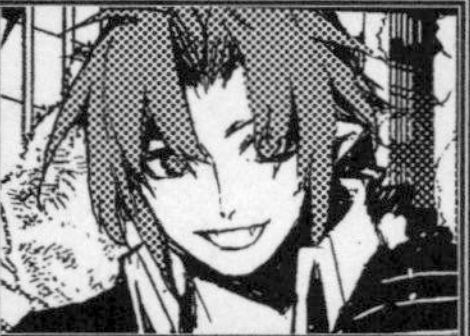

CROWLEY EUSFORD

A Thirteenth Progenitor vampire. Part of Ferid's faction.

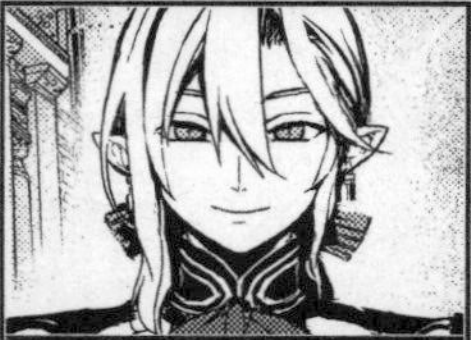

FERID BATHORY

A Seventh Progenitor vampire, he killed Mikaela.

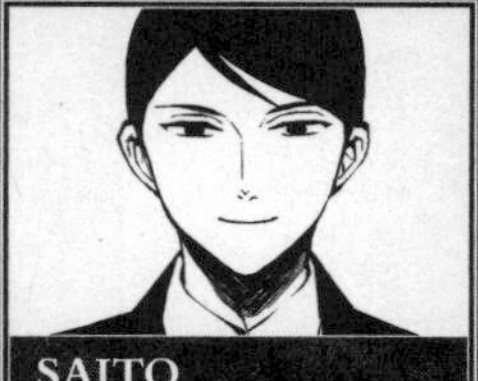

SAITO

A mysterious man somehow connected with the Hyakuya Sect. He was once a Second Progenitor vampire.

URD GEALES

Second Progenitor and ruler over the parts of Europe that used to be Russia.

KRUL TEPES

Third Progenitor and Queen of the Vampires. She is currently being held prisoner by Urd Geales.

GUREN ICHINOSE

Lt. Colonel of the Moon Demon Company. He recruited Yuichiro into the Demon Army. During the battle in Nagoya, he began acting strangely... His Cursed Gear is Mahiru-no-yo, a katana.

SHIKAMA DOJI

The being that inhabits Shinoa's scythe. He's actually the long-missing First Progenitor of the vampires.

ASHURAMARU

The demon that possesses Yuichiro's sword. A long time ago, he was a human boy named Ashera.

SHINYA HIRAGI

A Major General and adoptee into the Hiragi Family. He was Mahiru Hiragi's fiancé.

STORY

A mysterious virus decimates the human population, and vampires claim dominion over the world. Yuichiro and his adopted family of orphans are kept as vampire fodder in an underground city until the day Mikaela, Yuichiro's best friend, plots an ill-fated escape for the orphans. Only Yuichiro survives and reaches the surface.

Four years later, Yuichiro enters into the Moon Demon Company, a Vampire Extermination Unit in the Japanese Imperial Demon Army, to enact his revenge. There he gains Asuramaru, a demon-possessed weapon capable of killing vampires, and a squad of trusted friends—Shinoa, Yoichi, Kimizuki and Mitsuba.

In his battles against the vampires, Yuichiro discovers that not only is Mikaela alive, but he also has been turned into a vampire. After misunderstandings and near-misses, Yuichiro and Mikaela finally rejoin each other in Nagoya.

After the chaos and confusion of the Seraph of the End experiment and Guren's betrayal in Nagoya, Shinoa Squad deserts the Demon Army and accompanies Ferid to Osaka. There, Ferid and Krul are sentenced to exposure torture by Second Progenitor Urd Geales.

Meanwhile, Kureto carries out a successful coup d'état, taking control of the Demon Army from his father, Tenri. However, the godlike being Shikama Doji, which had been possessing Tenri, possesses him...

Back in Osaka, Shikama Doji invades Shinoa's heart and begins turning her into a vampire. What is it that he's plotting...?

Seraph of the End
— VAMPIRE REIGN —

19

CONTENTS

Chapter 75
Secret Distance

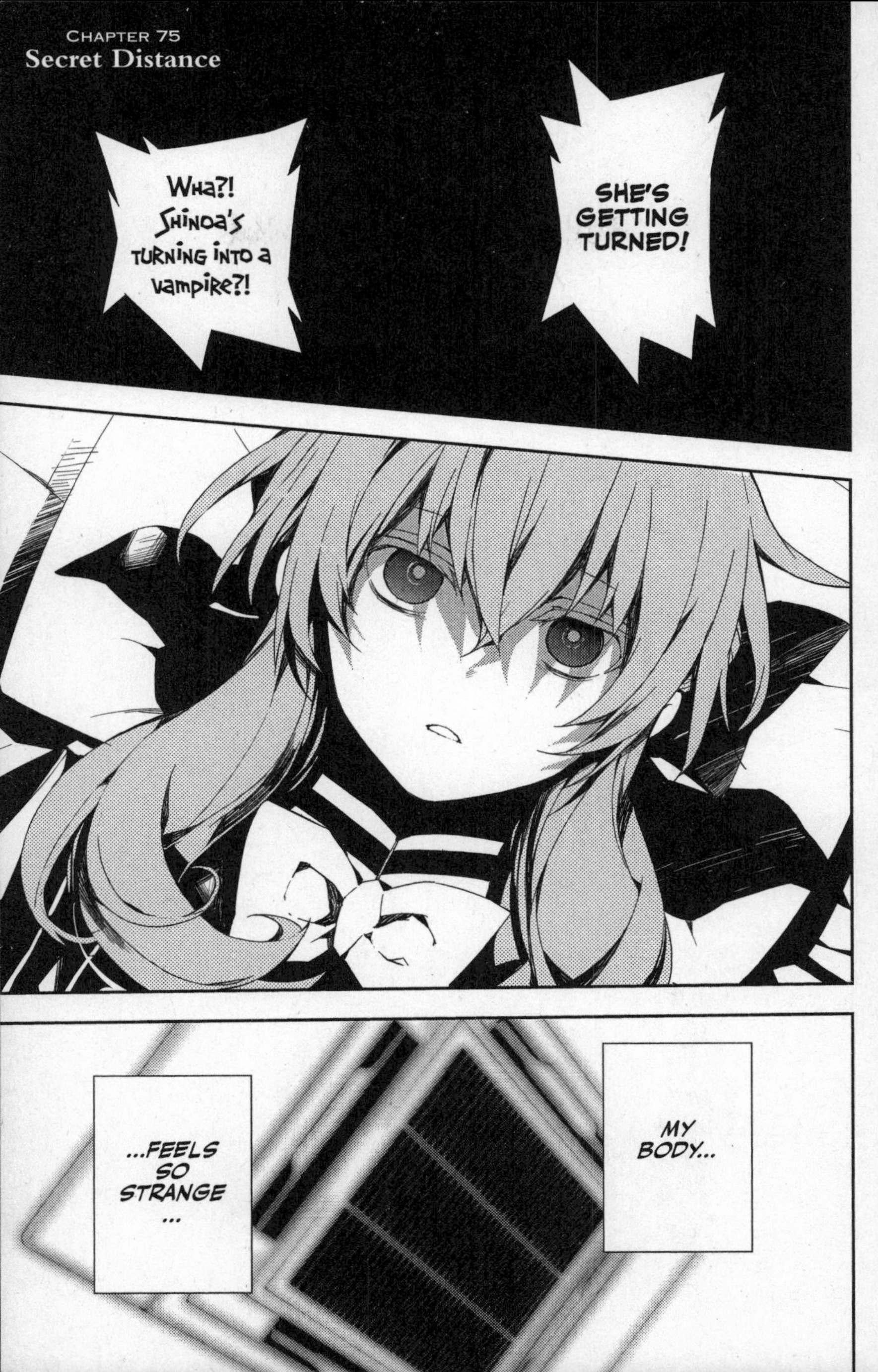
SHE'S GETTING TURNED!
Wha?! Shinoa's turning into a vampire?!
MY BODY...
...FEELS SO STRANGE ...

CHAPTER 75 Secret Distance

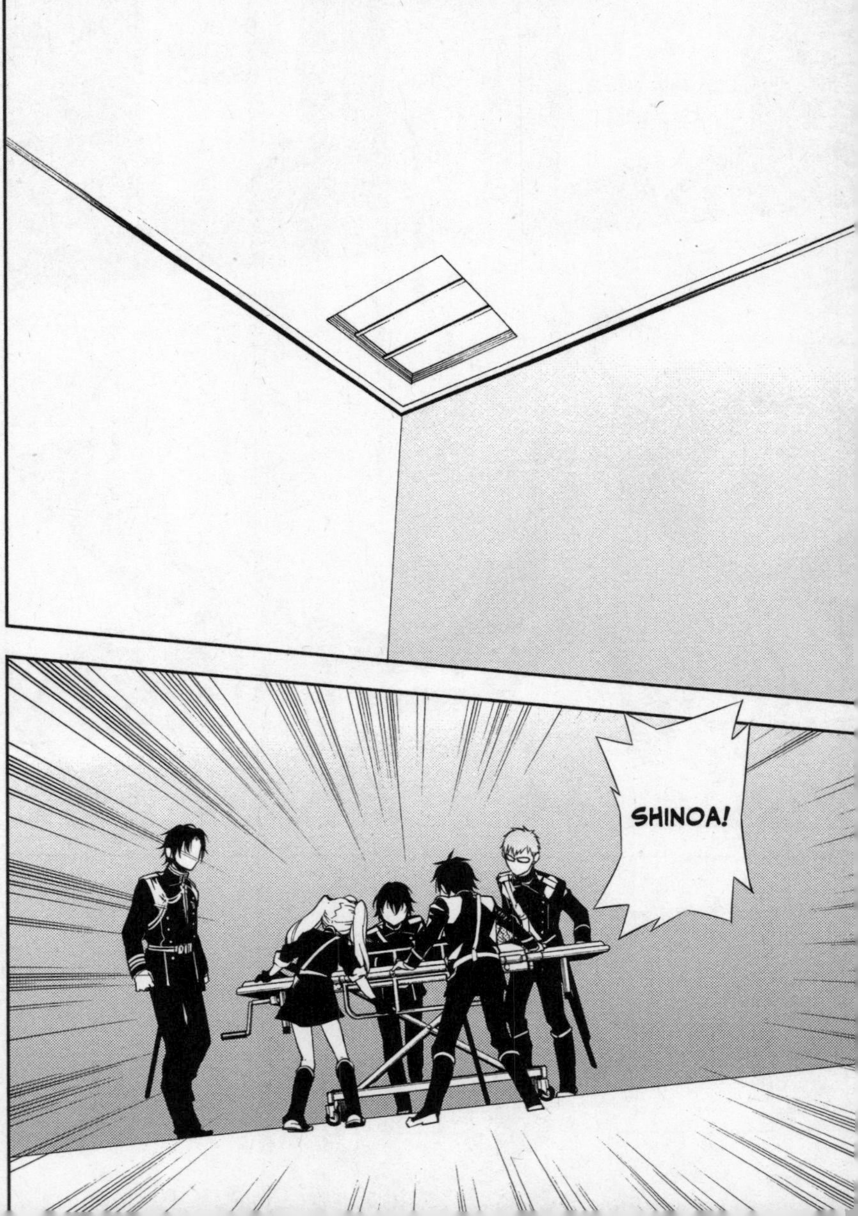
SHINOA!

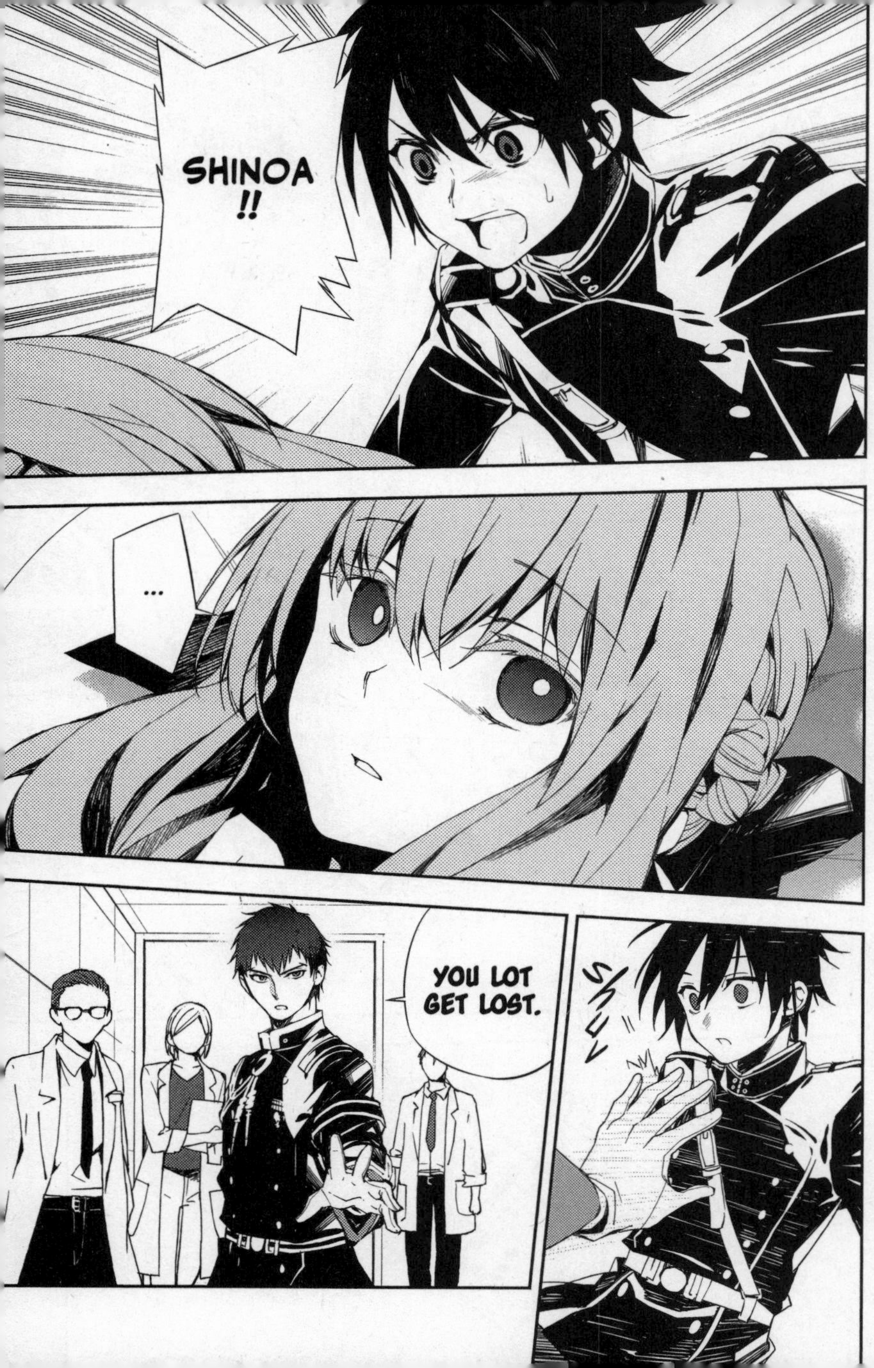
SHINOA !!
...
SHUV
YOU LOT GET LOST.

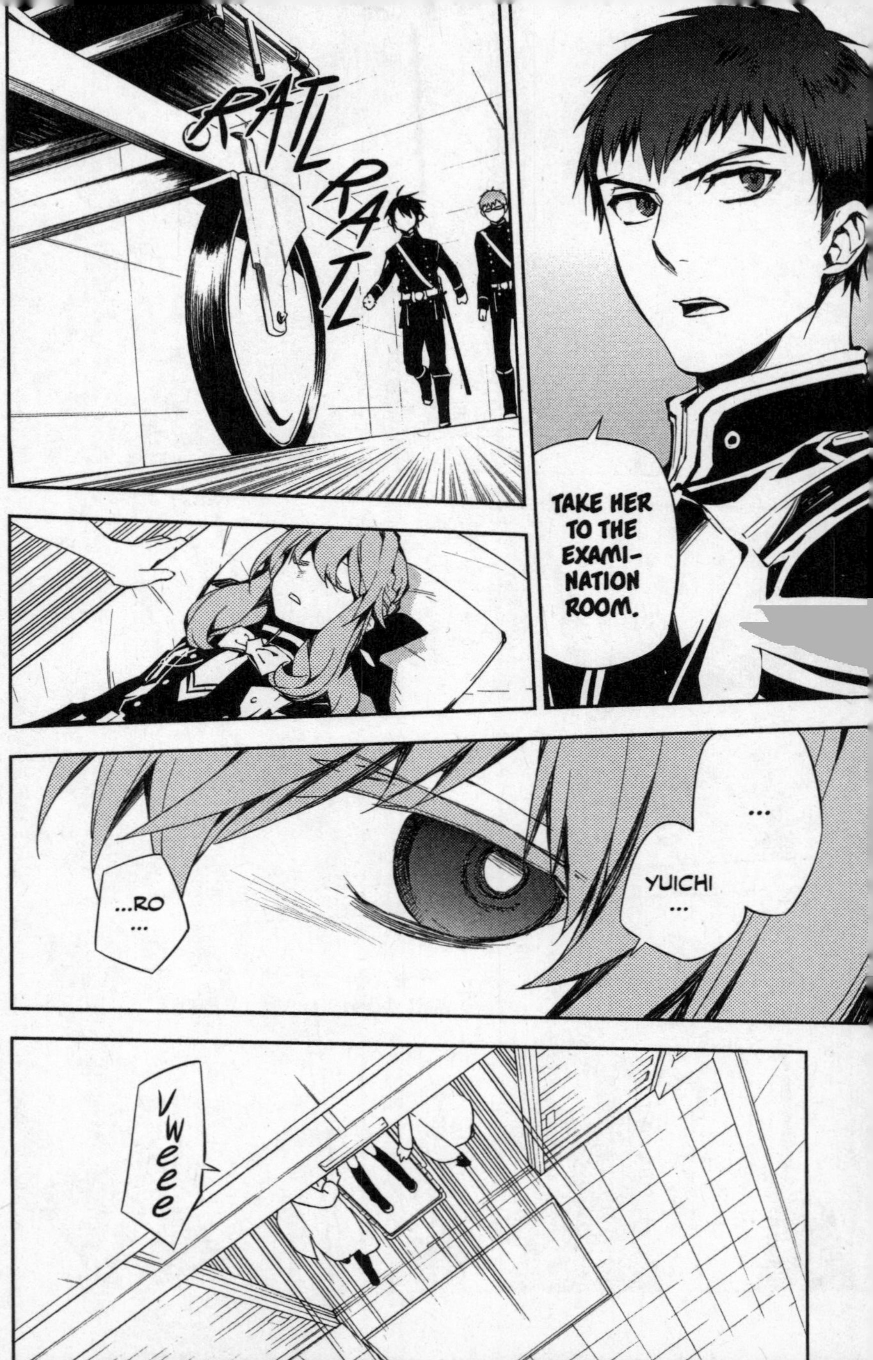
TAKE HER TO THE EXAMI-NATION ROOM.
RATL RATL
... YUICHI ...
...RO ...
Vweee

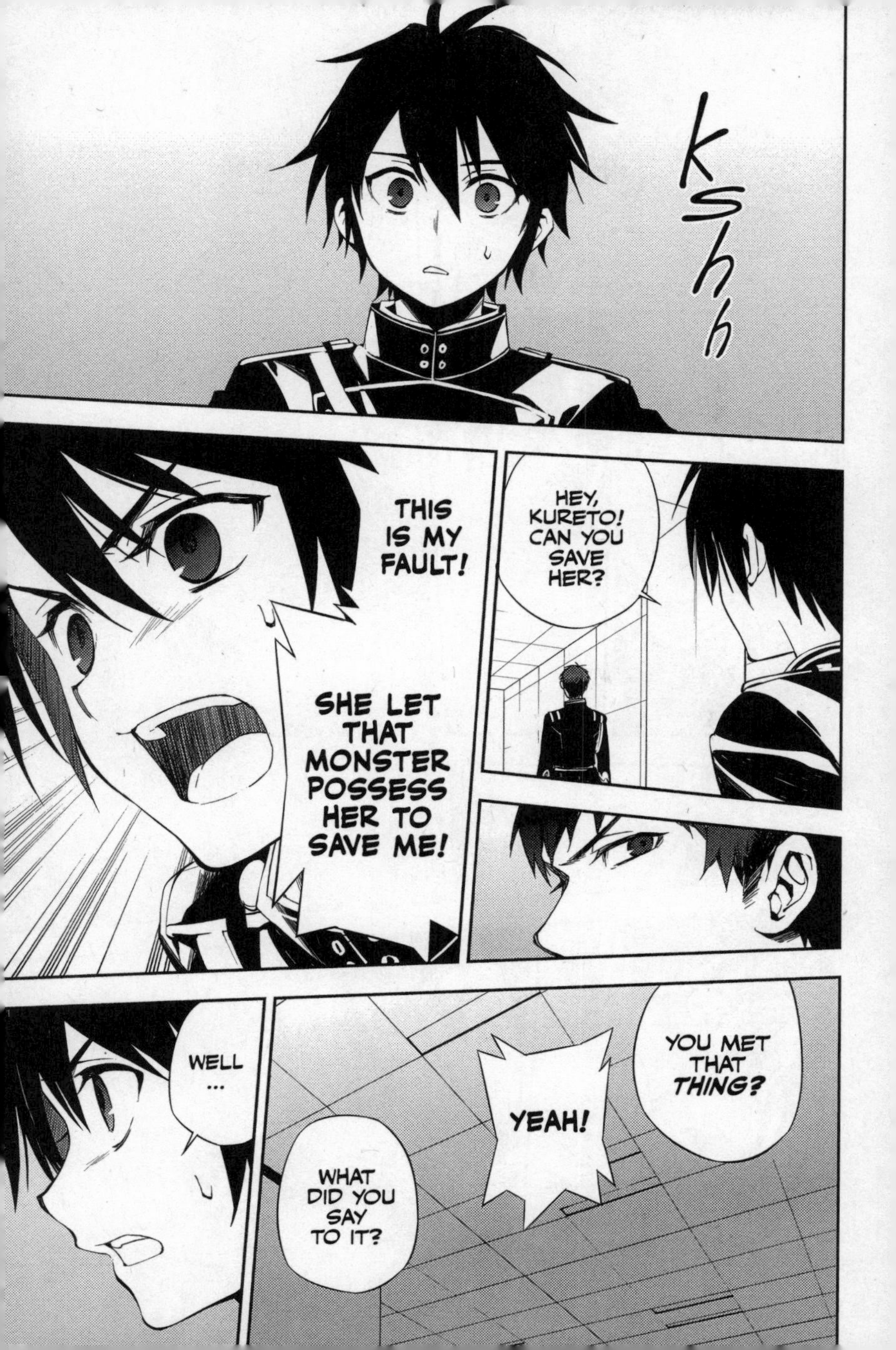
kshh
HEY, KURETO! CAN YOU SAVE HER?
THIS IS MY FAULT!
SHE LET THAT MONSTER POSSESS HER TO SAVE ME!
YOU MET THAT *THING*?
YEAH!
WHAT DID YOU SAY TO IT?
WELL ...

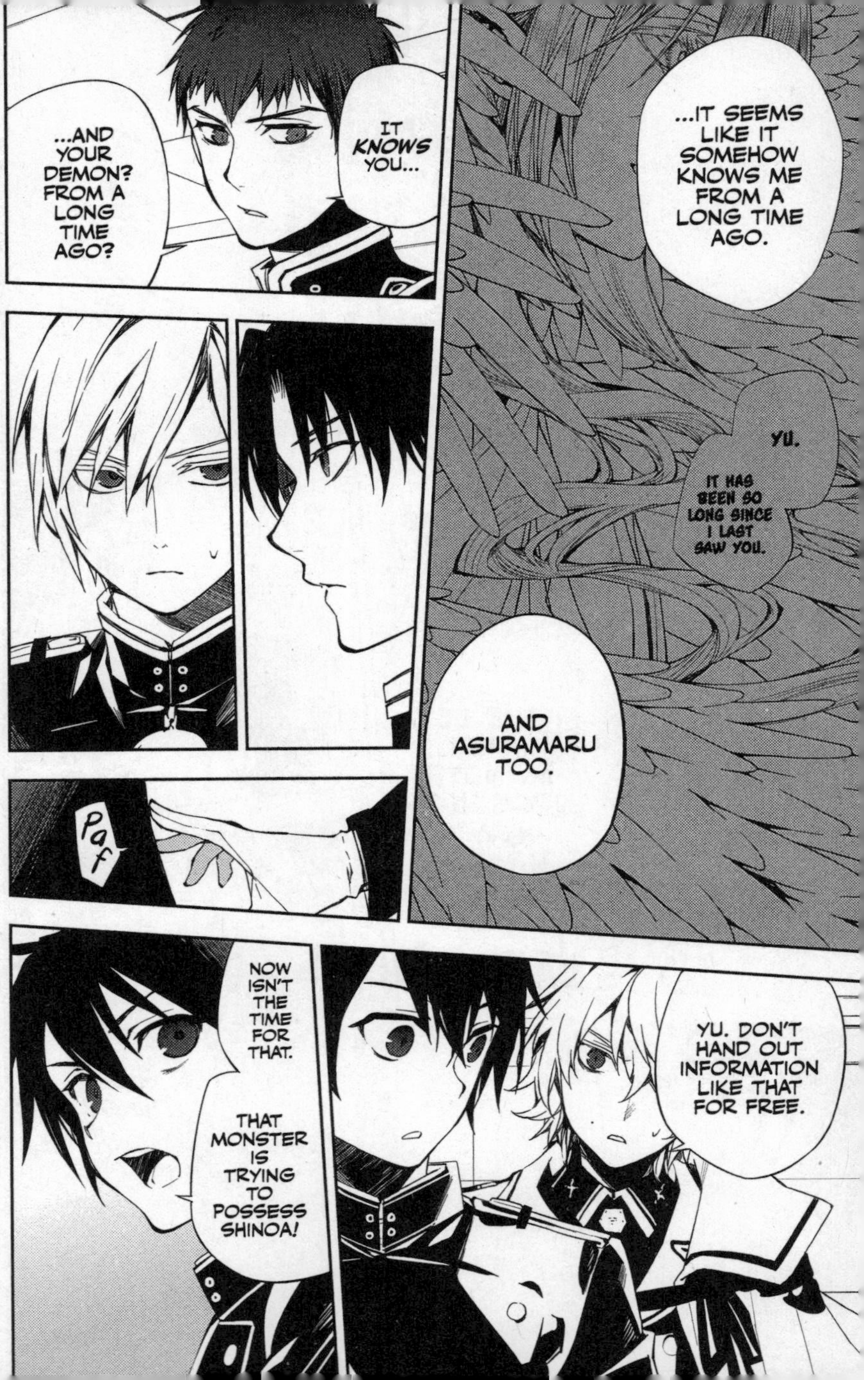
...IT SEEMS LIKE IT SOMEHOW KNOWS ME FROM A LONG TIME AGO.
YU.
IT HAS BEEN SO LONG SINCE I LAST SAW YOU.
AND ASURAMARU TOO.
IT KNOWS YOU...
...AND YOUR DEMON? FROM A LONG TIME AGO?
Paf
YU. DON'T HAND OUT INFORMATION LIKE THAT FOR FREE.
NOW ISN'T THE TIME FOR THAT.
THAT MONSTER IS TRYING TO POSSESS SHINOA!

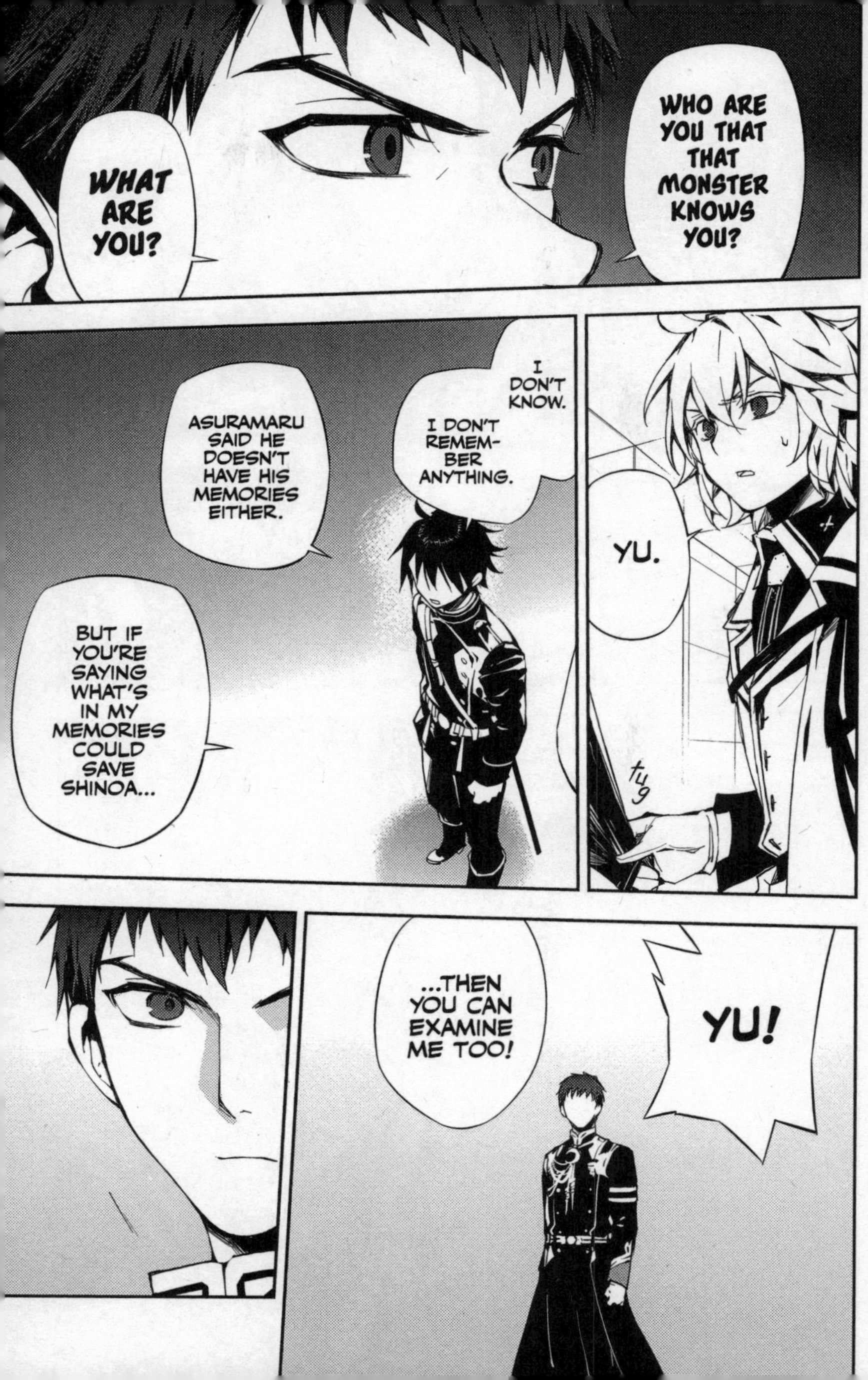
WHO ARE YOU THAT THAT MONSTER KNOWS YOU?
WHAT ARE YOU?
YU.
TUG
I DON'T KNOW.
I DON'T REMEM-BER ANYTHING.
ASURAMARU SAID HE DOESN'T HAVE HIS MEMORIES EITHER.
BUT IF YOU'RE SAYING WHAT'S IN MY MEMORIES COULD SAVE SHINOA...
YU!
...THEN YOU CAN EXAMINE ME TOO!

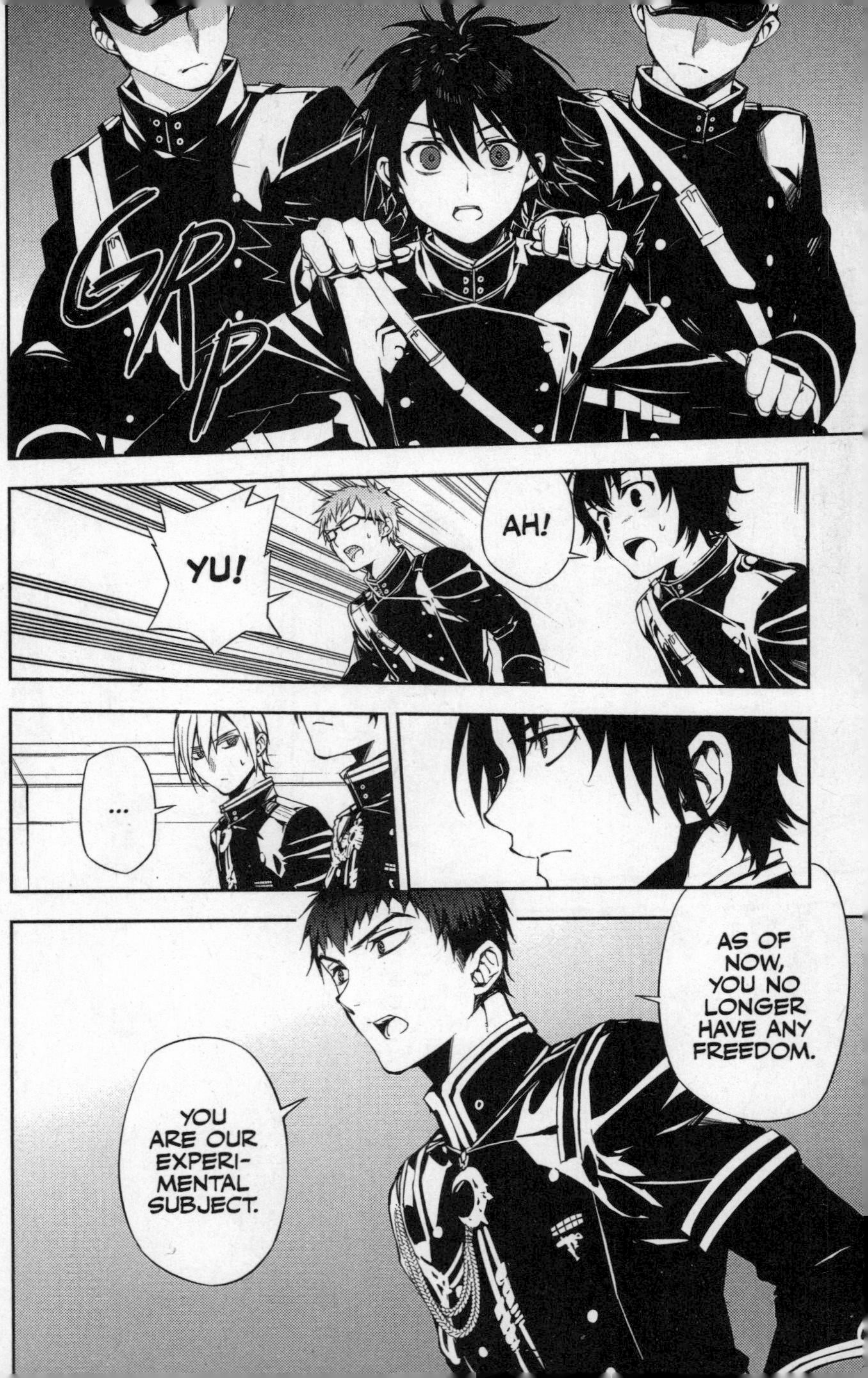
GRP
AH!
YU!
...
AS OF NOW, YOU NO LONGER HAVE ANY FREEDOM.
YOU ARE OUR EXPERIMENTAL SUBJECT.

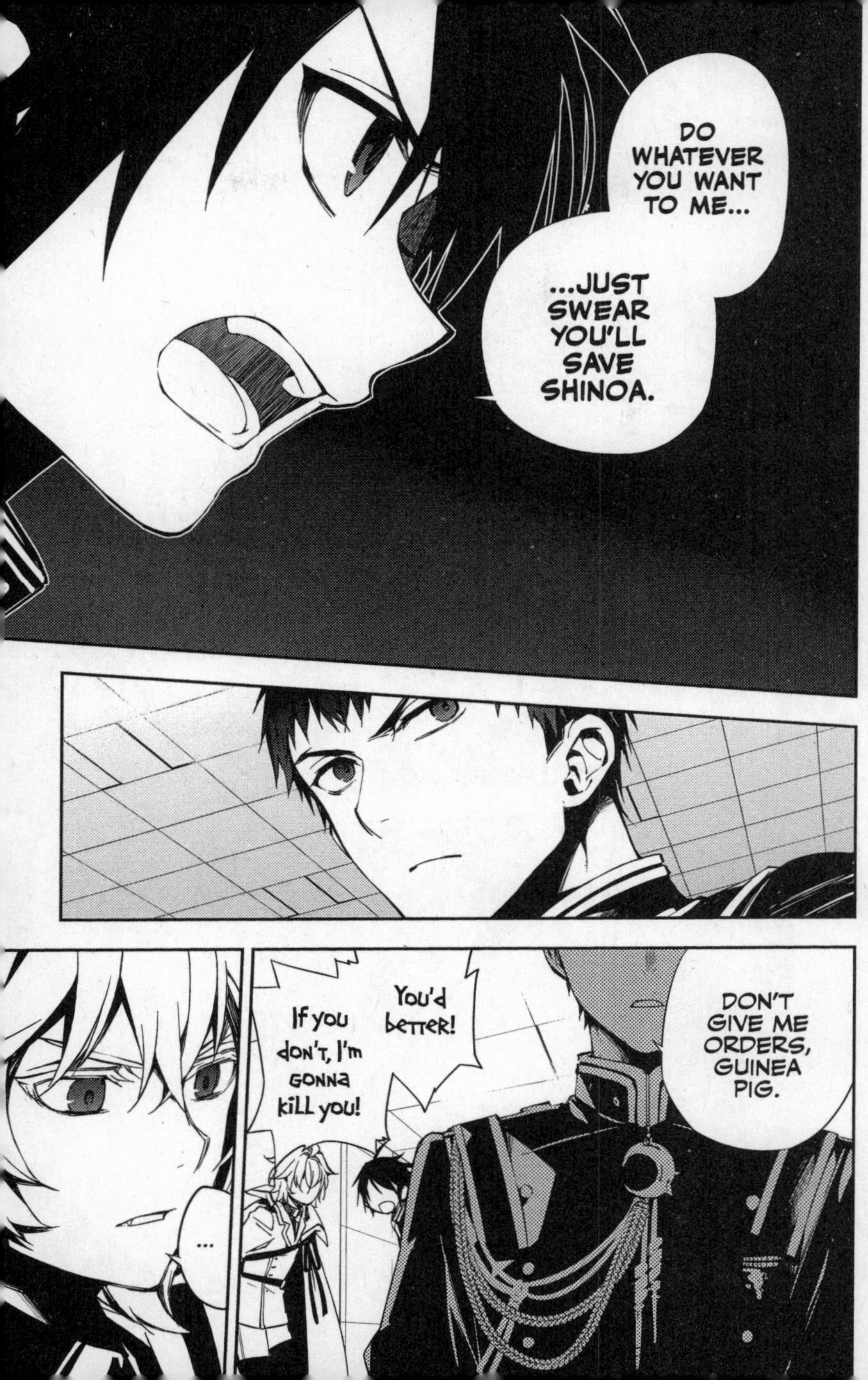
DO WHATEVER YOU WANT TO ME...
...JUST SWEAR YOU'LL SAVE SHINOA.
DON'T GIVE ME ORDERS, GUINEA PIG.
You'd better!
If you don't, I'm gonna kill you!
...

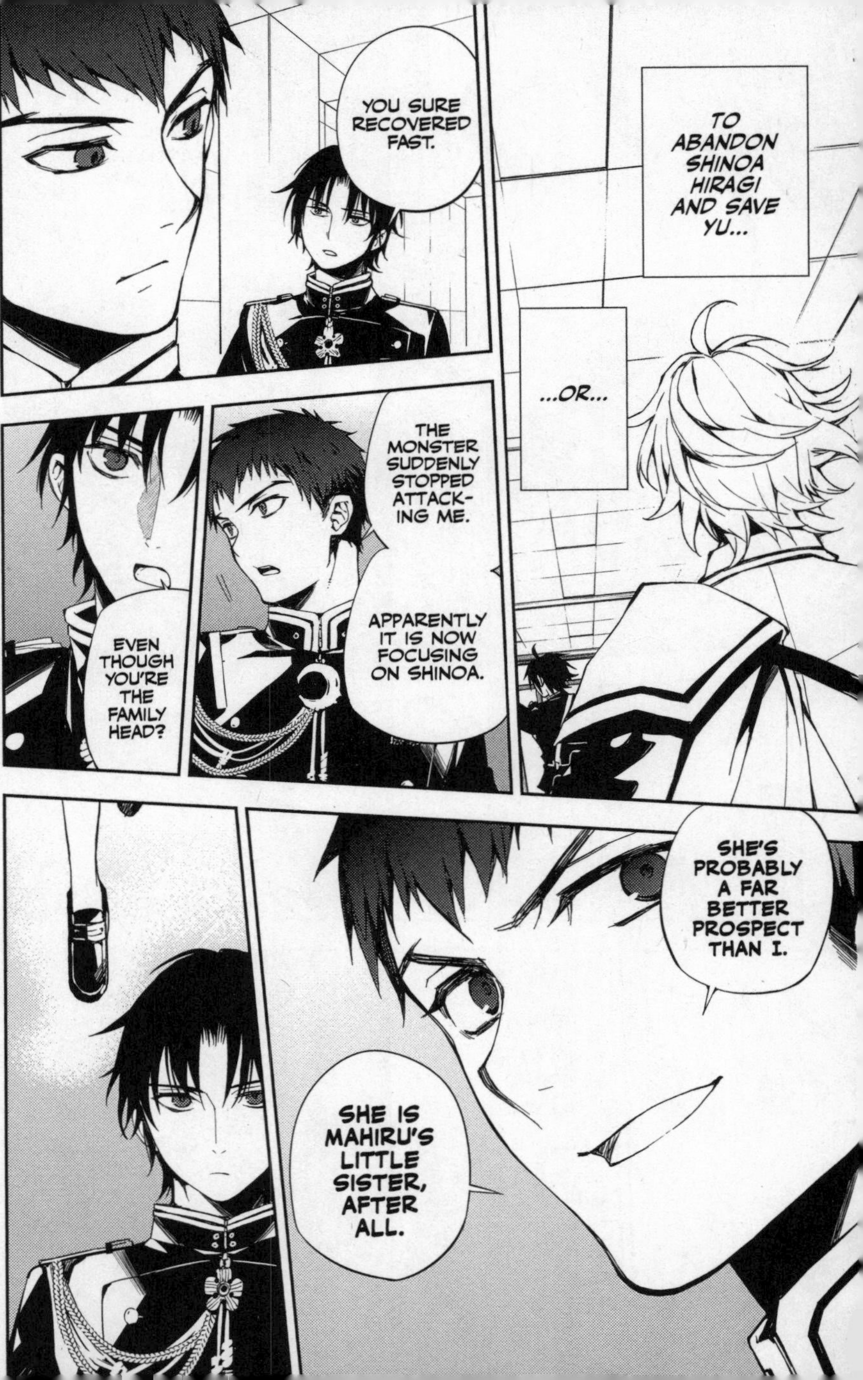
TO ABANDON SHINOA HIRAGI AND SAVE YU...
...OR...
YOU SURE RECOVERED FAST.
THE MONSTER SUDDENLY STOPPED ATTACK-ING ME.
APPARENTLY IT IS NOW FOCUSING ON SHINOA.
EVEN THOUGH YOU'RE THE FAMILY HEAD?
SHE'S PROBABLY A FAR BETTER PROSPECT THAN I.
SHE IS MAHIRU'S LITTLE SISTER, AFTER ALL.

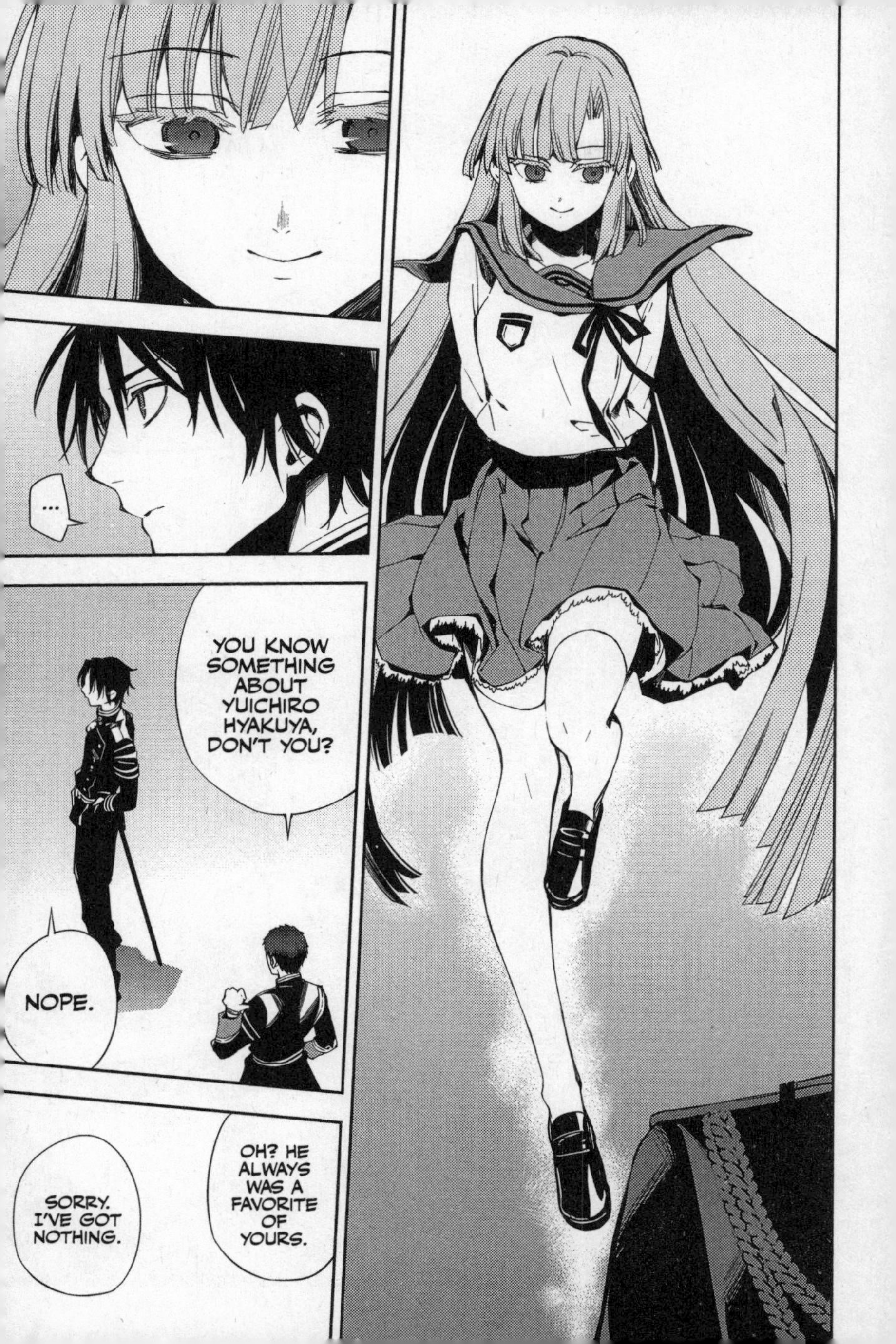
...
YOU KNOW SOMETHING ABOUT YUICHIRO HYAKUYA, DON'T YOU?
NOPE.
OH? HE ALWAYS WAS A FAVORITE OF YOURS.
SORRY. I'VE GOT NOTHING.

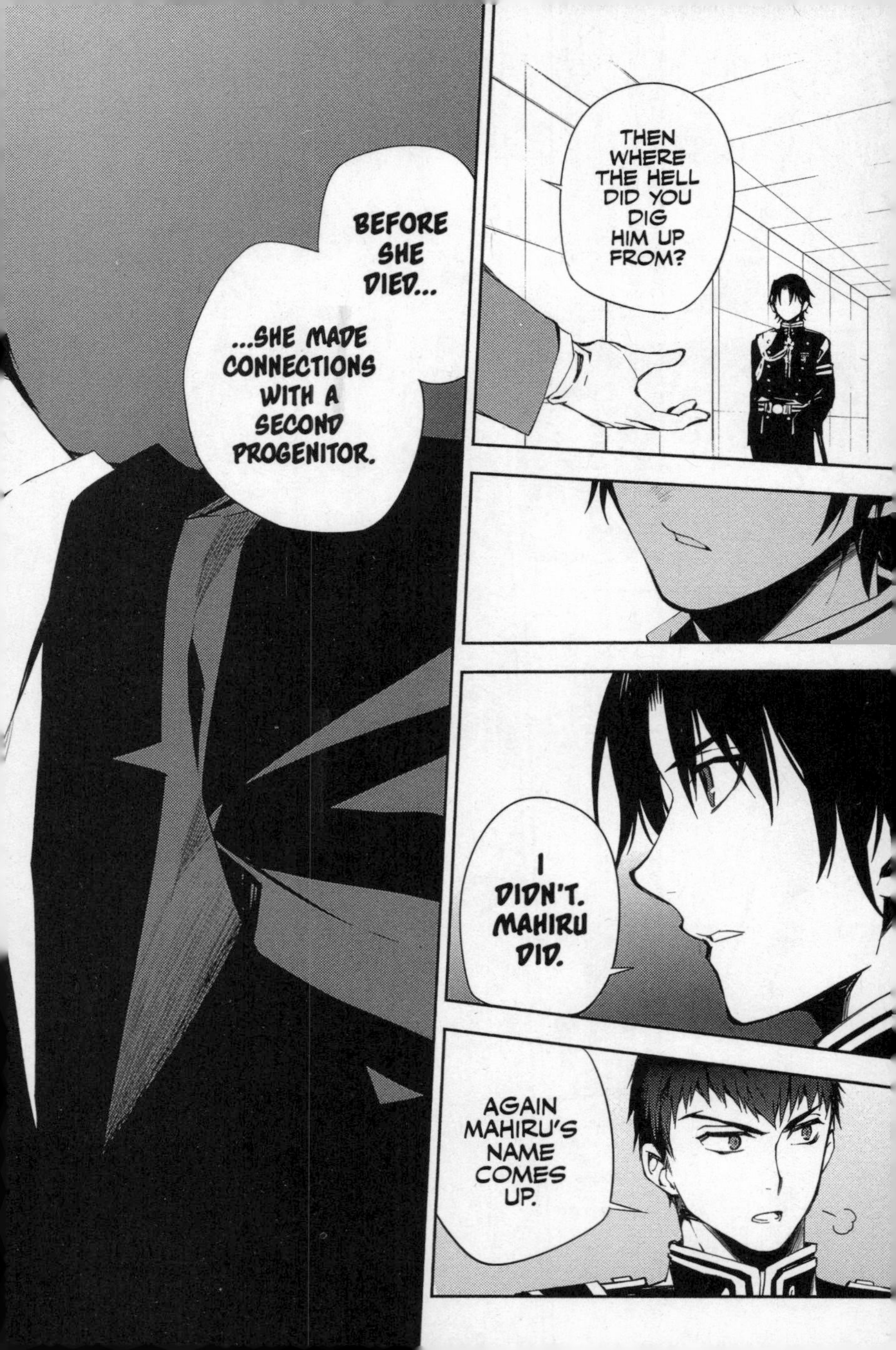
THEN WHERE THE HELL DID YOU DIG HIM UP FROM?
I DIDN'T. MAHIRU DID.
AGAIN MAHIRU'S NAME COMES UP.
BEFORE SHE DIED...
...SHE MADE CONNECTIONS WITH A SECOND PROGENITOR.

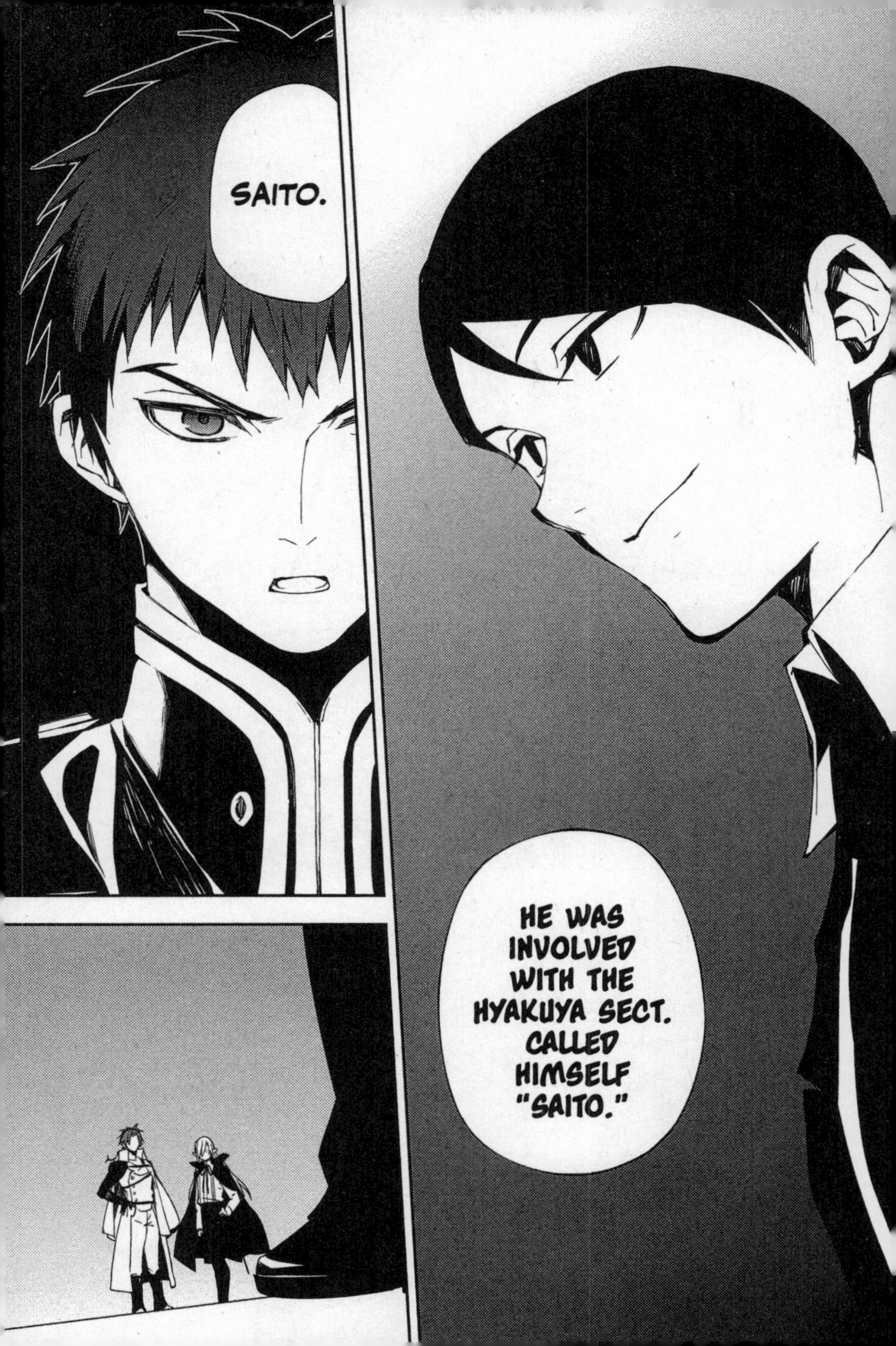
HE WAS INVOLVED WITH THE HYAKUYA SECT. CALLED HIMSELF "SAITO."
SAITO.

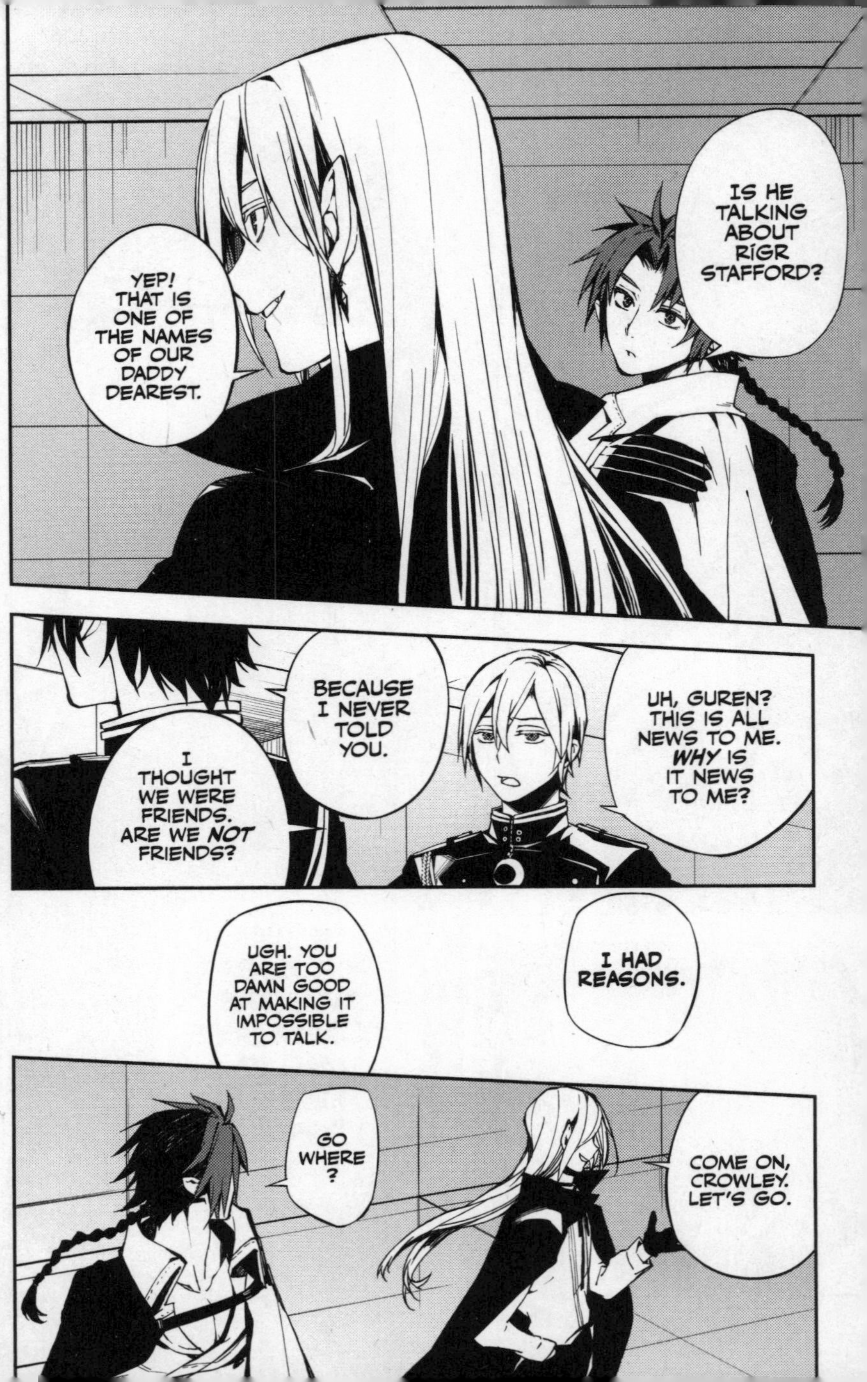
IS HE TALKING ABOUT RÍGR STAFFORD?
YEP! THAT IS ONE OF THE NAMES OF OUR DADDY DEAREST.
UH, GUREN? THIS IS ALL NEWS TO ME. *WHY* IS IT NEWS TO ME?
BECAUSE I NEVER TOLD YOU.
I THOUGHT WE WERE FRIENDS. ARE WE *NOT* FRIENDS?
I HAD REASONS.
UGH. YOU ARE TOO DAMN GOOD AT MAKING IT IMPOSSIBLE TO TALK.
COME ON, CROWLEY. LET'S GO.
GO WHERE?

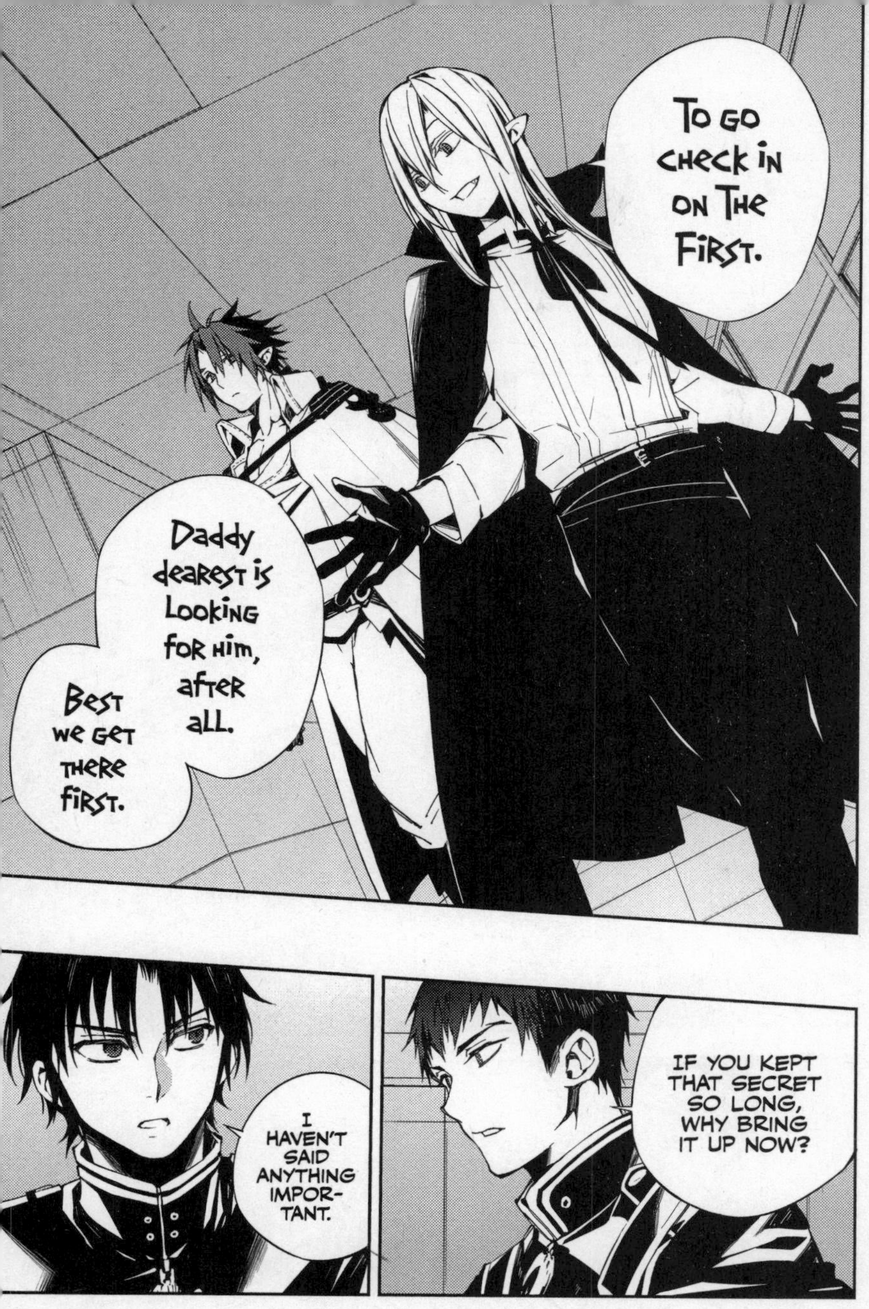
To go check in on the First.
Daddy dearest is looking for him, after all.
Best we get there first.
IF YOU KEPT THAT SECRET SO LONG, WHY BRING IT UP NOW?
I HAVEN'T SAID ANYTHING IMPORTANT.

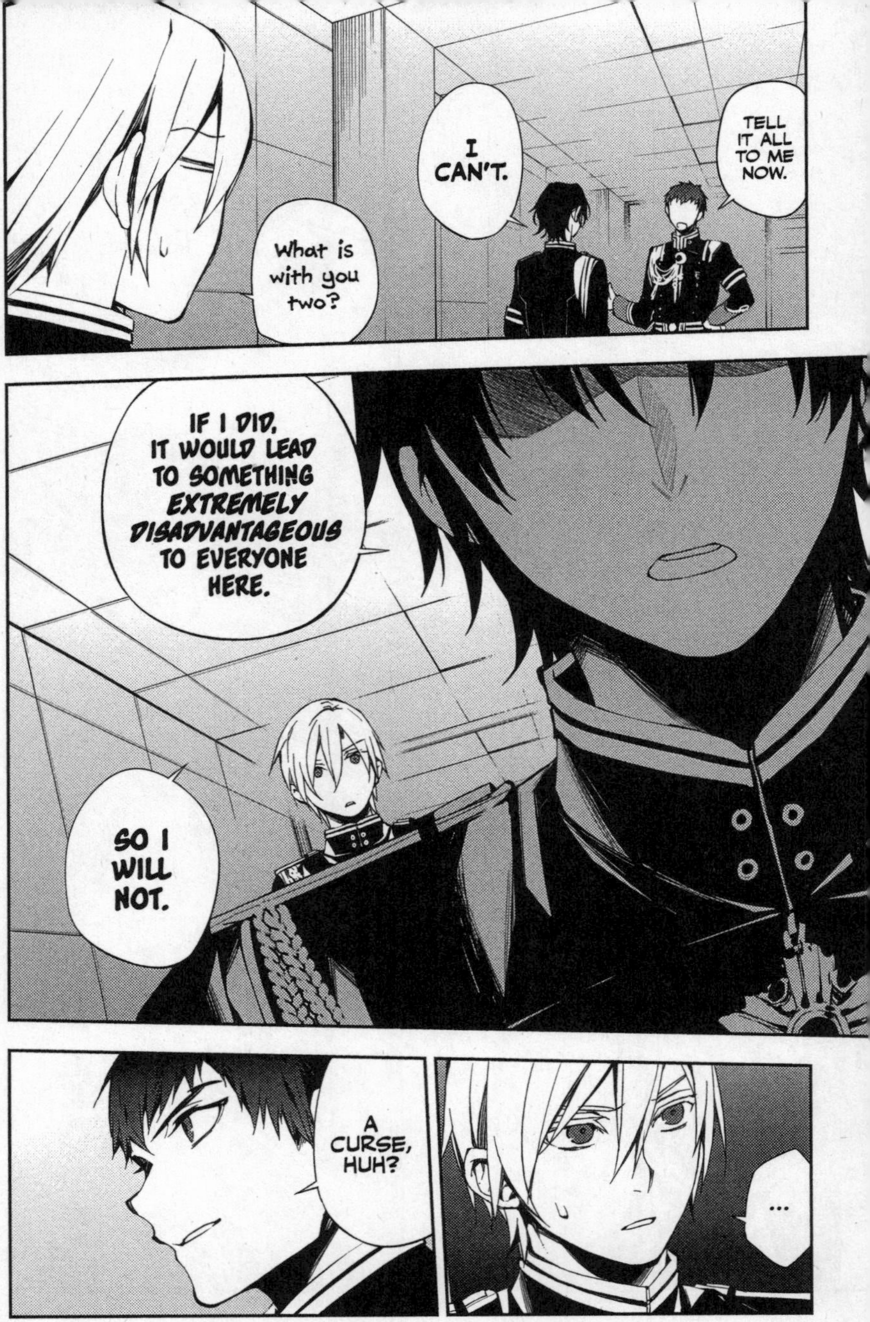
TELL IT ALL TO ME NOW.
I CAN'T.
What is with you two?
IF I DID, IT WOULD LEAD TO SOMETHING EXTREMELY DISADVANTAGEOUS TO EVERYONE HERE.
SO I WILL NOT.
...
A CURSE, HUH?

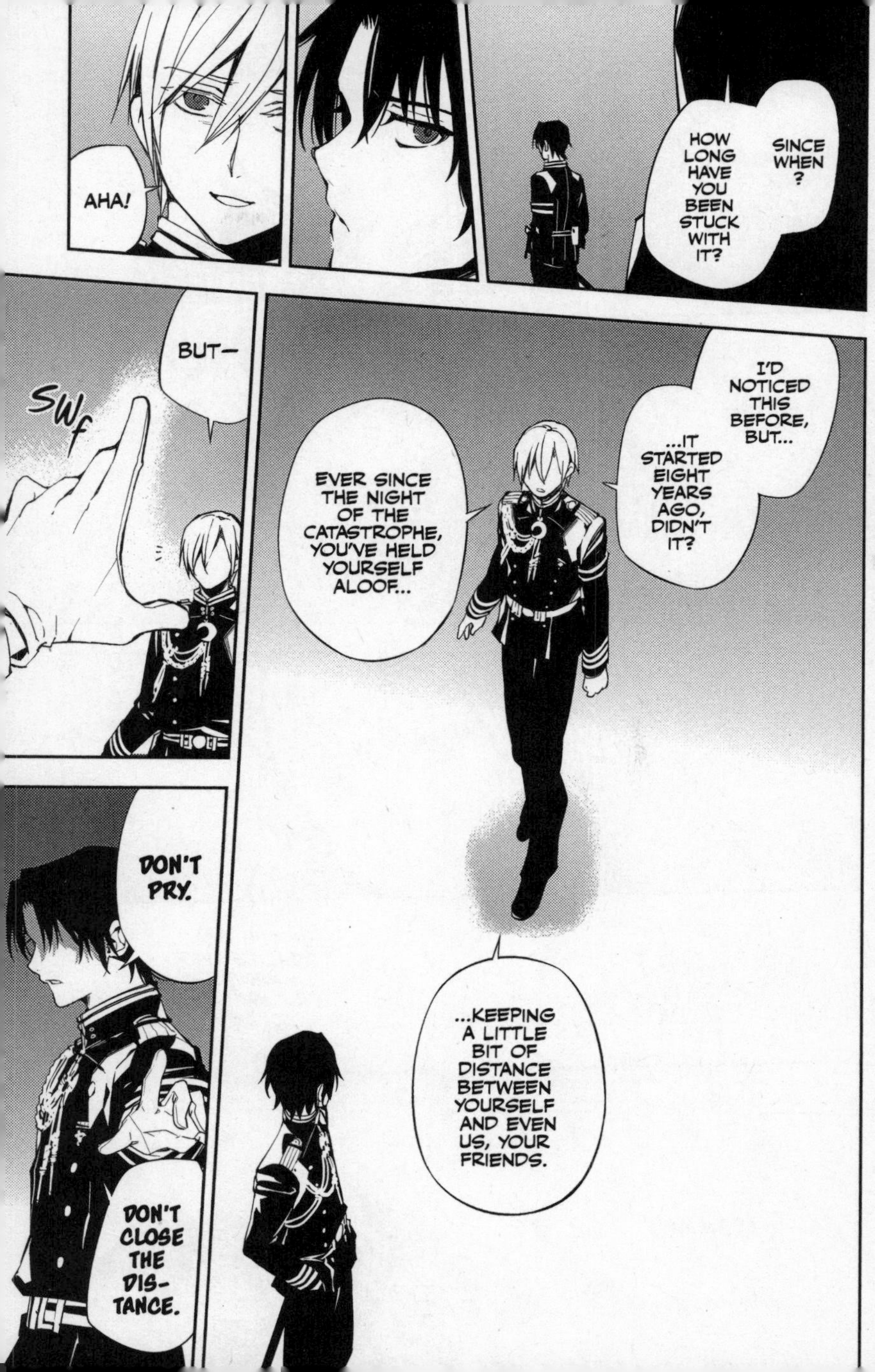
SINCE WHEN?
HOW LONG HAVE YOU BEEN STUCK WITH IT?
AHA!
I'D NOTICED THIS BEFORE, BUT...
...IT STARTED EIGHT YEARS AGO, DIDN'T IT?
EVER SINCE THE NIGHT OF THE CATASTROPHE, YOU'VE HELD YOURSELF ALOOF...
...KEEPING A LITTLE BIT OF DISTANCE BETWEEN YOURSELF AND EVEN US, YOUR FRIENDS.
BUT—
SWf
DON'T PRY.
DON'T CLOSE THE DIS-TANCE.

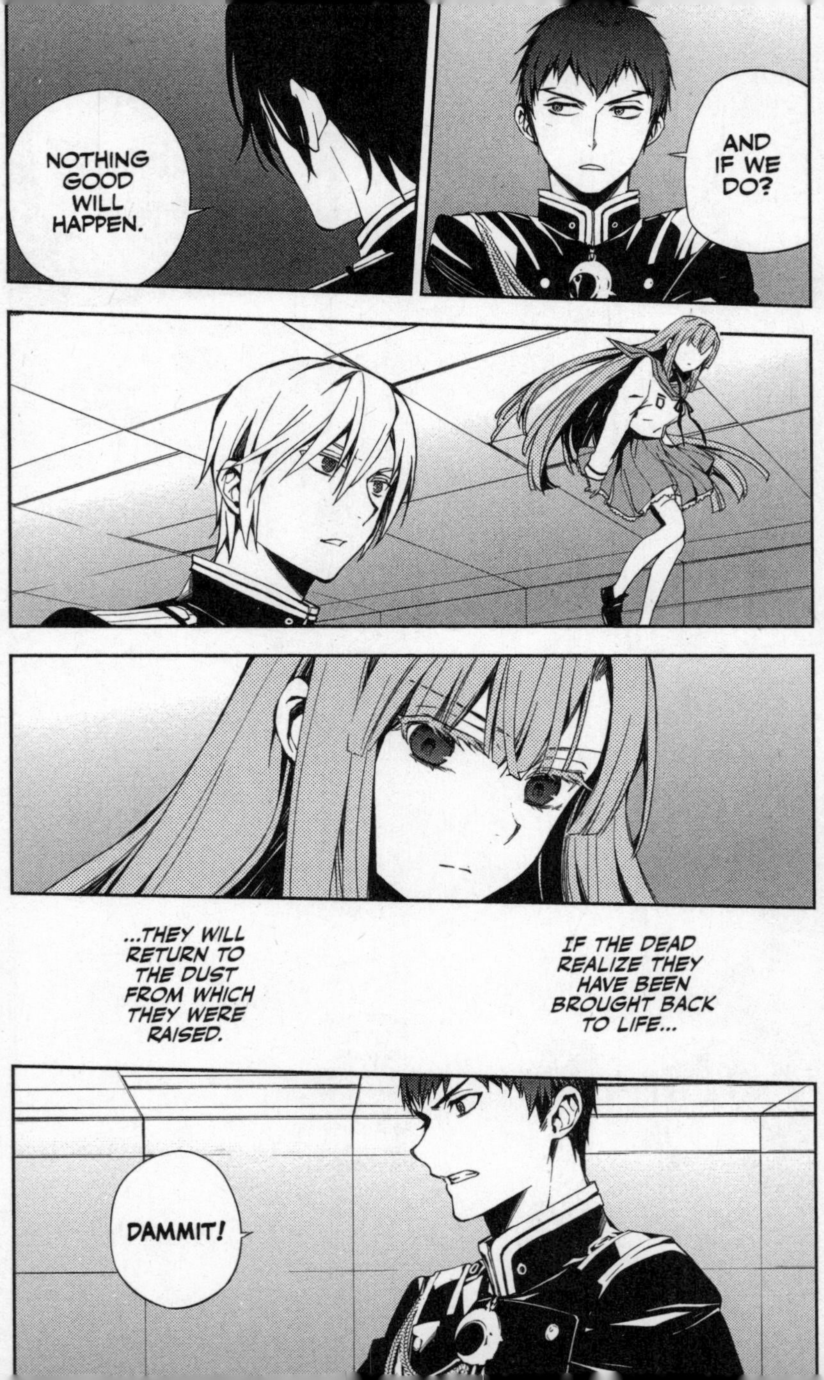
AND IF WE DO?
NOTHING GOOD WILL HAPPEN.
IF THE DEAD REALIZE THEY HAVE BEEN BROUGHT BACK TO LIFE...
...THEY WILL RETURN TO THE DUST FROM WHICH THEY WERE RAISED.
DAMMIT!

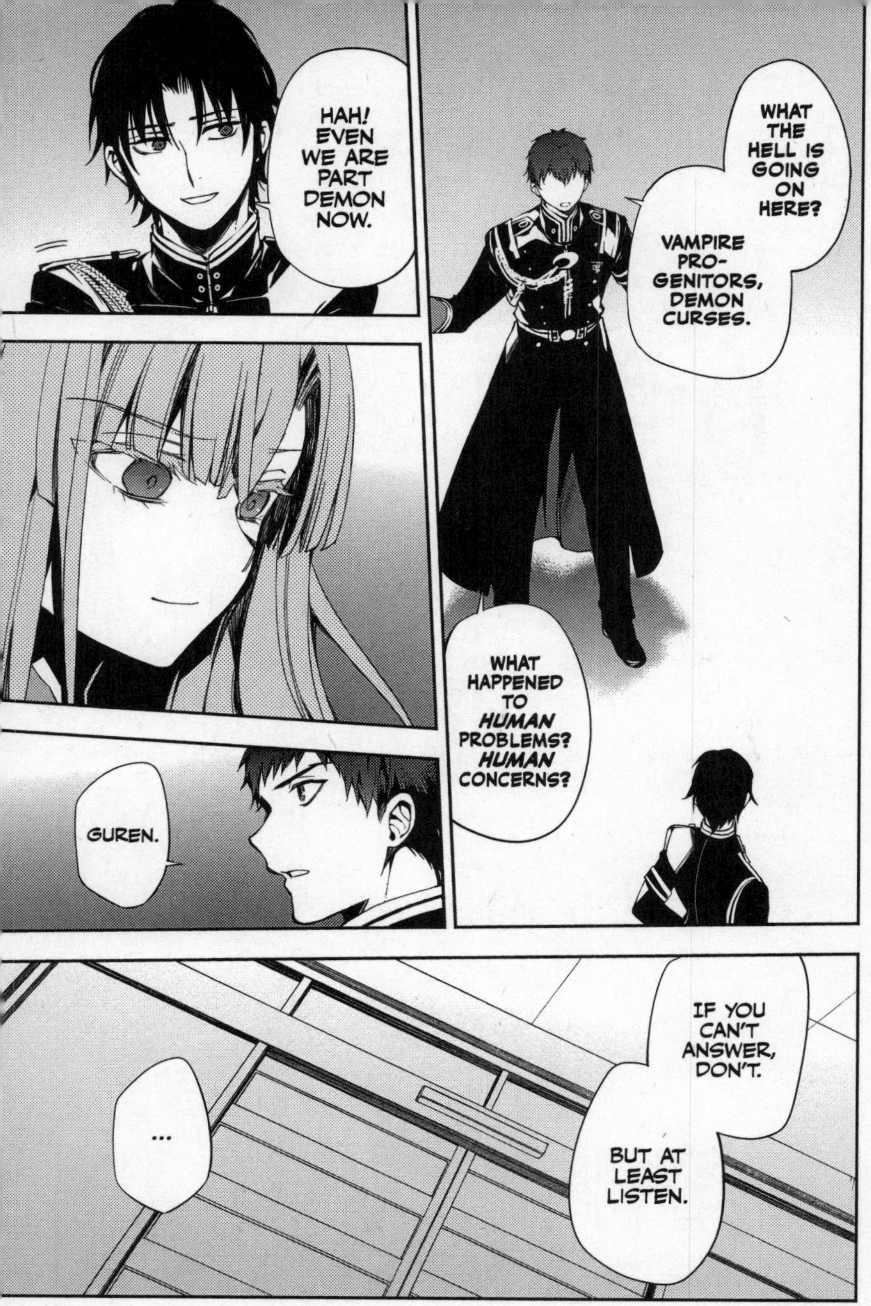
WHAT THE HELL IS GOING ON HERE?
VAMPIRE PRO-GENITORS, DEMON CURSES.
WHAT HAPPENED TO *HUMAN* PROBLEMS? *HUMAN* CONCERNS?
HAH! EVEN WE ARE PART DEMON NOW.
GUREN.
IF YOU CAN'T ANSWER, DON'T.
BUT AT LEAST LISTEN.
...

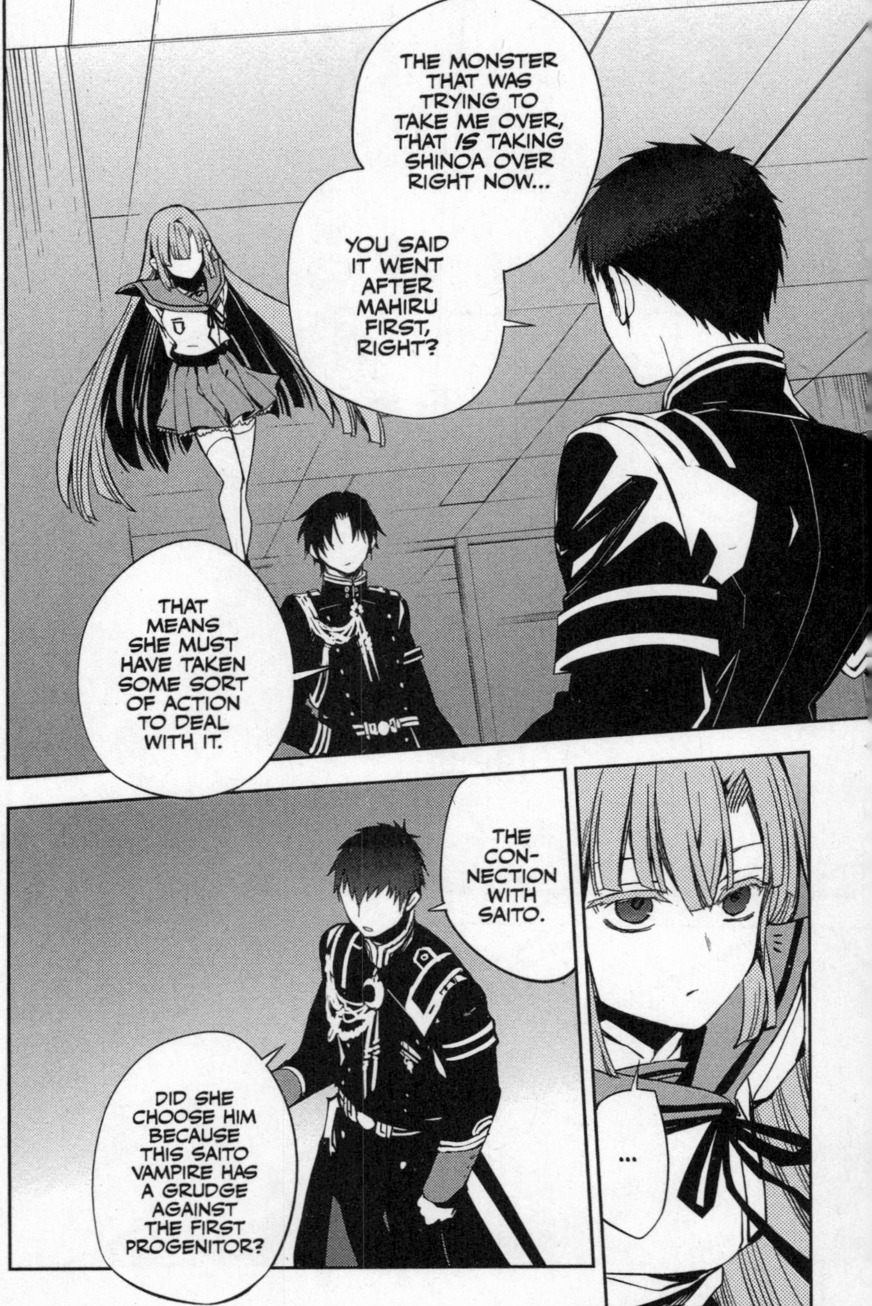
THE MONSTER THAT WAS TRYING TO TAKE ME OVER, THAT *IS* TAKING SHINOA OVER RIGHT NOW...
YOU SAID IT WENT AFTER MAHIRU FIRST, RIGHT?
THAT MEANS SHE MUST HAVE TAKEN SOME SORT OF ACTION TO DEAL WITH IT.
...
THE CON-NECTION WITH SAITO.
DID SHE CHOOSE HIM BECAUSE THIS SAITO VAMPIRE HAS A GRUDGE AGAINST THE FIRST PROGENITOR?

I DON'T KNOW.

SHE SAID HE WAS "AFTER IT."

PROB-ABLY.

YOU CAN TELL ME THAT?

I DON'T KNOW.

WHAT IS SAITO'S GOAL?

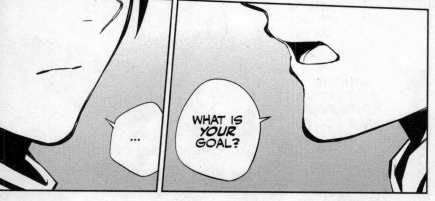

...

WHAT IS *YOUR* GOAL?

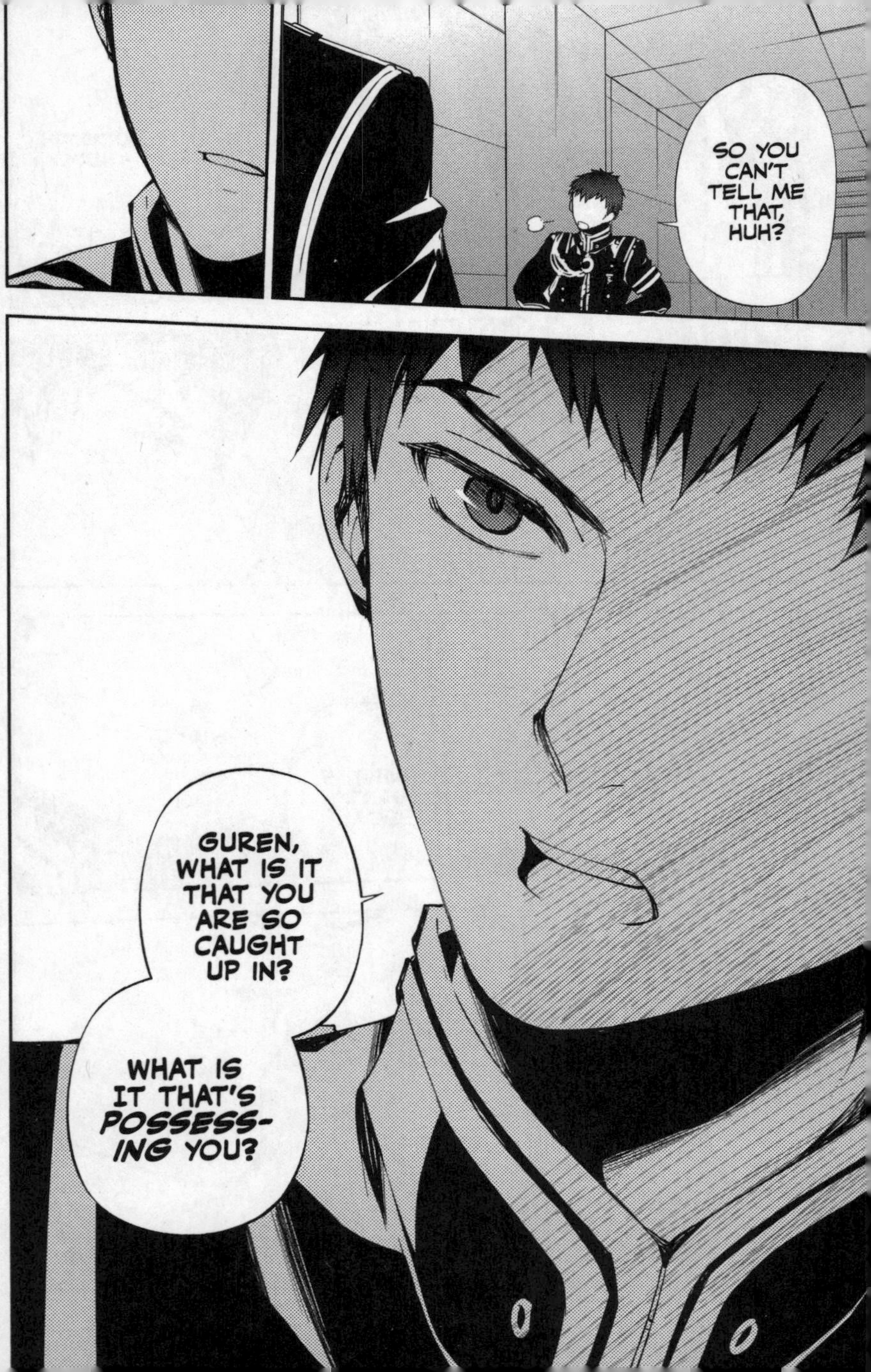
SO YOU CAN'T TELL ME THAT, HUH?
GUREN, WHAT IS IT THAT YOU ARE SO CAUGHT UP IN?
WHAT IS IT THAT'S *POSSESS-ING* YOU?

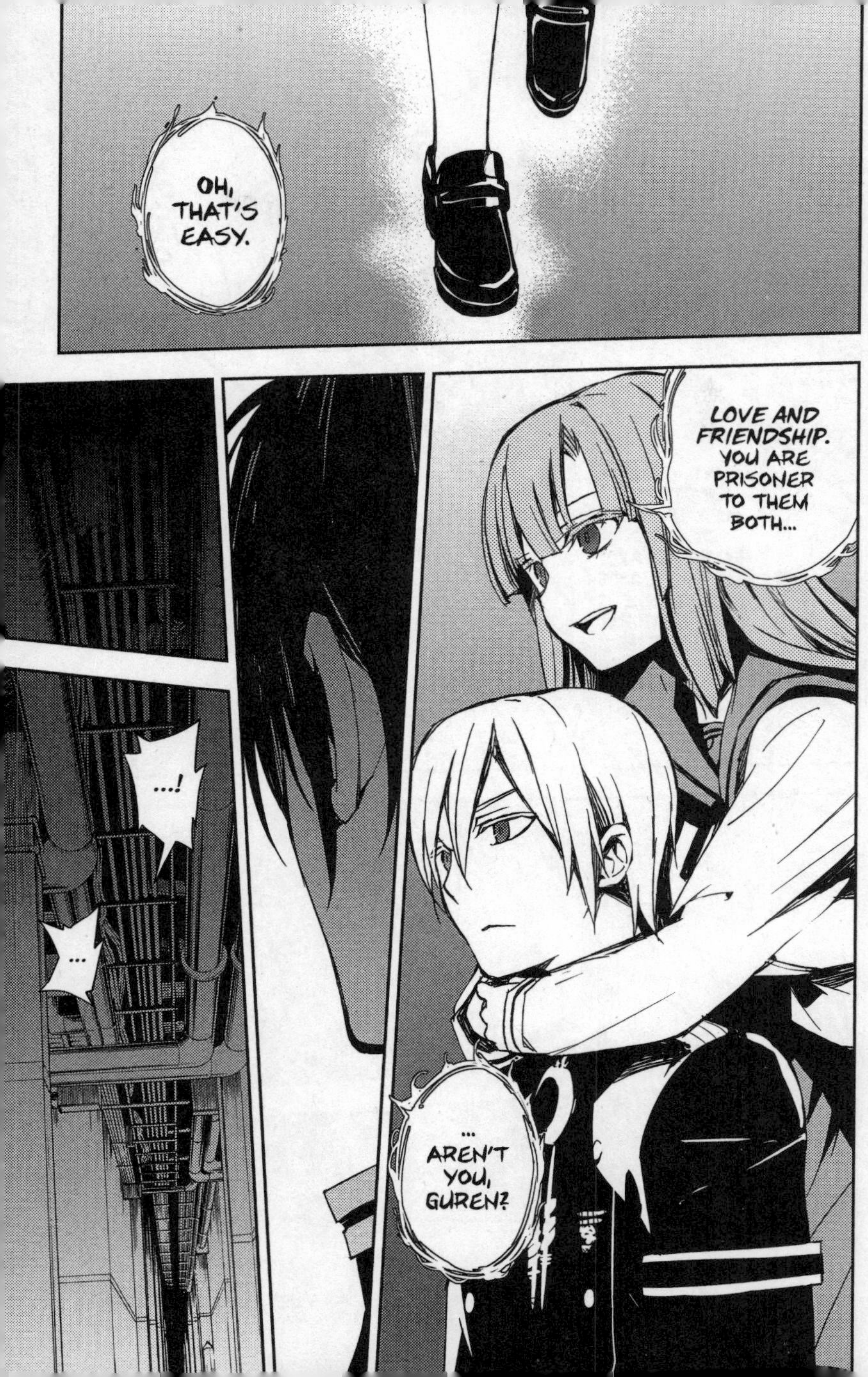
OH, THAT'S EASY.
LOVE AND FRIENDSHIP. YOU ARE PRISONER TO THEM BOTH...
... AREN'T YOU, GUREN?
...!
...

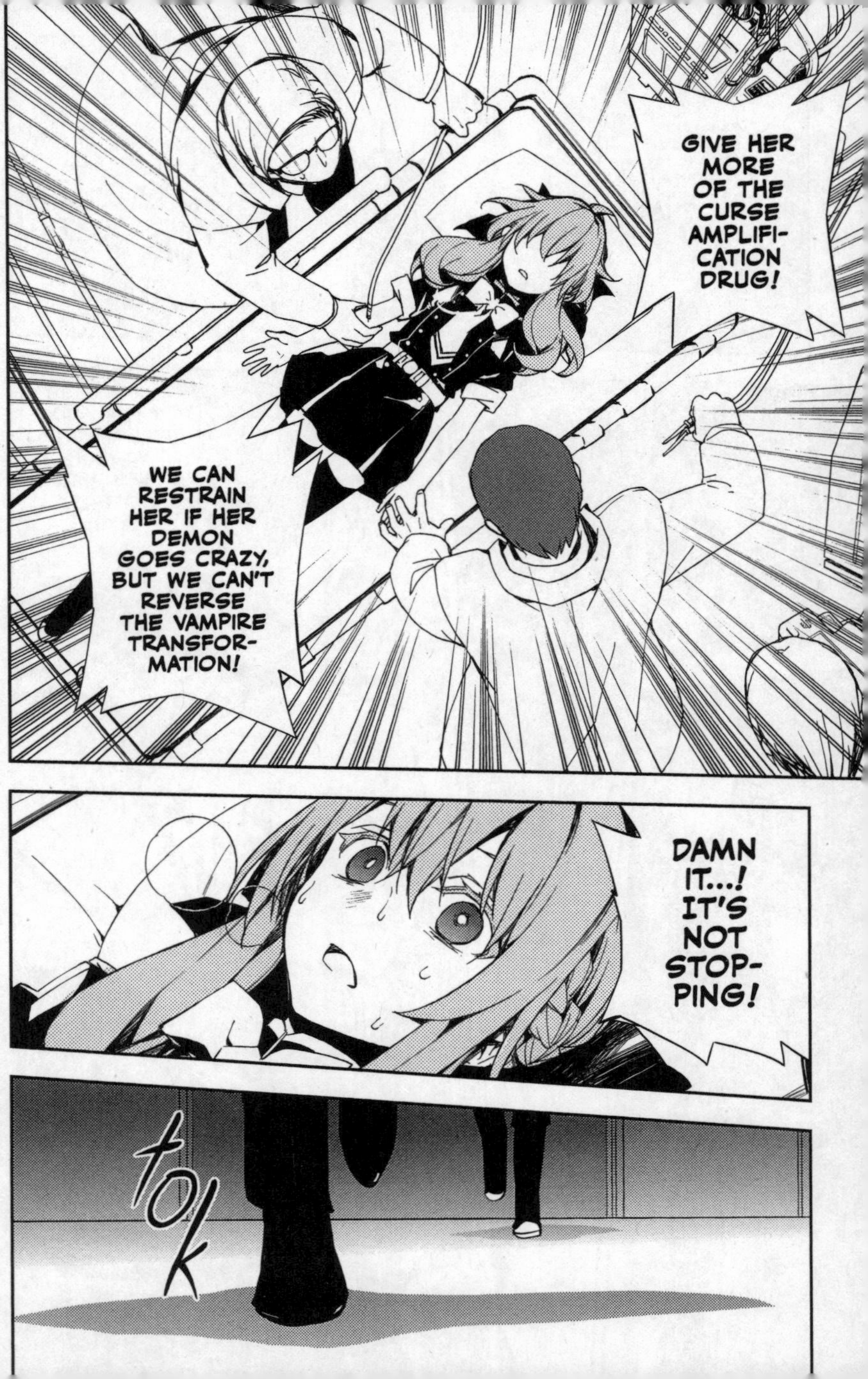
GIVE HER MORE OF THE CURSE AMPLIFICATION DRUG!
WE CAN RESTRAIN HER IF HER DEMON GOES CRAZY, BUT WE CAN'T REVERSE THE VAMPIRE TRANSFORMATION!
DAMN IT...! IT'S NOT STOPPING!
tok

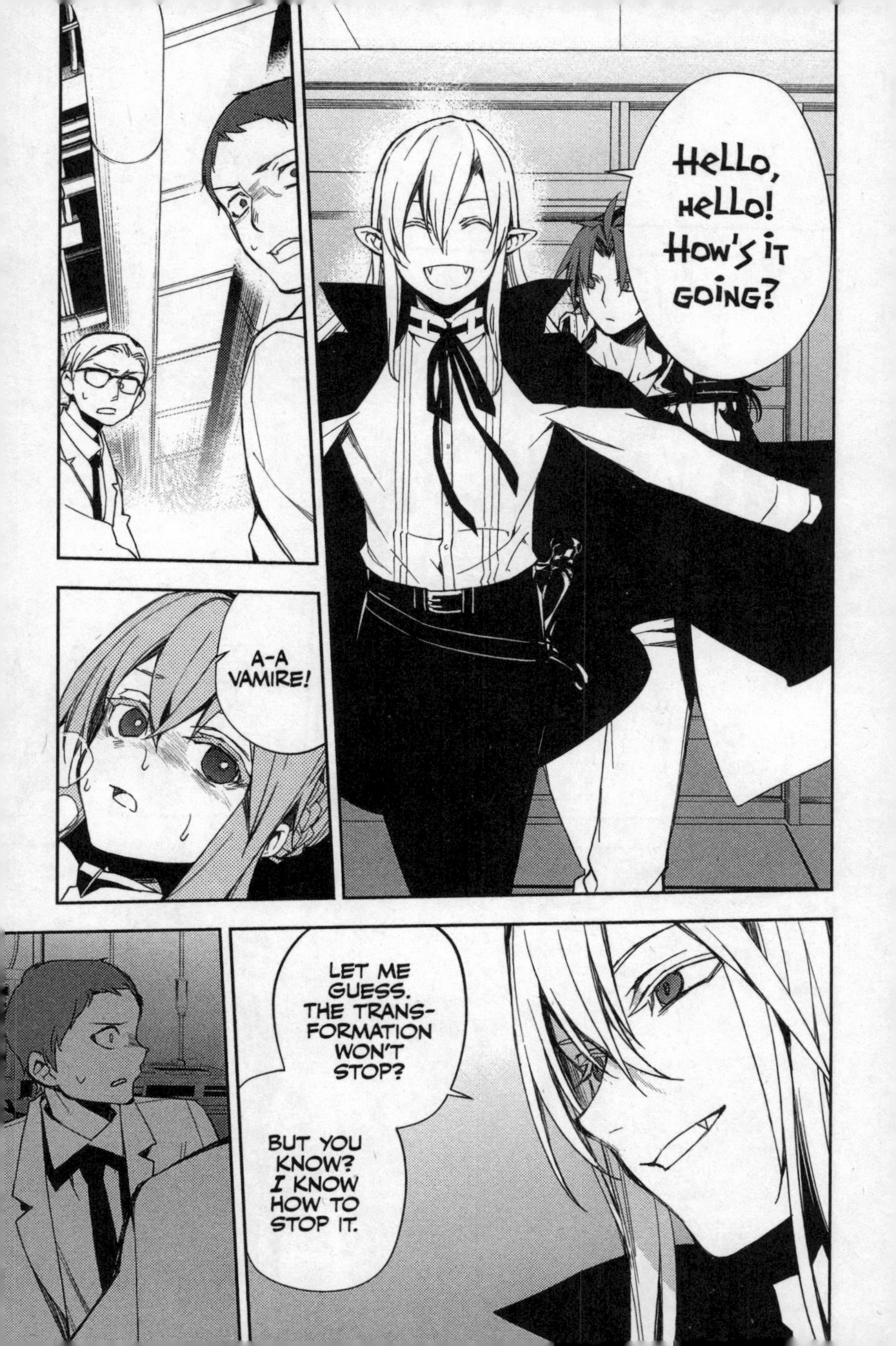
HELLO, HELLO! HOW'S IT GOING?
A-A VAMIRE!
LET ME GUESS. THE TRANS-FORMATION WON'T STOP?
BUT YOU KNOW? I KNOW HOW TO STOP IT.

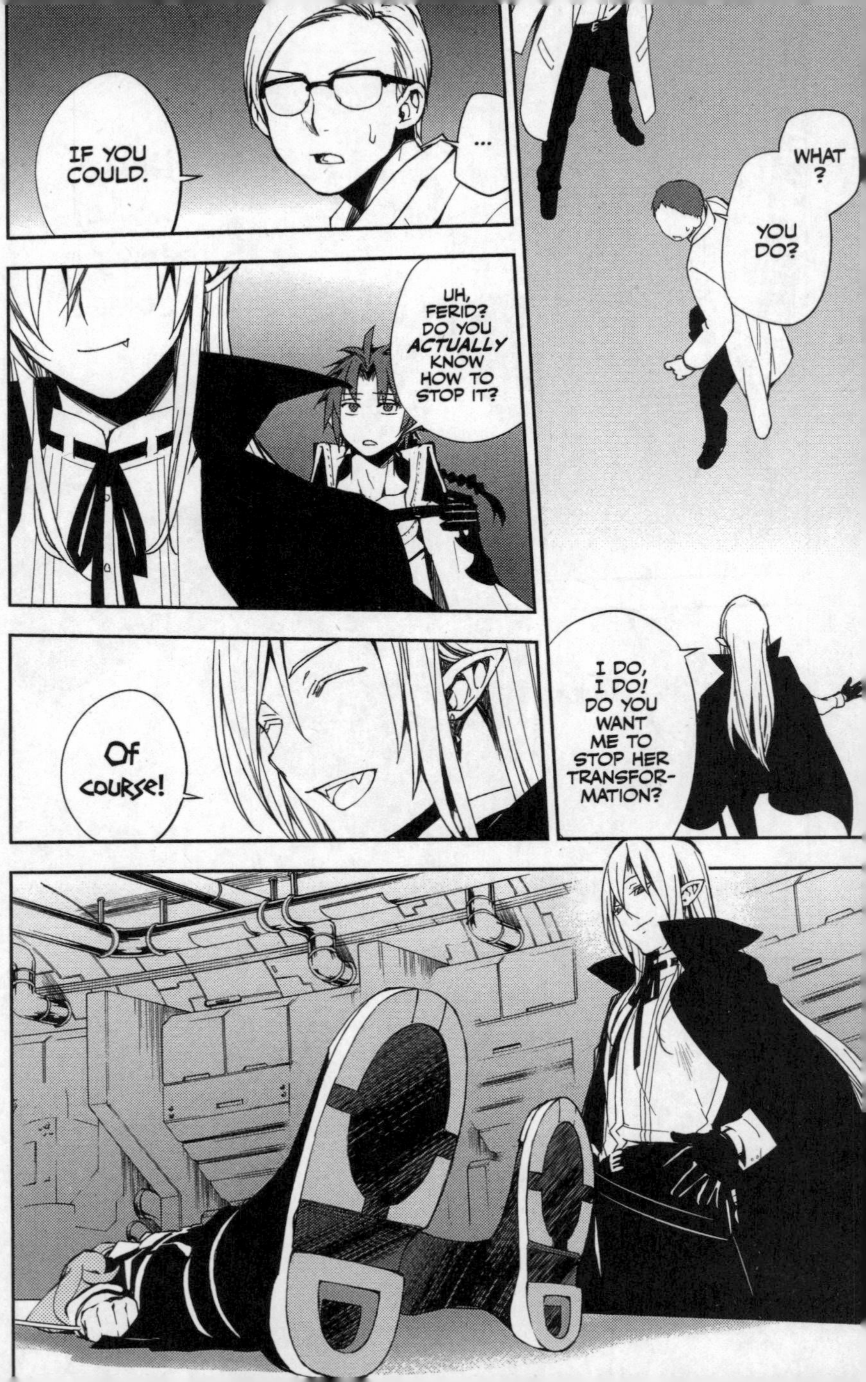
WHAT? YOU DO?
...
IF YOU COULD.
UH, FERID? DO YOU ACTUALLY KNOW HOW TO STOP IT?
I DO, I DO! DO YOU WANT ME TO STOP HER TRANSFORMATION?
Of course!

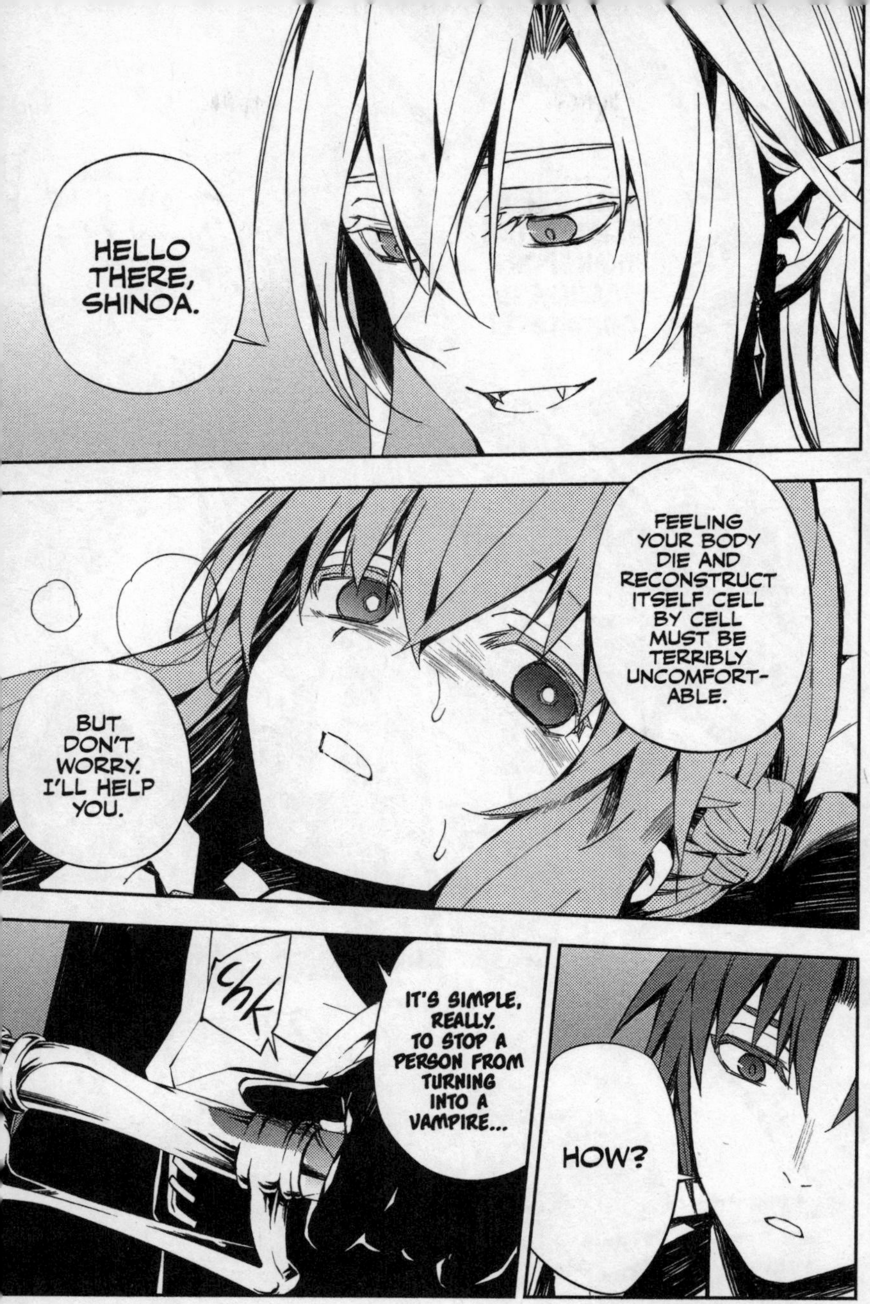
HELLO THERE, SHINOA.
FEELING YOUR BODY DIE AND RECONSTRUCT ITSELF CELL BY CELL MUST BE TERRIBLY UNCOMFORT-ABLE.
BUT DON'T WORRY. I'LL HELP YOU.
HOW?
IT'S SIMPLE, REALLY. TO STOP A PERSON FROM TURNING INTO A VAMPIRE...
chk

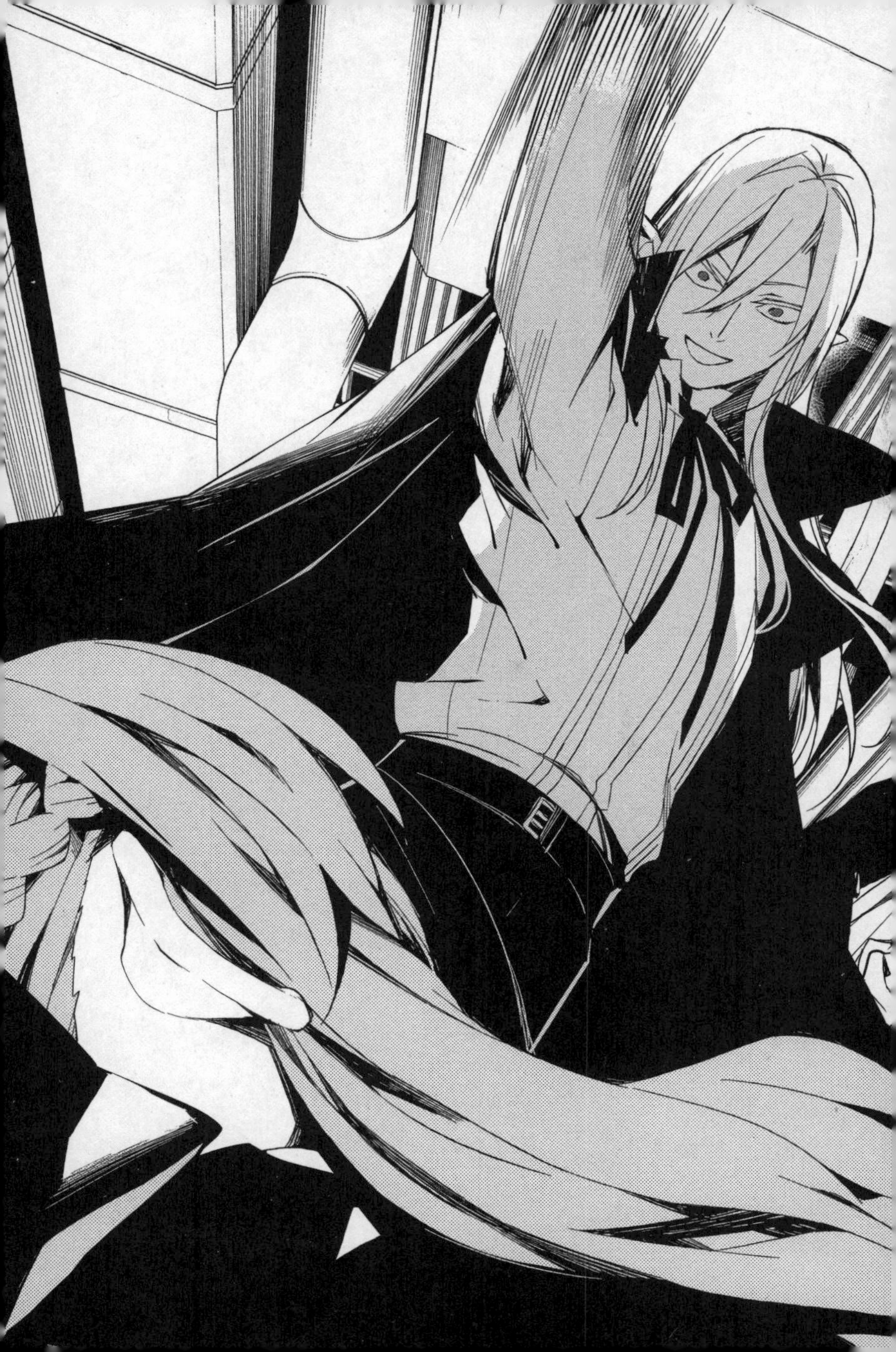

Seraph of the End
—VAMPIRE REIGN—

Chapter 76
Age of Immortals

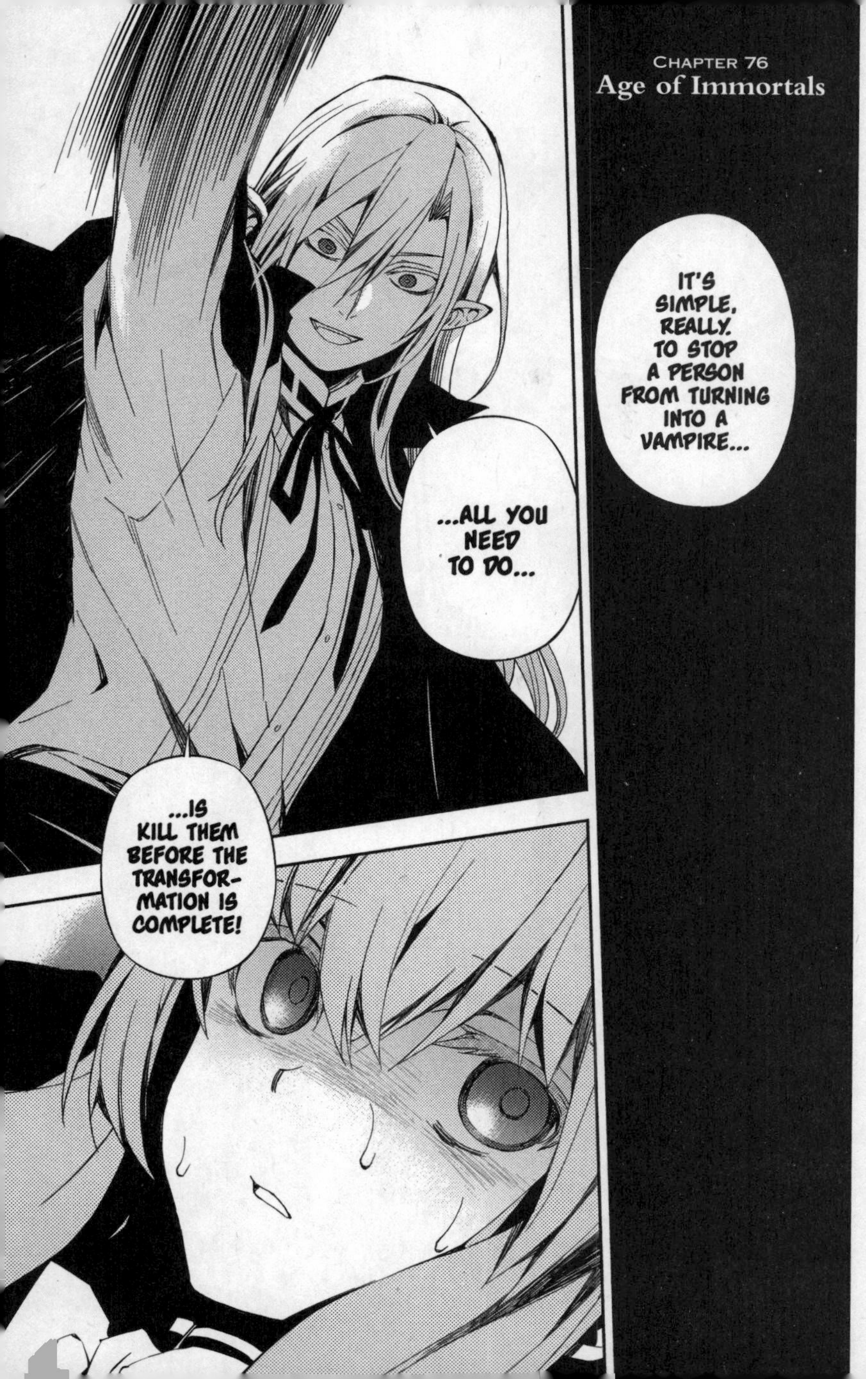
IT'S SIMPLE, REALLY. TO STOP A PERSON FROM TURNING INTO A VAMPIRE...
...ALL YOU NEED TO DO...
...IS KILL THEM BEFORE THE TRANSFORMATION IS COMPLETE!

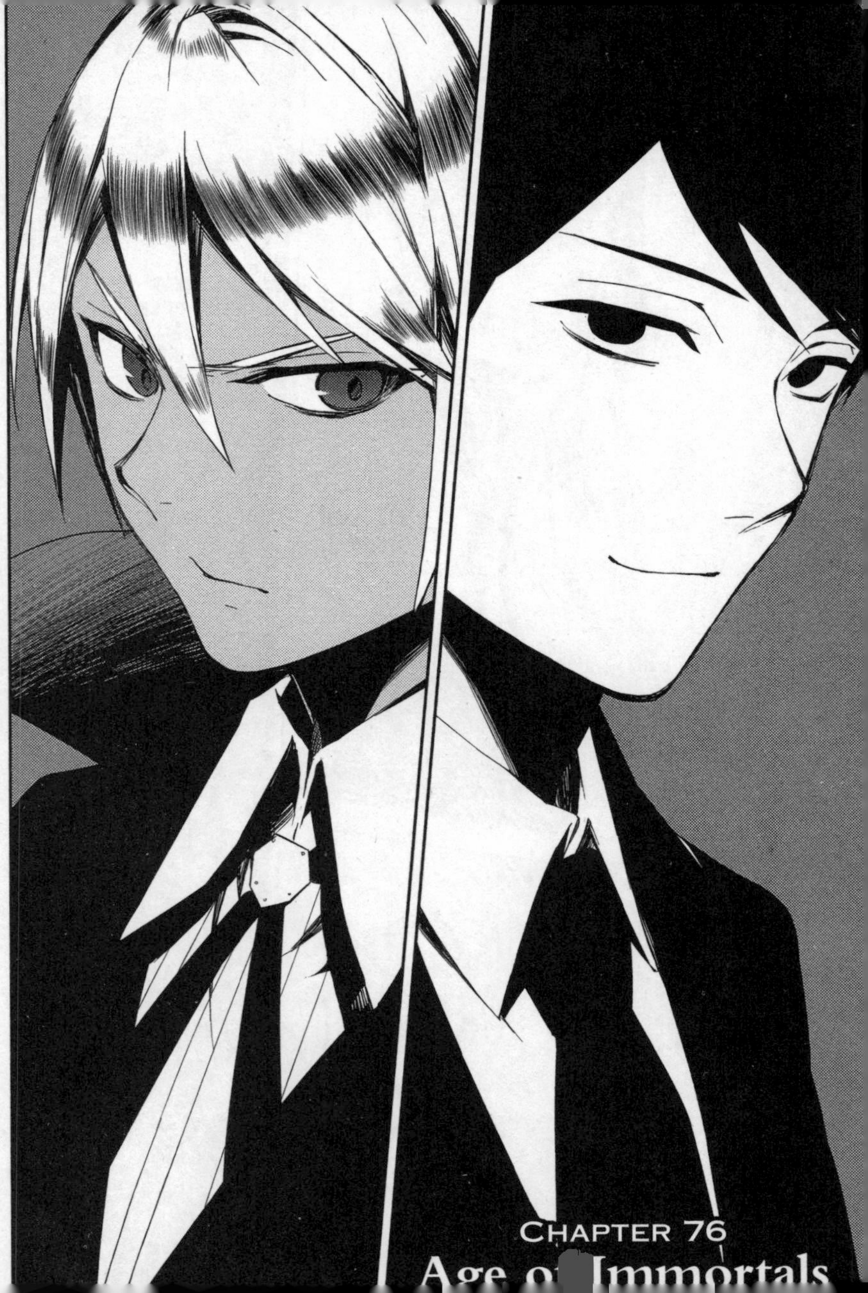

CHAPTER 76
Age of Immortals

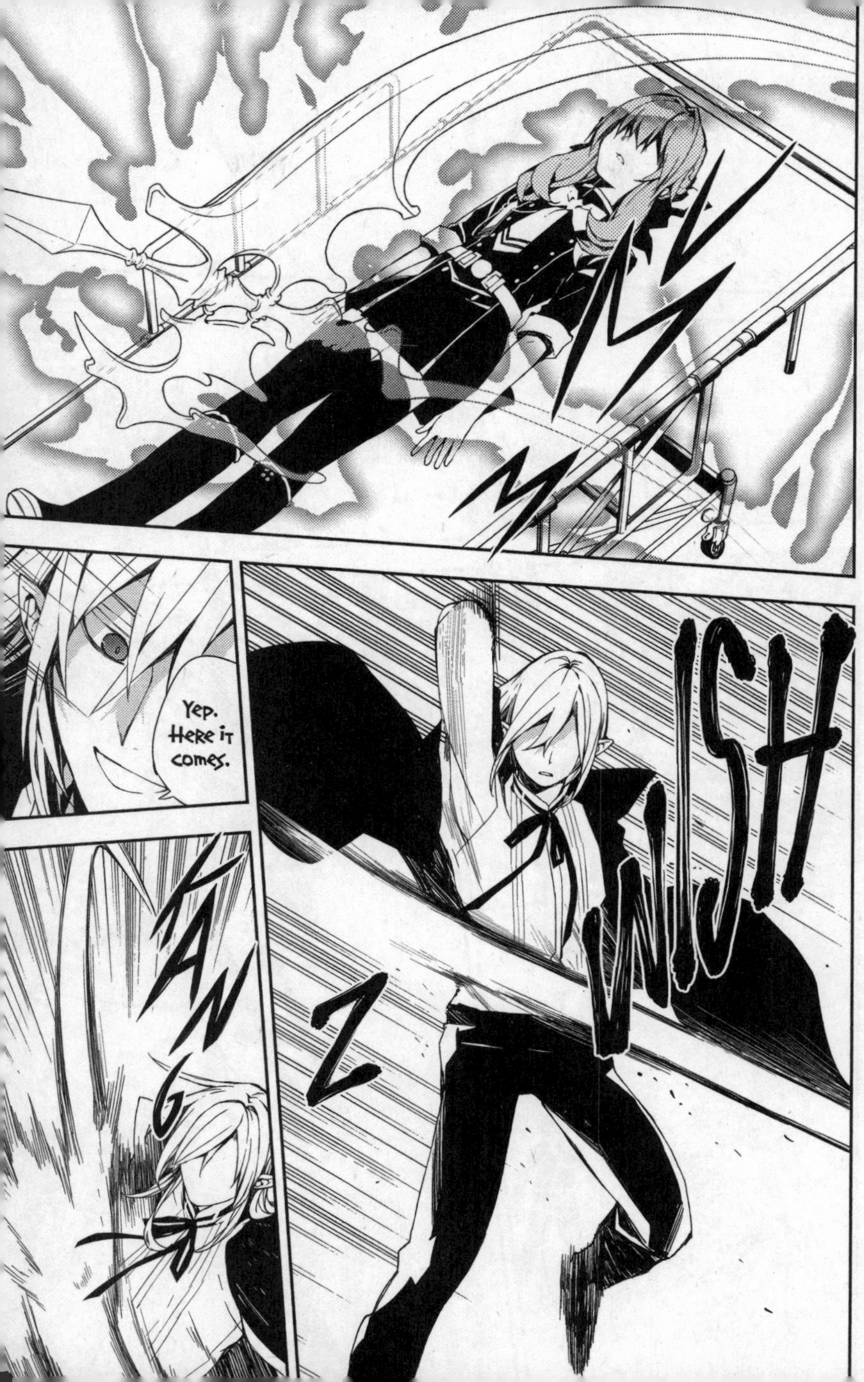
Yep. Here it comes.

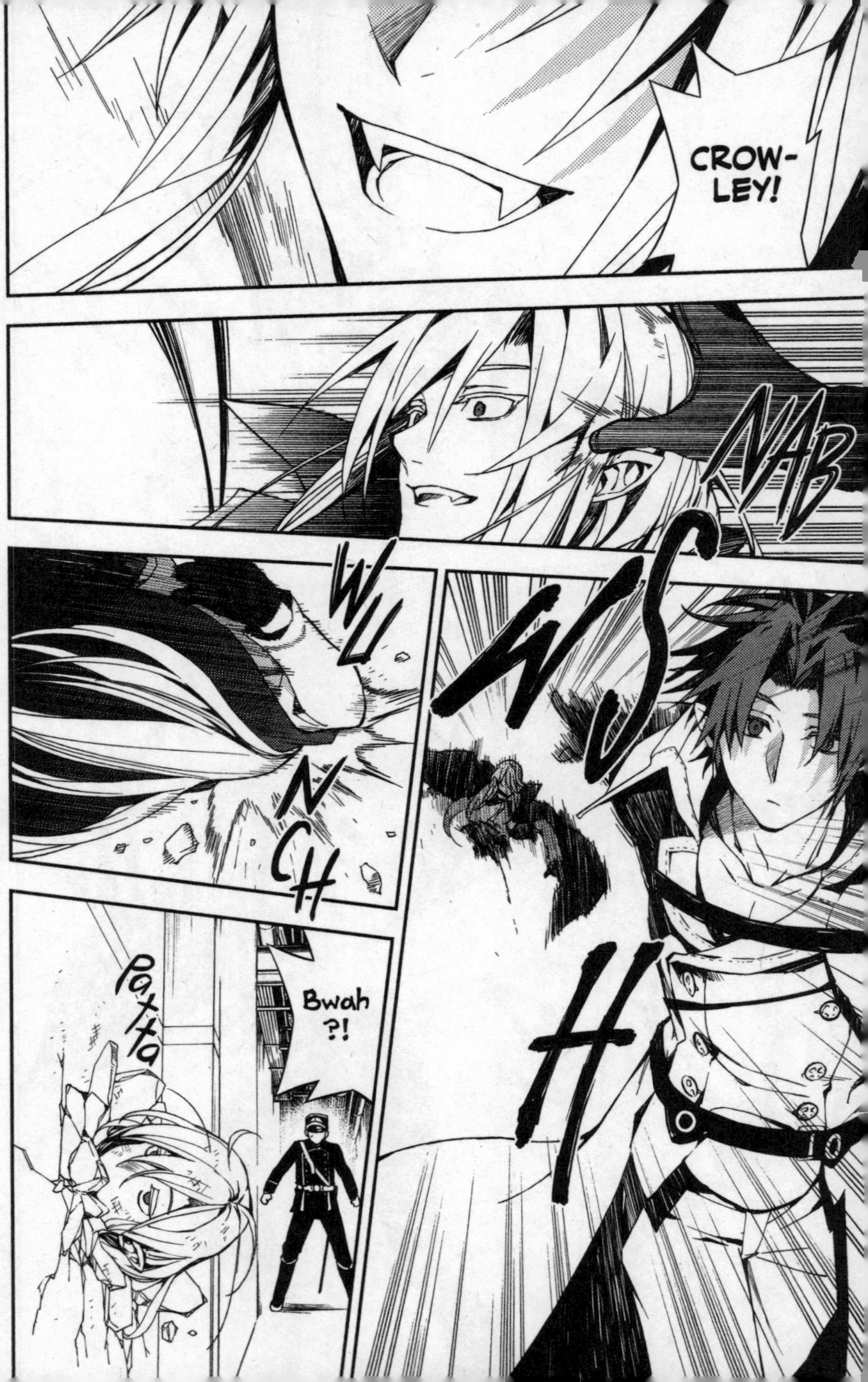
CROW-
LEY!
NAB
Bwah
?!
Patta

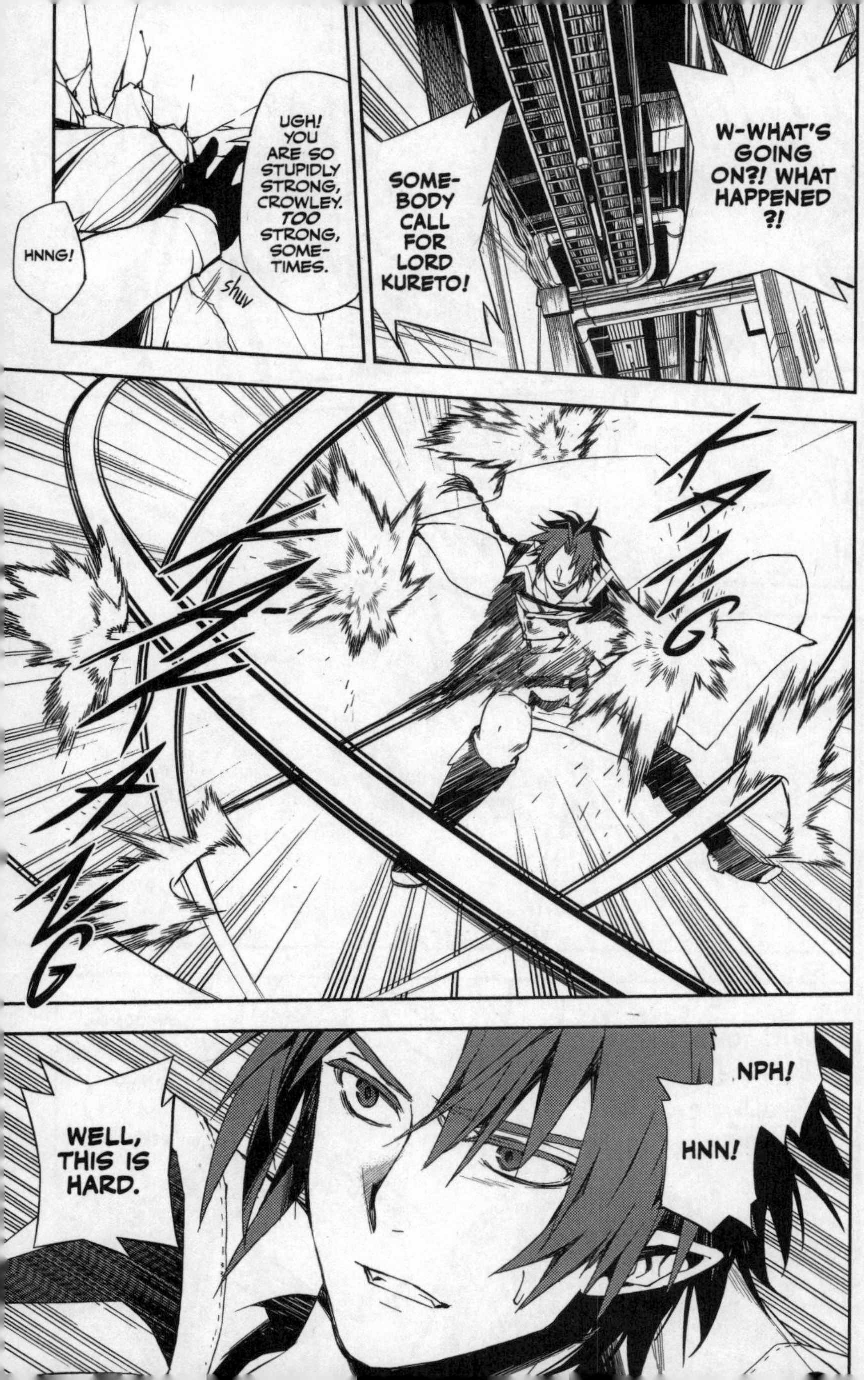
W-WHAT'S GOING ON?! WHAT HAPPENED ?!
SOME-BODY CALL FOR LORD KURETO!
UGH! YOU ARE SO STUPIDLY STRONG, CROWLEY. *TOO* STRONG, SOME-TIMES.
HNNG!
shuv
KANG
NPH!
HNN!
WELL, THIS IS HARD.

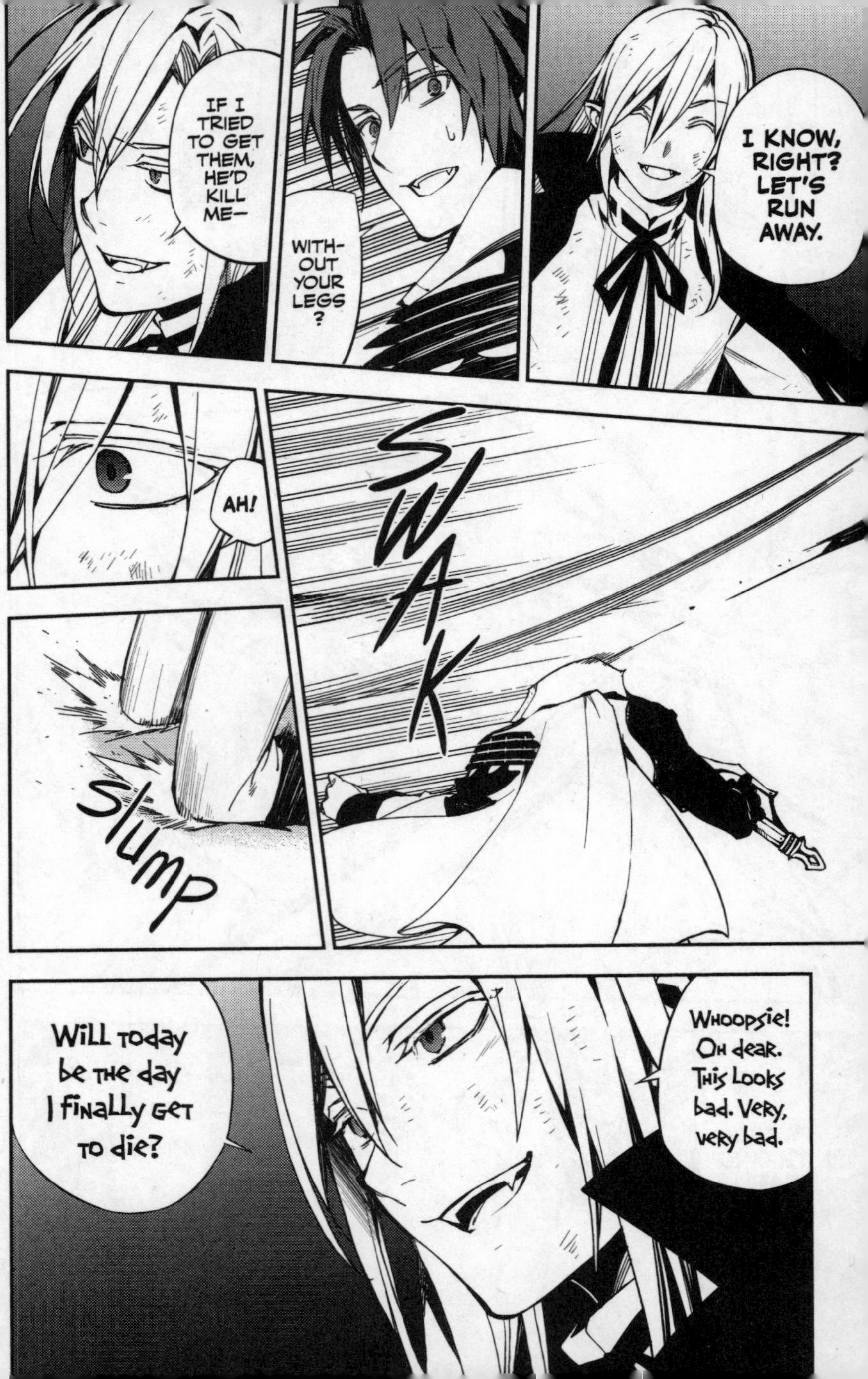
I KNOW, RIGHT? LET'S RUN AWAY.
WITH-OUT YOUR LEGS?
IF I TRIED TO GET THEM, HE'D KILL ME—
SWAK
AH!
SLUMP
Whoopsie! Oh dear. This looks bad. Very, very bad.
Will today be the day I finally get to die?

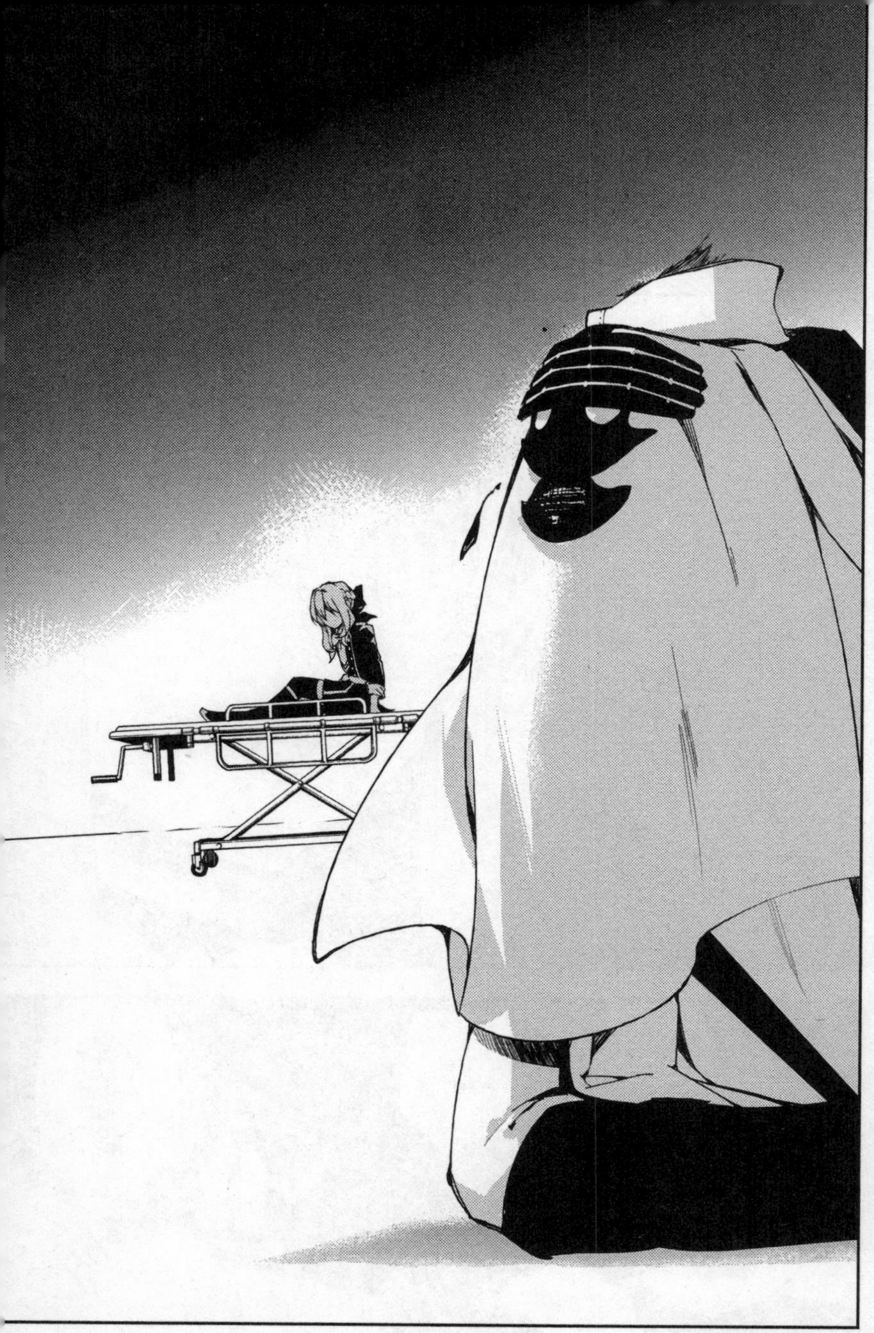

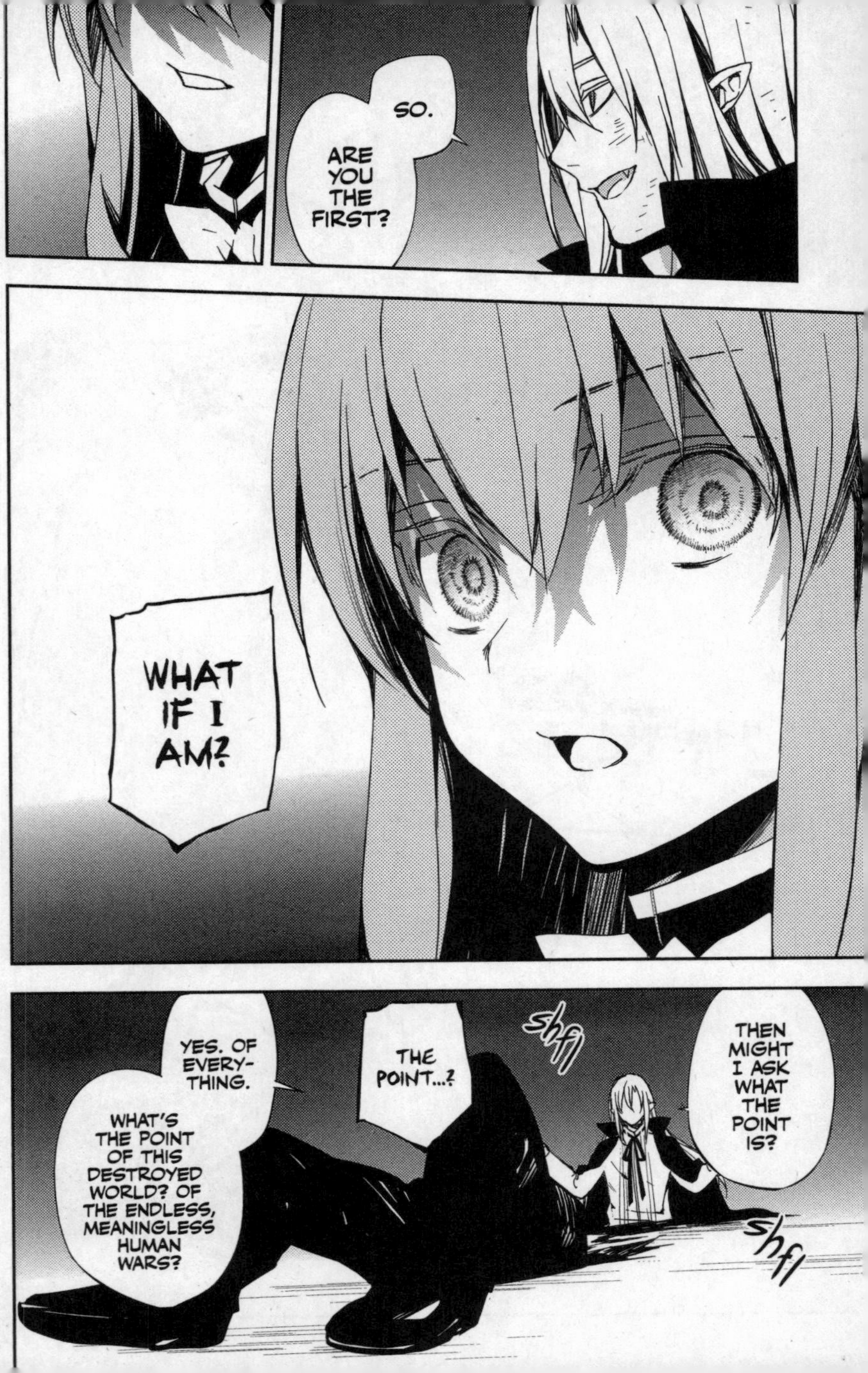
SO.
ARE YOU THE FIRST?
WHAT IF I AM?
THEN MIGHT I ASK WHAT THE POINT IS?
shfl
THE POINT...?
YES. OF EVERY-THING.
WHAT'S THE POINT OF THIS DESTROYED WORLD? OF THE ENDLESS, MEANINGLESS HUMAN WARS?
shfl

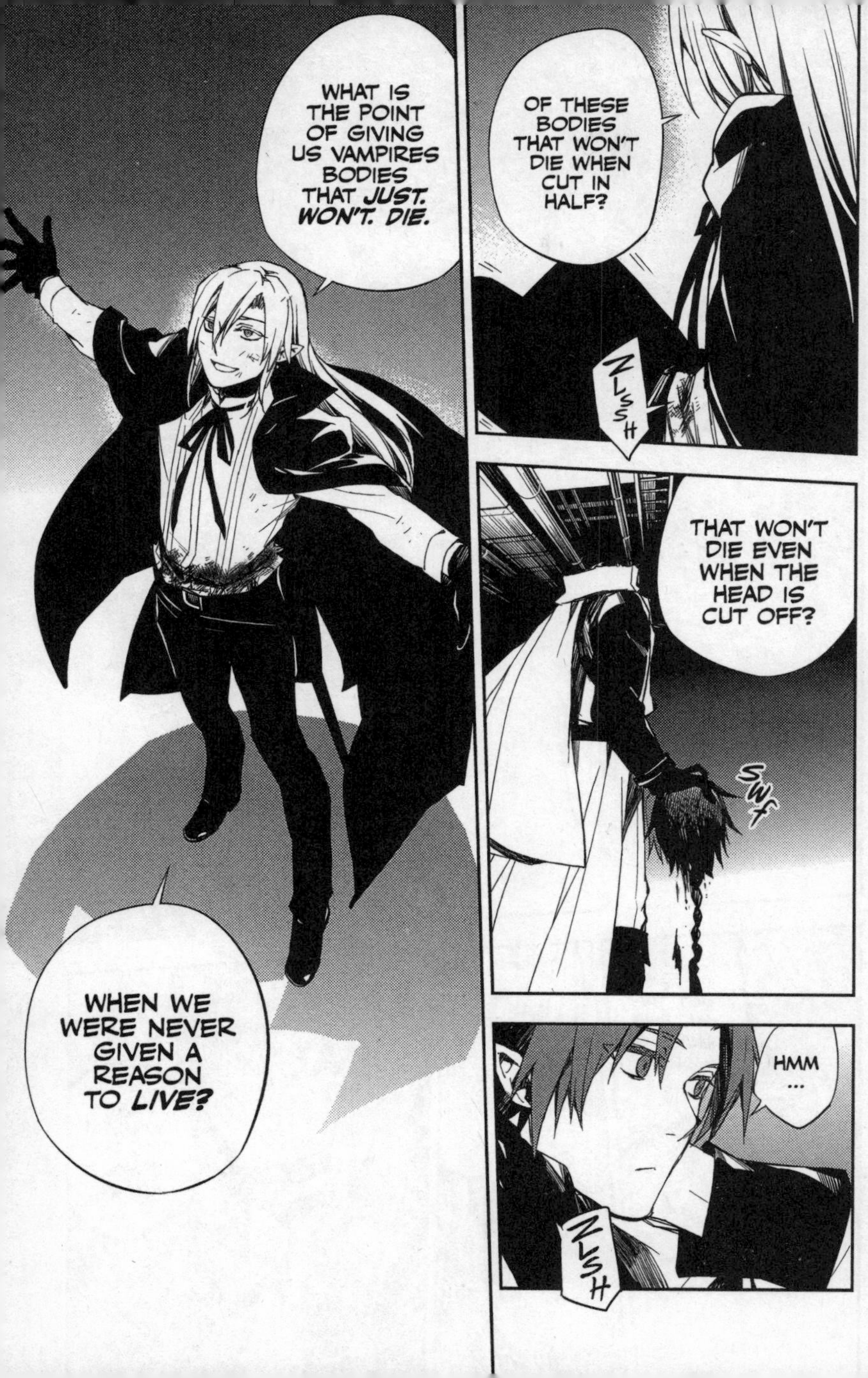
WHAT IS THE POINT OF GIVING US VAMPIRES BODIES THAT *JUST. WON'T. DIE.*
OF THESE BODIES THAT WON'T DIE WHEN CUT IN HALF?
ZLSH
THAT WON'T DIE EVEN WHEN THE HEAD IS CUT OFF?
SWF
WHEN WE WERE NEVER GIVEN A REASON TO *LIVE?*
HMM ...
ZLSH

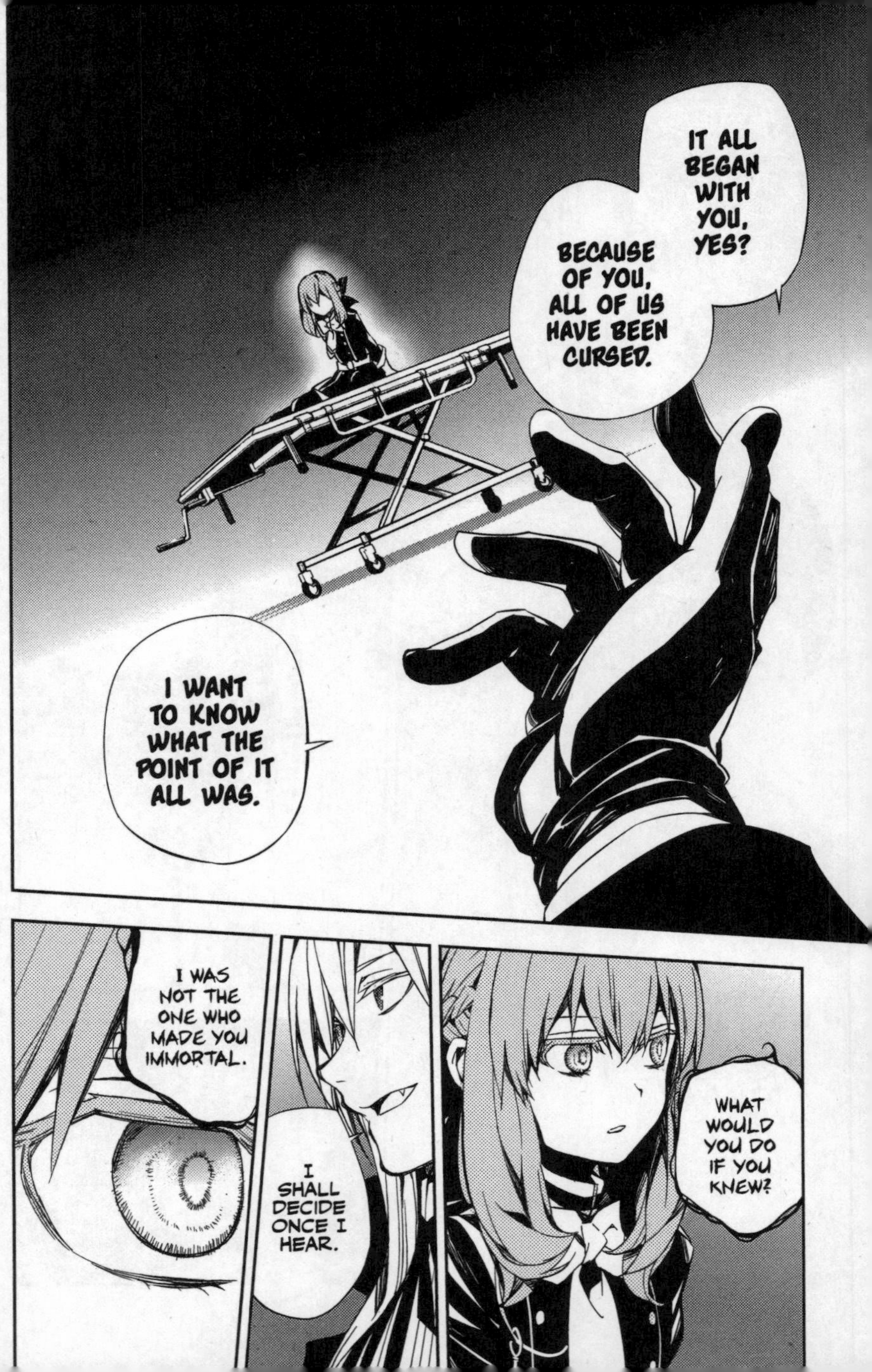
IT ALL BEGAN WITH YOU, YES?
BECAUSE OF YOU, ALL OF US HAVE BEEN CURSED.
I WANT TO KNOW WHAT THE POINT OF IT ALL WAS.
WHAT WOULD YOU DO IF YOU KNEW?
I SHALL DECIDE ONCE I HEAR.
I WAS NOT THE ONE WHO MADE YOU IMMORTAL.

TRUE. MY FATHER DID. BUT YOU CURSED *HIM.*
THE RIPPLE EFFECT FROM THAT IS WHY WE'RE HERE TODAY.
AAH...
WHO IS YOUR FATHER?
RIGR STAFFORD.
I SEE.
THEN WAS IT HE WHO CREATED THIS HUMAN ORGANI-ZATION?

Tokyo, Ikebukuro Station East Exit

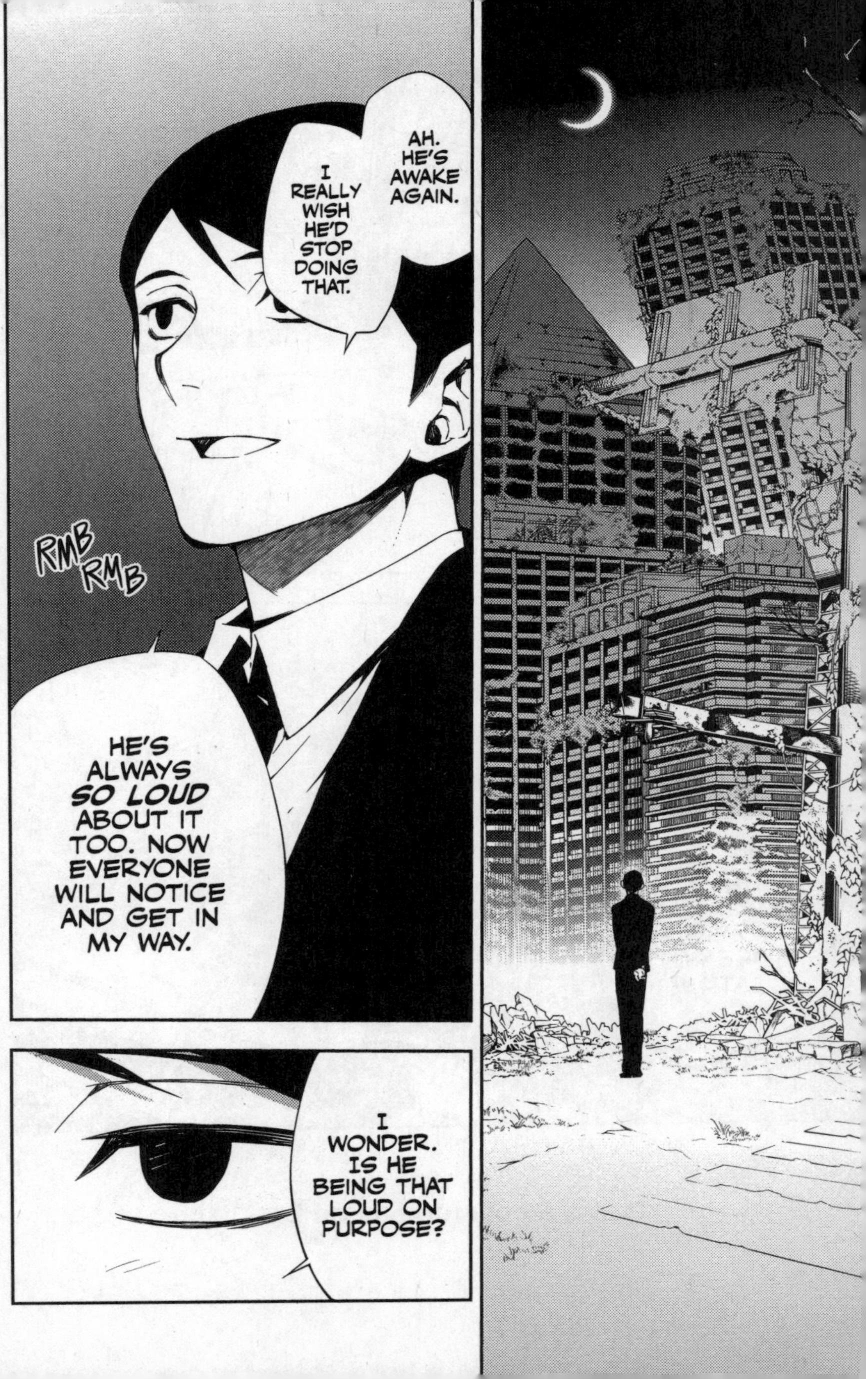
AH. HE'S AWAKE AGAIN.
I REALLY WISH HE'D STOP DOING THAT.
RMB RMB
HE'S ALWAYS *SO LOUD* ABOUT IT TOO. NOW EVERYONE WILL NOTICE AND GET IN MY WAY.
I WONDER. IS HE BEING THAT LOUD ON PURPOSE?

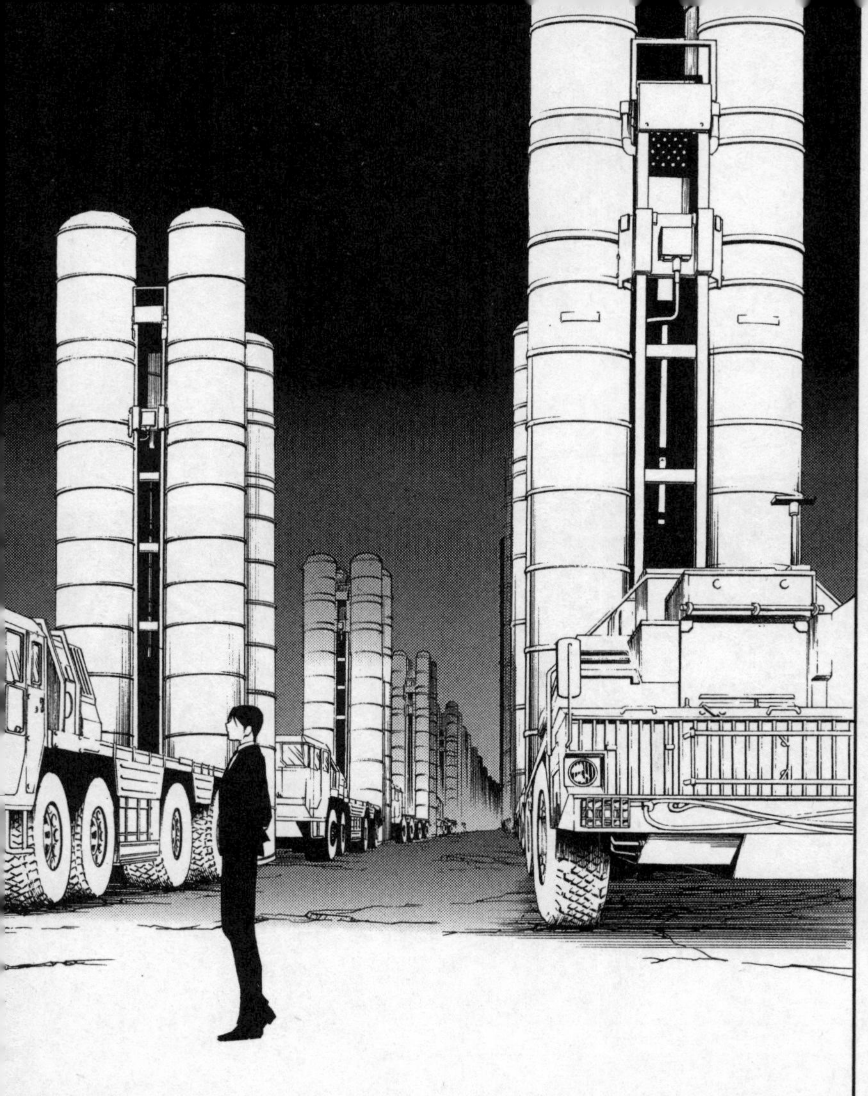

Ikebukuro, Old Hyakuya Sect Underground Headquarters

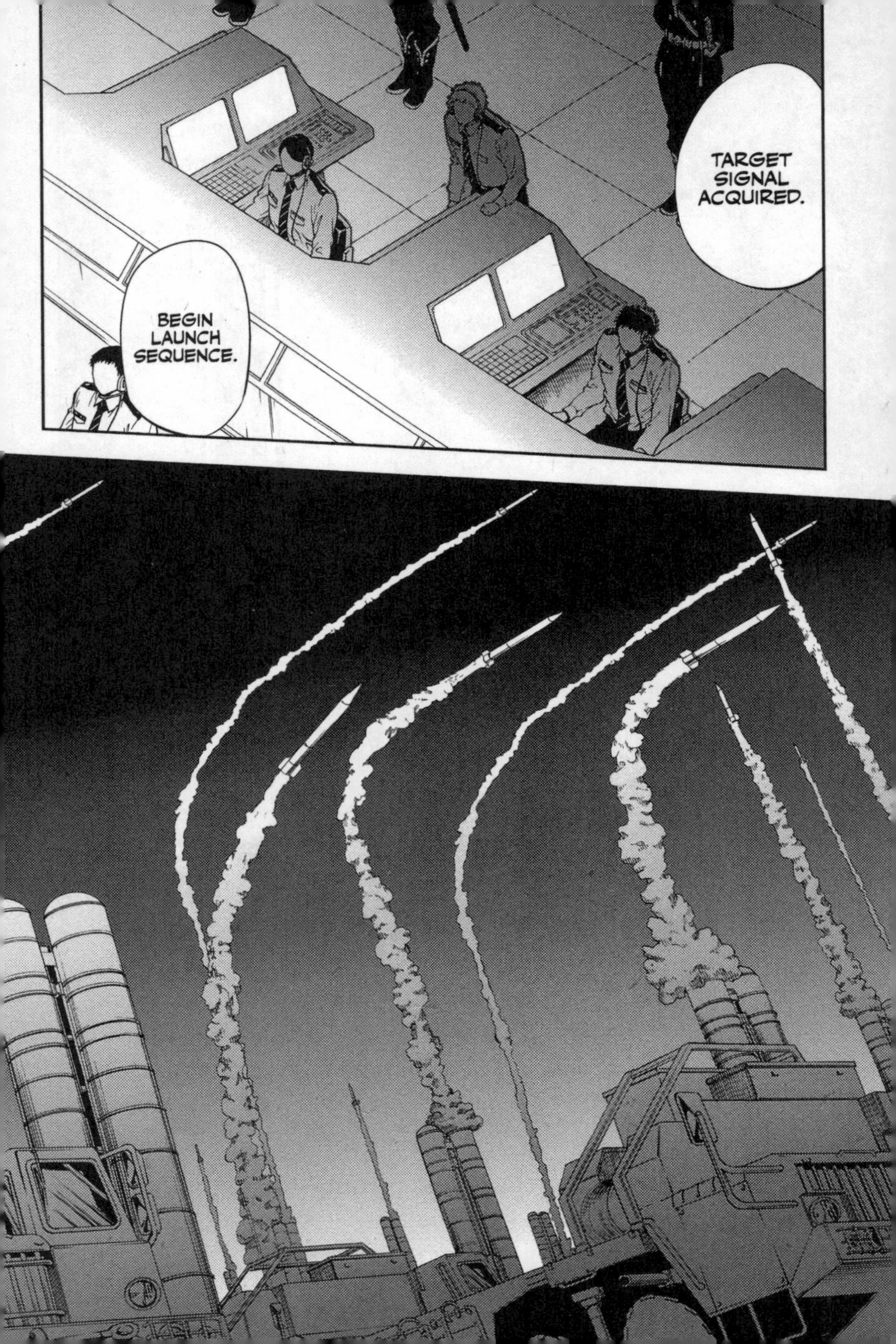
TARGET SIGNAL ACQUIRED.
BEGIN LAUNCH SEQUENCE.

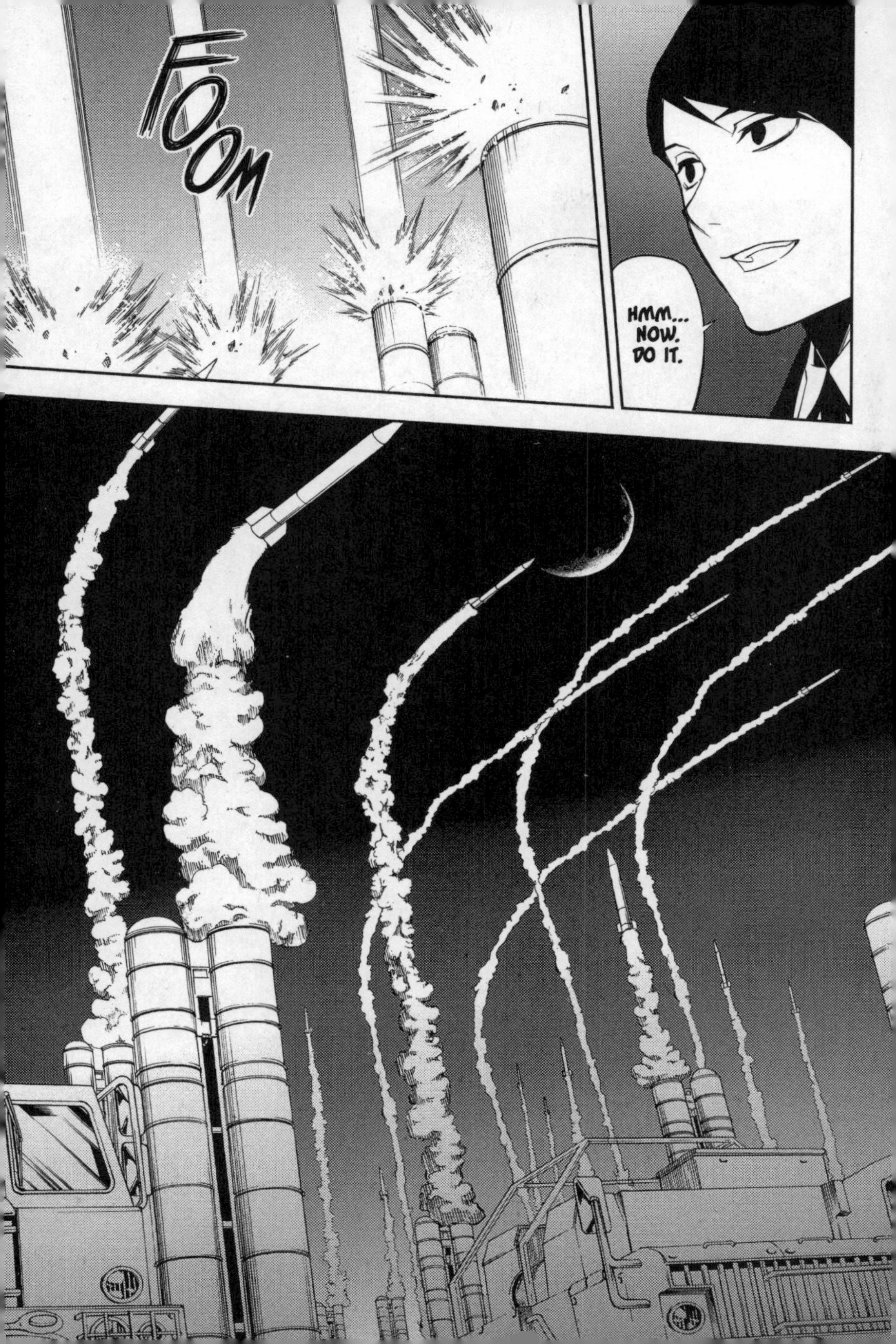
HMM... NOW. DO IT.
FOOM

Above Osaka

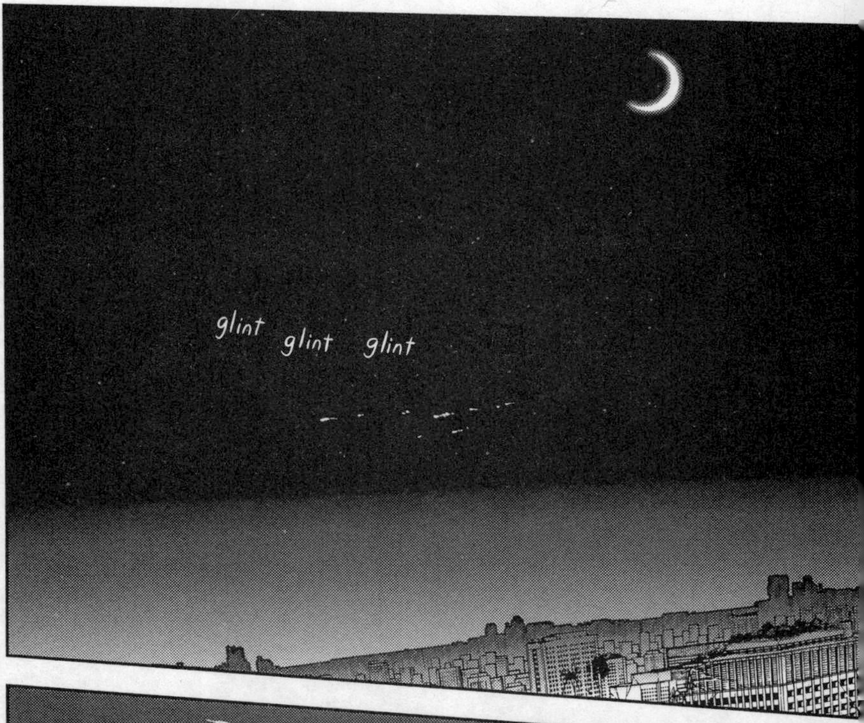
glint glint glint

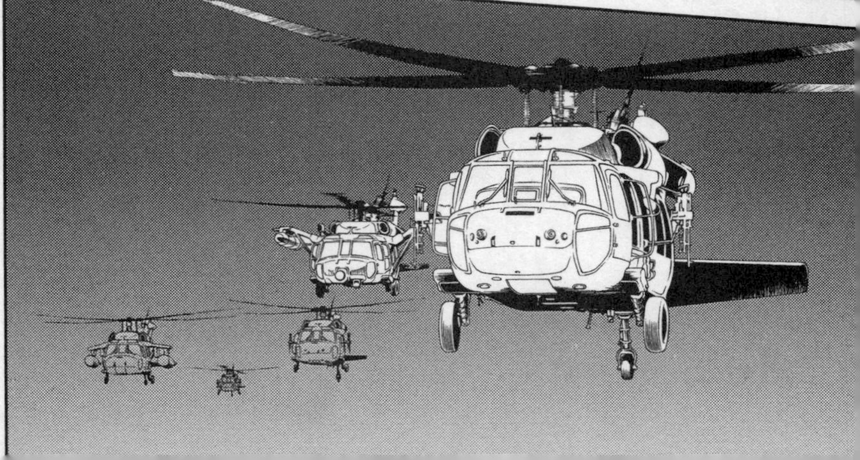

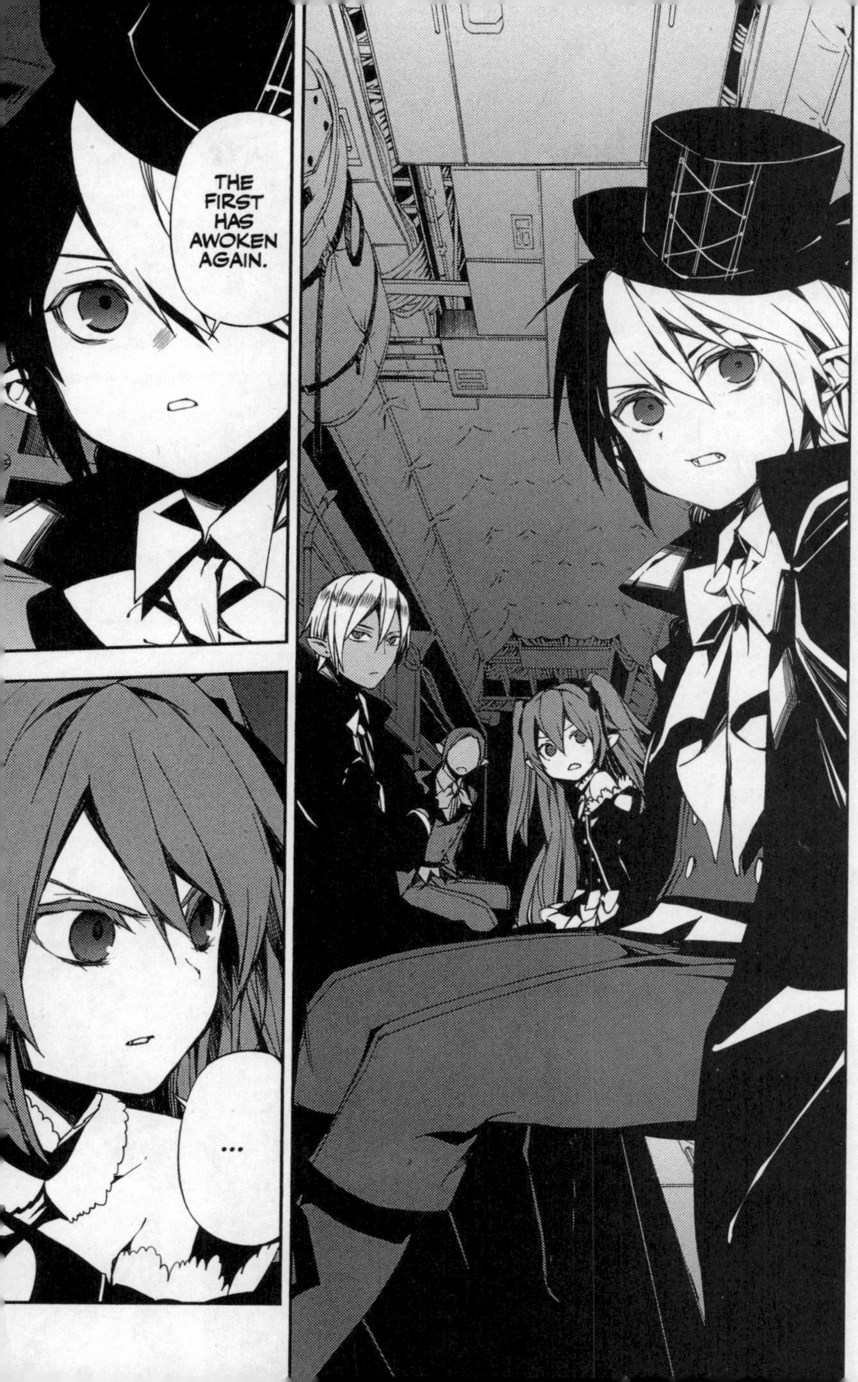
THE FIRST HAS AWOKEN AGAIN.
...

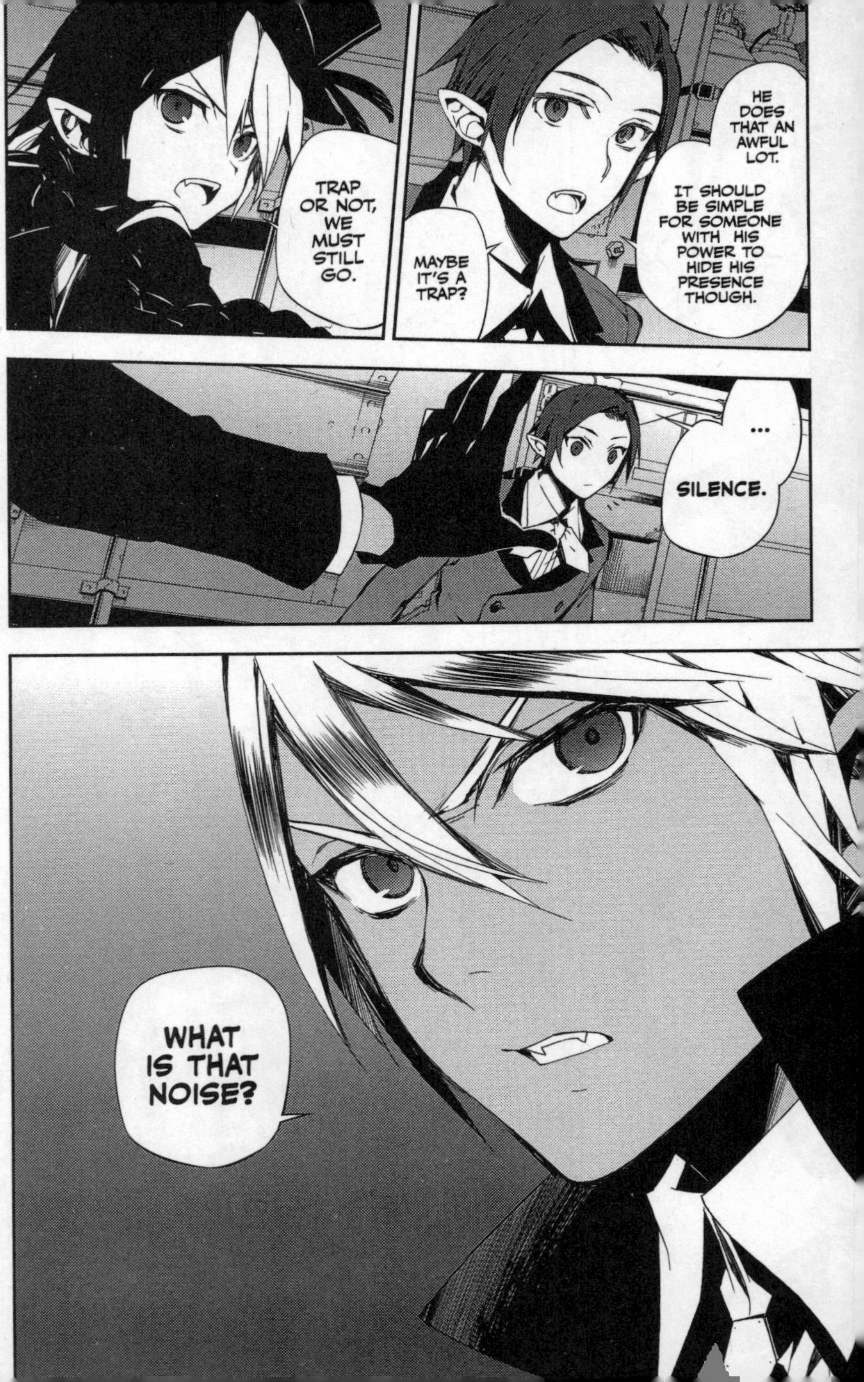
HE DOES THAT AN AWFUL LOT.
IT SHOULD BE SIMPLE FOR SOMEONE WITH HIS POWER TO HIDE HIS PRESENCE THOUGH.
MAYBE IT'S A TRAP?
TRAP OR NOT, WE MUST STILL GO.
...
SILENCE.
WHAT IS THAT NOISE?

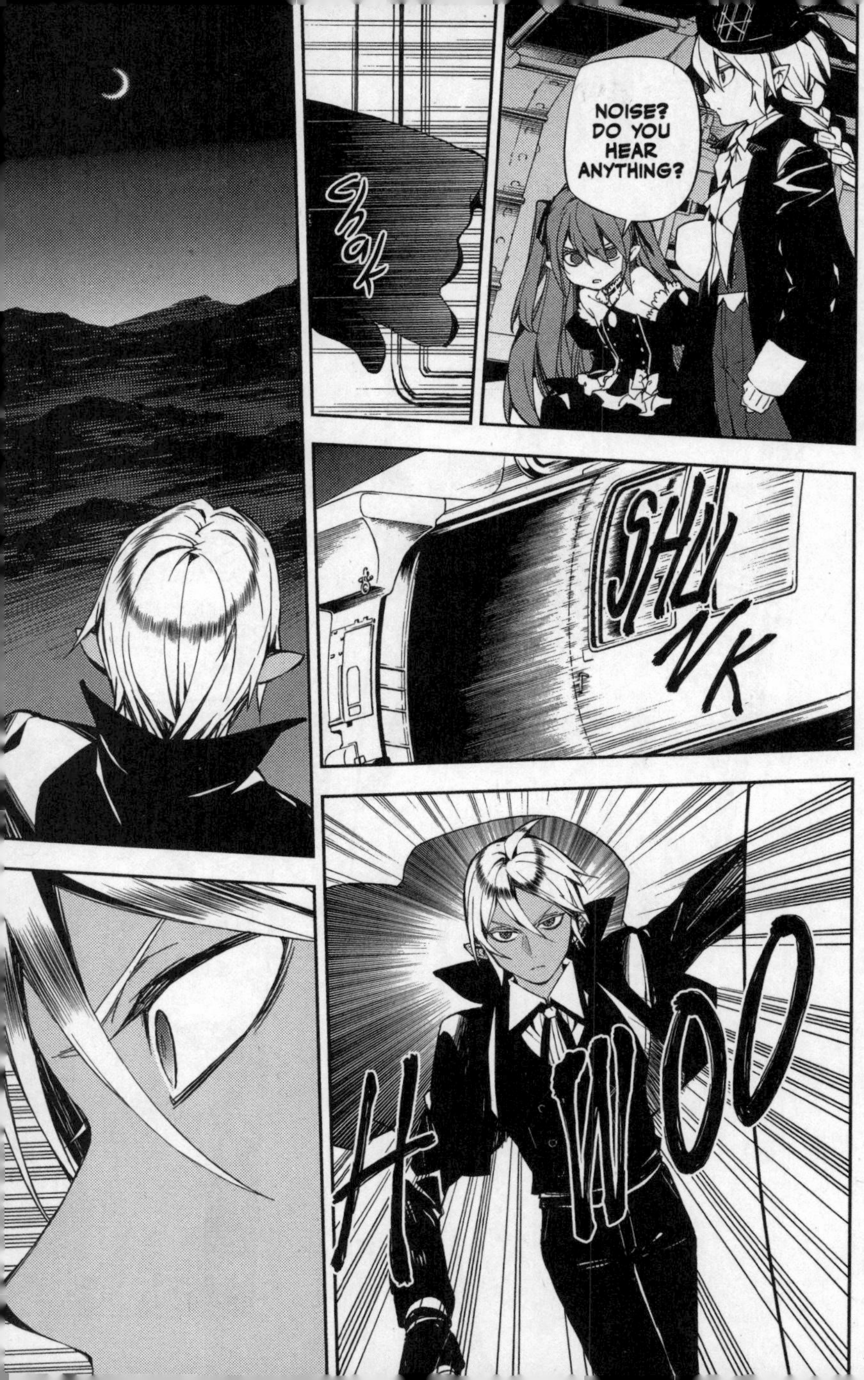
NOISE? DO YOU HEAR ANYTHING?
Shak
SHUNK
HWOO

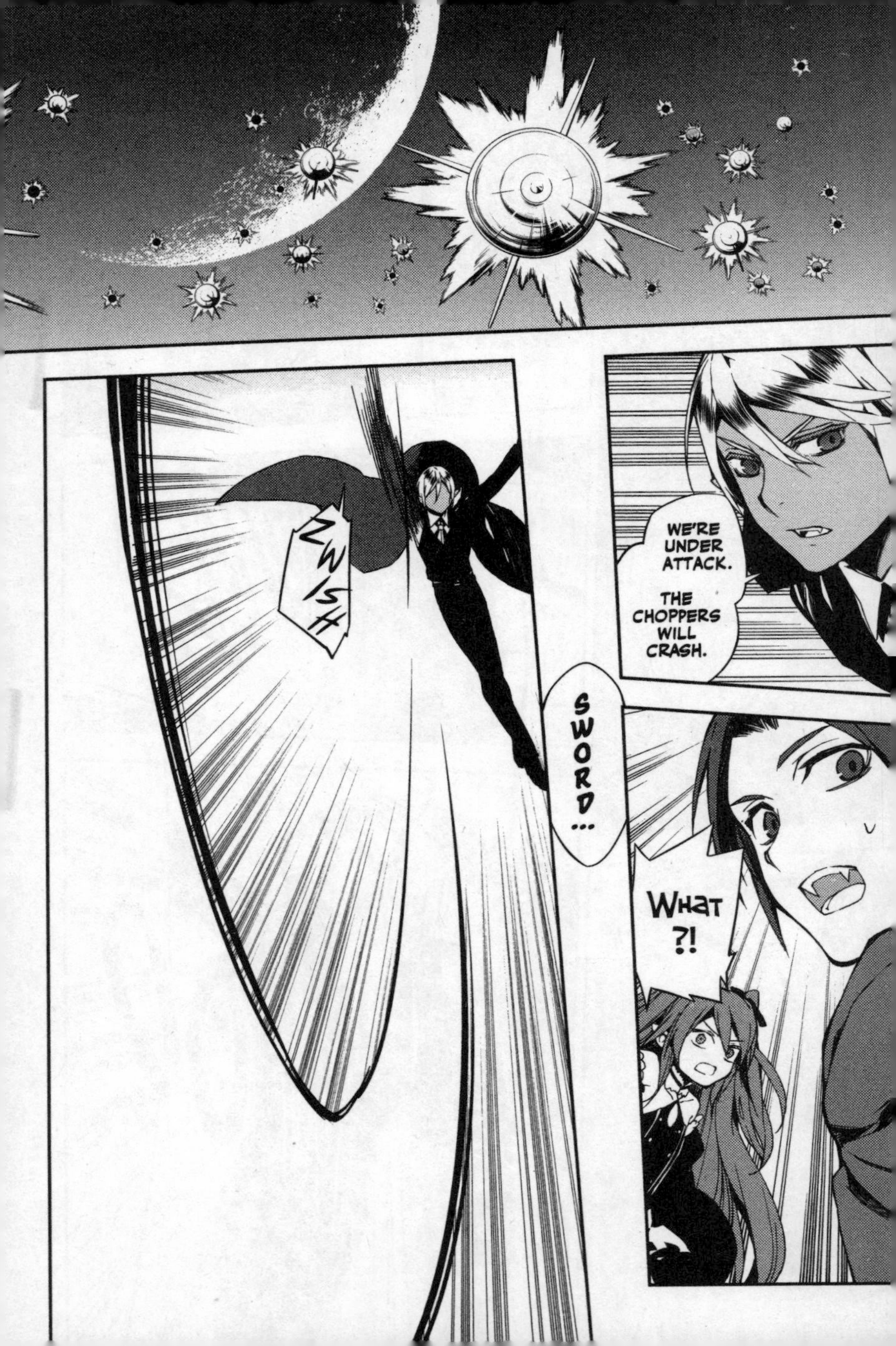
WE'RE UNDER ATTACK.
THE CHOPPERS WILL CRASH.
SWORD...
WHAT?!
ZWISH

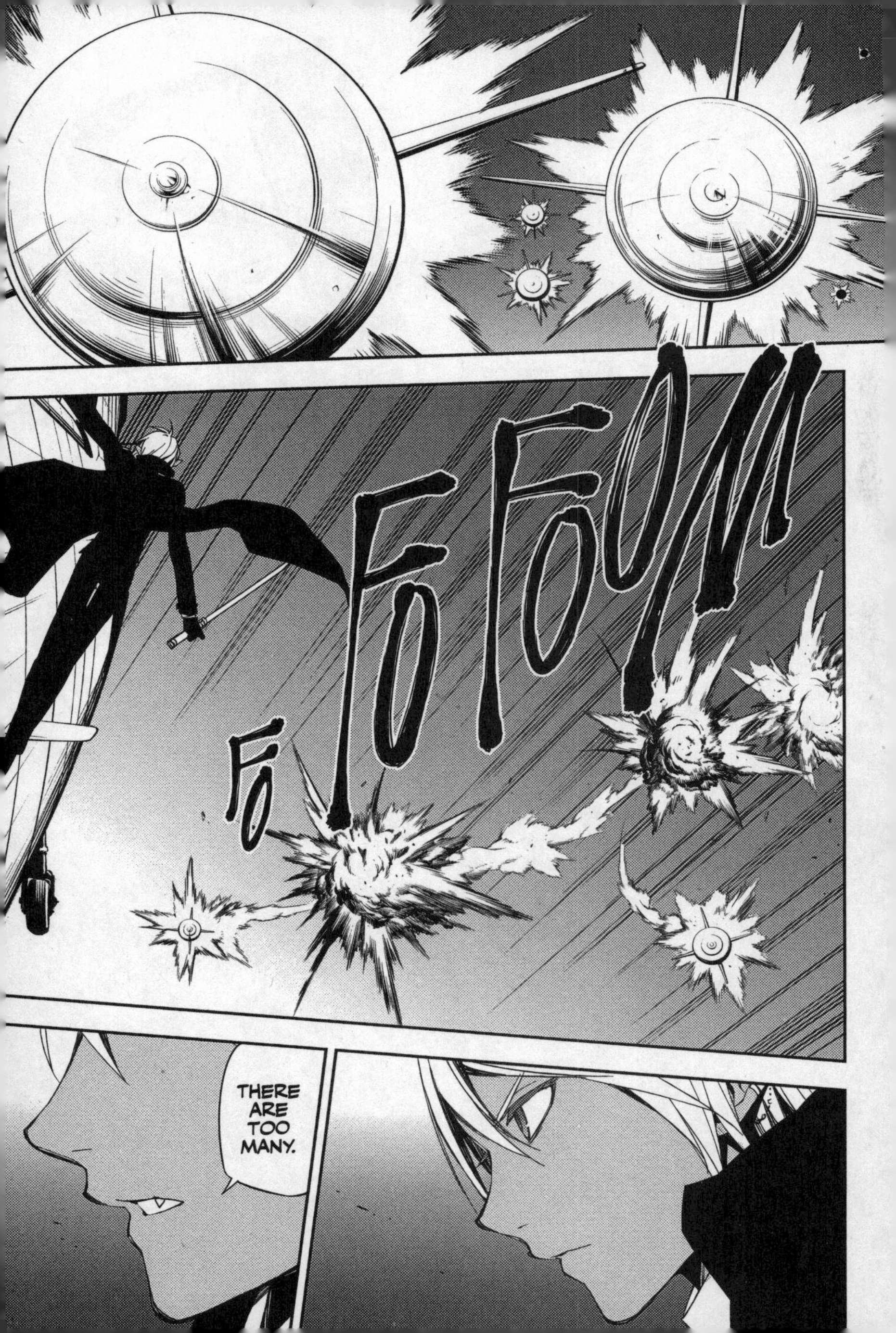
FO FOFOOM
THERE ARE TOO MANY.

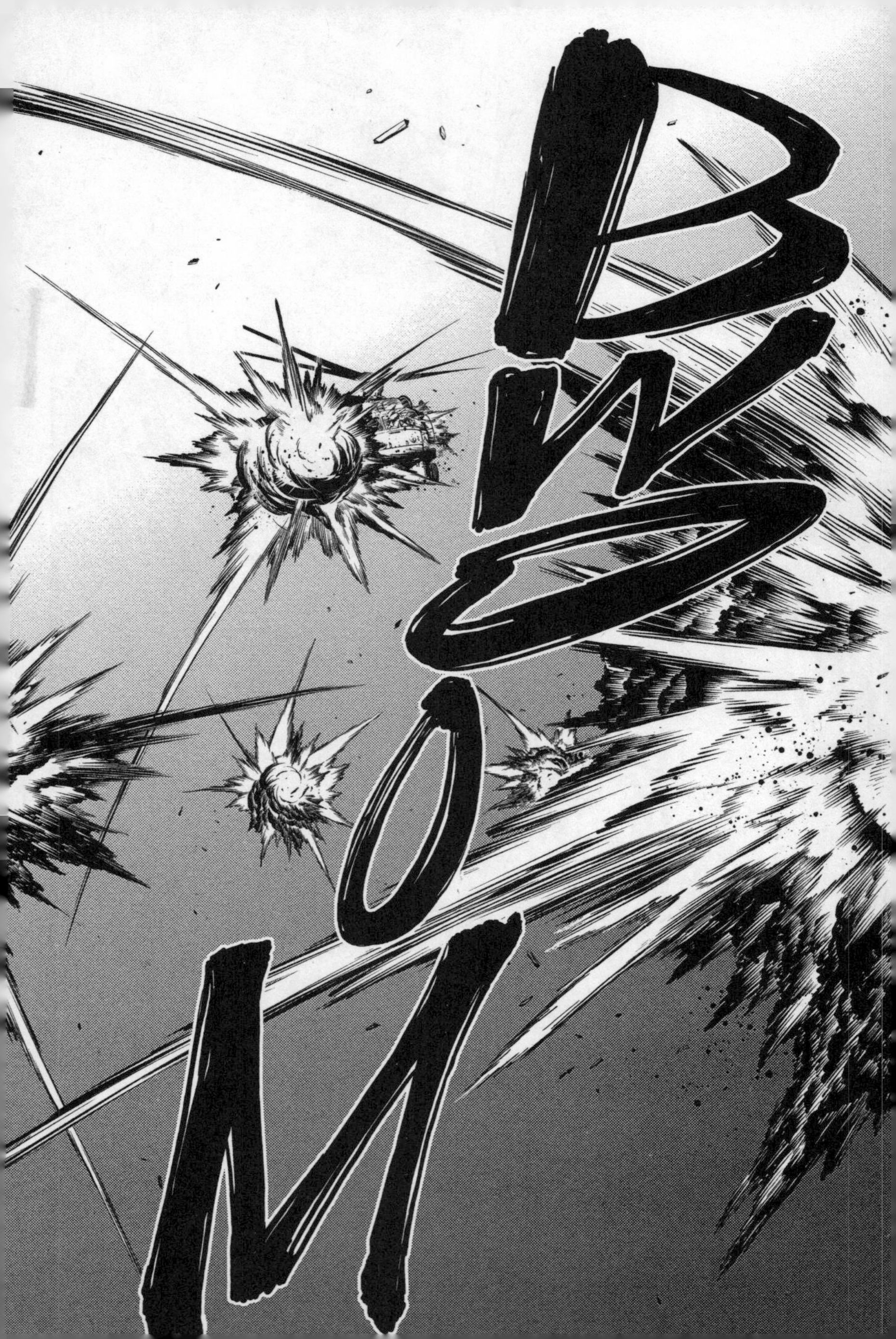
BWOOM

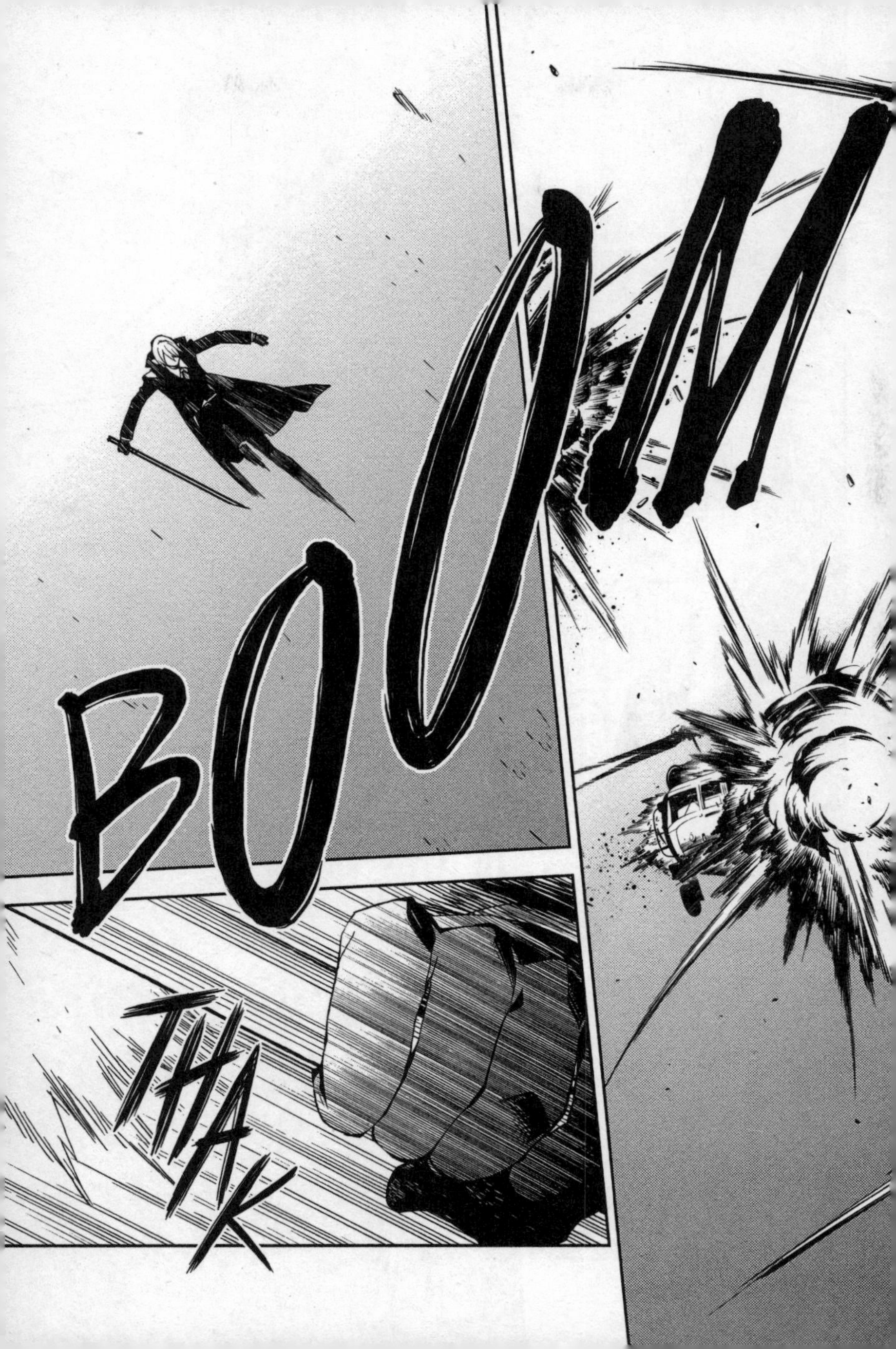
BOOM
THAK

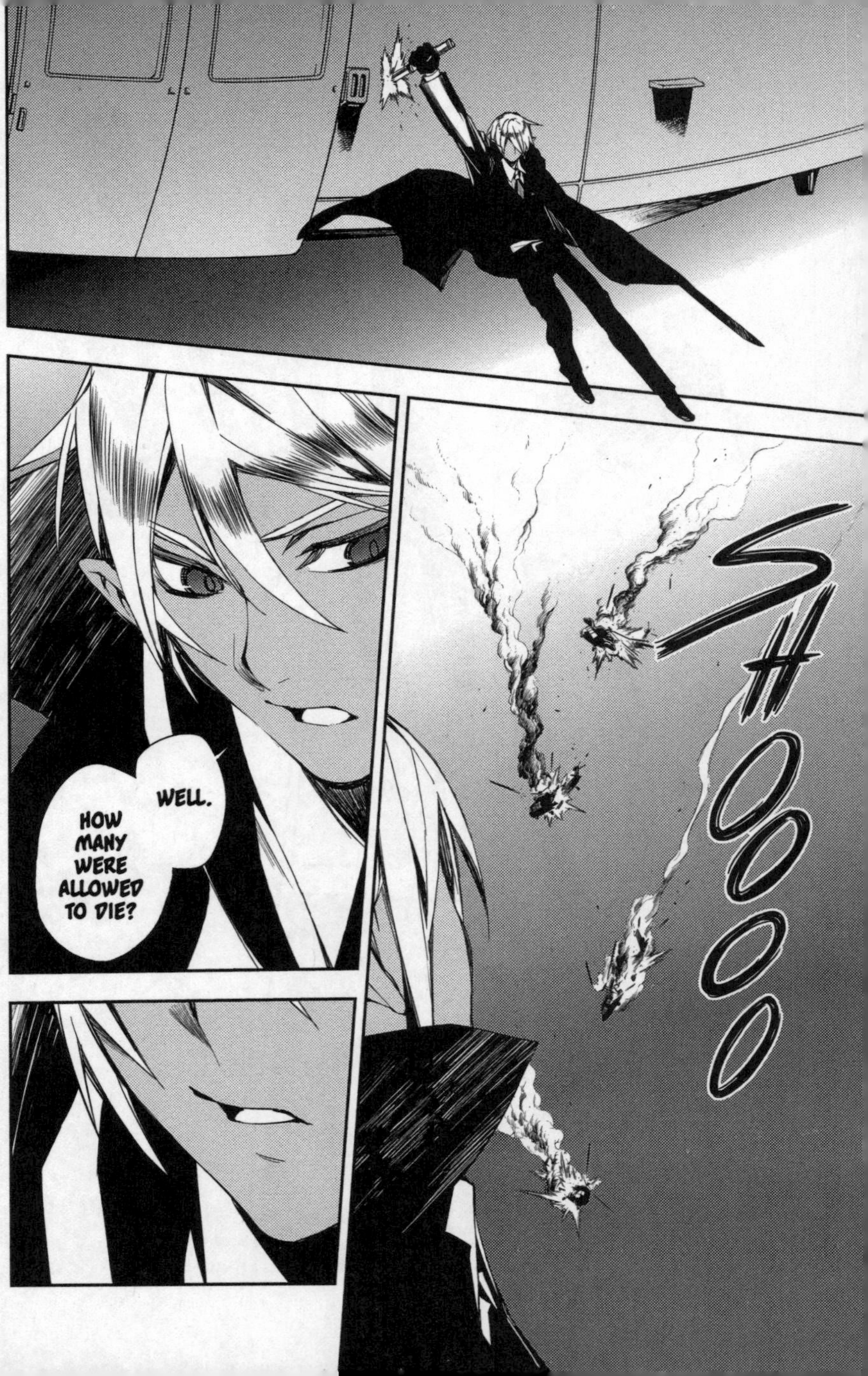
SHOOOOO
WELL. HOW MANY WERE ALLOWED TO DIE?

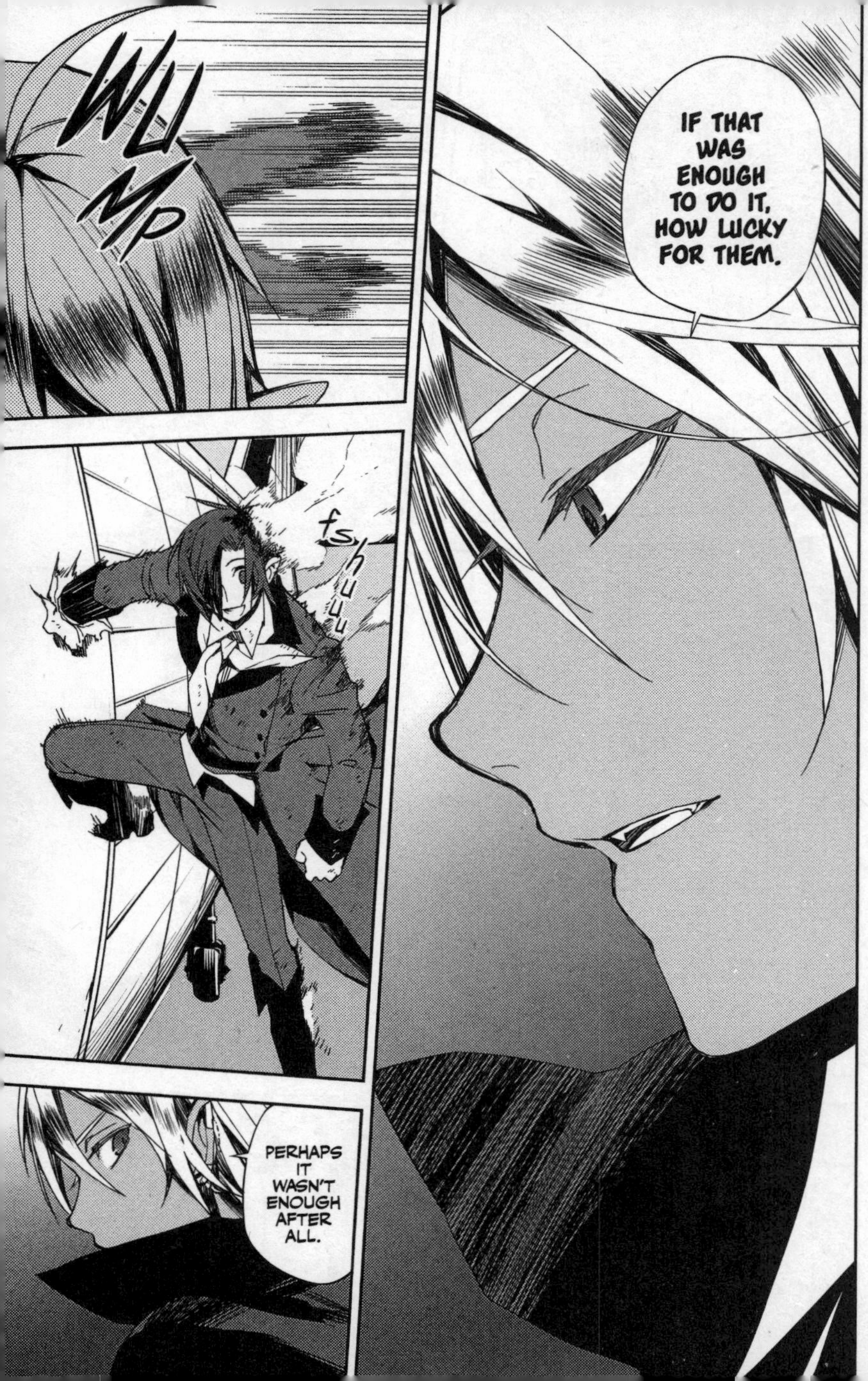
IF THAT WAS ENOUGH TO DO IT, HOW LUCKY FOR THEM.
WUMP
fshuuu
PERHAPS IT WASN'T ENOUGH AFTER ALL.

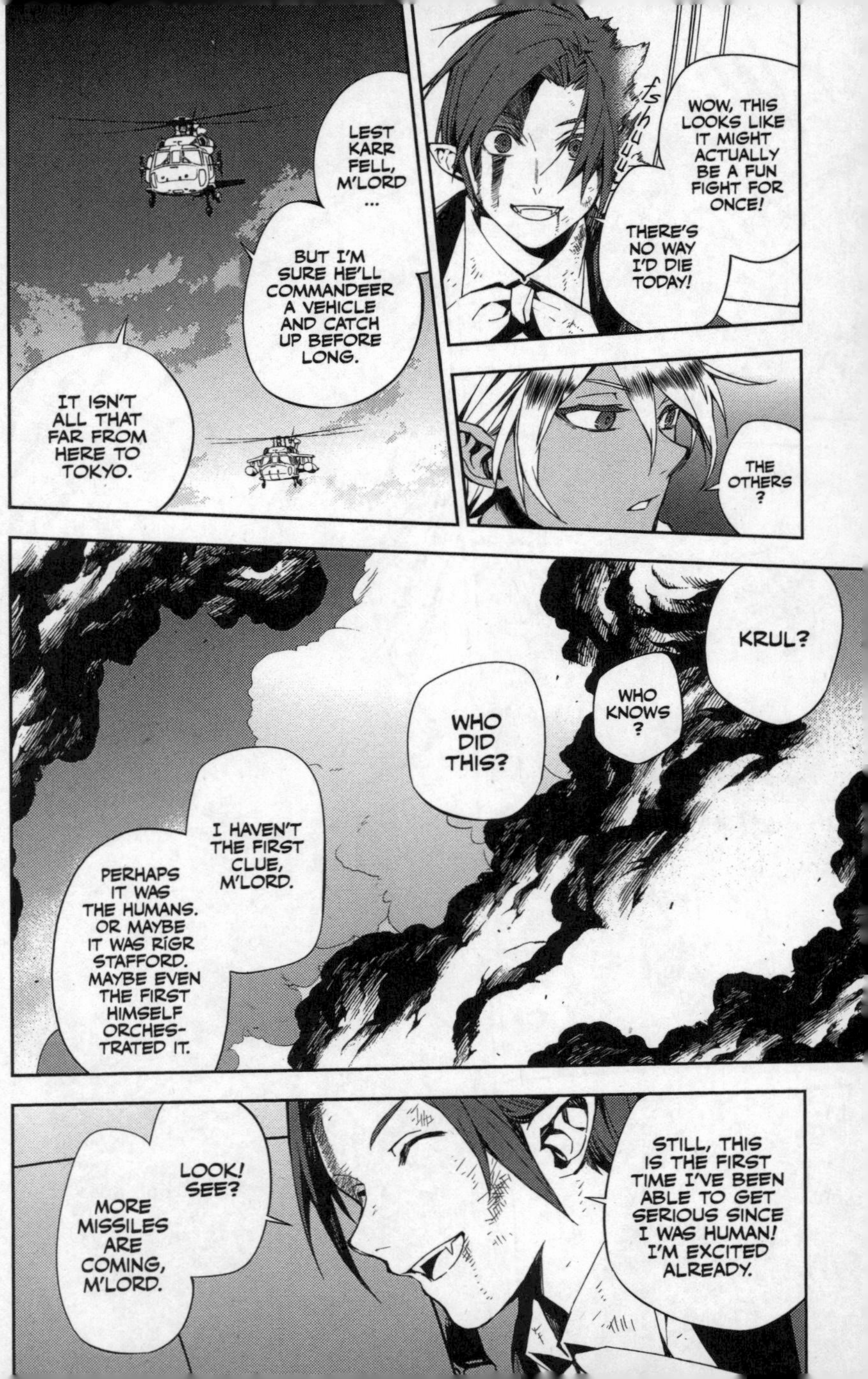
WOW, THIS LOOKS LIKE IT MIGHT ACTUALLY BE A FUN FIGHT FOR ONCE!
THERE'S NO WAY I'D DIE TODAY!
THE OTHERS?
LEST KARR FELL, M'LORD...
BUT I'M SURE HE'LL COMMANDEER A VEHICLE AND CATCH UP BEFORE LONG.
IT ISN'T ALL THAT FAR FROM HERE TO TOKYO.
KRUL?
WHO KNOWS?
WHO DID THIS?
I HAVEN'T THE FIRST CLUE, M'LORD.
PERHAPS IT WAS THE HUMANS. OR MAYBE IT WAS RIGR STAFFORD. MAYBE EVEN THE FIRST HIMSELF ORCHESTRATED IT.
STILL, THIS IS THE FIRST TIME I'VE BEEN ABLE TO GET SERIOUS SINCE I WAS HUMAN! I'M EXCITED ALREADY.
LOOK! SEE?
MORE MISSILES ARE COMING, M'LORD.

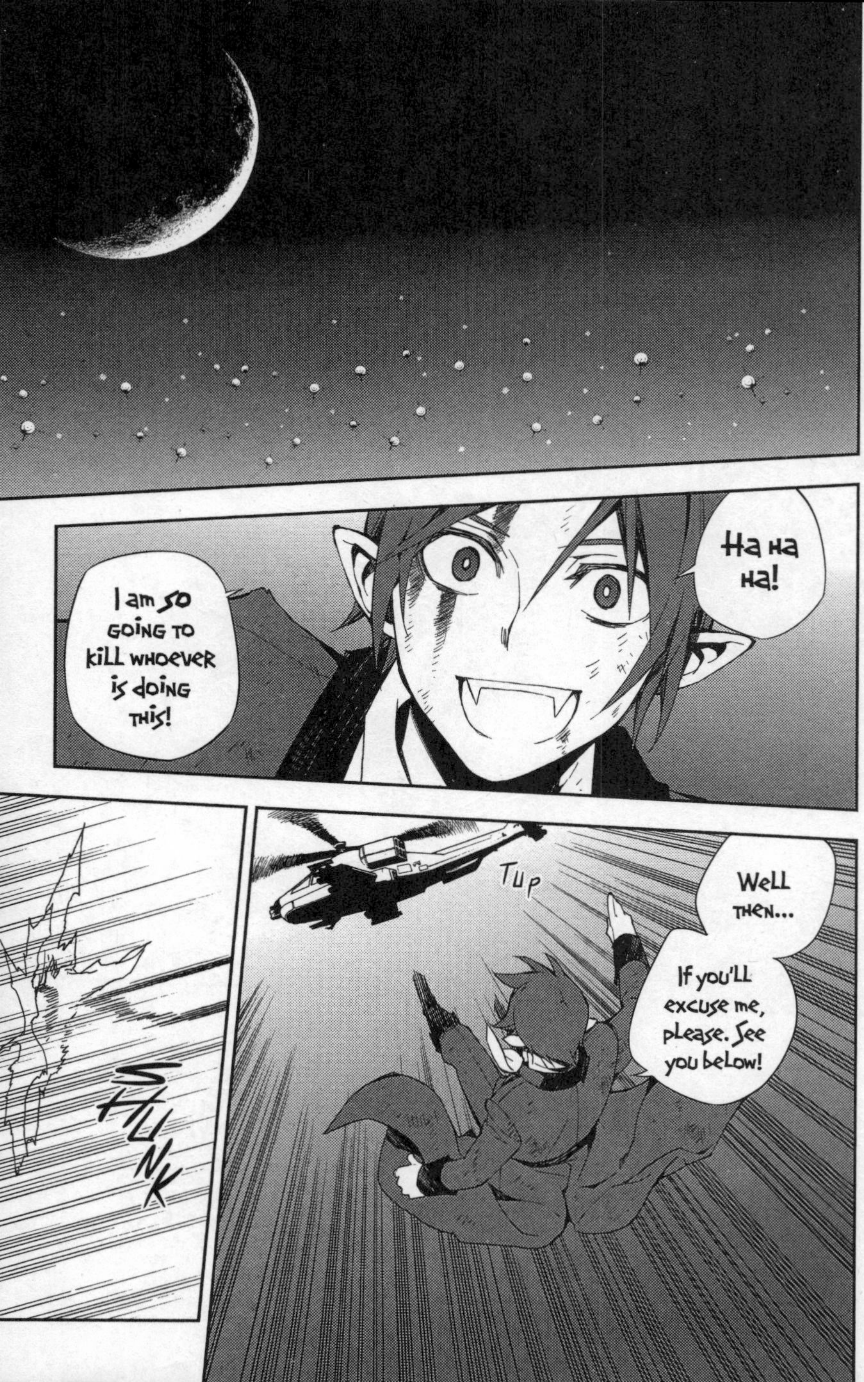
Ha ha ha!
I am SO going to kill whoever is doing this!
Well then...
If you'll excuse me, please. See you below!
TUP
SHUNK

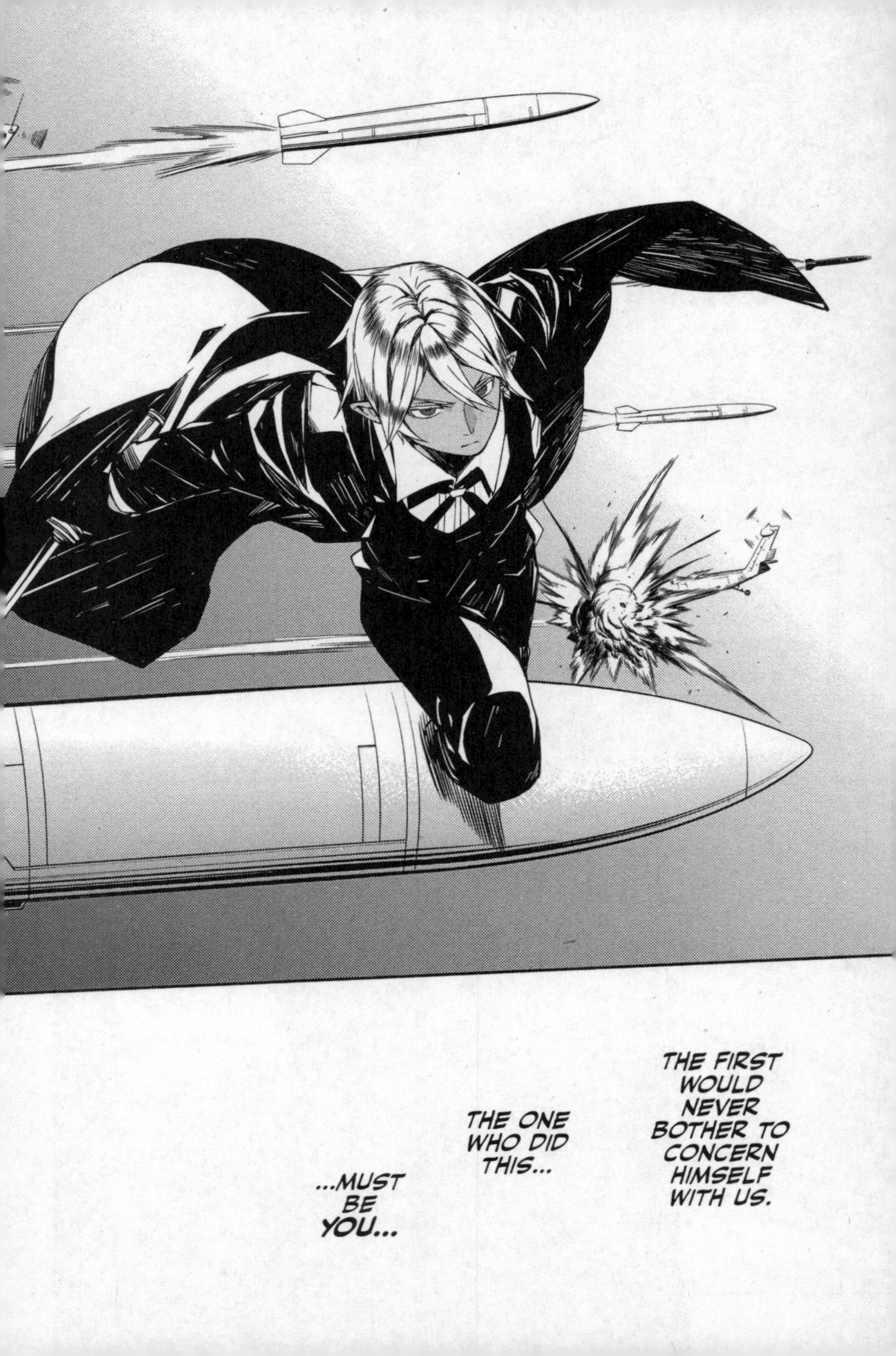
THE FIRST WOULD NEVER BOTHER TO CONCERN HIMSELF WITH US.
THE ONE WHO DID THIS...
...MUST BE YOU...

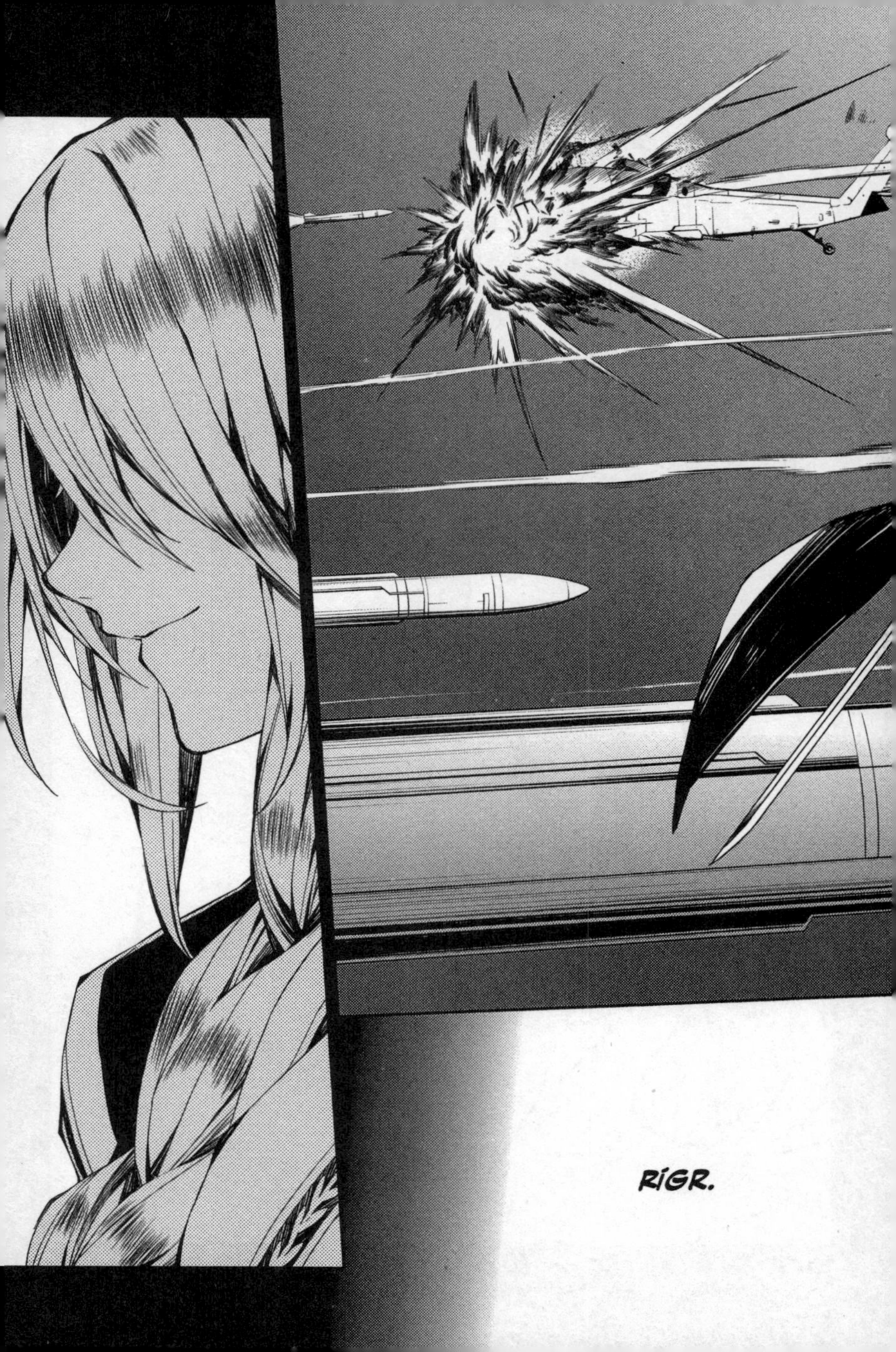
RÍGR.

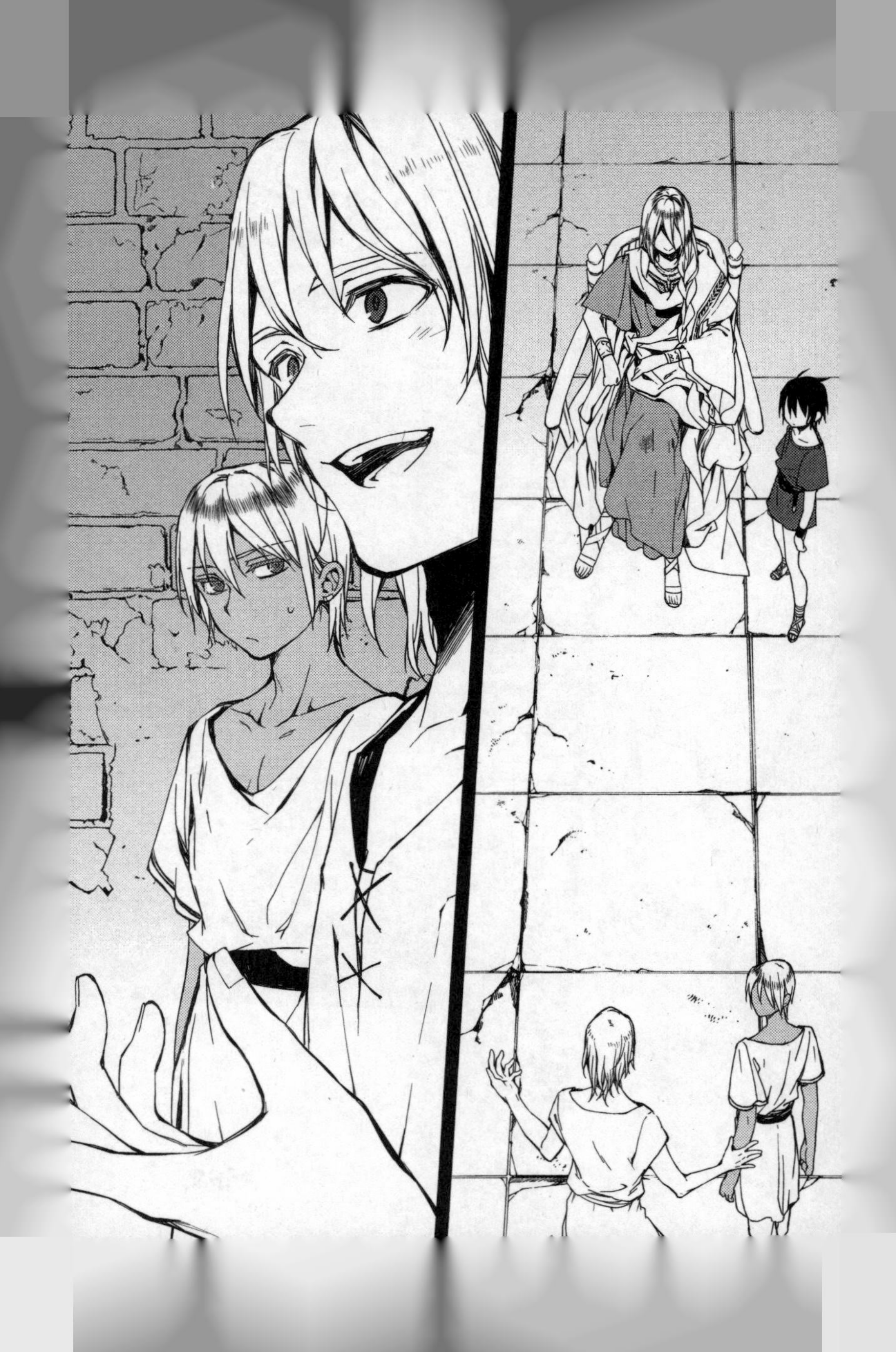

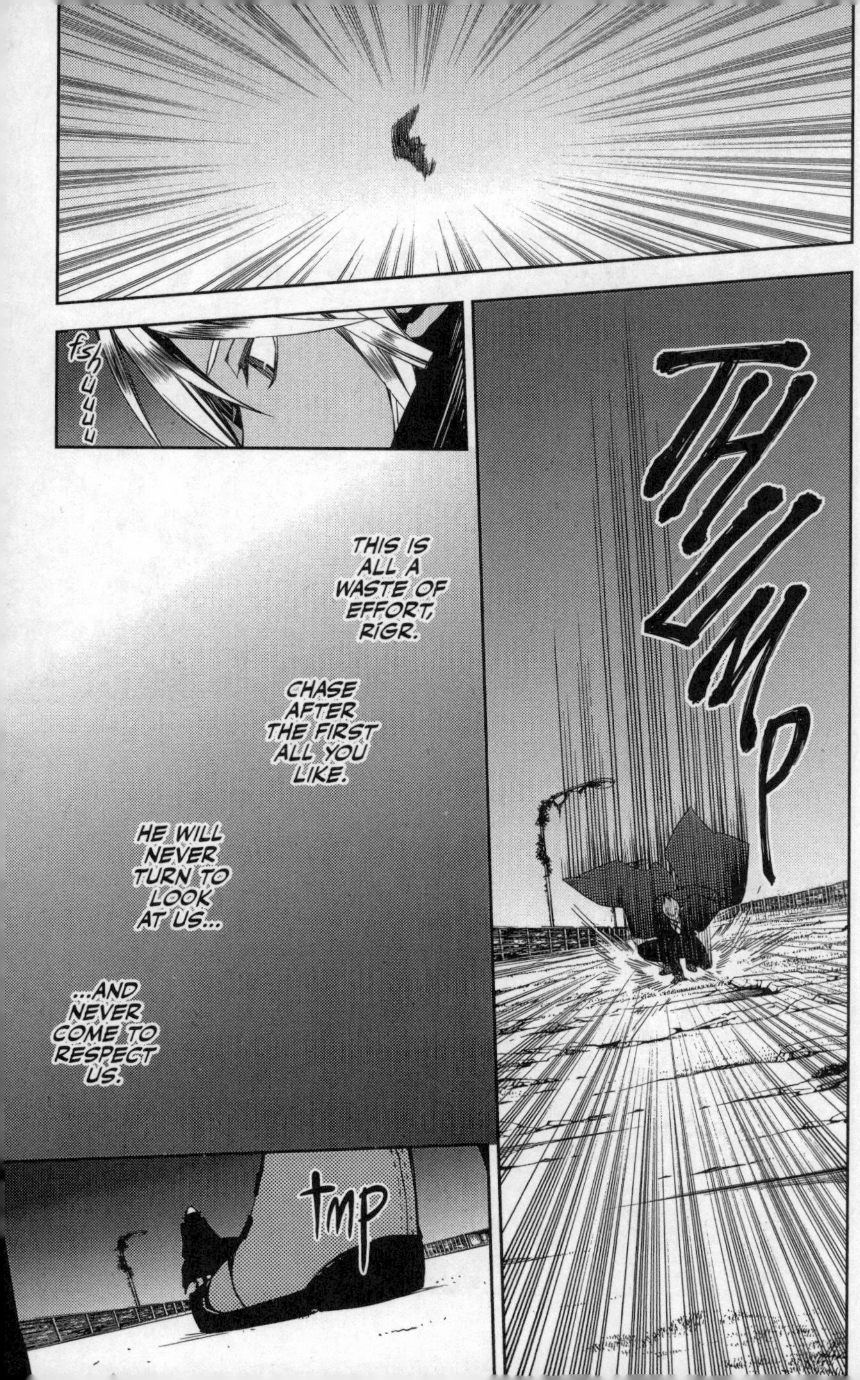
THUMP
fshuuuu
THIS IS ALL A WASTE OF EFFORT, RIGR.
CHASE AFTER THE FIRST ALL YOU LIKE.
HE WILL NEVER TURN TO LOOK AT US...
...AND NEVER COME TO RESPECT US.
tmp

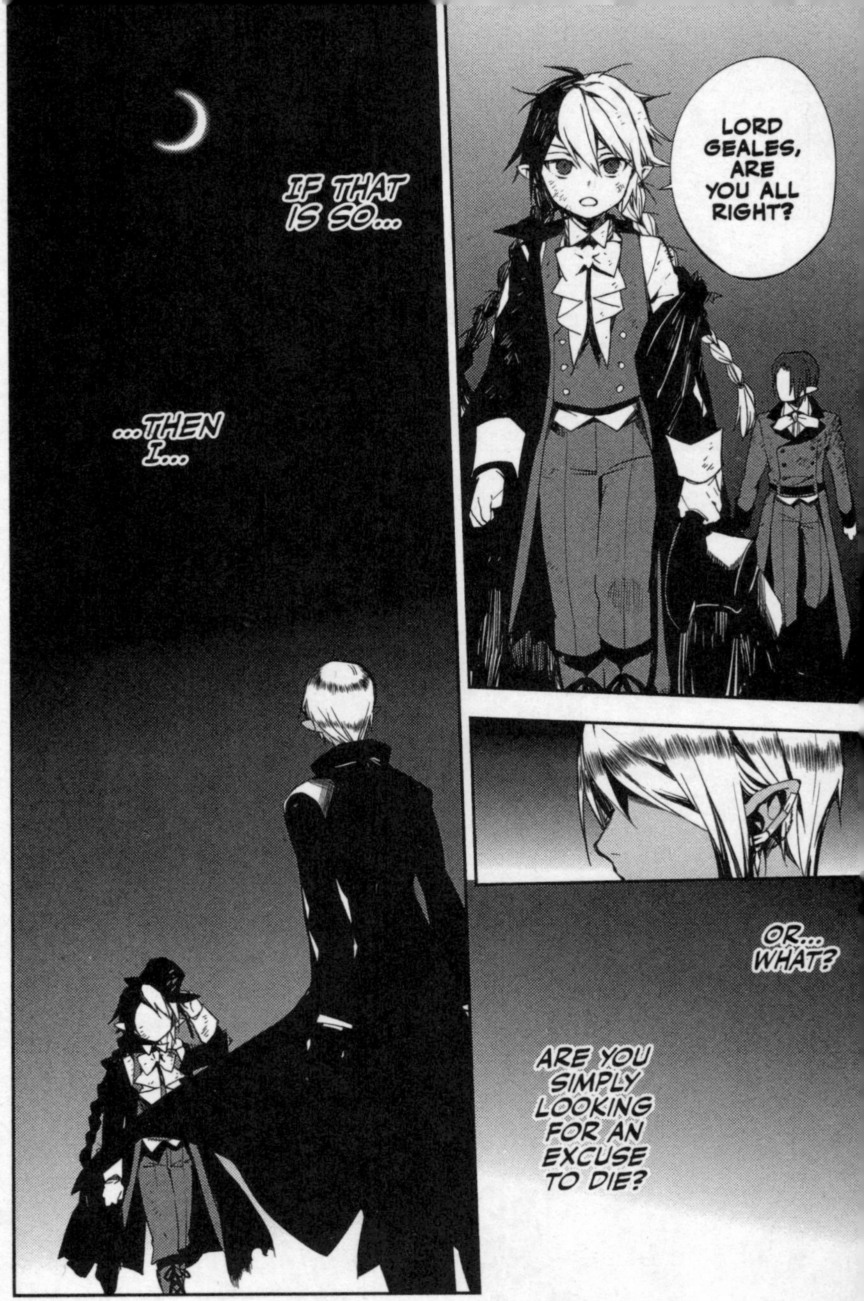
LORD GEALES, ARE YOU ALL RIGHT?
OR... WHAT?
ARE YOU SIMPLY LOOKING FOR AN EXCUSE TO DIE?
IF THAT IS SO...
...THEN I...

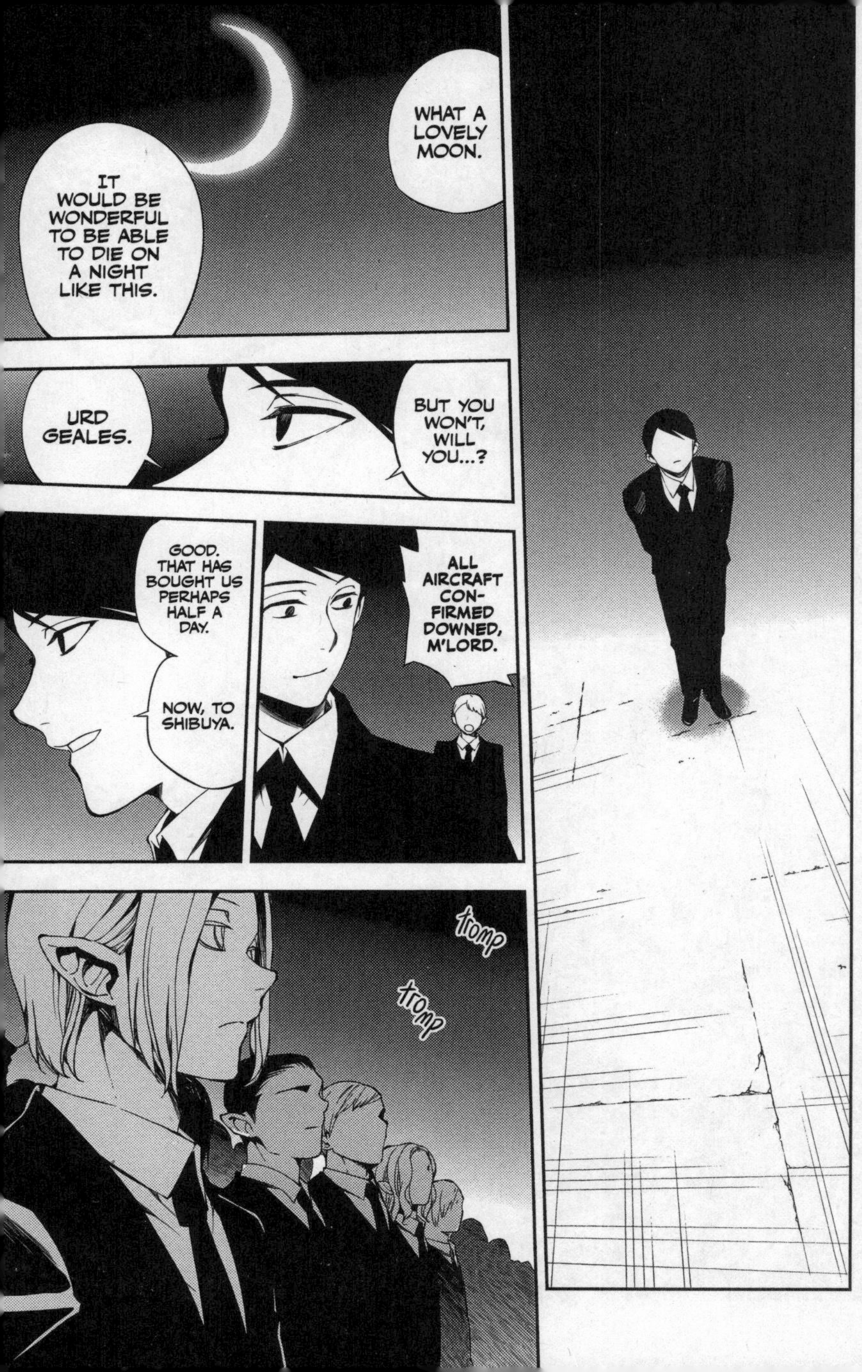
WHAT A LOVELY MOON.
IT WOULD BE WONDERFUL TO BE ABLE TO DIE ON A NIGHT LIKE THIS.
BUT YOU WON'T, WILL YOU...?
URD GEALES.
ALL AIRCRAFT CON-FIRMED DOWNED, M'LORD.
GOOD. THAT HAS BOUGHT US PERHAPS HALF A DAY.
NOW, TO SHIBUYA.
tromp
tromp

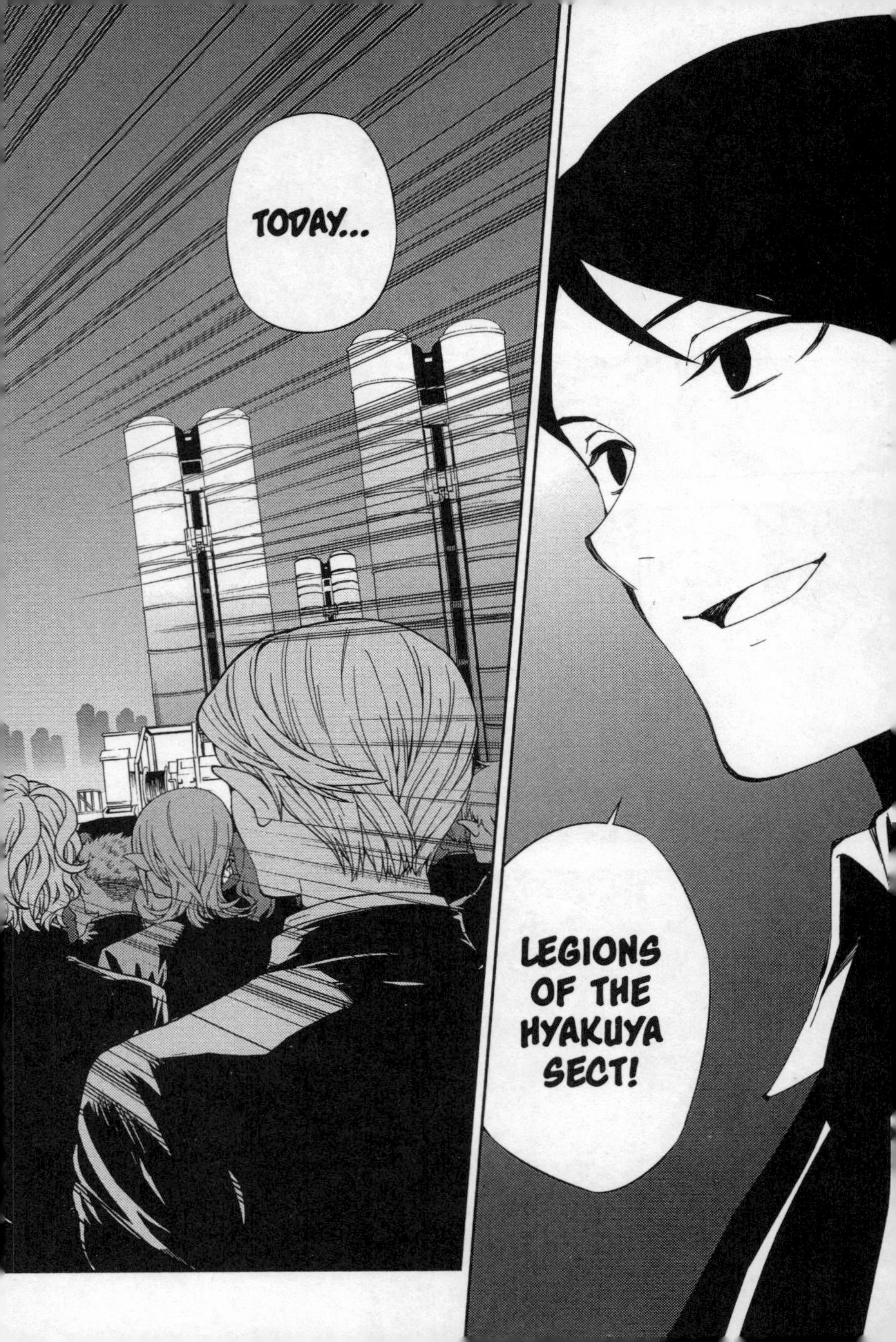
TODAY...
LEGIONS OF THE HYAKUYA SECT!

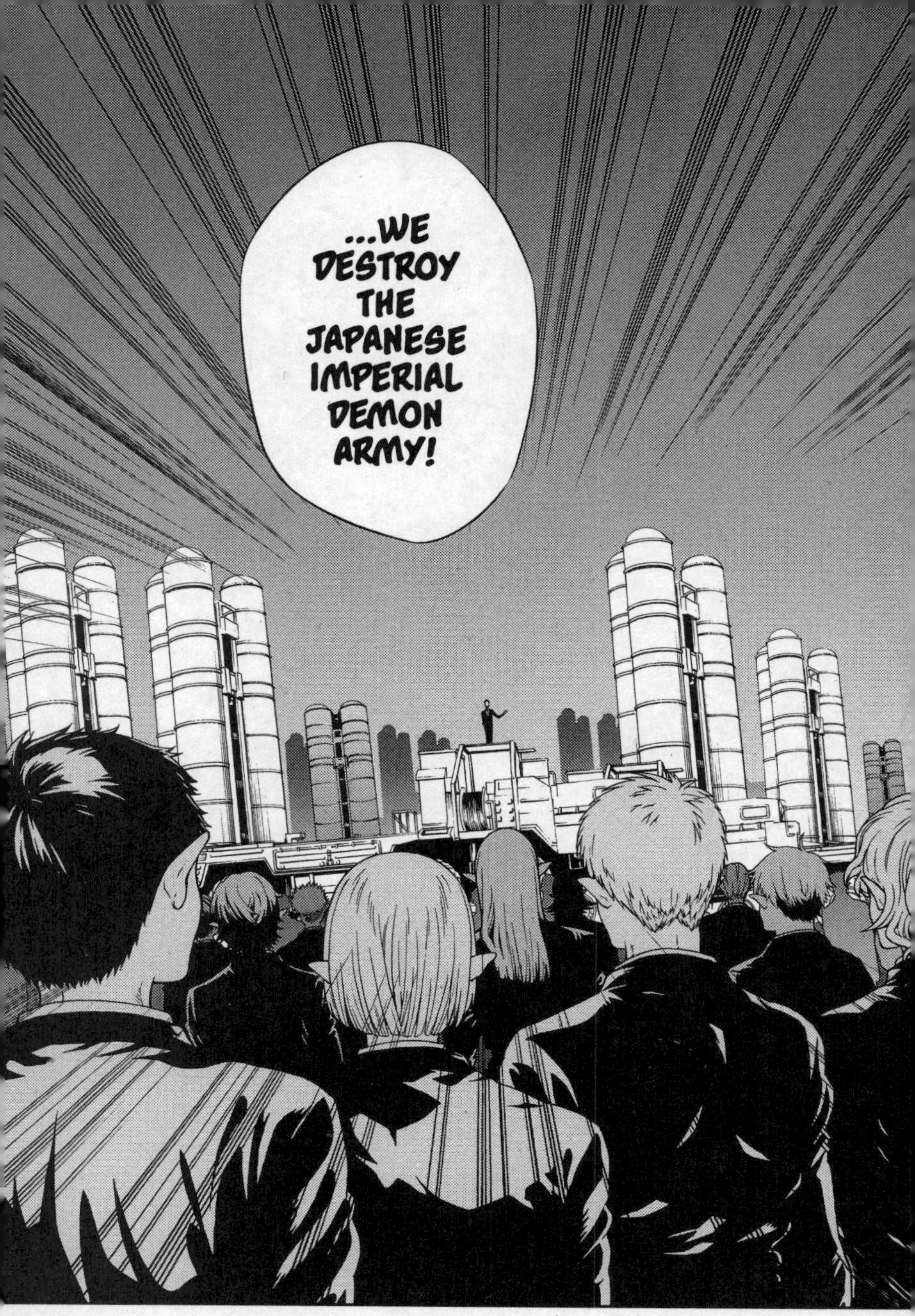
...WE DESTROY THE JAPANESE IMPERIAL DEMON ARMY!

Seraph of the End
—VAMPIRE REIGN—

Rescue for the Devil

HEY! QUIT STRUGGLING AND WALK!

FORGET ABOUT ME!

JUST PROMISE ME YOU'LL FIND SOME WAY TO KEEP SHINOA FROM TURNING INTO A VAMPIRE!

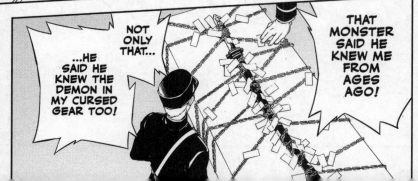

THAT MONSTER SAID HE KNEW ME FROM AGES AGO!

NOT ONLY THAT...

...HE SAID HE KNEW THE DEMON IN MY CURSED GEAR TOO!

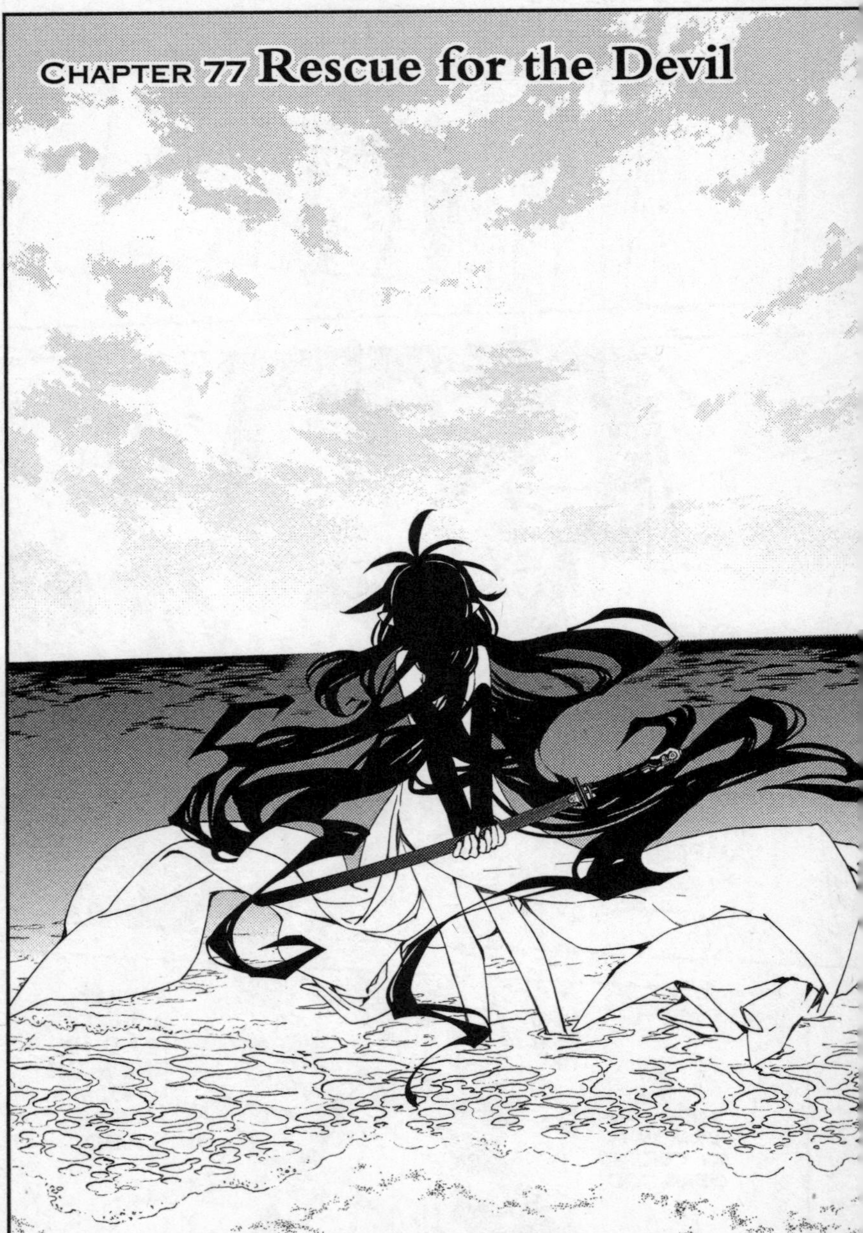
CHAPTER 77 Rescue for the Devil

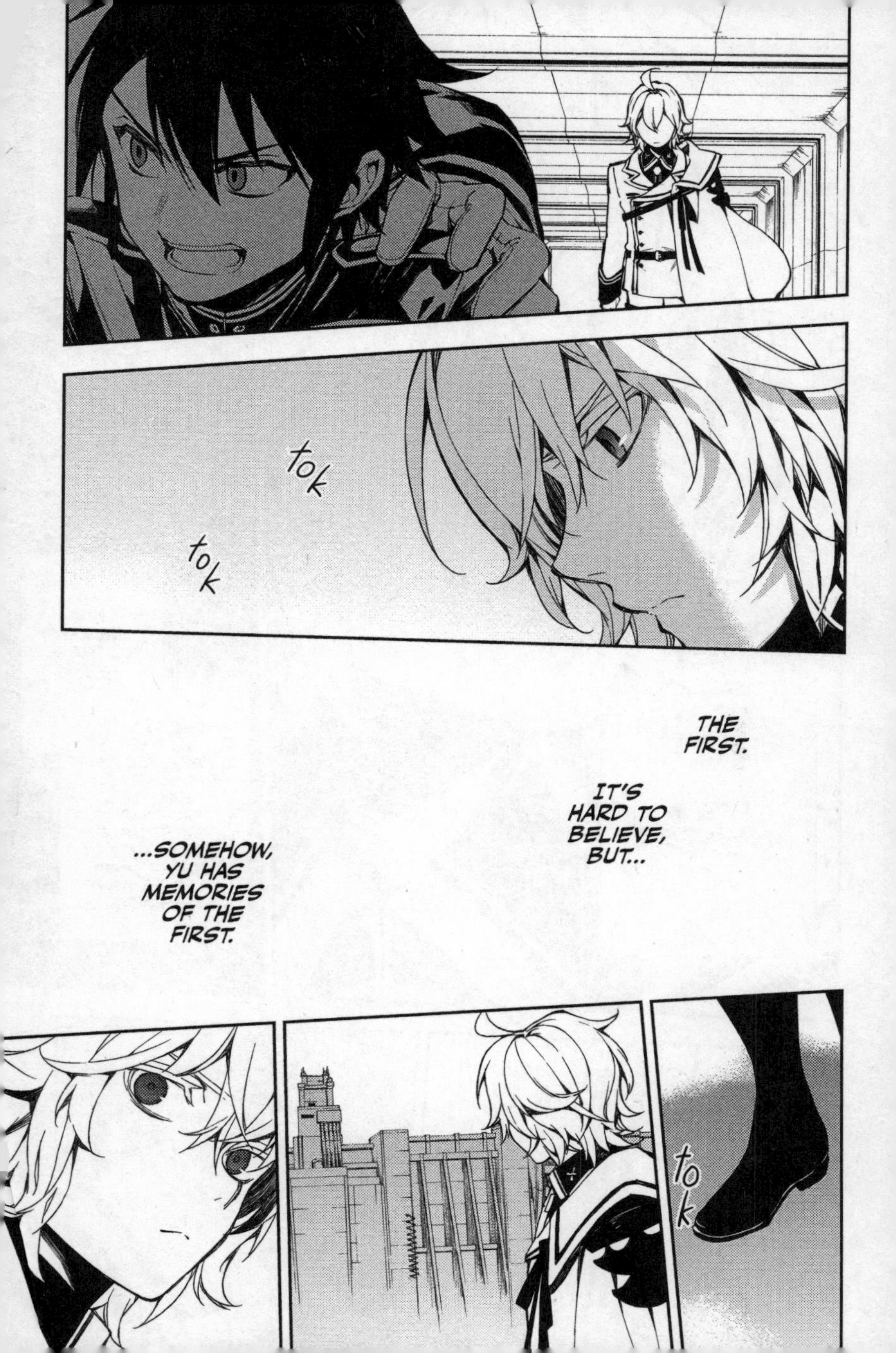
tok
tok
THE FIRST.
IT'S HARD TO BELIEVE, BUT...
...SOMEHOW, YU HAS MEMORIES OF THE FIRST.
tok

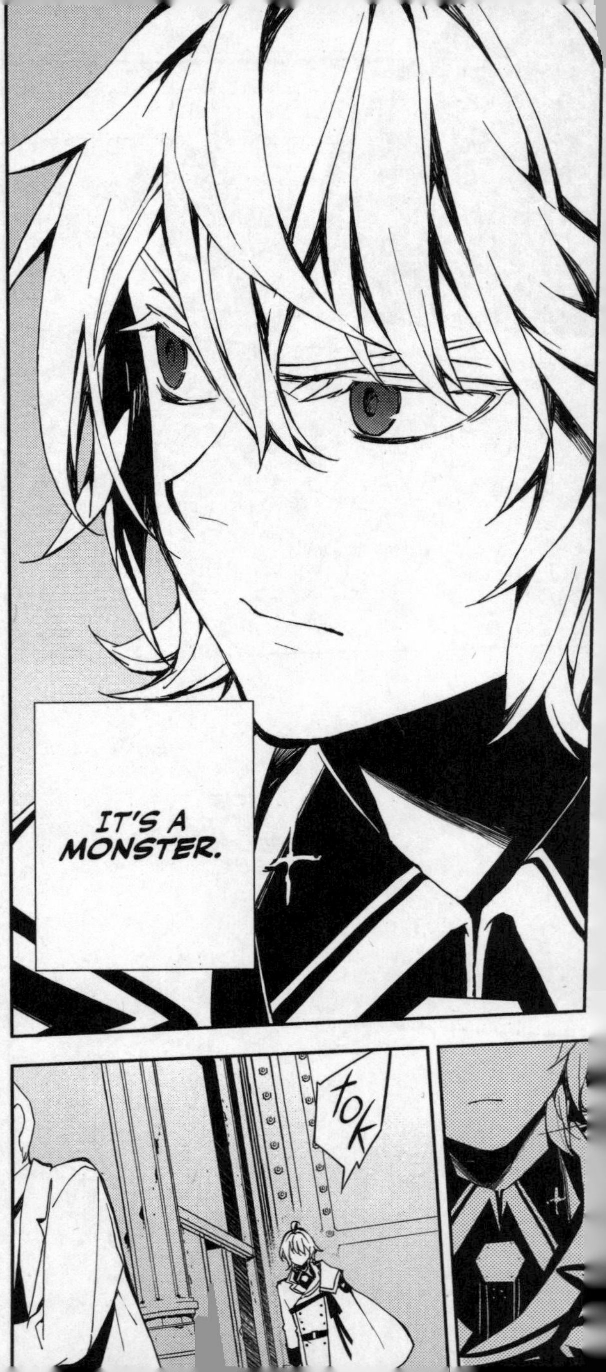
IT'S A MONSTER.
TOK

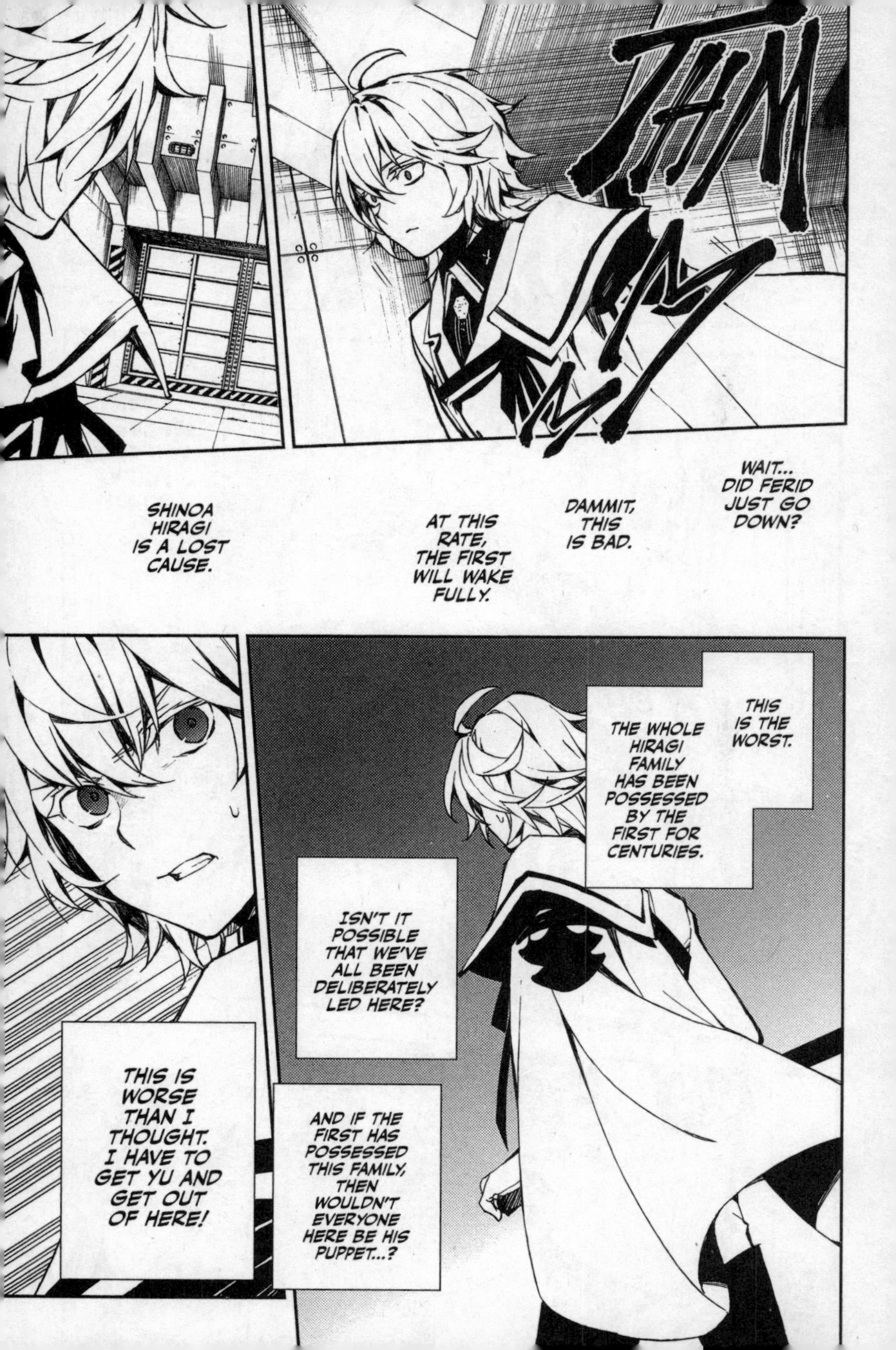
THMMM
WAIT... DID FERID JUST GO DOWN?
DAMMIT, THIS IS BAD.
AT THIS RATE, THE FIRST WILL WAKE FULLY.
SHINOA HIRAGI IS A LOST CAUSE.
THIS IS THE WORST.
THE WHOLE HIRAGI FAMILY HAS BEEN POSSESSED BY THE FIRST FOR CENTURIES.
ISN'T IT POSSIBLE THAT WE'VE ALL BEEN DELIBERATELY LED HERE?
AND IF THE FIRST HAS POSSESSED THIS FAMILY, THEN WOULDN'T EVERYONE HERE BE HIS PUPPET...?
THIS IS WORSE THAN I THOUGHT. I HAVE TO GET YU AND GET OUT OF HERE!

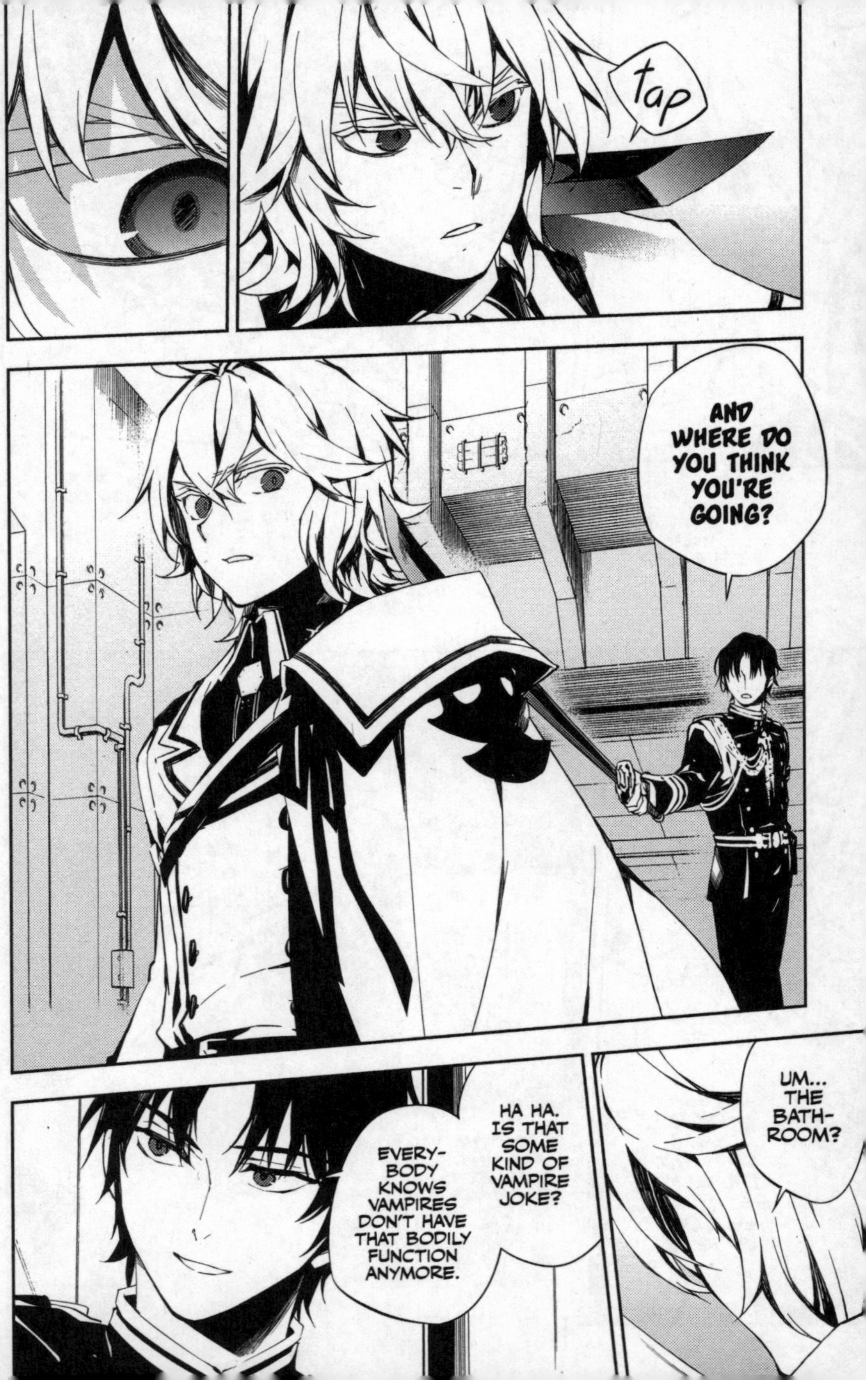
tap
AND WHERE DO YOU THINK YOU'RE GOING?
UM... THE BATH-ROOM?
HA HA. IS THAT SOME KIND OF VAMPIRE JOKE?
EVERY-BODY KNOWS VAMPIRES DON'T HAVE THAT BODILY FUNCTION ANYMORE.

JUST SO YOU KNOW, YOU AREN'T TAKING YU ANYWHERE.

AN- OTHER PUPPET OF THE FIRST, HM?

I WON'T LET YOU USE YU.

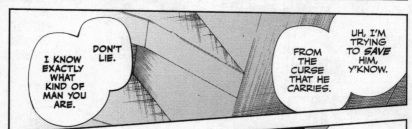

UH, I'M TRYING TO *SAVE* HIM, Y'KNOW.

FROM THE CURSE THAT HE CARRIES.

DON'T LIE.

I KNOW EXACTLY WHAT KIND OF MAN YOU ARE.

UH-HUH. SO, IF YOU RAN, WHERE WOULD YOU GO?

DO YOU THINK YOU WOULD GET AWAY CLEAN WITH YU ALL ON YOUR OWN?

...

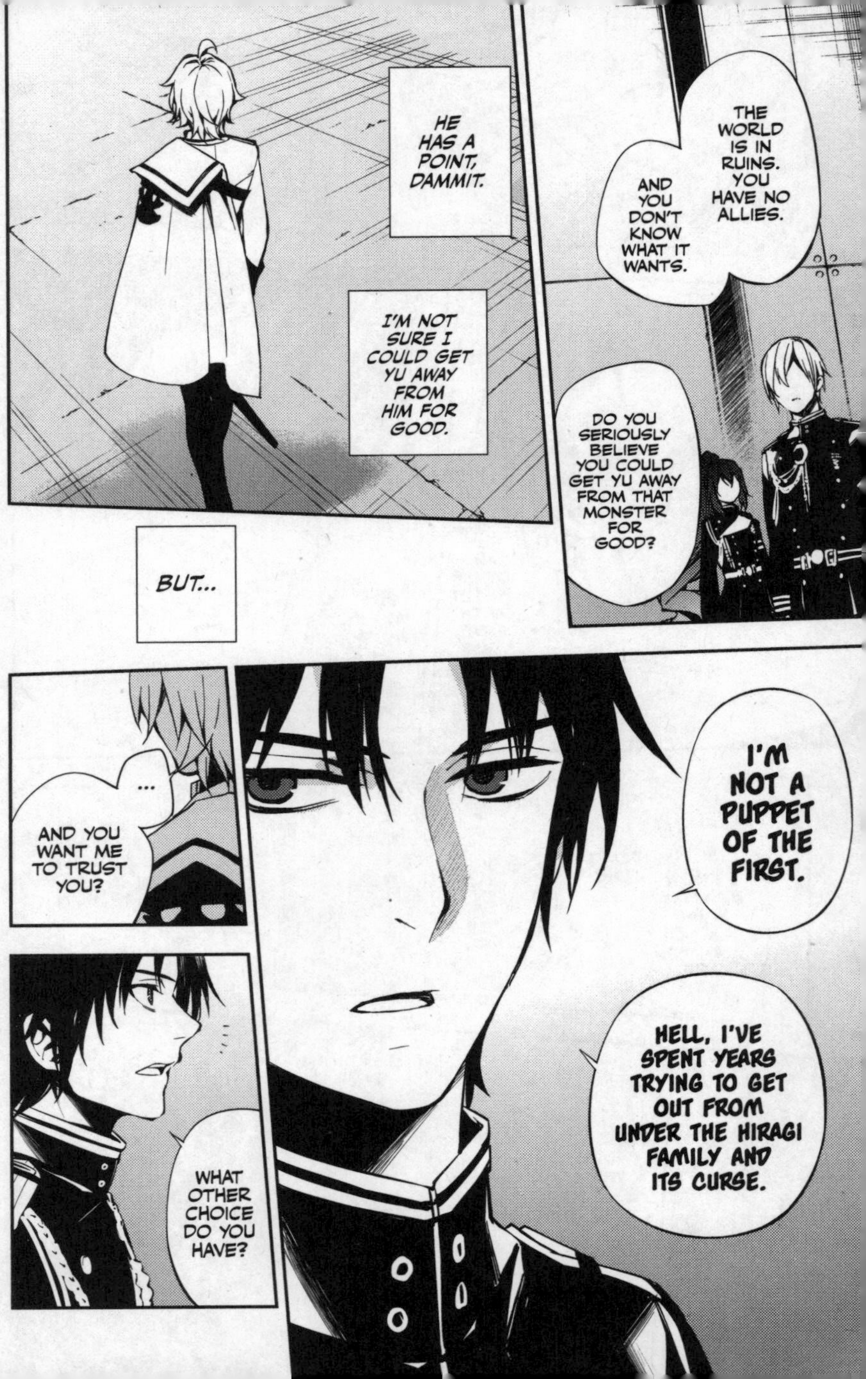
THE WORLD IS IN RUINS. YOU HAVE NO ALLIES.
AND YOU DON'T KNOW WHAT IT WANTS.
DO YOU SERIOUSLY BELIEVE YOU COULD GET YU AWAY FROM THAT MONSTER FOR GOOD?
HE HAS A POINT, DAMMIT.
I'M NOT SURE I COULD GET YU AWAY FROM HIM FOR GOOD.
BUT...
I'M NOT A PUPPET OF THE FIRST.
HELL, I'VE SPENT YEARS TRYING TO GET OUT FROM UNDER THE HIRAGI FAMILY AND ITS CURSE.
...
AND YOU WANT ME TO TRUST YOU?
WHAT OTHER CHOICE DO YOU HAVE?

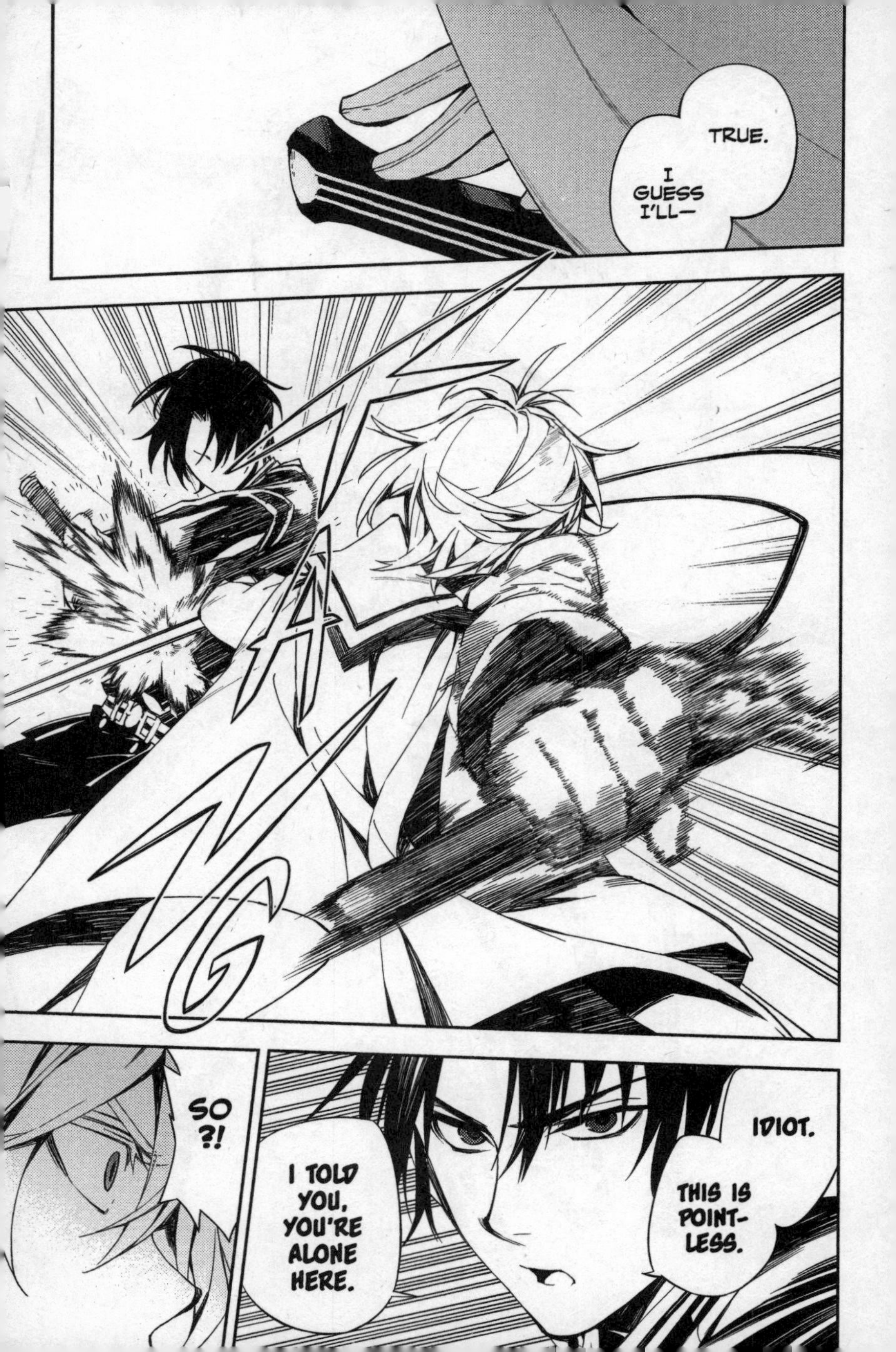
TRUE.
I GUESS I'LL—
IDIOT.
THIS IS POINT-LESS.
I TOLD YOU, YOU'RE ALONE HERE.
SO ?!

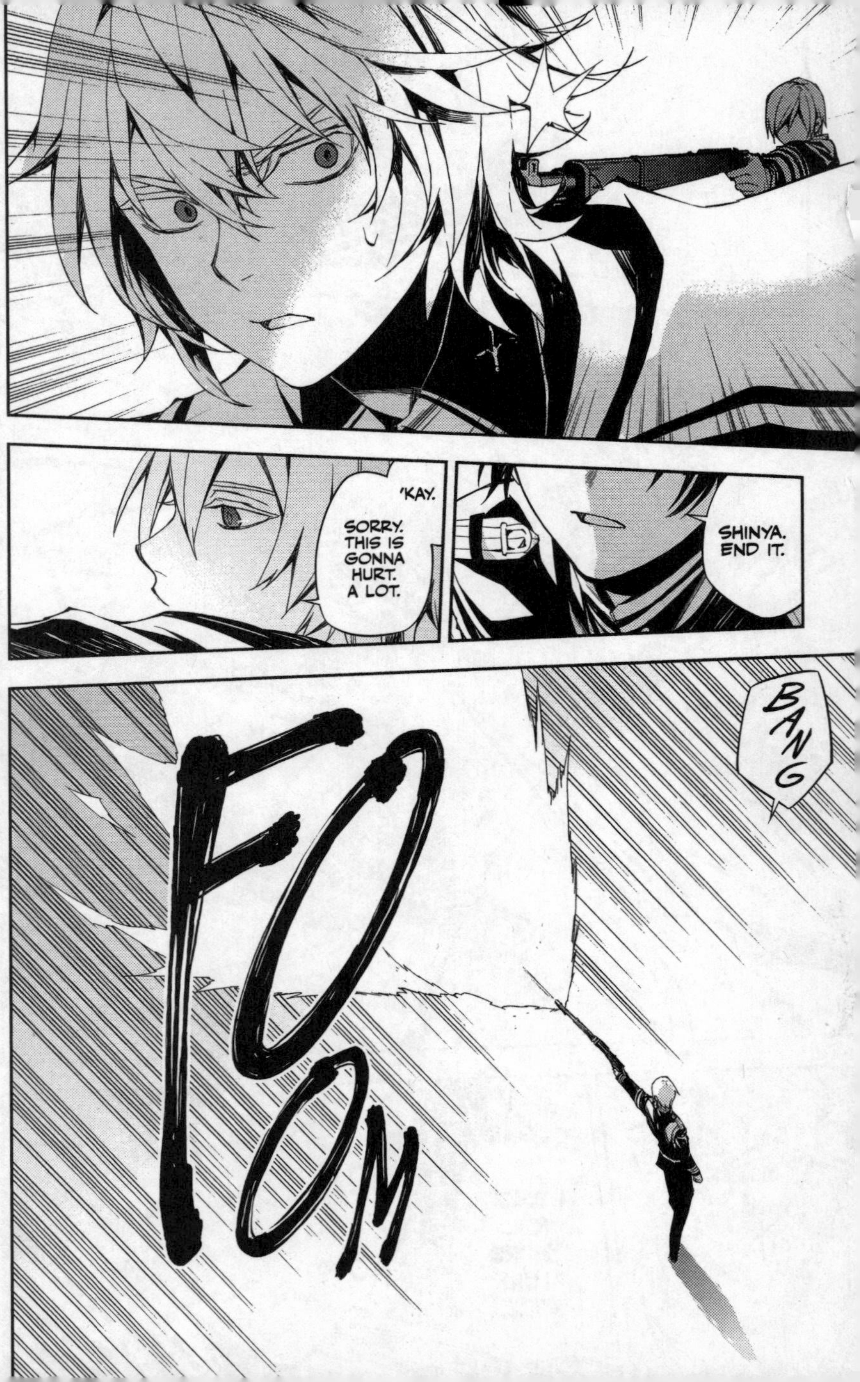
SHINYA. END IT.
'KAY.
SORRY. THIS IS GONNA HURT. A LOT.
BANG
FOOM

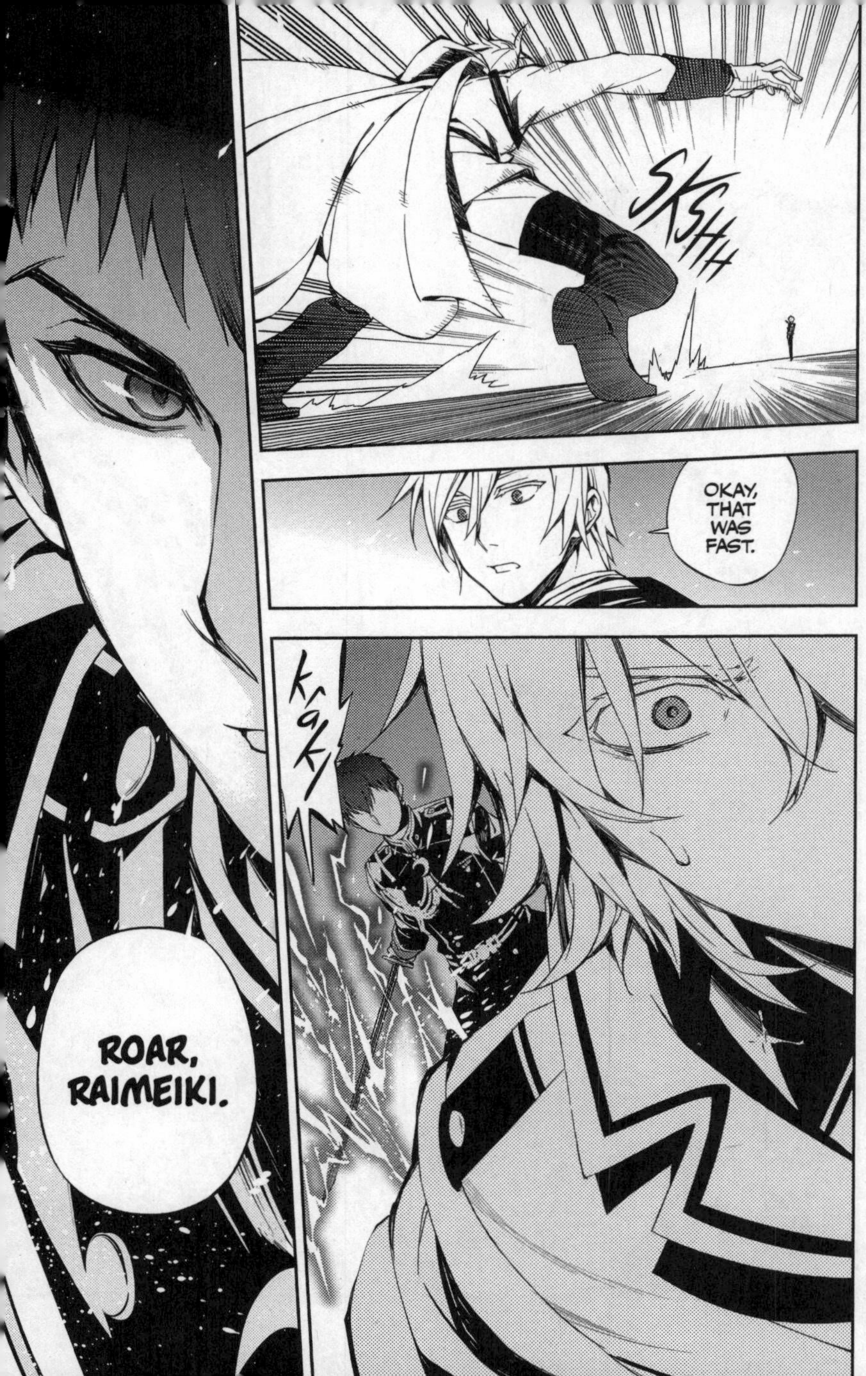
SKSHH
OKAY, THAT WAS FAST.
krak!
ROAR, RAIMEIKI.

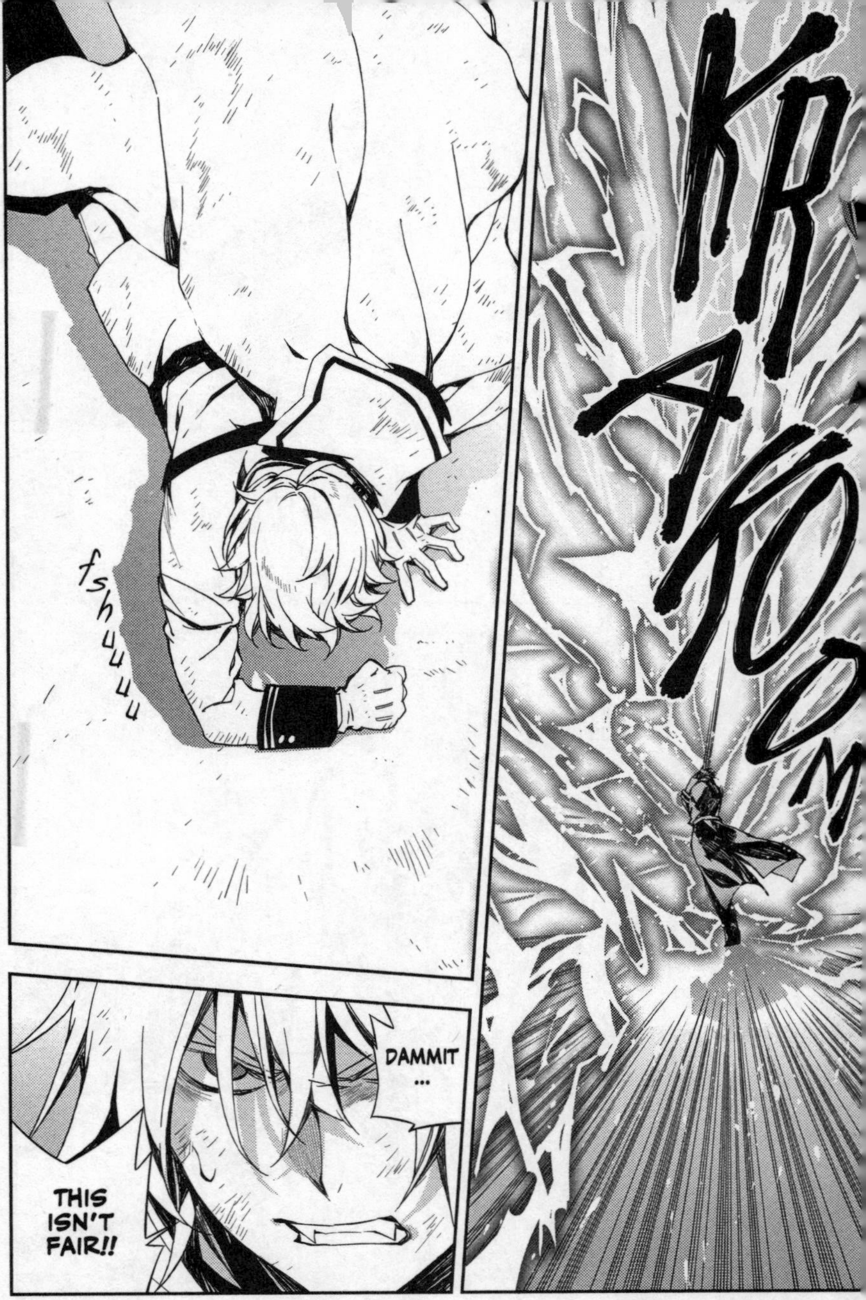
KRAKOOM
fshuuuu
DAMMIT
...
THIS ISN'T FAIR!!

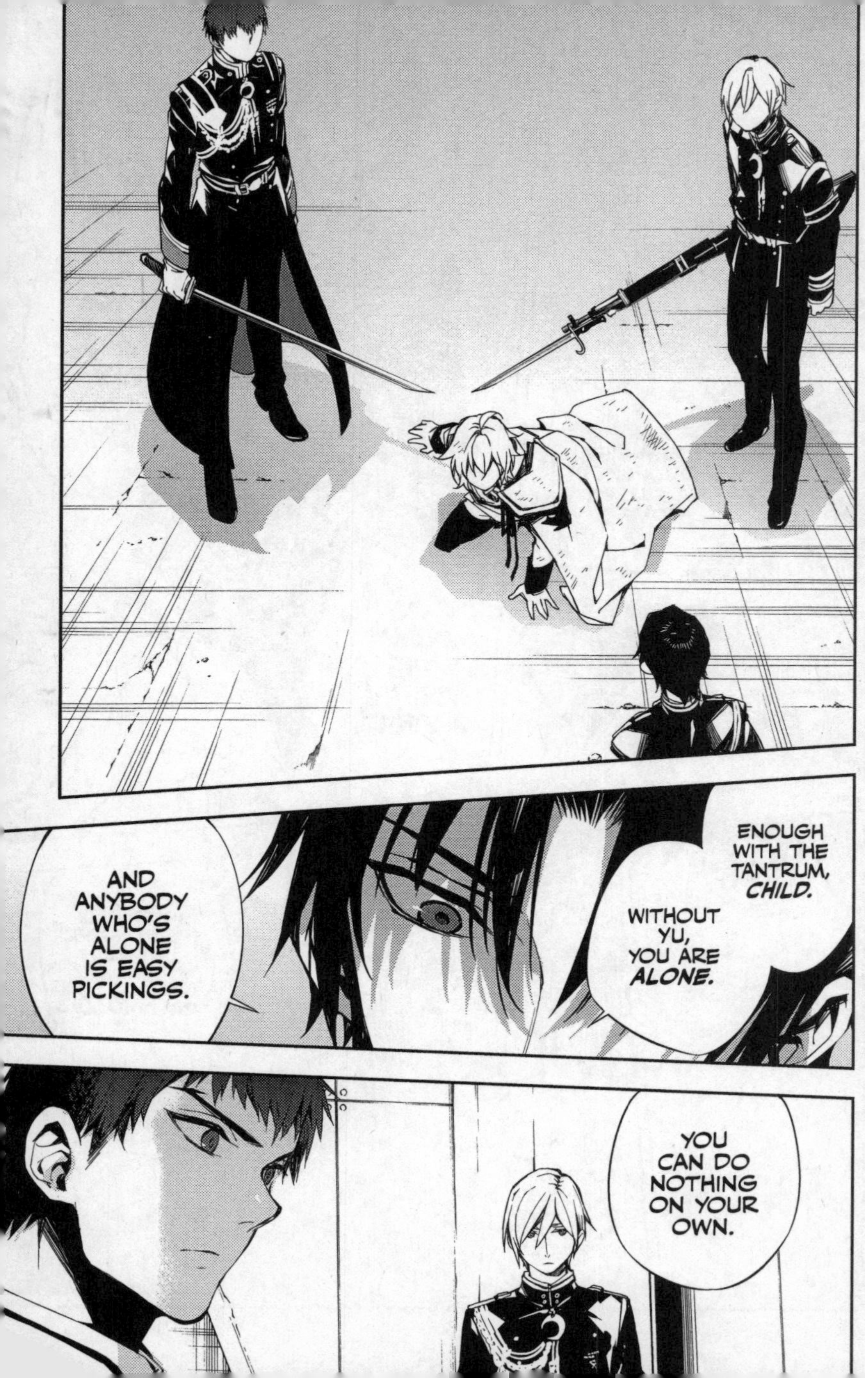
ENOUGH WITH THE TANTRUM, *CHILD.*
WITHOUT YU, YOU ARE *ALONE.*
AND ANYBODY WHO'S ALONE IS EASY PICKINGS.
YOU CAN DO NOTHING ON YOUR OWN.

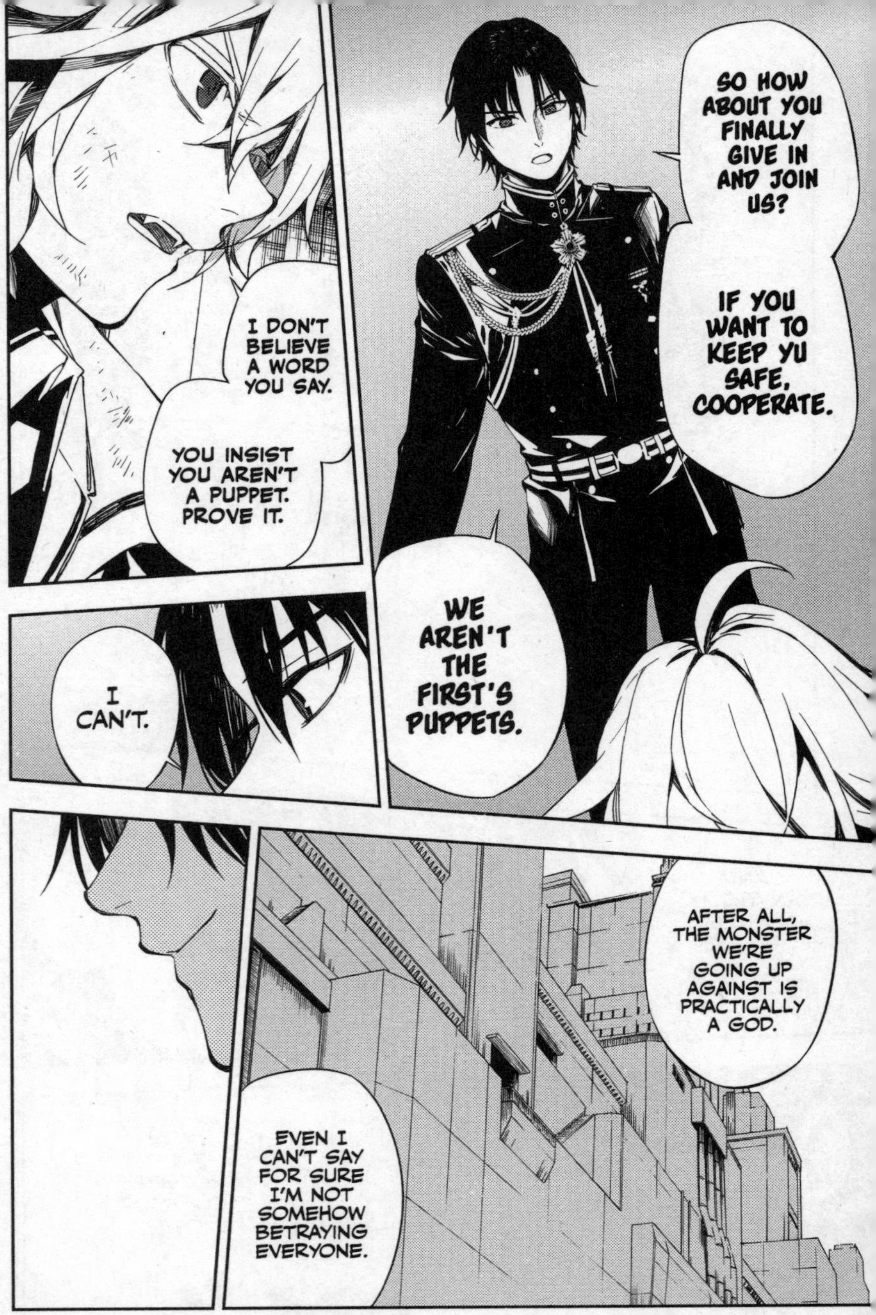
SO HOW ABOUT YOU FINALLY GIVE IN AND JOIN US?
IF YOU WANT TO KEEP YU SAFE, COOPERATE.
WE AREN'T THE FIRST'S PUPPETS.
I DON'T BELIEVE A WORD YOU SAY.
YOU INSIST YOU AREN'T A PUPPET. PROVE IT.
I CAN'T.
AFTER ALL, THE MONSTER WE'RE GOING UP AGAINST IS PRACTICALLY A GOD.
EVEN I CAN'T SAY FOR SURE I'M NOT SOMEHOW BETRAYING EVERYONE.

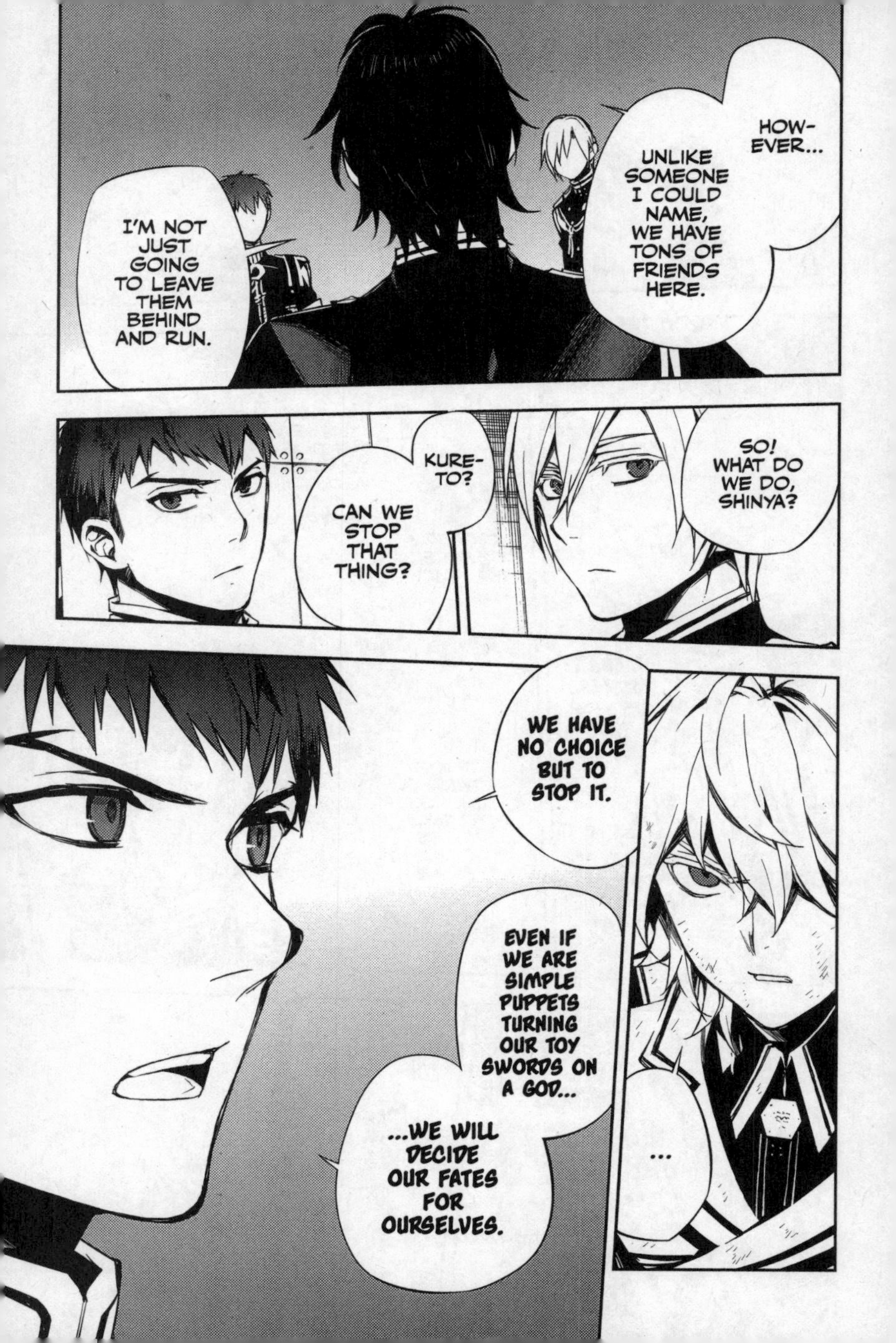
HOW-EVER...
UNLIKE SOMEONE I COULD NAME, WE HAVE TONS OF FRIENDS HERE.
I'M NOT JUST GOING TO LEAVE THEM BEHIND AND RUN.
SO! WHAT DO WE DO, SHINYA?
KURE-TO?
CAN WE STOP THAT THING?
WE HAVE NO CHOICE BUT TO STOP IT.
EVEN IF WE ARE SIMPLE PUPPETS TURNING OUR TOY SWORDS ON A GOD...
...
...WE WILL DECIDE OUR FATES FOR OURSELVES.

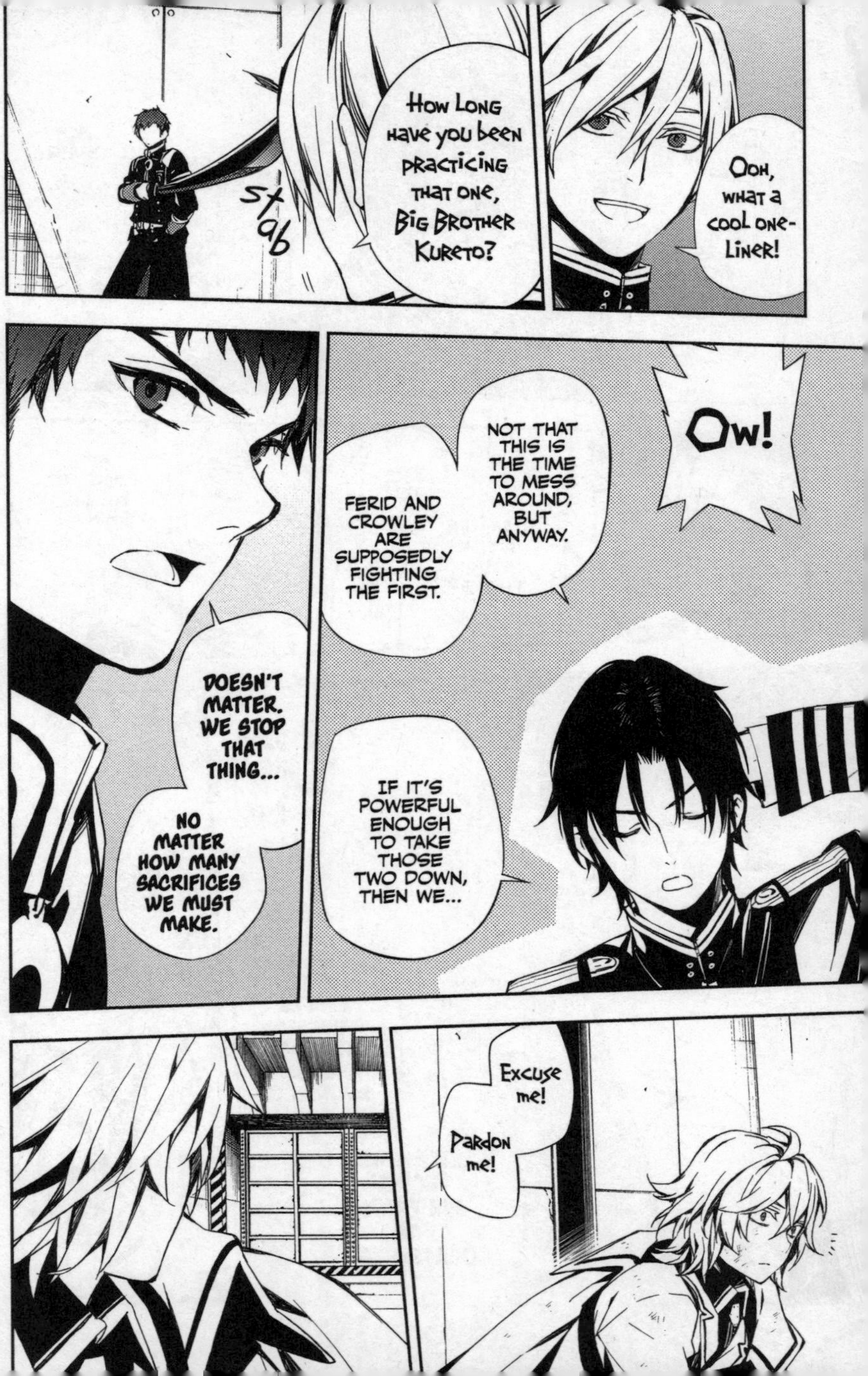
Ooh, what a cool one-liner!
How long have you been practicing that one, Big Brother Kureto?
stab
Ow!
Not that this is the time to mess around, but anyway.
Ferid and Crowley are supposedly fighting the First.
If it's powerful enough to take those two down, then we...
Doesn't matter. We stop that thing...
No matter how many sacrifices we must make.
Excuse me!
Pardon me!

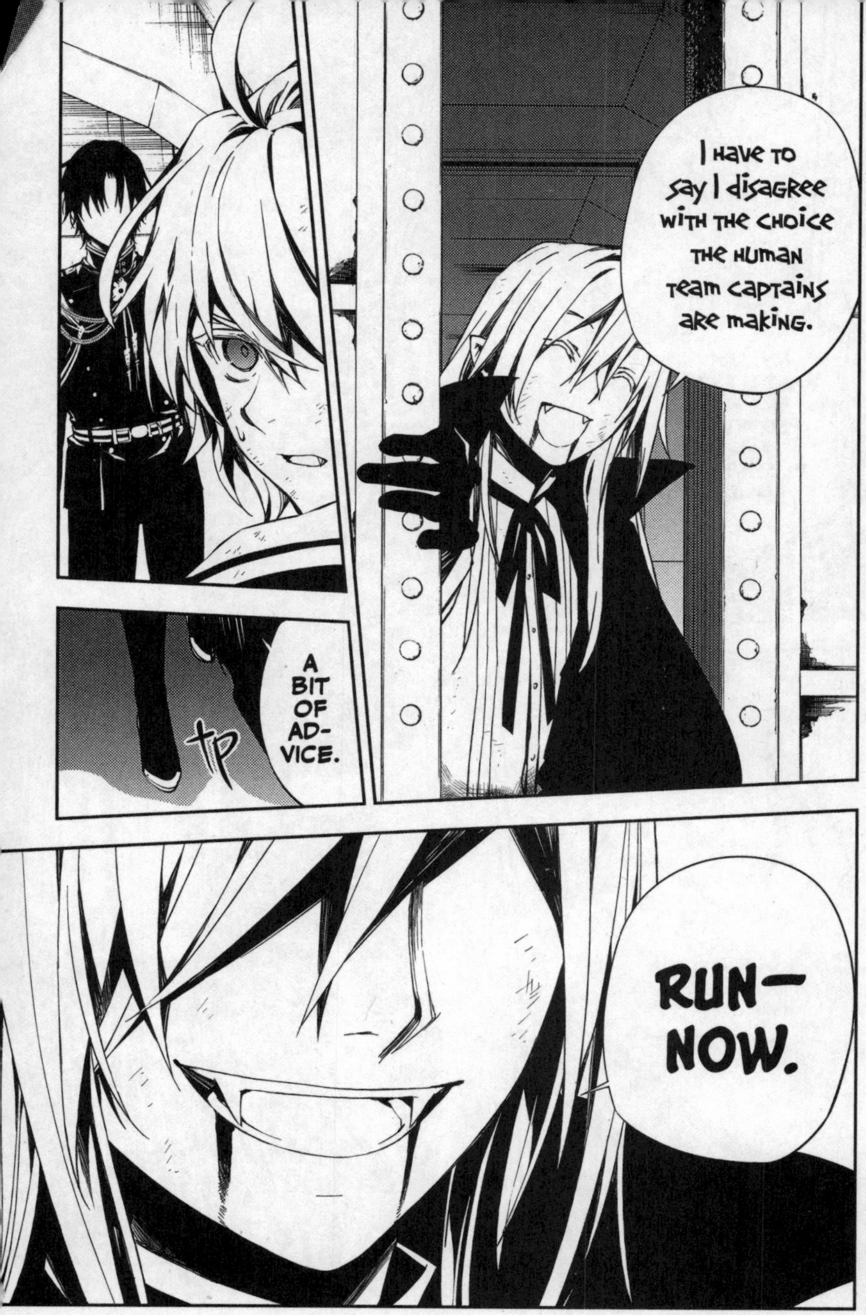
I have to say I disagree with the choice the human team captains are making.
A BIT OF AD-VICE.
tp
RUN—NOW.

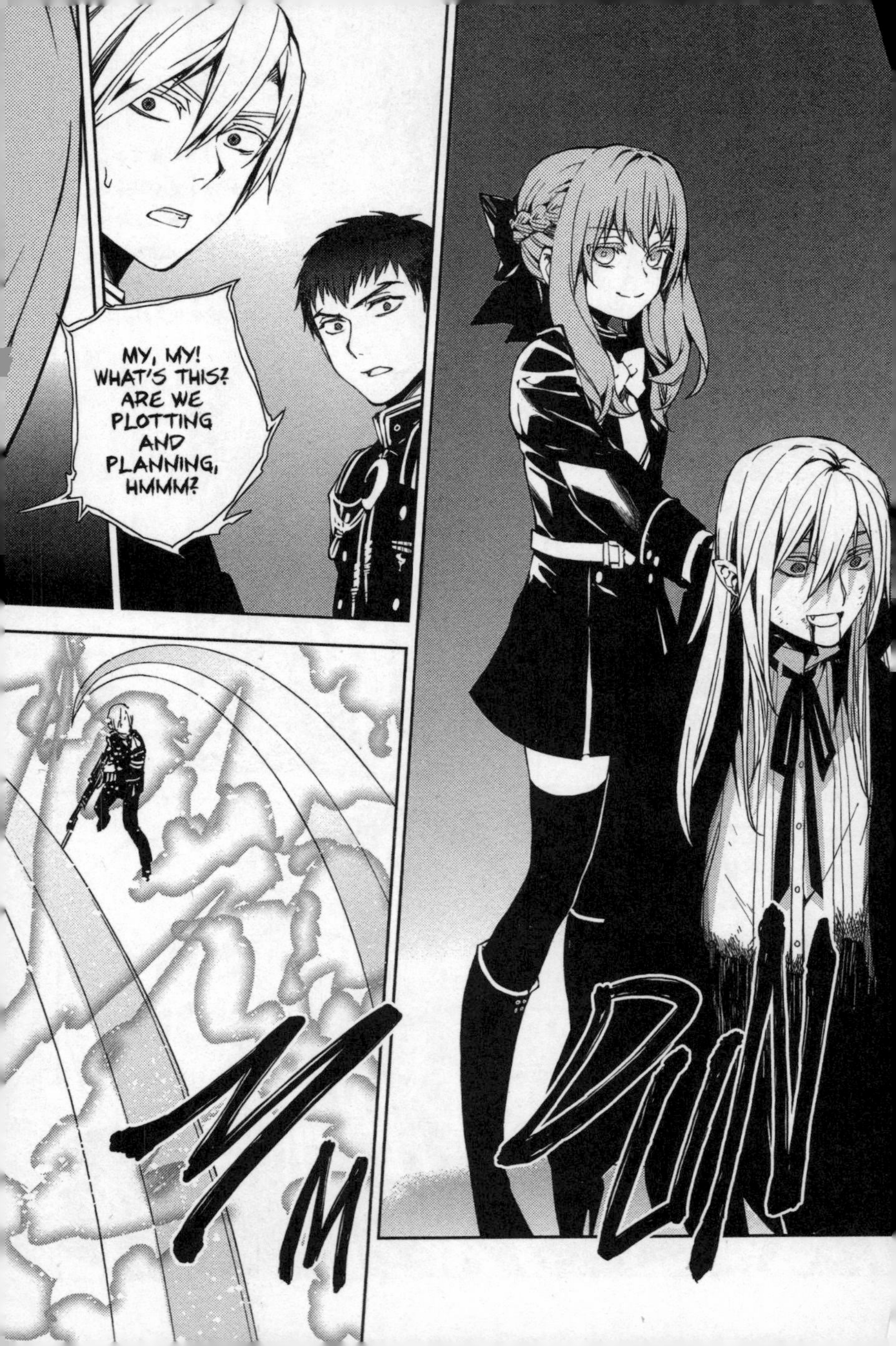
MY, MY! WHAT'S THIS? ARE WE PLOTTING AND PLANNING, HMMM?
MMM
NNN

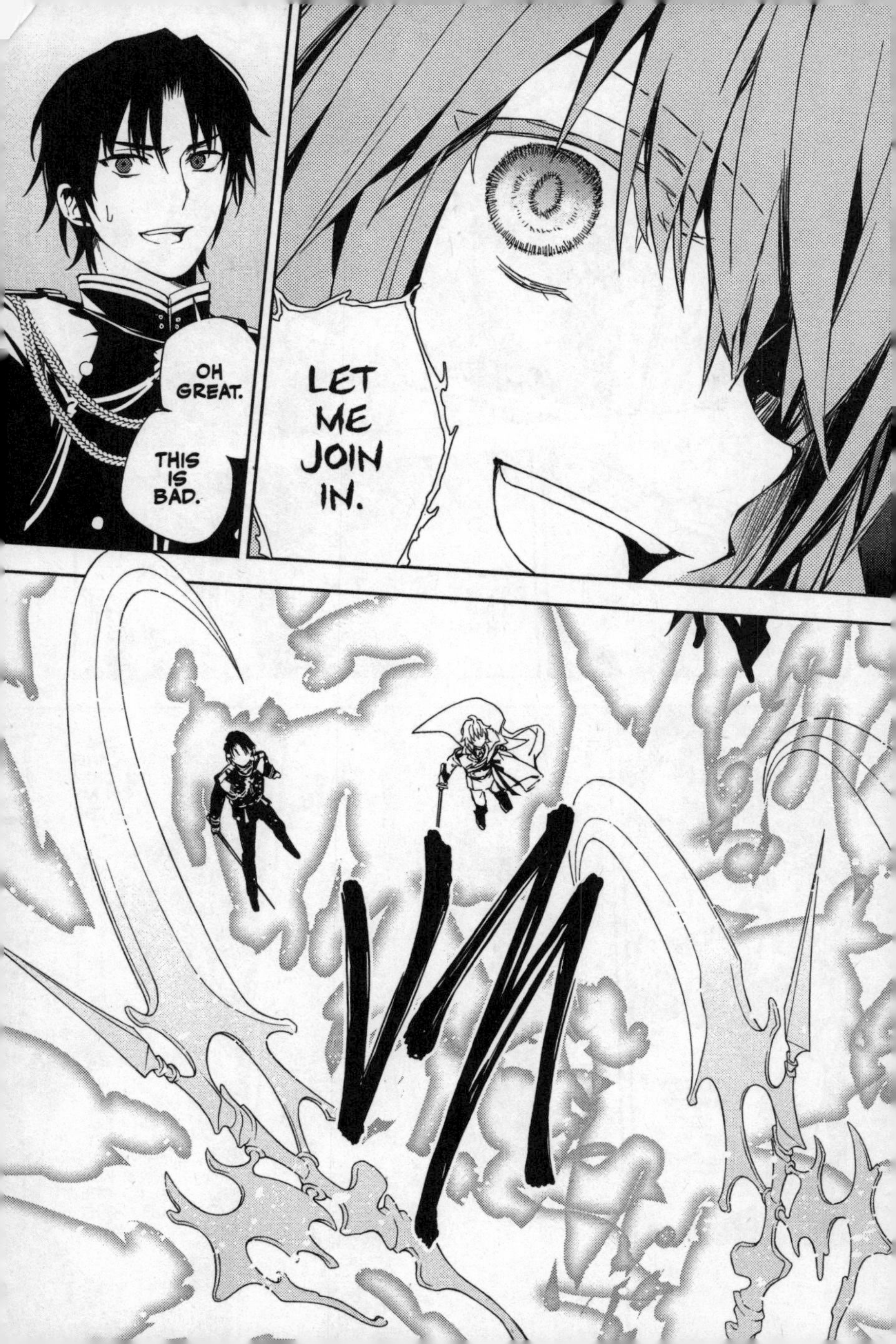
LET ME JOIN IN.
OH GREAT.
THIS IS BAD.

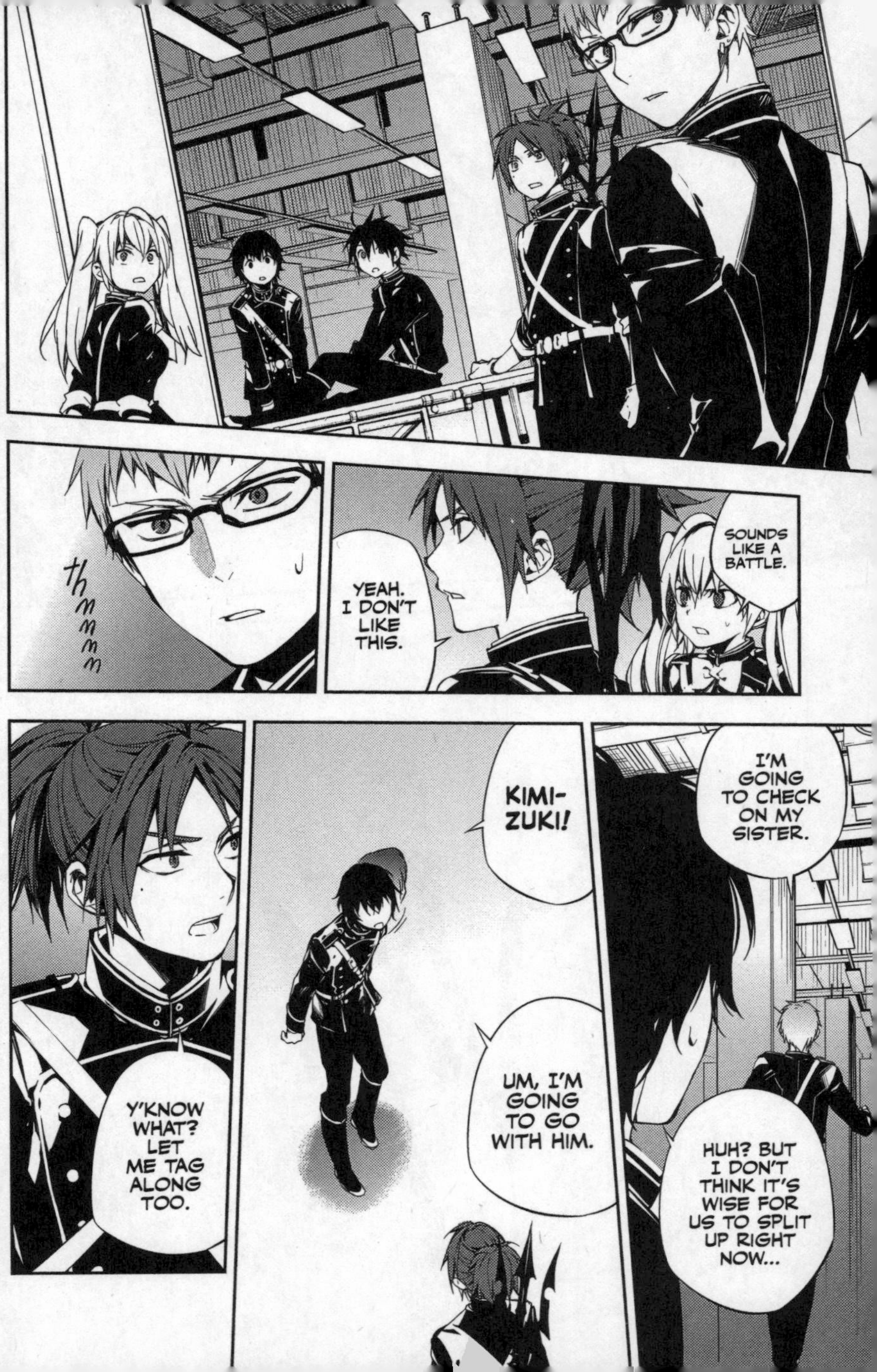
SOUNDS LIKE A BATTLE.
YEAH. I DON'T LIKE THIS.
thmmmm
I'M GOING TO CHECK ON MY SISTER.
HUH? BUT I DON'T THINK IT'S WISE FOR US TO SPLIT UP RIGHT NOW...
KIMI-ZUKI!
UM, I'M GOING TO GO WITH HIM.
Y'KNOW WHAT? LET ME TAG ALONG TOO.

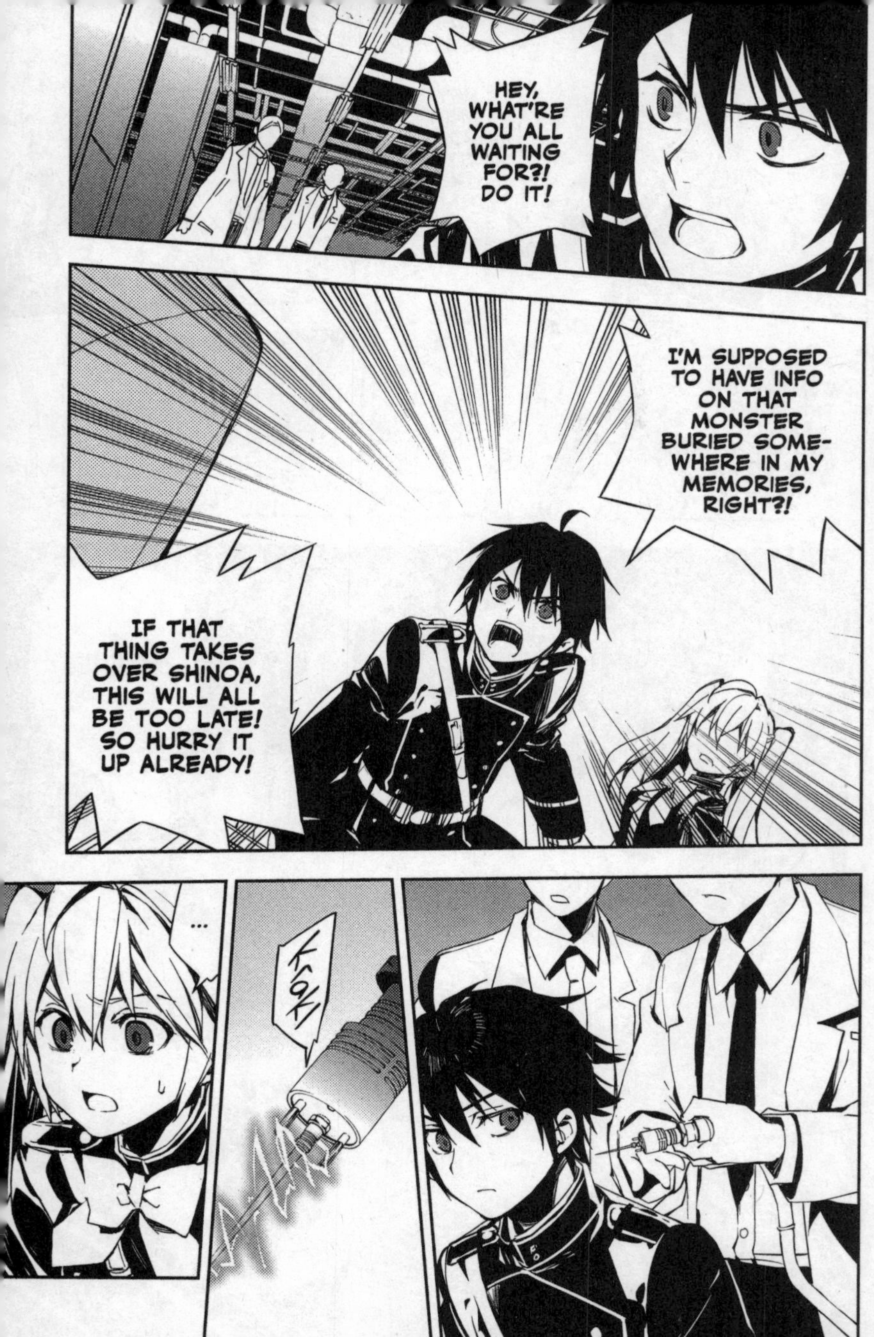
HEY, WHAT'RE YOU ALL WAITING FOR?! DO IT!
I'M SUPPOSED TO HAVE INFO ON THAT MONSTER BURIED SOME-WHERE IN MY MEMORIES, RIGHT?!
IF THAT THING TAKES OVER SHINOA, THIS WILL ALL BE TOO LATE! SO HURRY IT UP ALREADY!
KRAK!
...

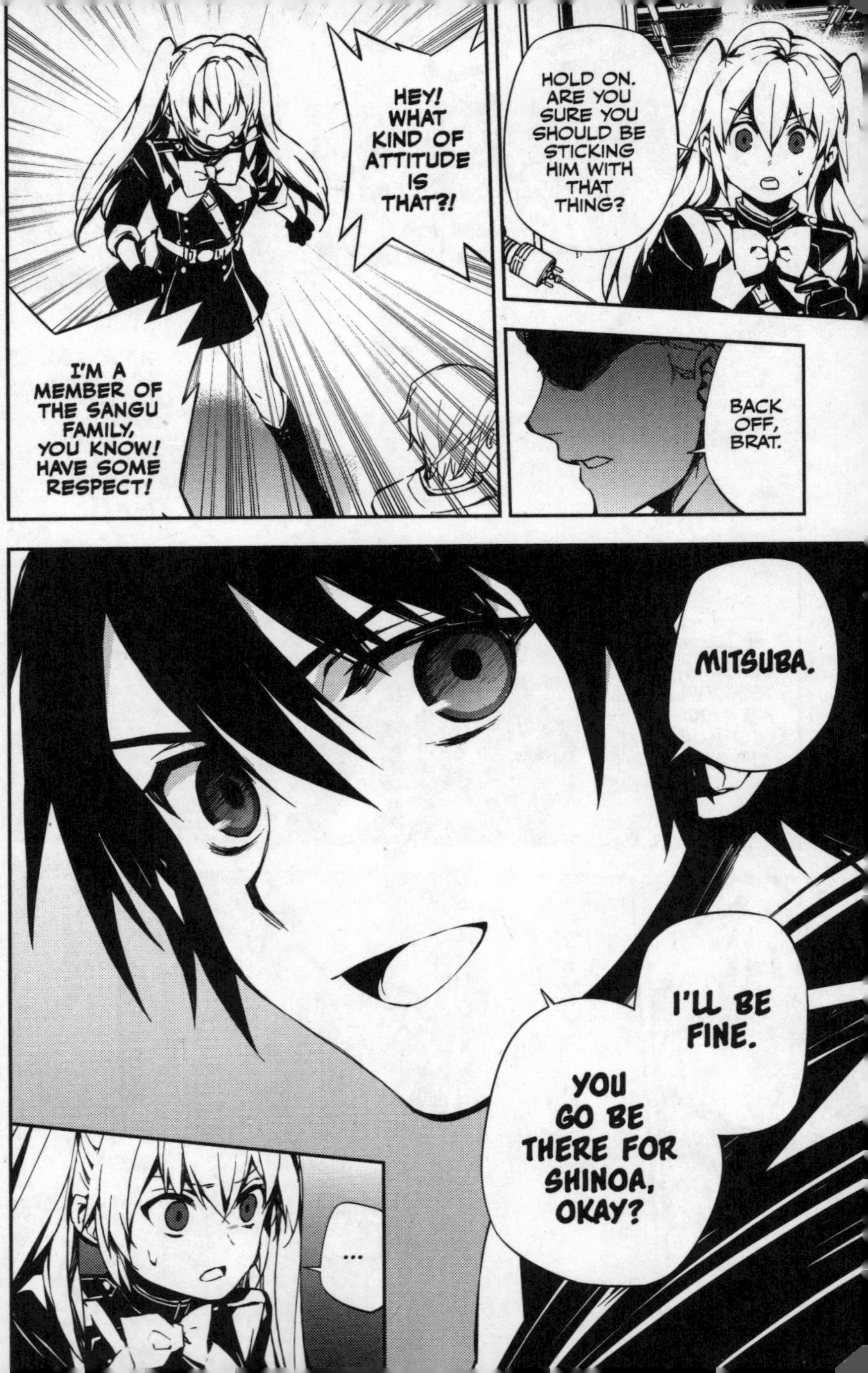
HOLD ON. ARE YOU SURE YOU SHOULD BE STICKING HIM WITH THAT THING?
BACK OFF, BRAT.
HEY! WHAT KIND OF ATTITUDE IS THAT?!
I'M A MEMBER OF THE SANGU FAMILY, YOU KNOW! HAVE SOME RESPECT!
MITSUBA.
I'LL BE FINE.
YOU GO BE THERE FOR SHINOA, OKAY?
...

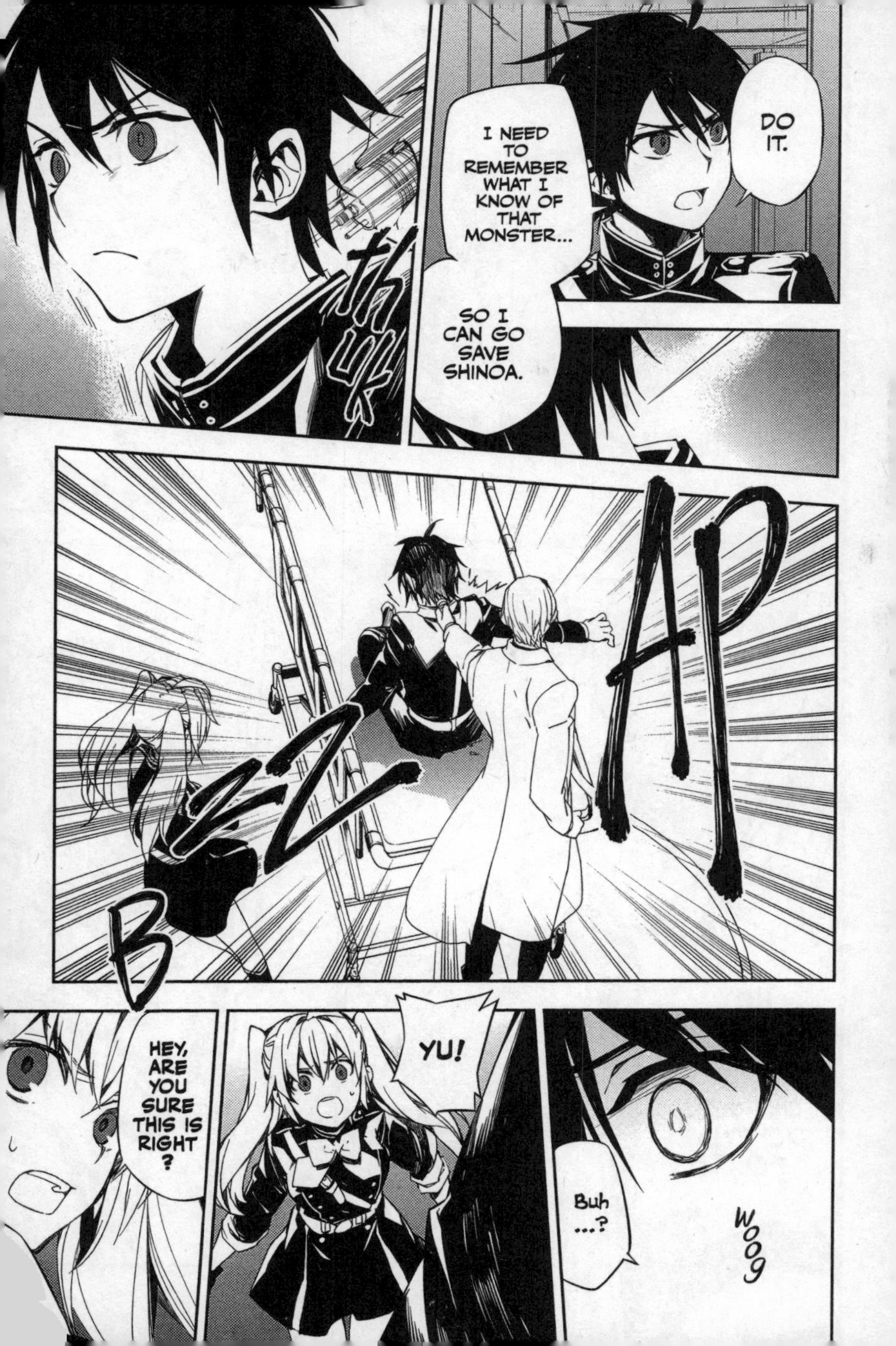
DO IT.
I NEED TO REMEMBER WHAT I KNOW OF THAT MONSTER...
SO I CAN GO SAVE SHINOA.
thuk
BZZAP
Buh ...?
Woog
YU!
HEY, ARE YOU SURE THIS IS RIGHT ?

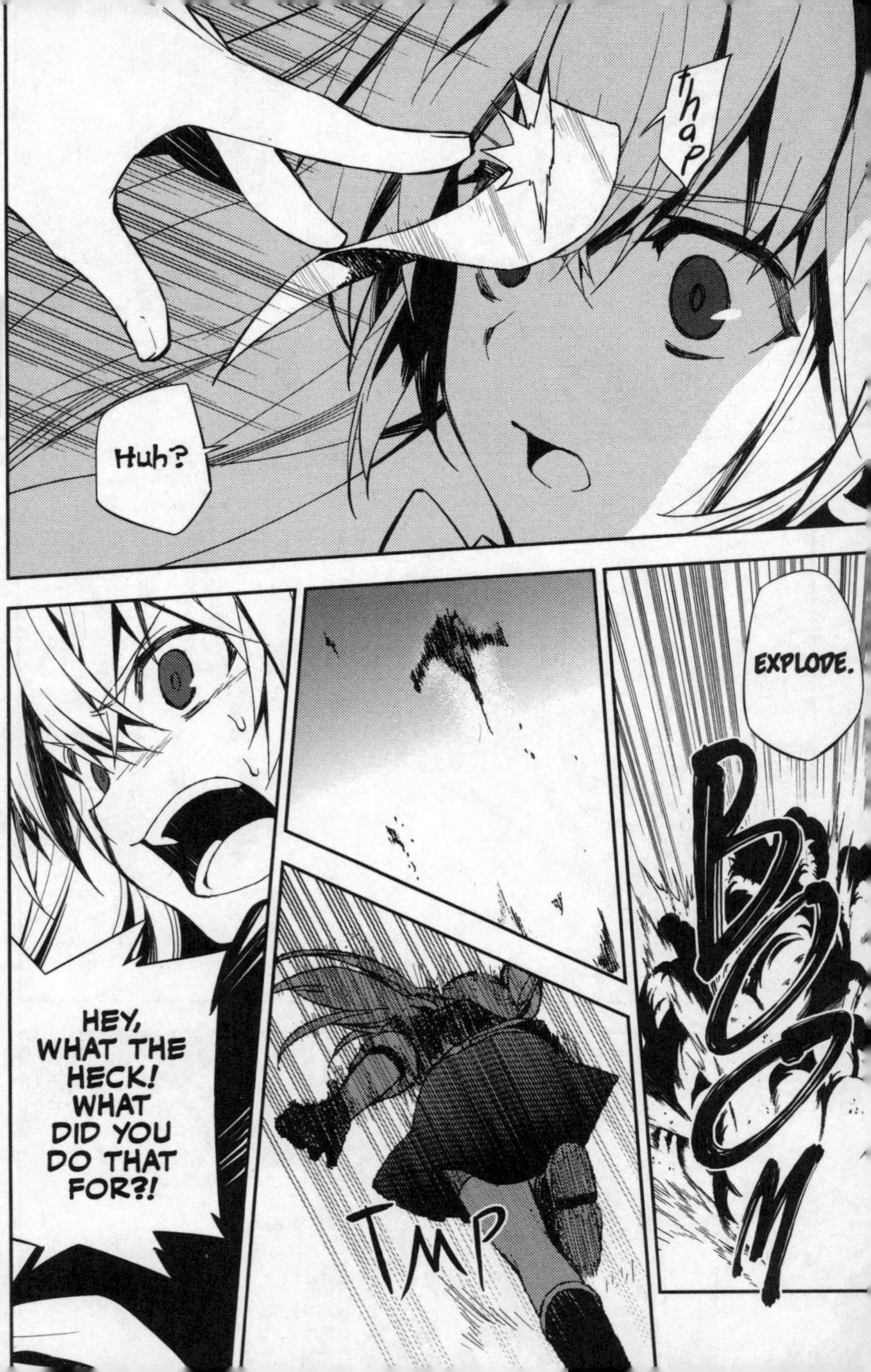
thap
Huh?
EXPLODE.
BOOM
TMP
HEY, WHAT THE HECK! WHAT DID YOU DO THAT FOR?!

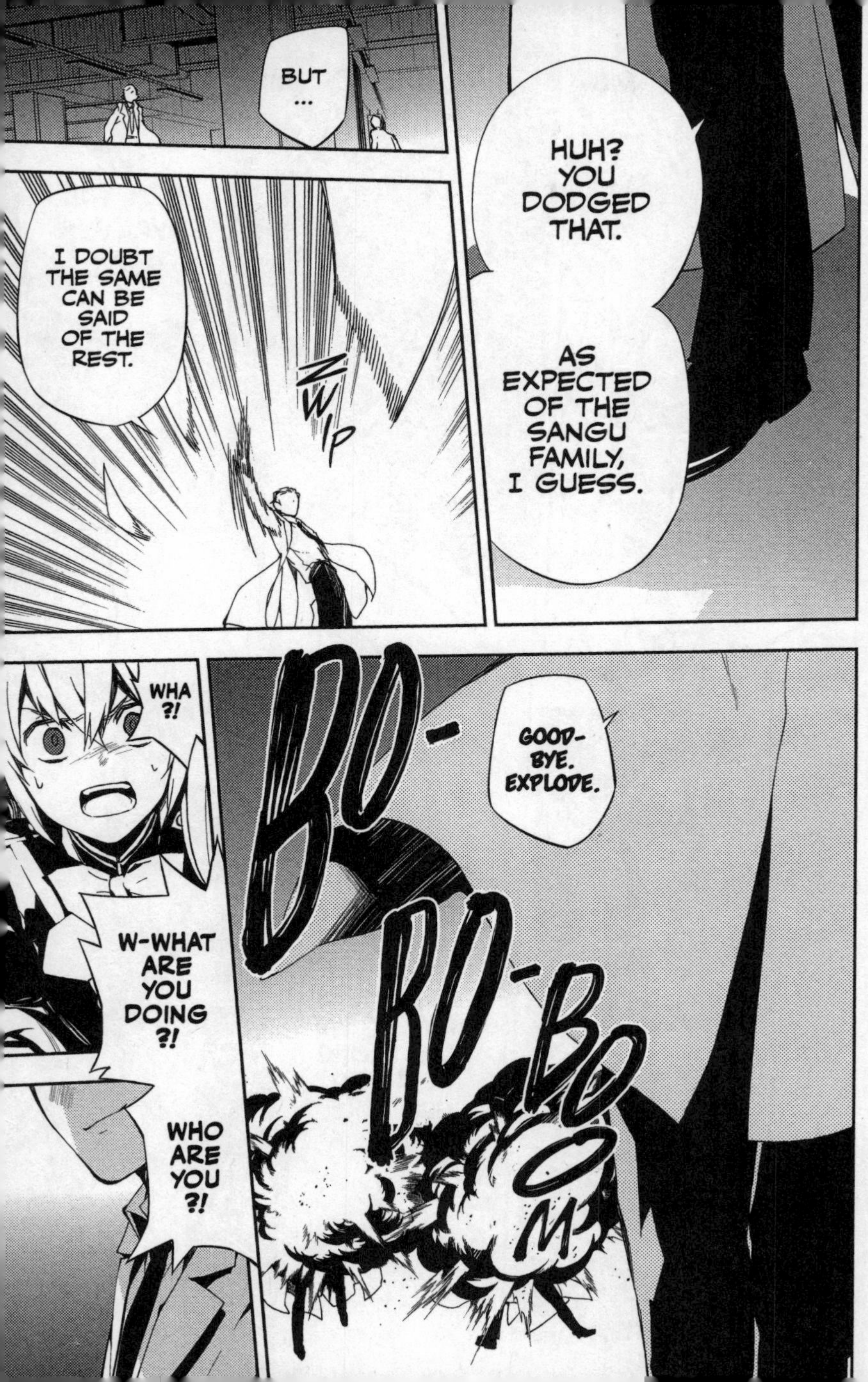
HUH? YOU DODGED THAT.
AS EXPECTED OF THE SANGU FAMILY, I GUESS.
BUT ...
I DOUBT THE SAME CAN BE SAID OF THE REST.
ZWIP
GOOD-BYE. EXPLODE.
BO-BO-BO-BOOM
WHA?!
W-WHAT ARE YOU DOING?!
WHO ARE YOU?!

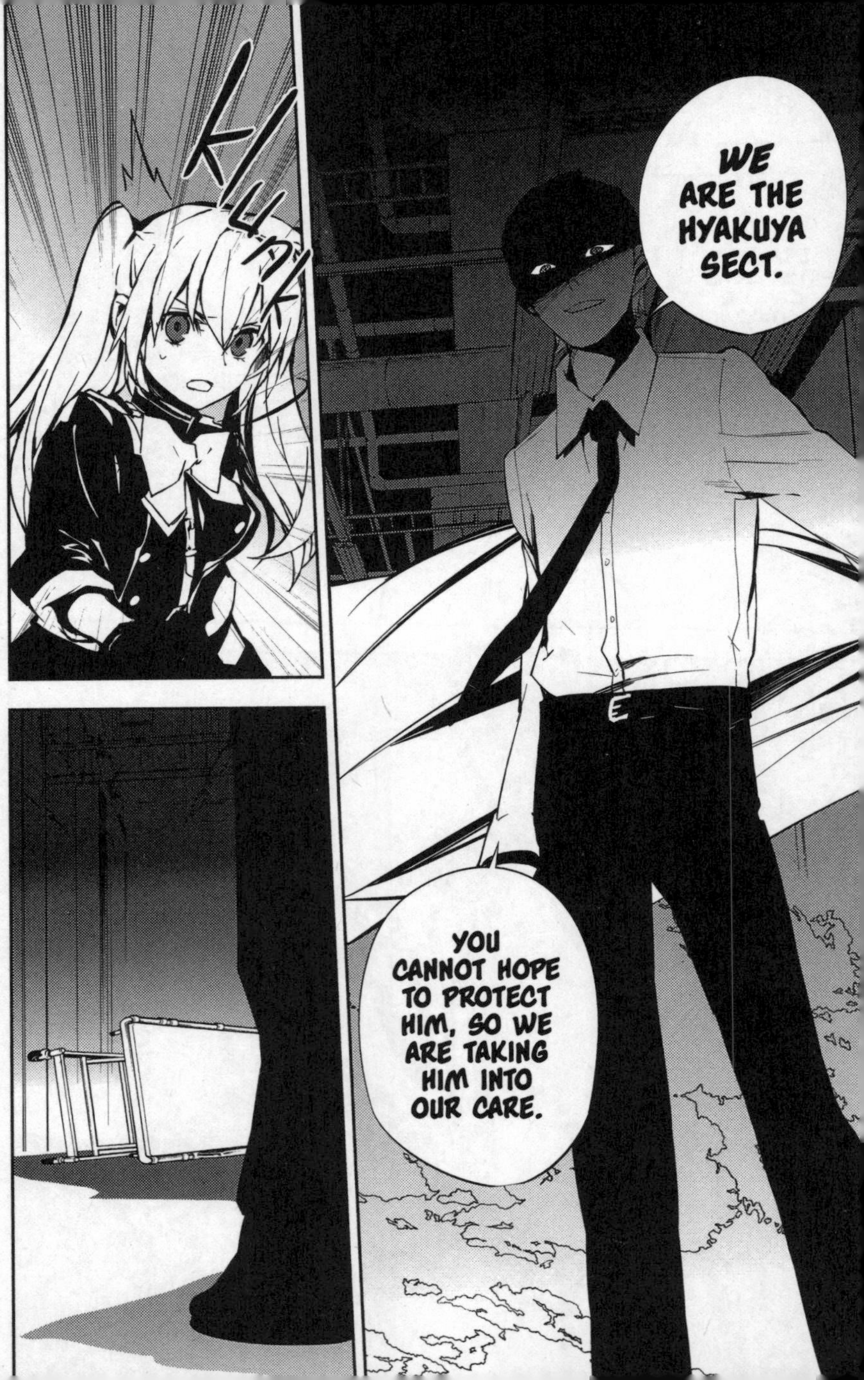
WE ARE THE HYAKUYA SECT.
YOU CANNOT HOPE TO PROTECT HIM, SO WE ARE TAKING HIM INTO OUR CARE.
KLUNK

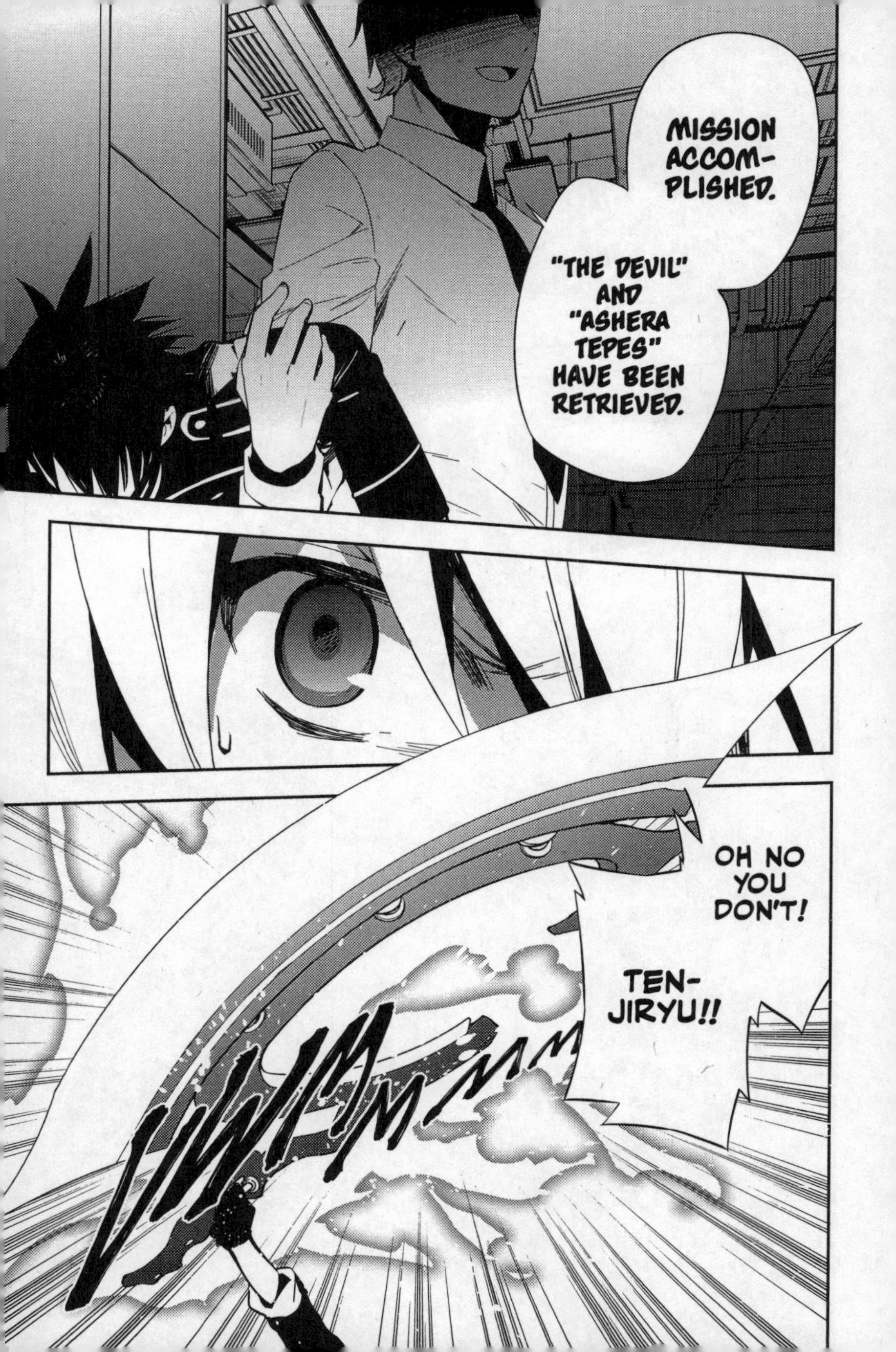
MISSION ACCOMPLISHED.
"THE DEVIL" AND "ASHERA TEPES" HAVE BEEN RETRIEVED.
OH NO YOU DON'T!
TEN-JIRYU!!
VWMmmm

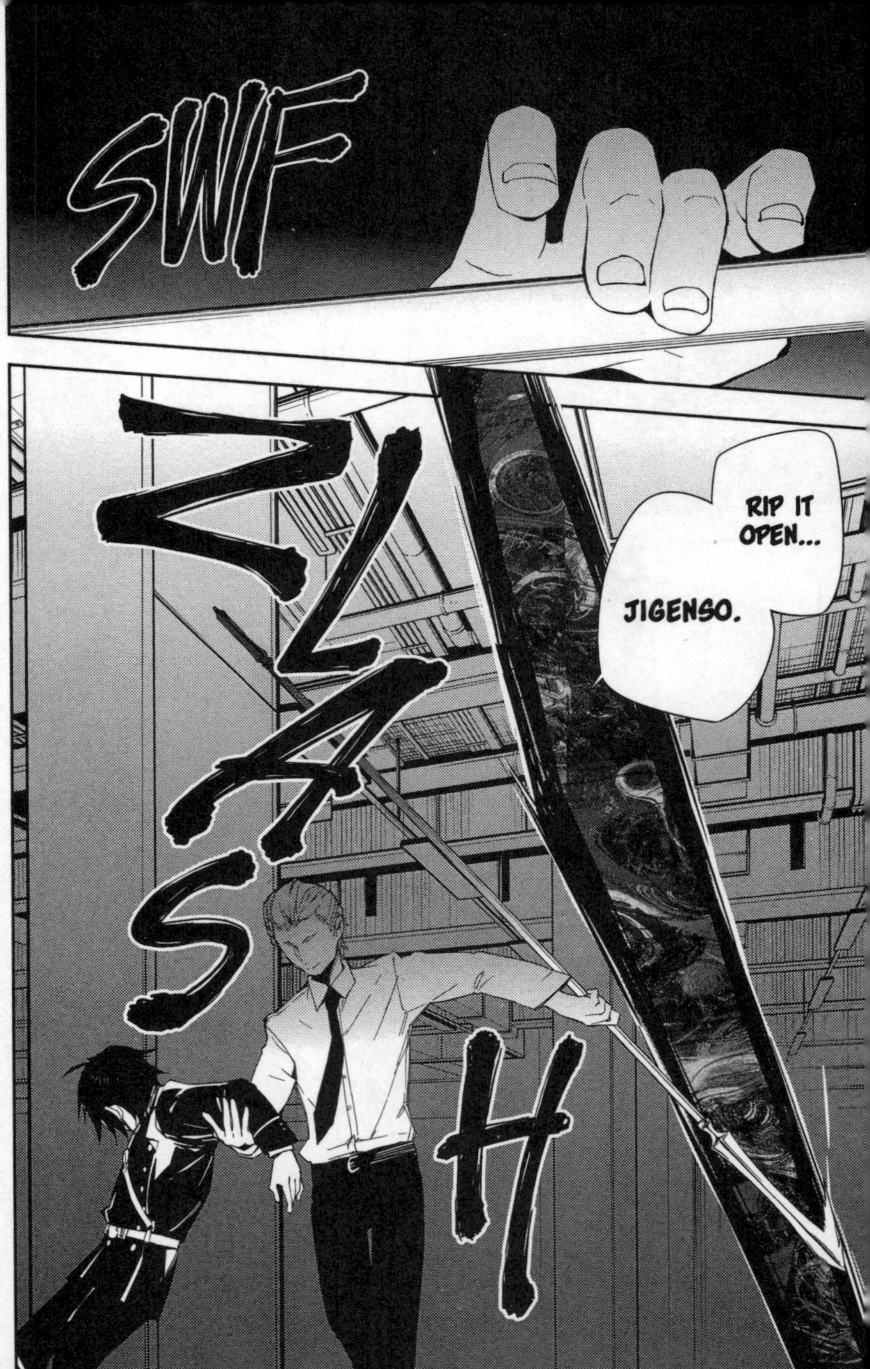
SWF
RIP IT OPEN... JIGENSO.
SMASH

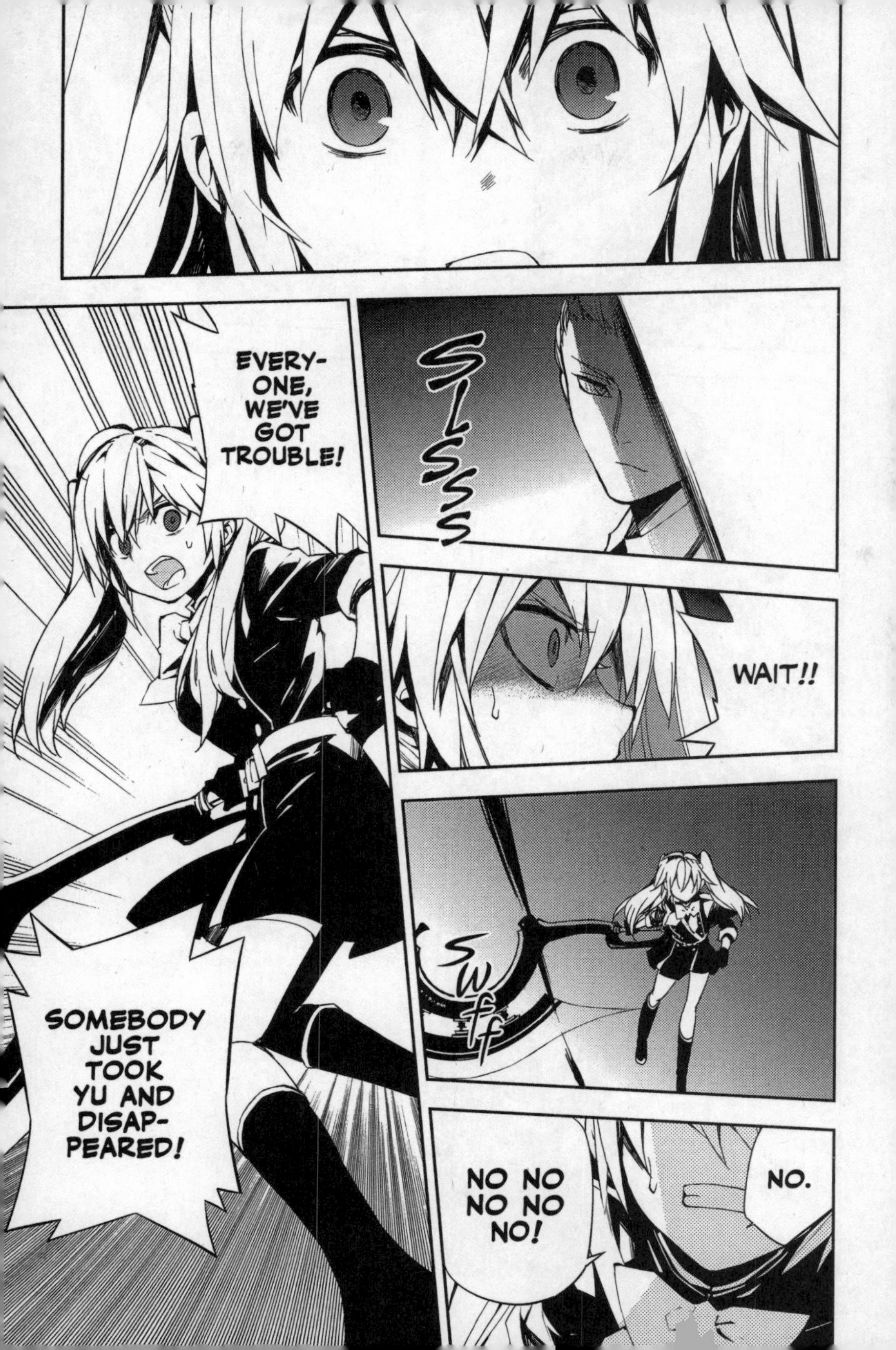
SISSS
WAIT!!
SWFF
NO.
NO NO NO NO NO!
EVERY-ONE, WE'VE GOT TROUBLE!
SOMEBODY JUST TOOK YU AND DISAP-PEARED!

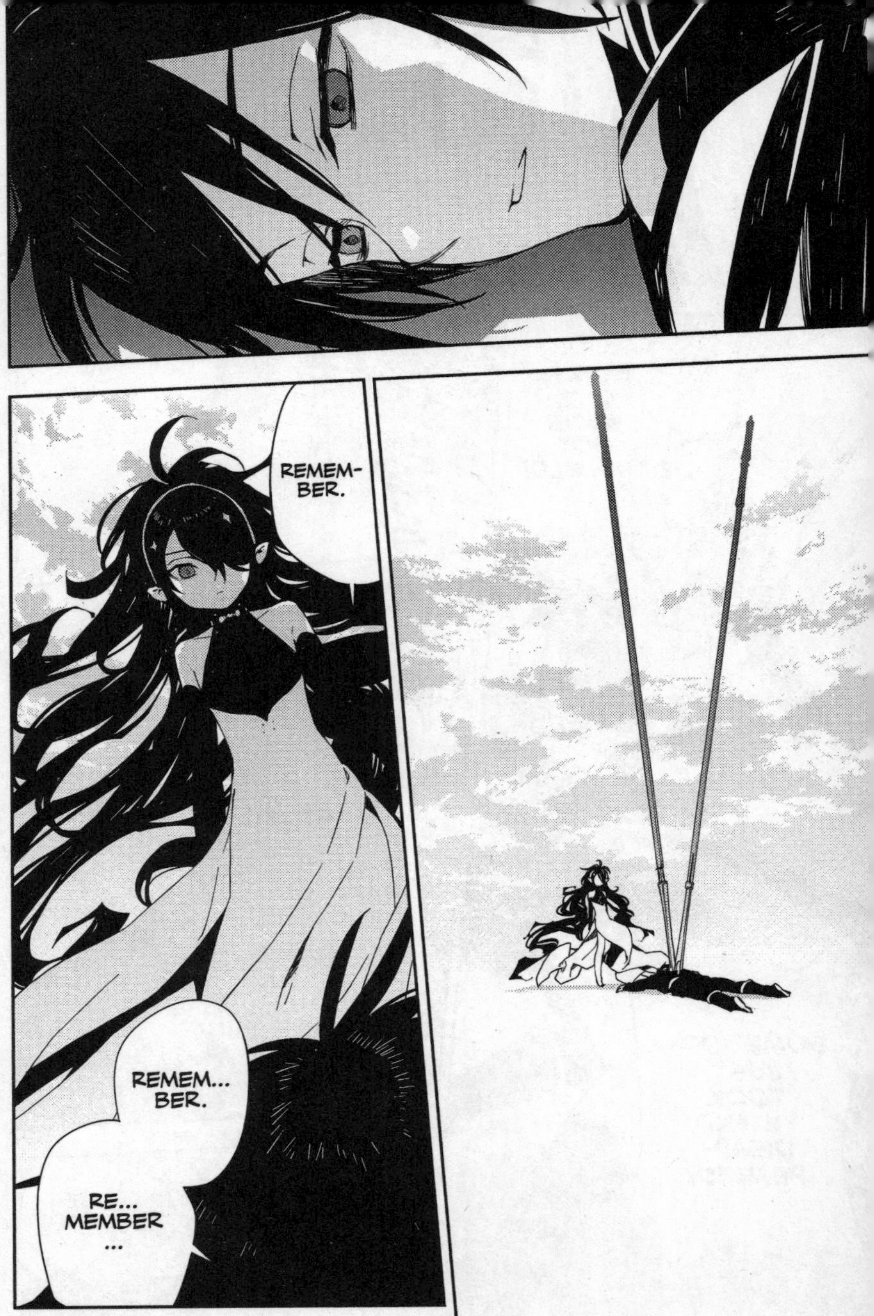
REMEM-
BER.
REMEM...
BER.
RE...
MEMBER
...

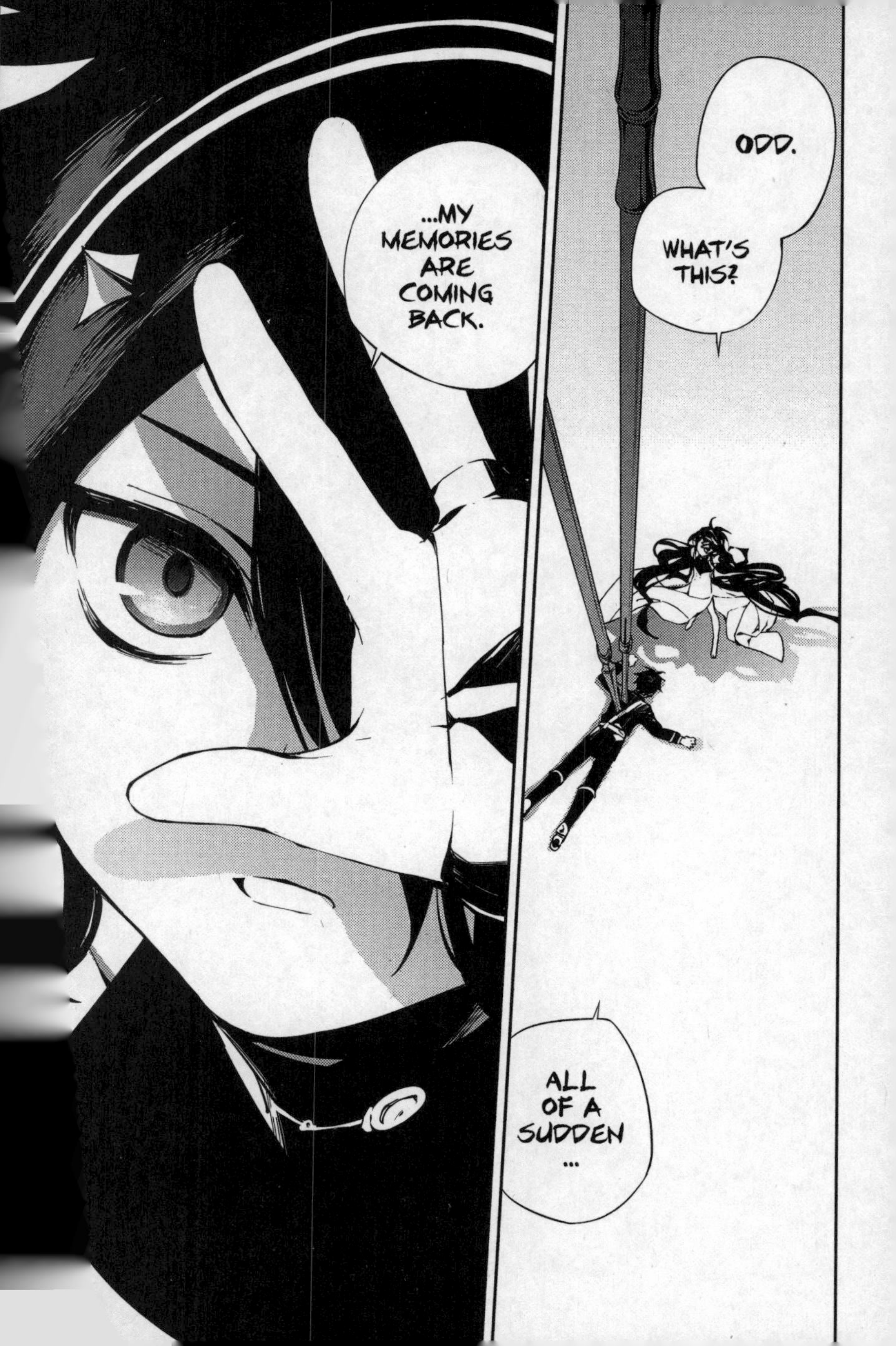
ODD.
WHAT'S THIS?
ALL OF A SUDDEN ...
...MY MEMORIES ARE COMING BACK.

Seraph of the End

—VAMPIRE REIGN—

Chapter 78
The Dark Ages of Greece

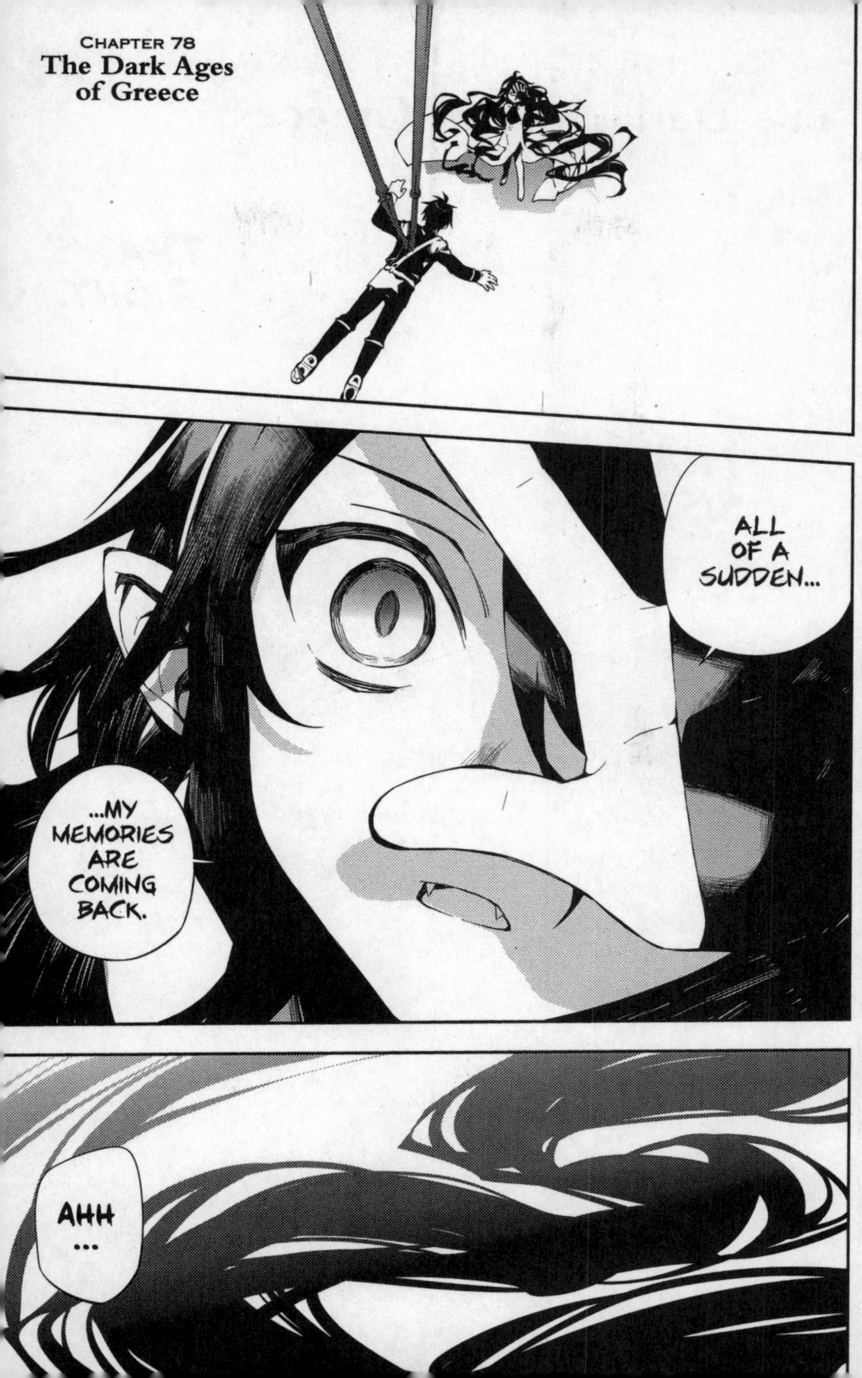
ALL OF A SUDDEN...
...MY MEMORIES ARE COMING BACK.
AHH ...

Chapter 78
The Dark Ages of Greece

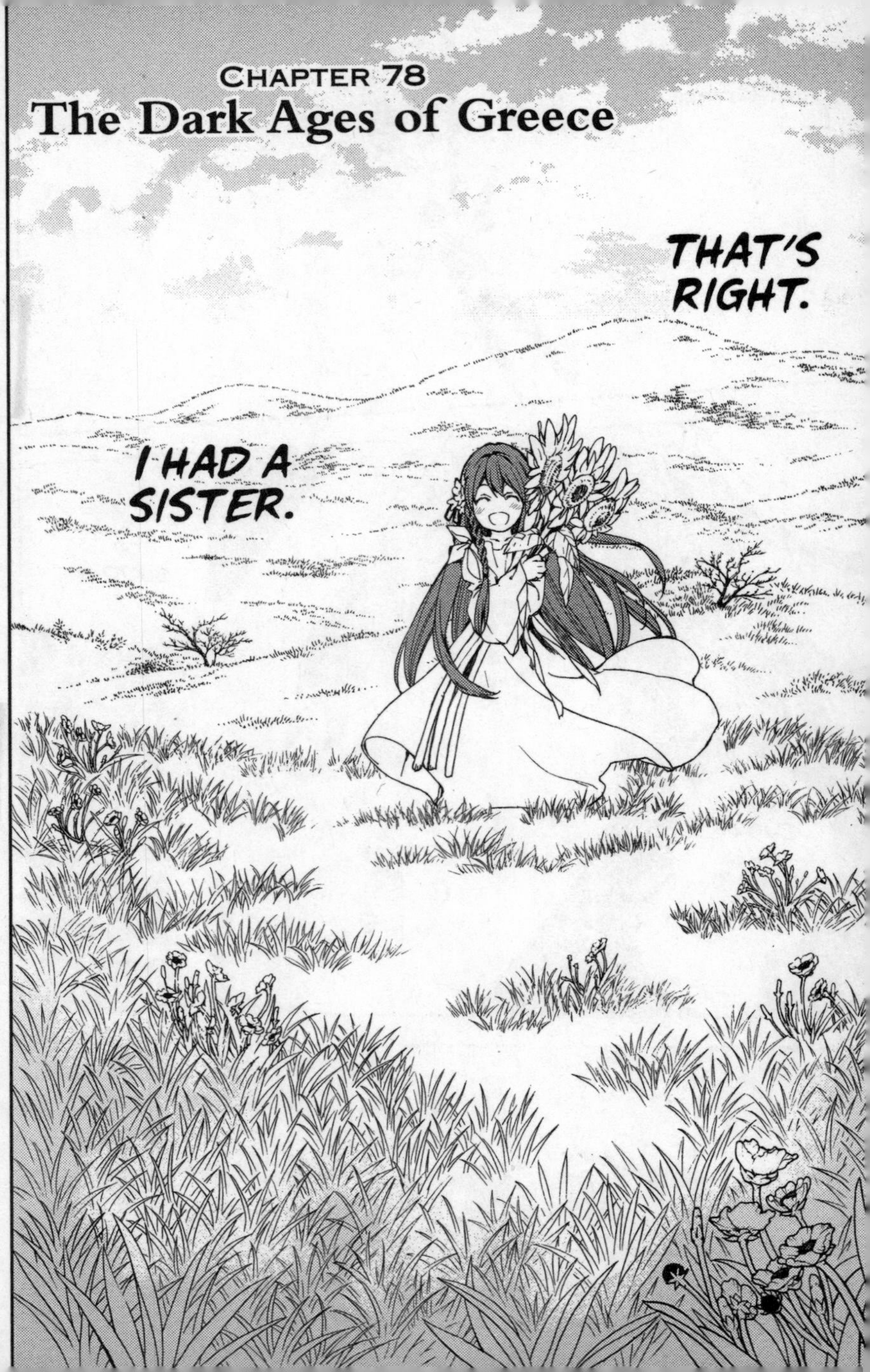
THAT'S RIGHT.
I HAD A SISTER.

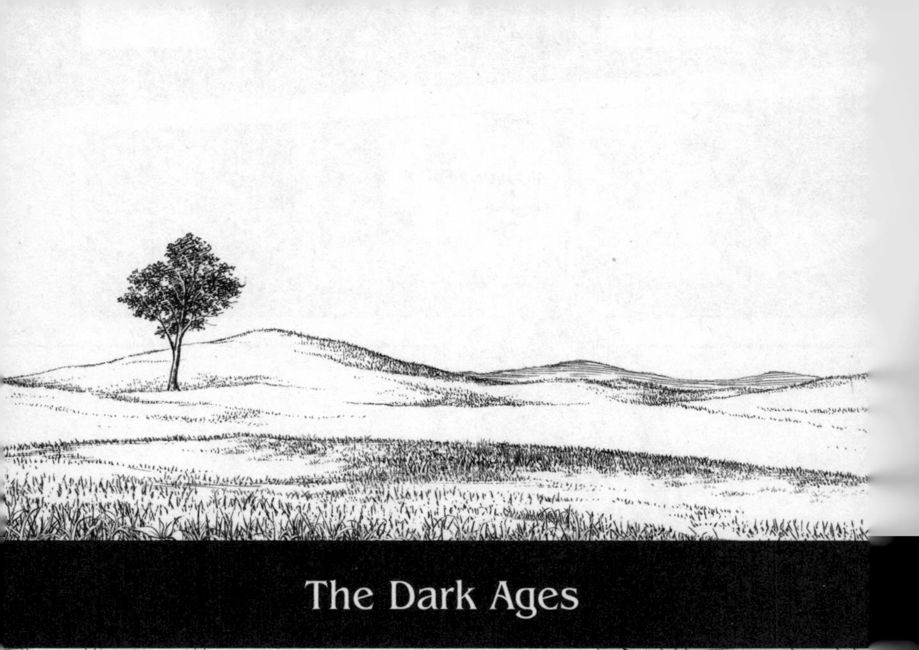

The Dark Ages

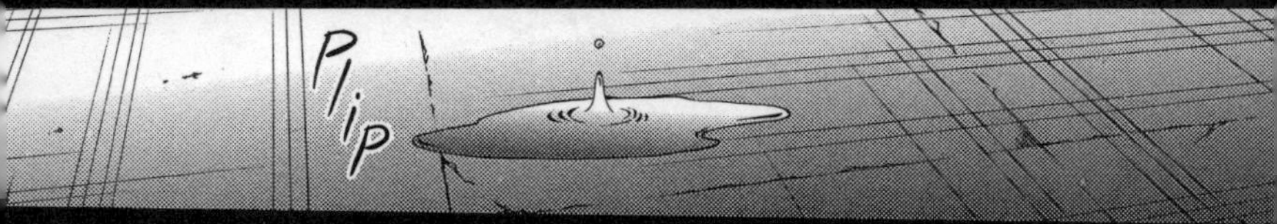
Plip

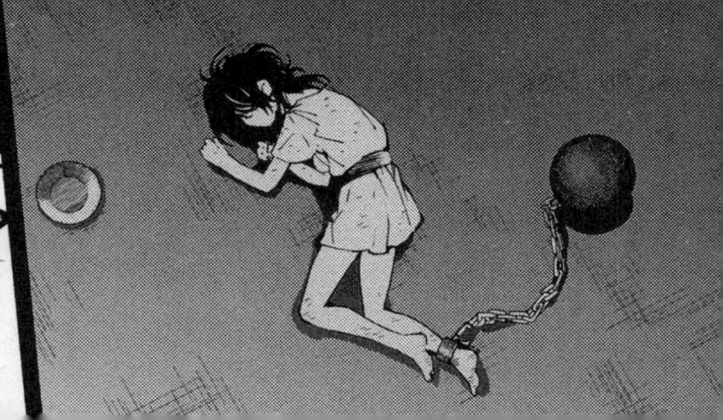

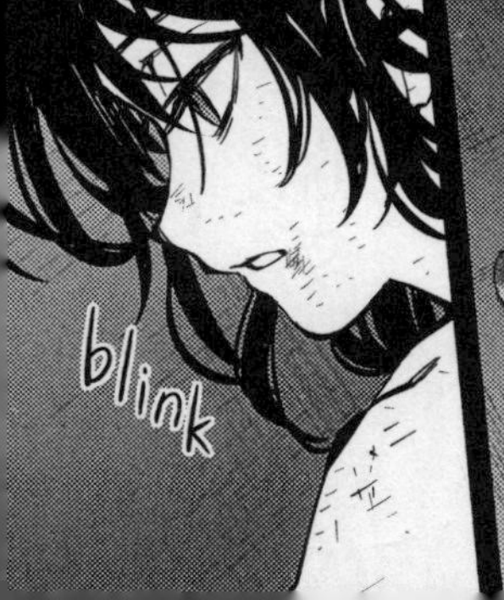
blink

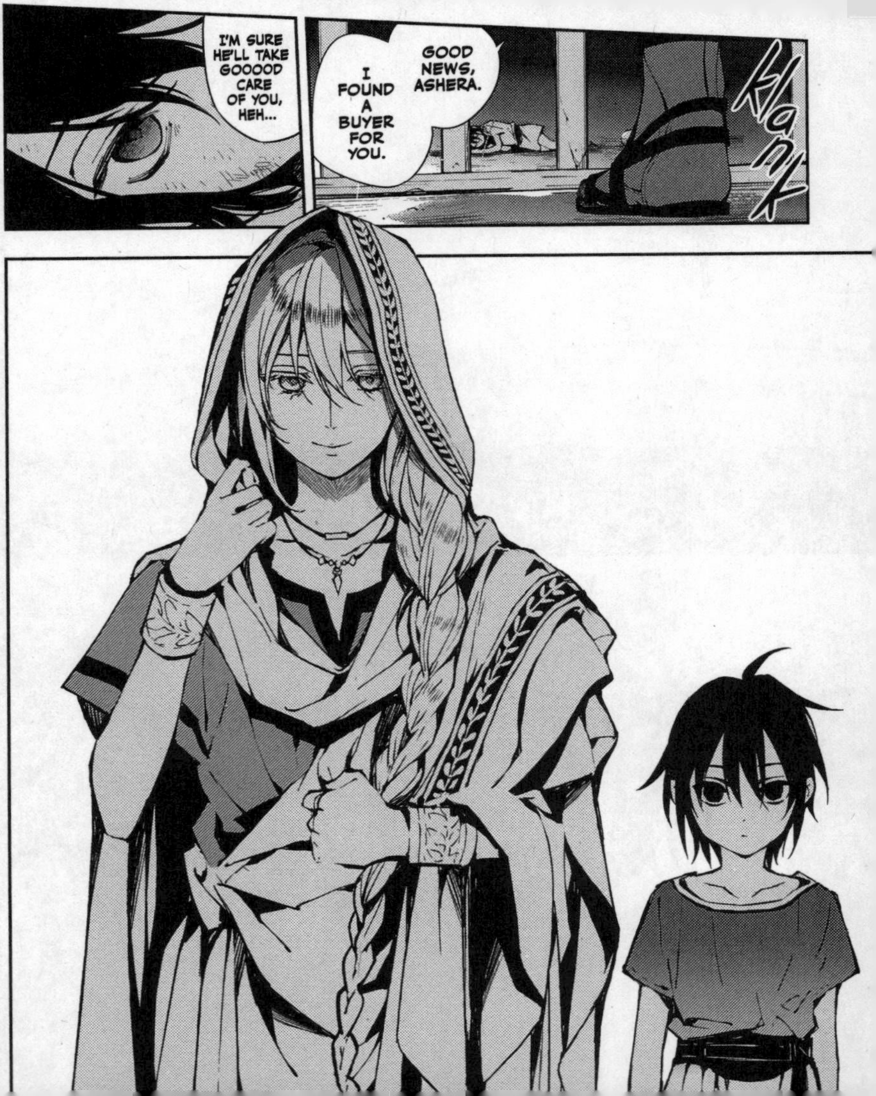
klank
GOOD NEWS, ASHERA.
I FOUND A BUYER FOR YOU.
I'M SURE HE'LL TAKE GOOOOD CARE OF YOU, HEH...

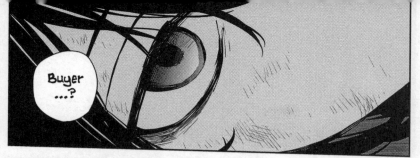

Buyer
....?

SWf

YU.
KINDLY
TAKE
OFF HIS
CHAINS.

YES-
SIR.

YOU.
WERE
YOU
BOUGHT
BY HIM
TOO?

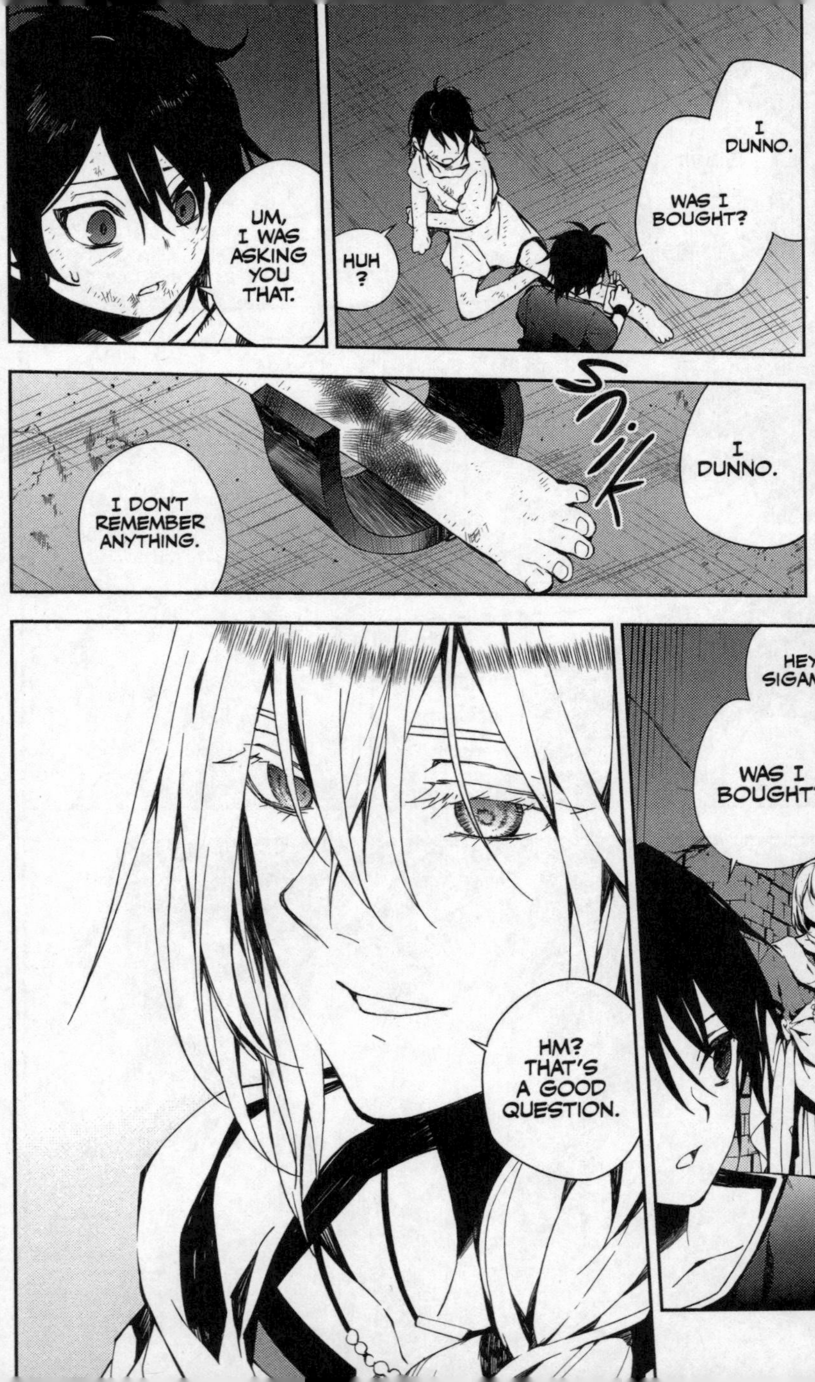
I DUNNO.
WAS I BOUGHT?
HUH?
UM, I WAS ASKING YOU THAT.
I DUNNO.
SNIK
I DON'T REMEMBER ANYTHING.
HEY, SIGAMA.
WAS I BOUGHT?
HM? THAT'S A GOOD QUESTION.

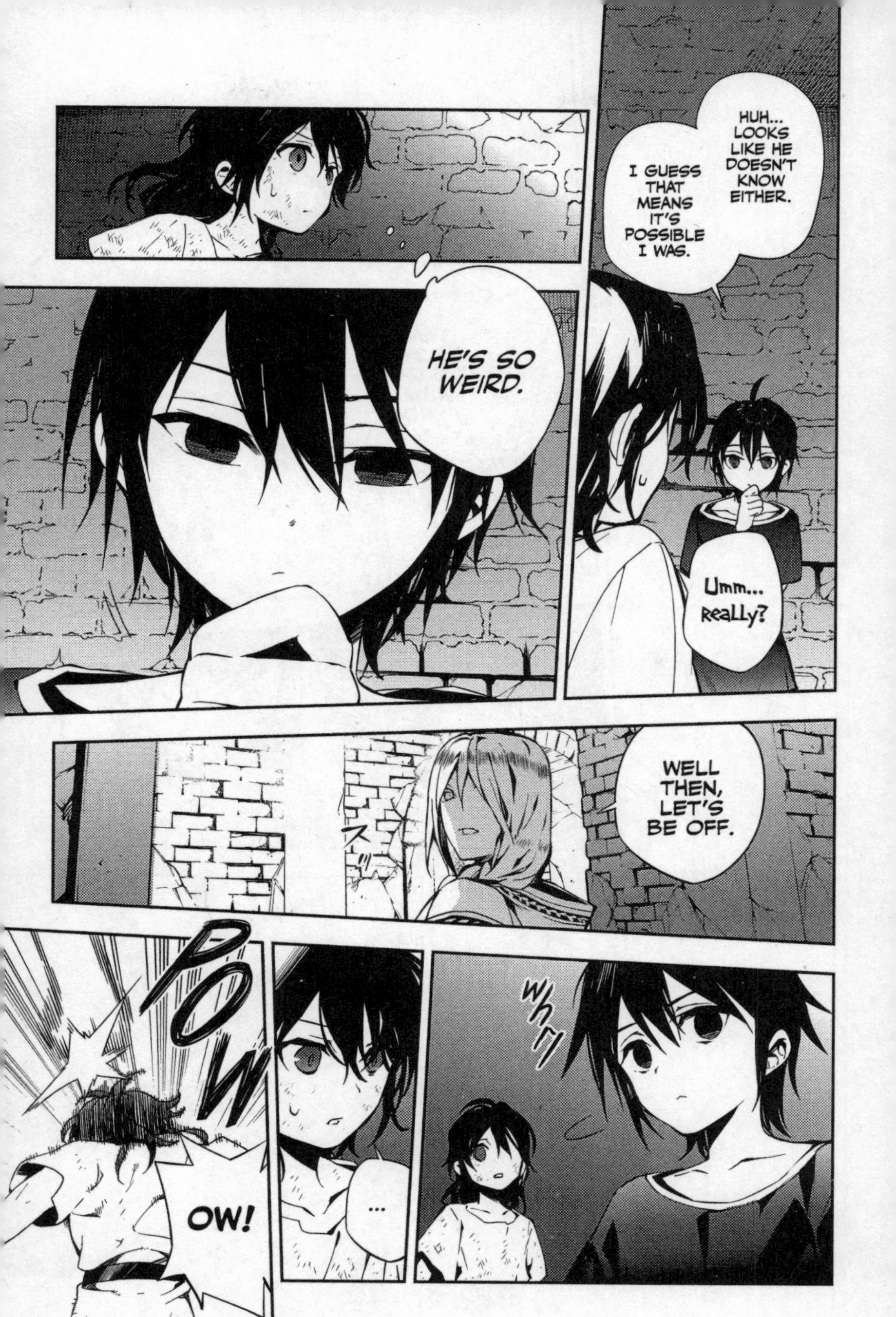
HUH... LOOKS LIKE HE DOESN'T KNOW EITHER.
I GUESS THAT MEANS IT'S POSSIBLE I WAS.
Umm... really?
HE'S SO WEIRD.
WELL THEN, LET'S BE OFF.
ズッ
whirl
...
POW
OW!

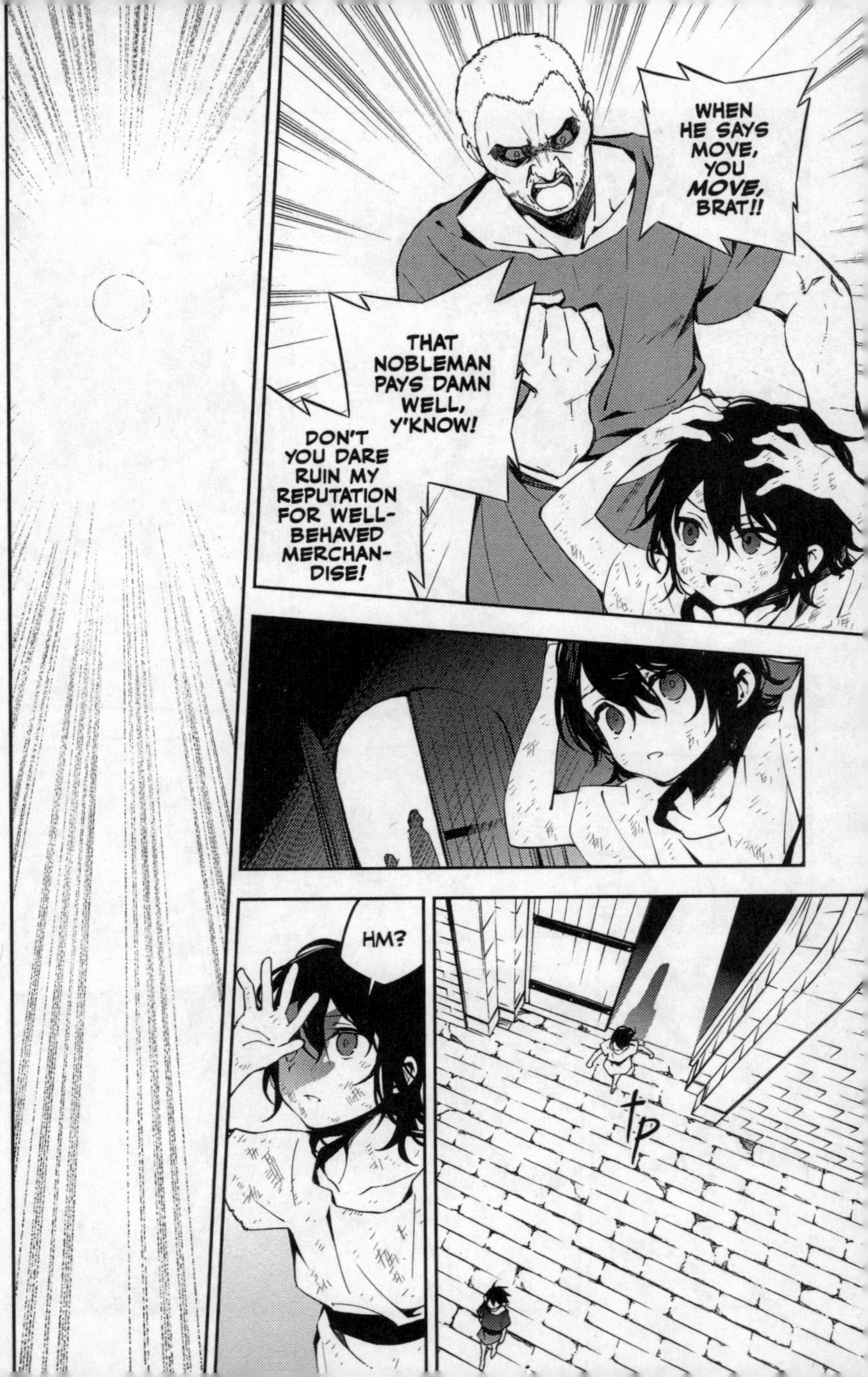

WHEN HE SAYS MOVE, YOU *MOVE*, BRAT!!
THAT NOBLEMAN PAYS DAMN WELL, Y'KNOW!
DON'T YOU DARE RUIN MY REPUTATION FOR WELL-BEHAVED MERCHANDISE!
TP
HM?

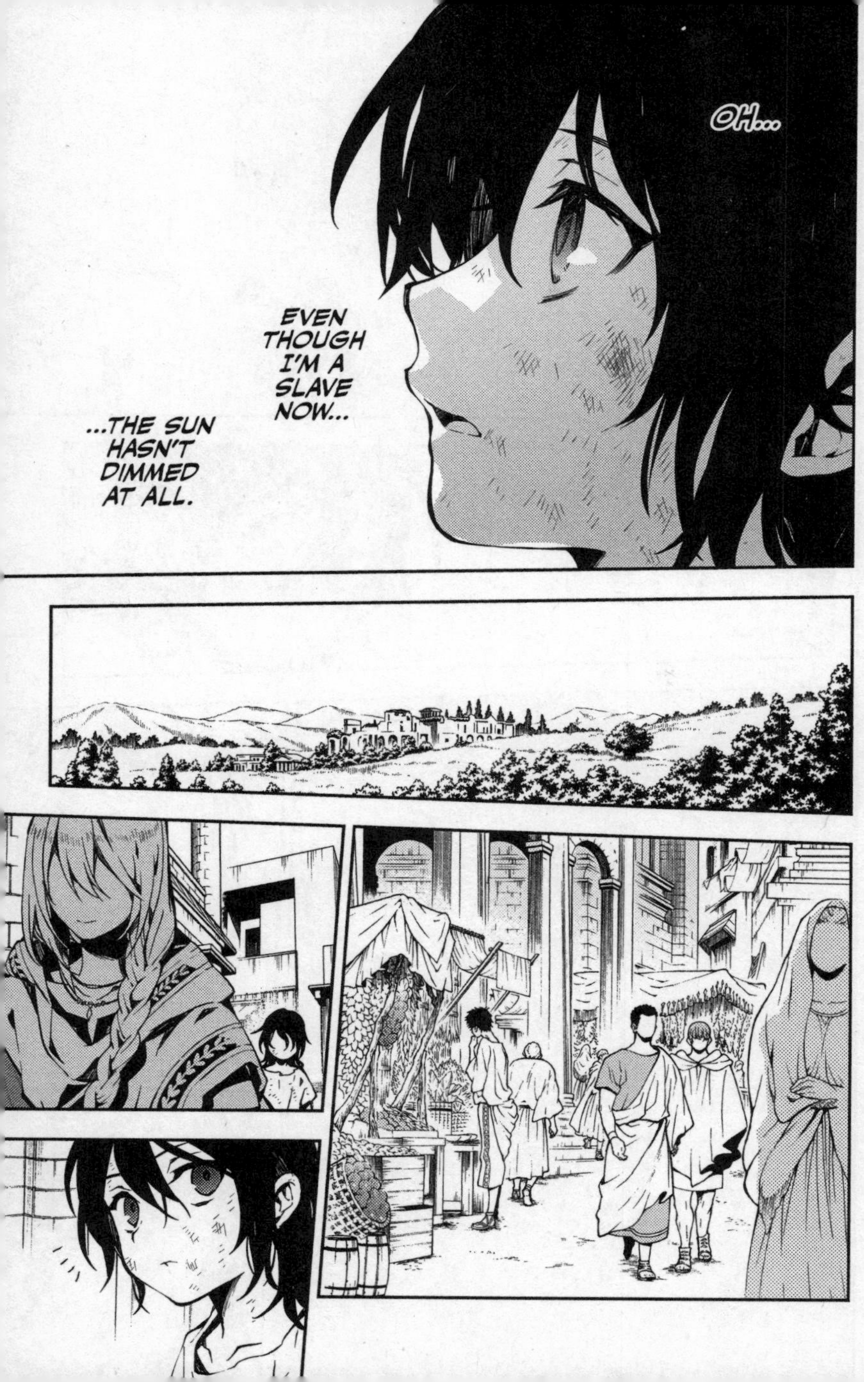
OH...
EVEN THOUGH I'M A SLAVE NOW...
...THE SUN HASN'T DIMMED AT ALL.

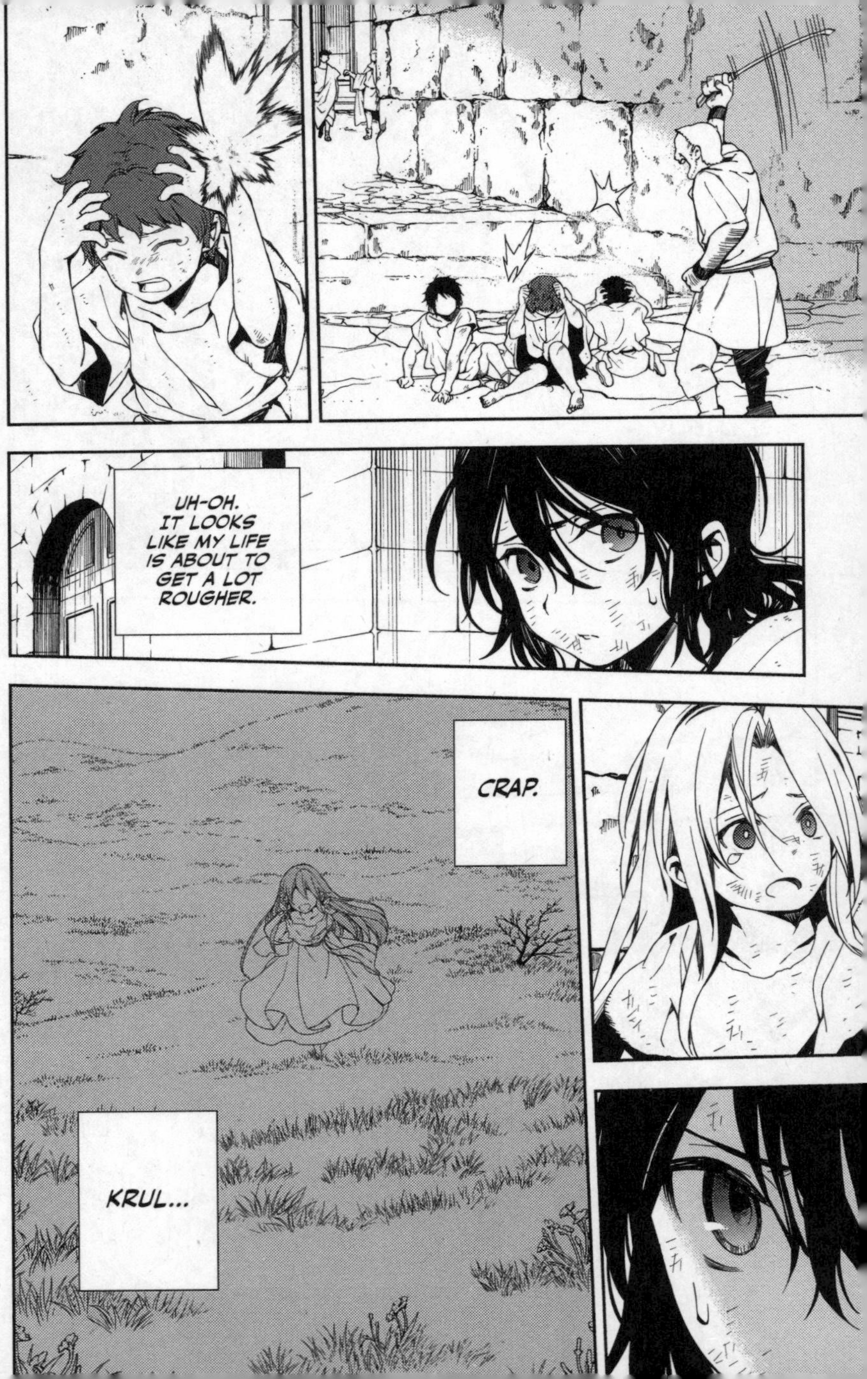
UH-OH. IT LOOKS LIKE MY LIFE IS ABOUT TO GET A LOT ROUGHER.
CRAP.
KRUL...

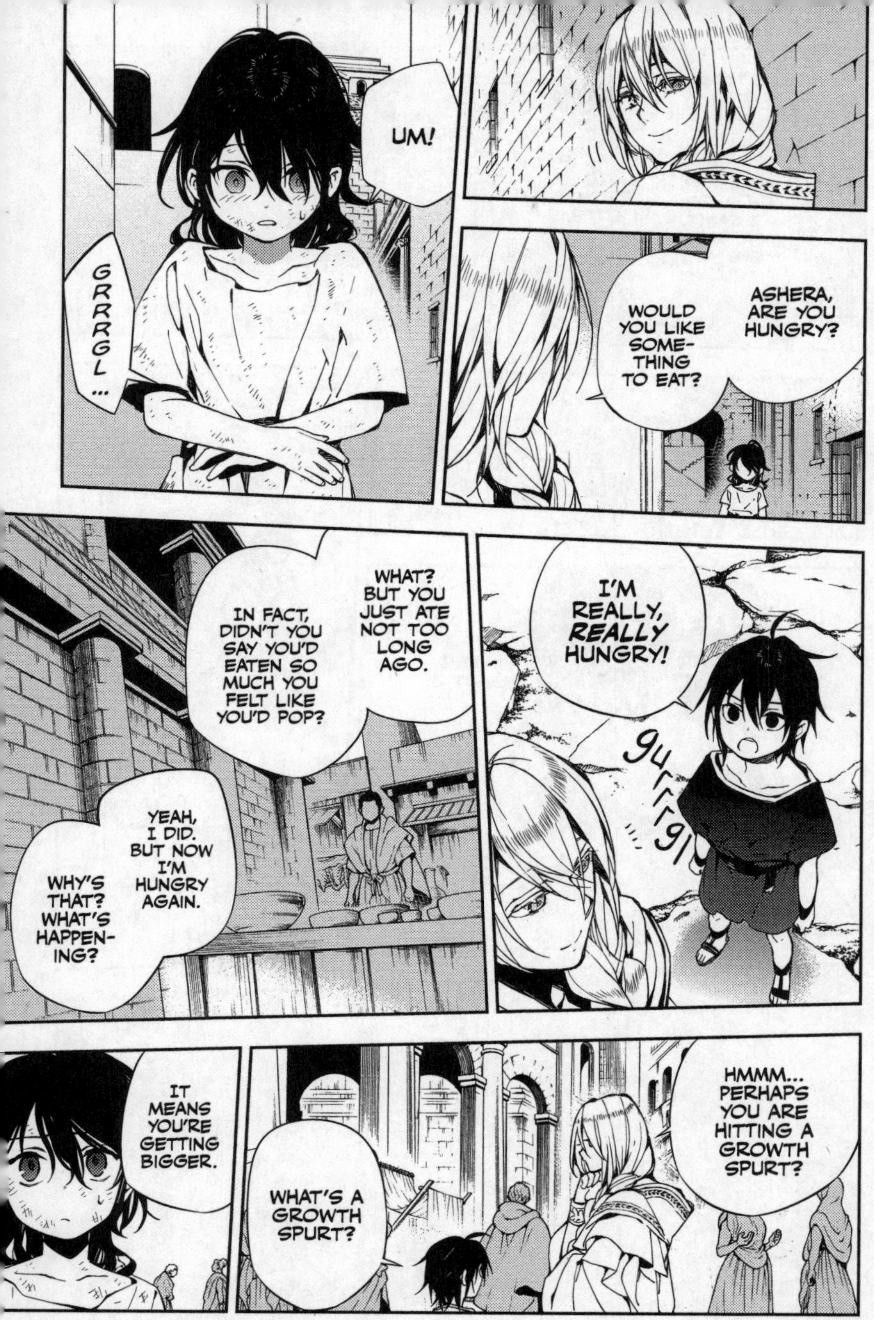
ASHERA, ARE YOU HUNGRY?
WOULD YOU LIKE SOME-THING TO EAT?
UM!
GRRRGL...
I'M REALLY, *REALLY* HUNGRY!
gurrrgl...
WHAT? BUT YOU JUST ATE NOT TOO LONG AGO.
IN FACT, DIDN'T YOU SAY YOU'D EATEN SO MUCH YOU FELT LIKE YOU'D POP?
YEAH, I DID. BUT NOW I'M HUNGRY AGAIN.
WHY'S THAT? WHAT'S HAPPEN-ING?
HMMM... PERHAPS YOU ARE HITTING A GROWTH SPURT?
WHAT'S A GROWTH SPURT?
IT MEANS YOU'RE GETTING BIGGER.

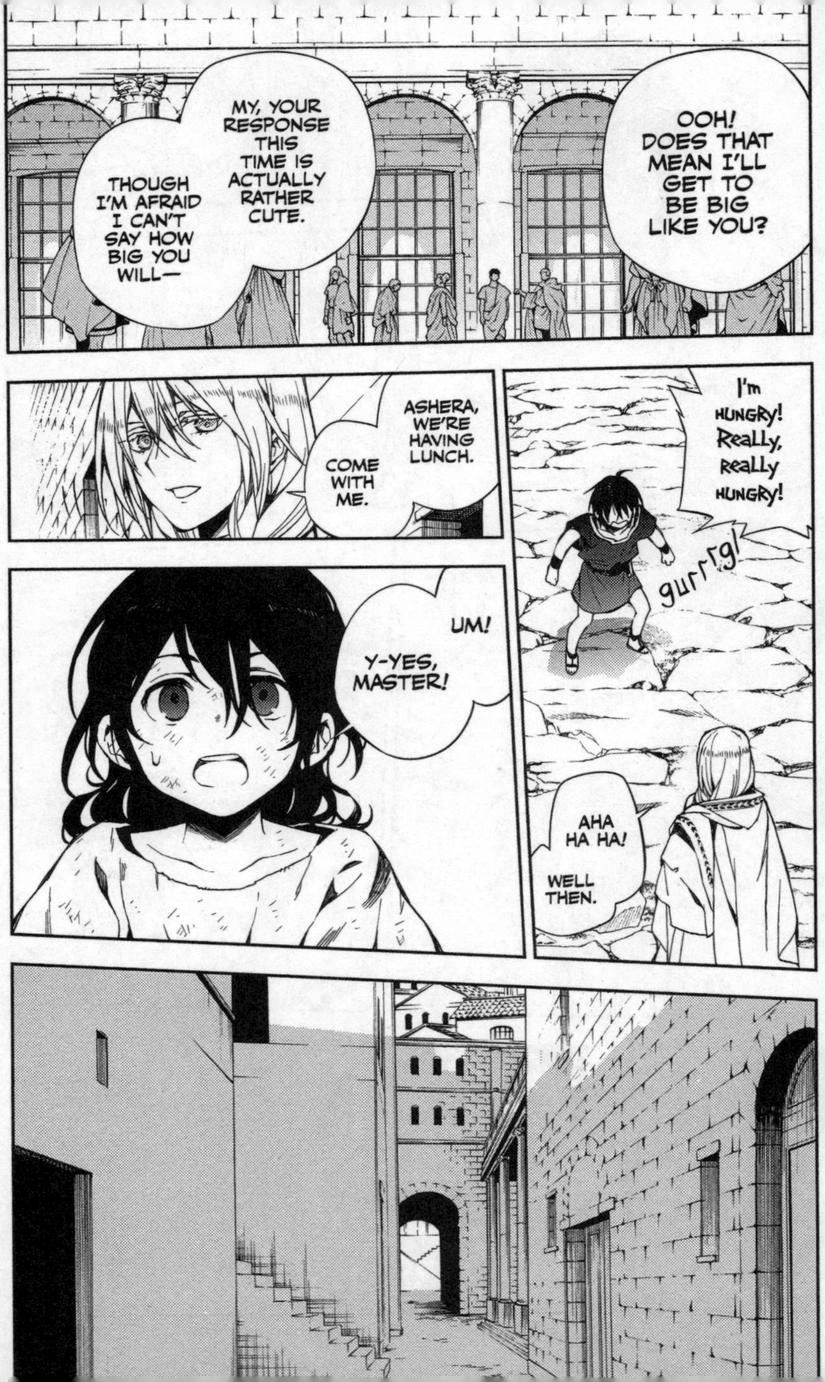
OOH! DOES THAT MEAN I'LL GET TO BE BIG LIKE YOU?
MY, YOUR RESPONSE THIS TIME IS ACTUALLY RATHER CUTE.
THOUGH I'M AFRAID I CAN'T SAY HOW BIG YOU WILL—
I'm HUNGRY! Really, really HUNGRY!
gurrrg!
AHA HA HA!
WELL THEN.
ASHERA, WE'RE HAVING LUNCH.
COME WITH ME.
UM!
Y-YES, MASTER!

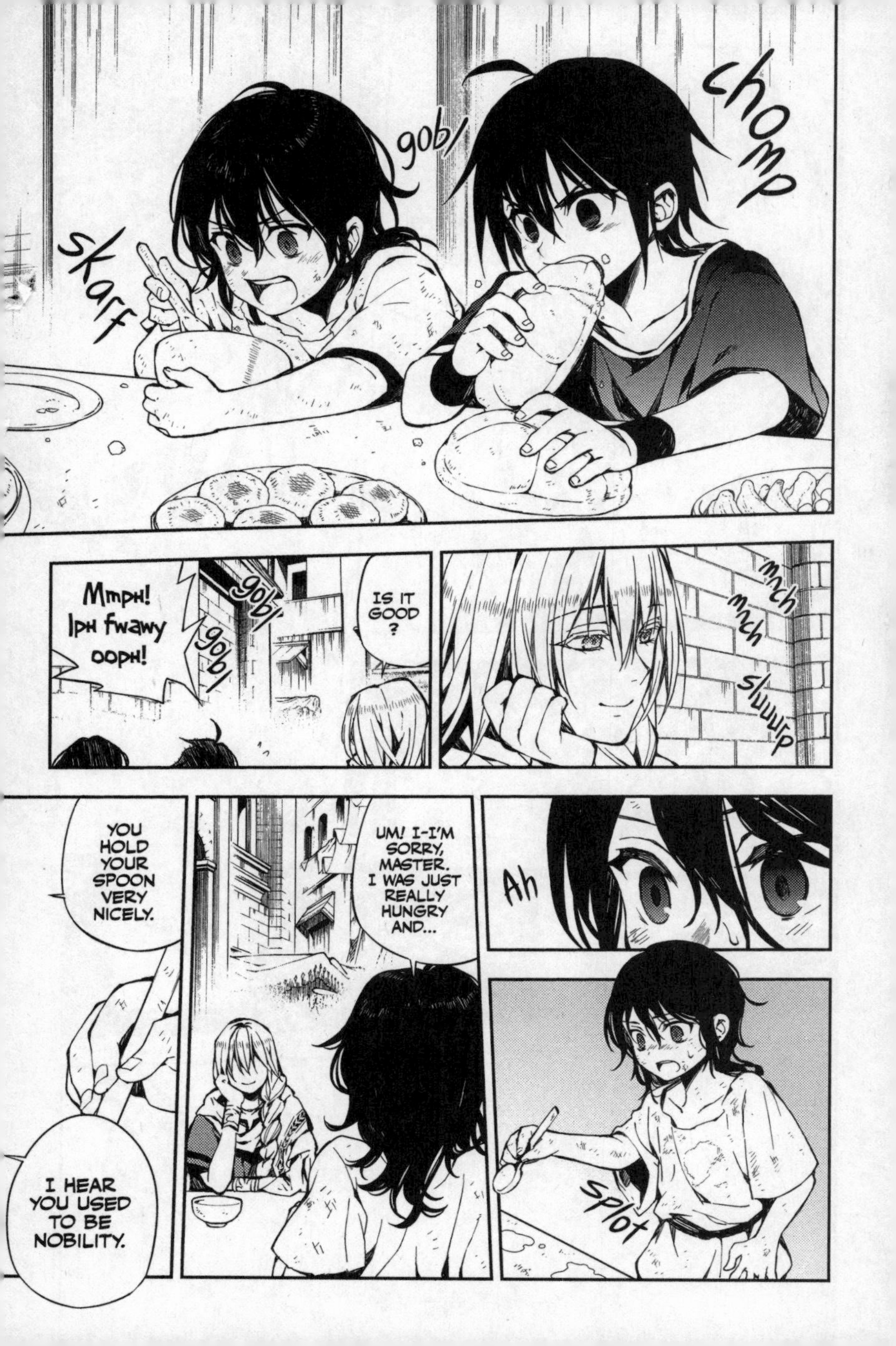
chomp
gob
skarf
mnch
mnch
sluuurp
IS IT GOOD?
gob
gob
Mmph! Iph fwawy ooph!
Ah
splot
UM! I-I'M SORRY, MASTER. I WAS JUST REALLY HUNGRY AND...
YOU HOLD YOUR SPOON VERY NICELY.
I HEAR YOU USED TO BE NOBILITY.

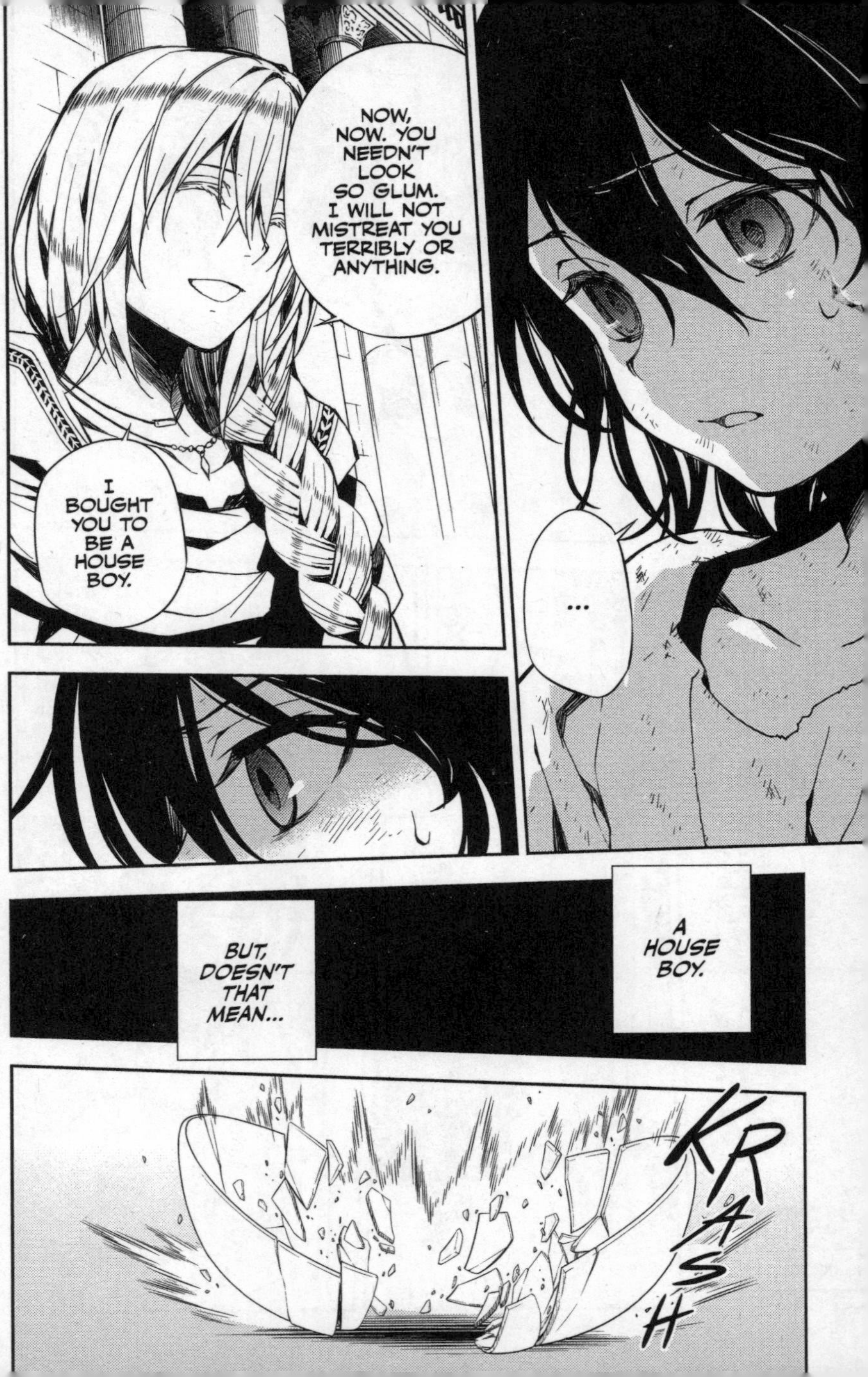
...
NOW, NOW. YOU NEEDN'T LOOK SO GLUM. I WILL NOT MISTREAT YOU TERRIBLY OR ANYTHING.
I BOUGHT YOU TO BE A HOUSE BOY.
A HOUSE BOY.
BUT, DOESN'T THAT MEAN...
KRASH

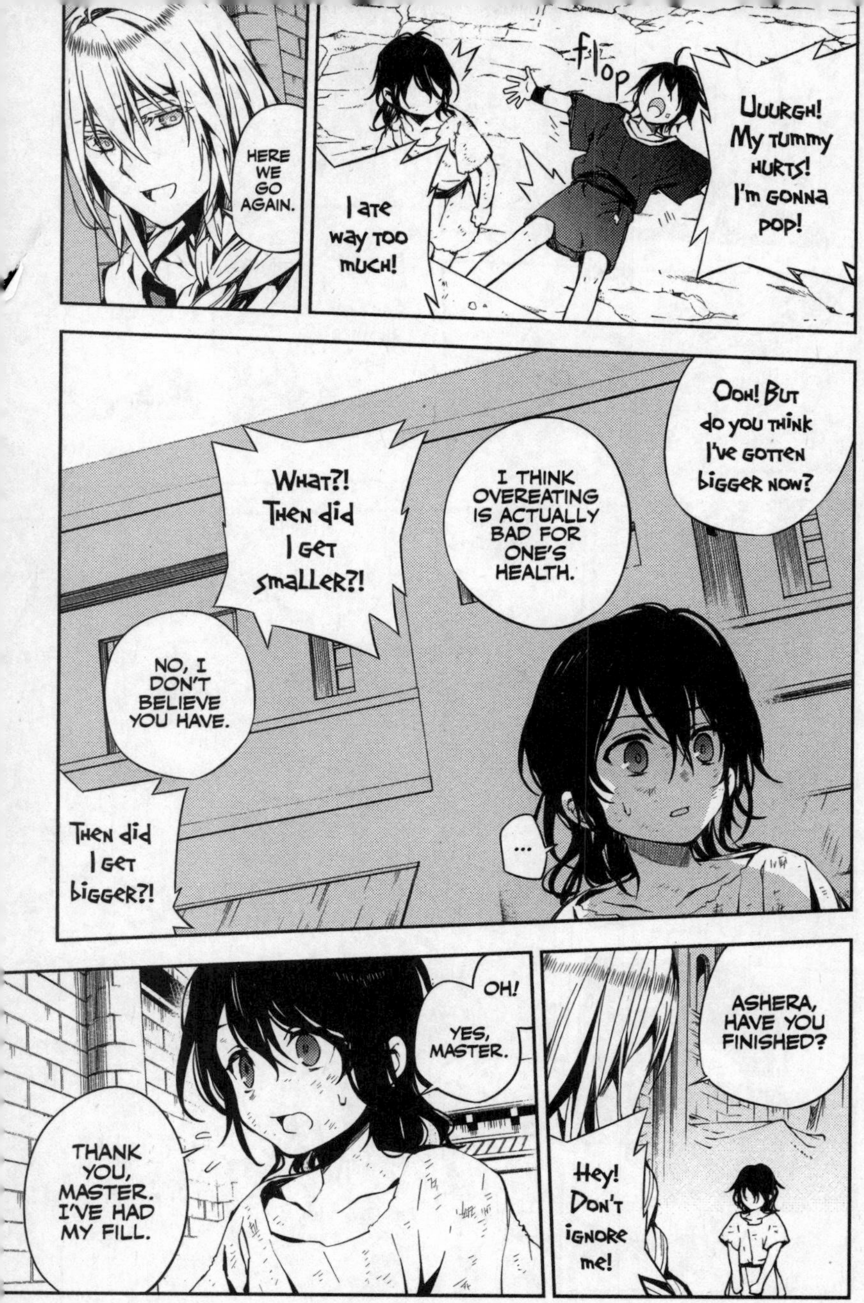
flop
Uuurgh! My tummy hurts! I'm gonna pop!
I ate way too much!
Here we go again.
Ooh! But do you think I've gotten bigger now?
I think overeating is actually bad for one's health.
What?! Then did I get smaller?!
No, I don't believe you have.
...
Then did I get bigger?!
Ashera, have you finished?
Hey! Don't ignore me!
Oh!
Yes, Master.
Thank you, Master. I've had my fill.

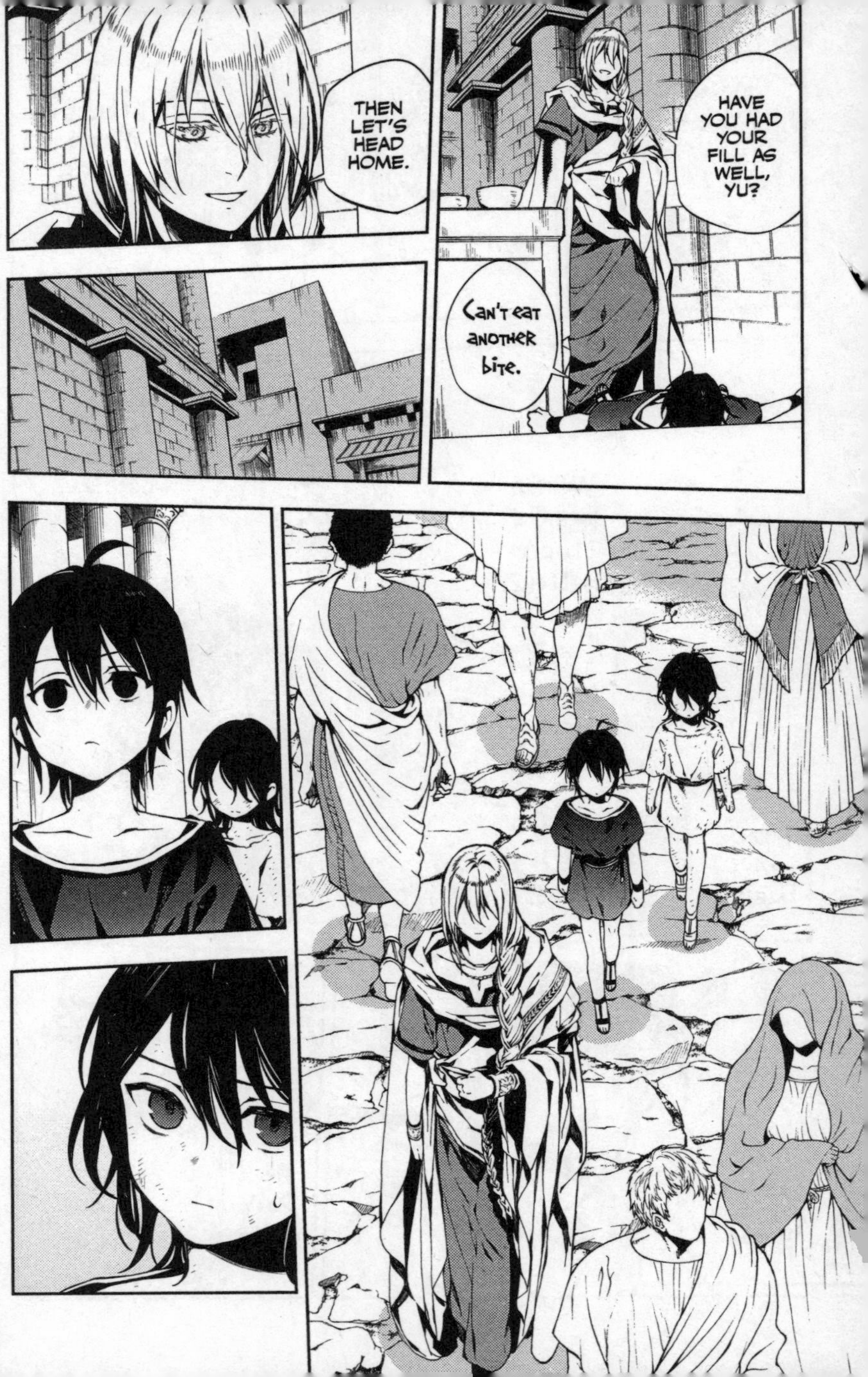
HAVE YOU HAD YOUR FILL AS WELL, YU?
Can't eat another bite.
THEN LET'S HEAD HOME.

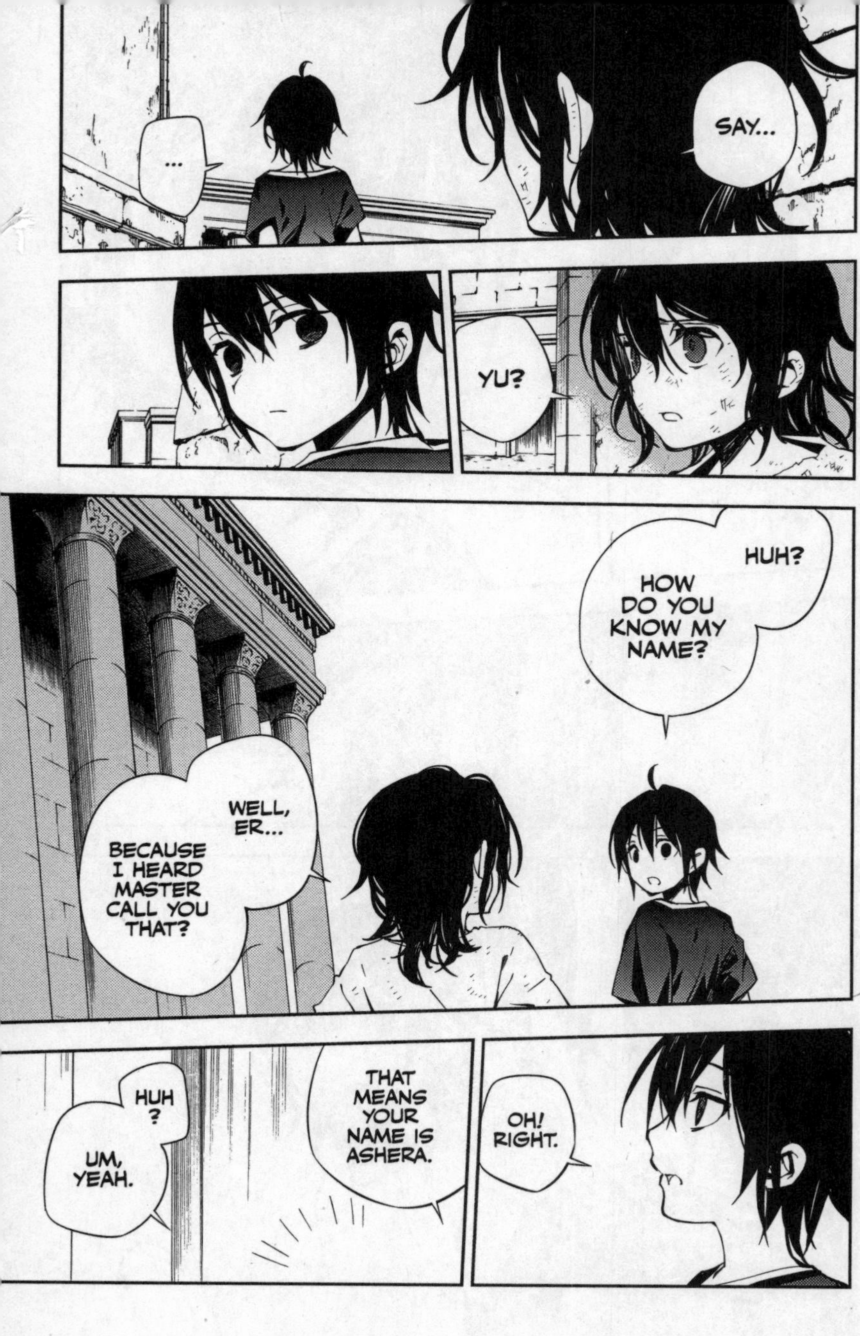
SAY...
...
YU?
HUH?
HOW DO YOU KNOW MY NAME?
WELL, ER...
BECAUSE I HEARD MASTER CALL YOU THAT?
OH! RIGHT.
THAT MEANS YOUR NAME IS ASHERA.
HUH?
UM, YEAH.

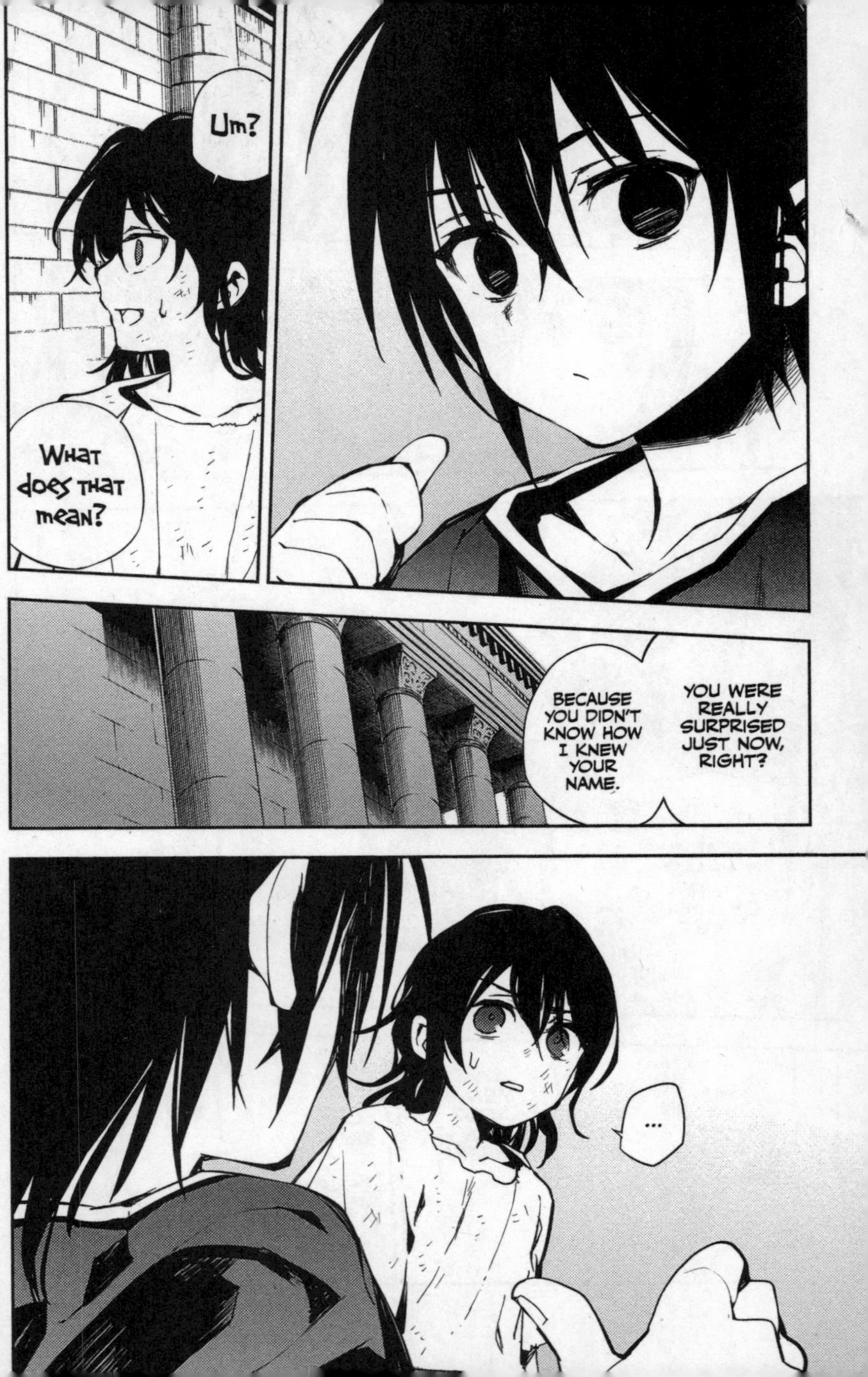
Um?
What does that mean?
YOU WERE REALLY SURPRISED JUST NOW, RIGHT?
BECAUSE YOU DIDN'T KNOW HOW I KNEW YOUR NAME.
...

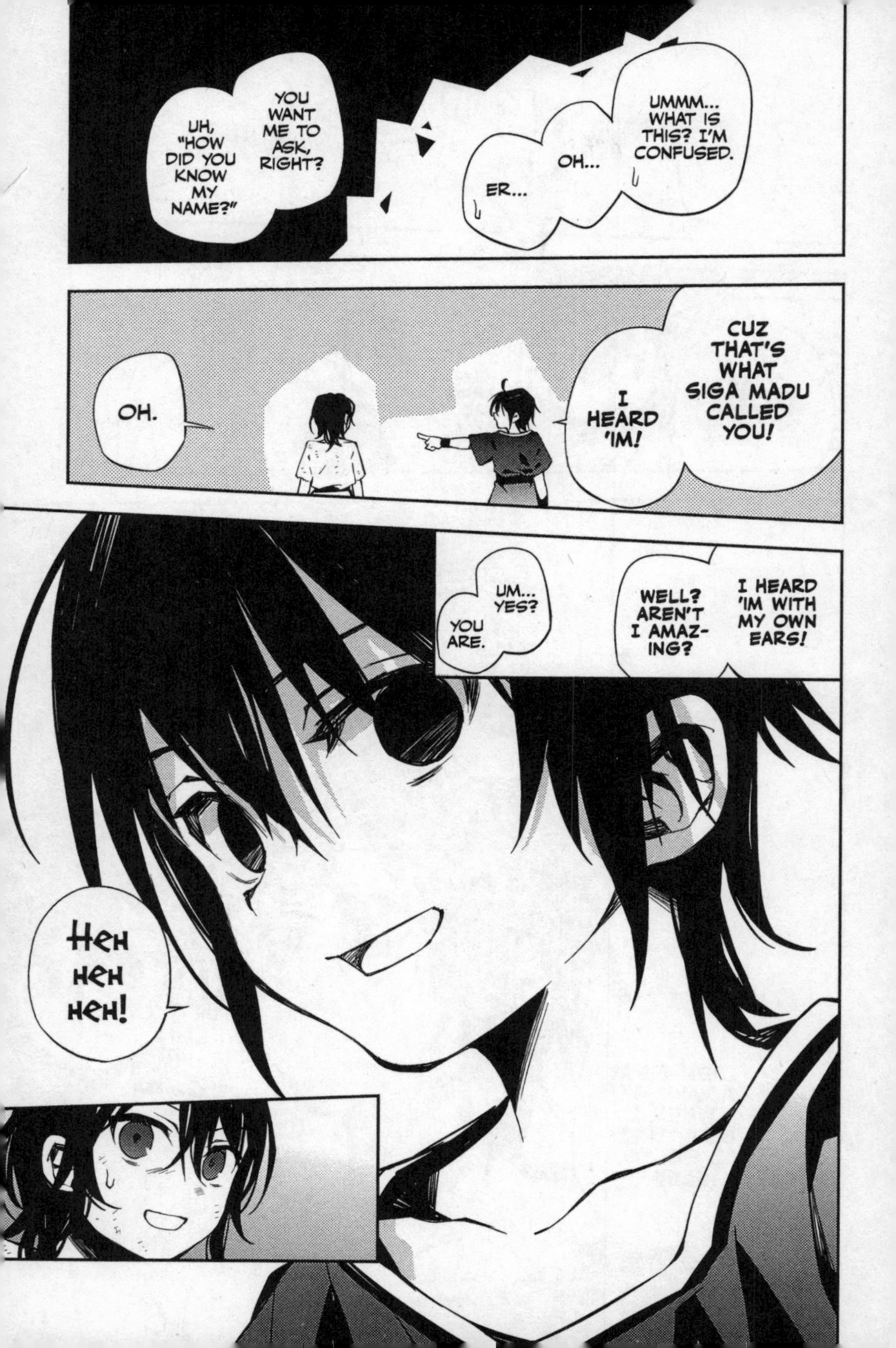
UMMM... WHAT IS THIS? I'M CONFUSED.
OH...
ER...
YOU WANT ME TO ASK, RIGHT?
UH, "HOW DID YOU KNOW MY NAME?"
CUZ THAT'S WHAT SIGA MADU CALLED YOU!
I HEARD 'IM!
OH.
I HEARD 'IM WITH MY OWN EARS!
WELL? AREN'T I AMAZ-ING?
UM... YES? YOU ARE.
HEH HEH HEH!

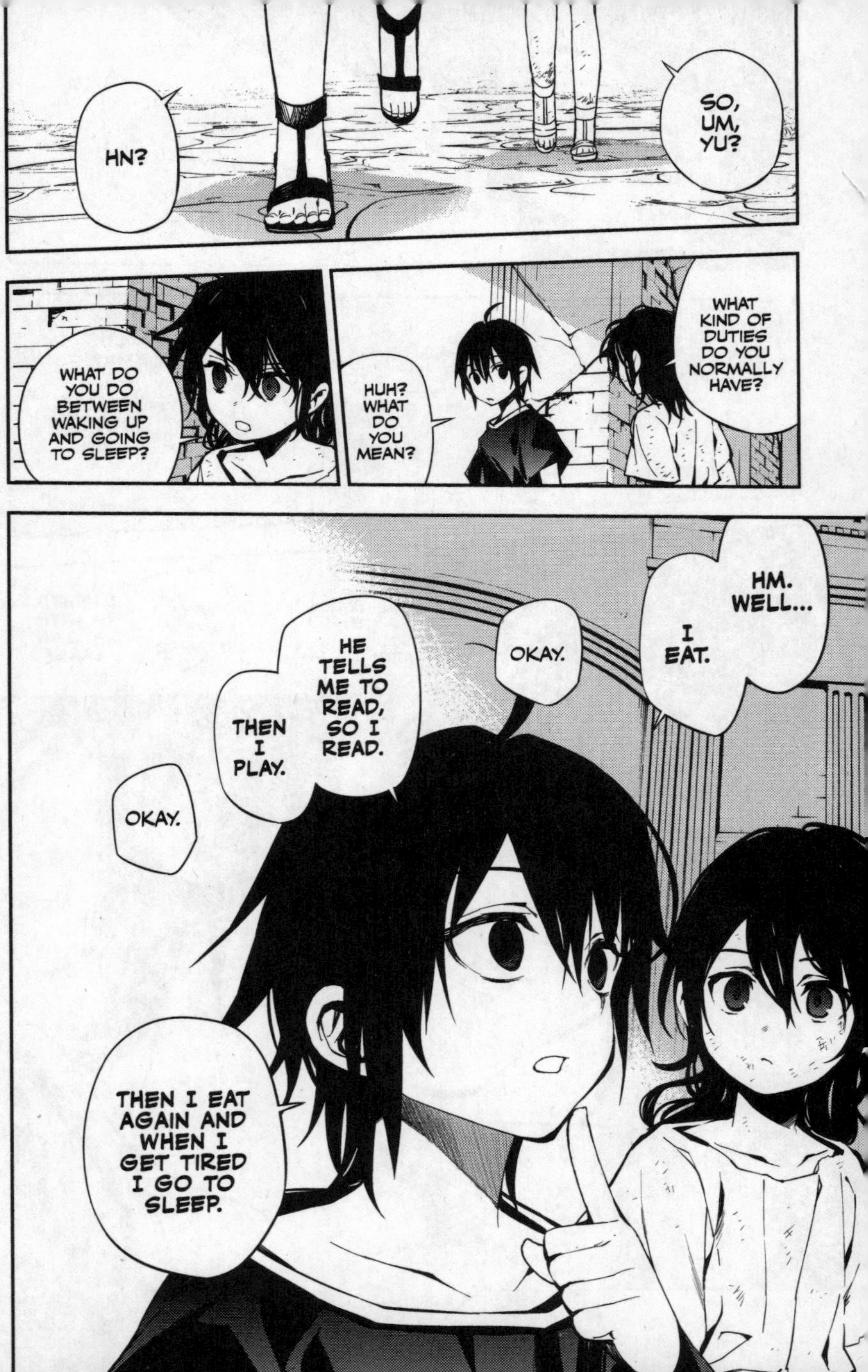
SO, UM, YU?
HN?
WHAT KIND OF DUTIES DO YOU NORMALLY HAVE?
HUH? WHAT DO YOU MEAN?
WHAT DO YOU DO BETWEEN WAKING UP AND GOING TO SLEEP?
HM. WELL...
I EAT.
OKAY.
HE TELLS ME TO READ, SO I READ.
THEN I PLAY.
OKAY.
THEN I EAT AGAIN AND WHEN I GET TIRED I GO TO SLEEP.

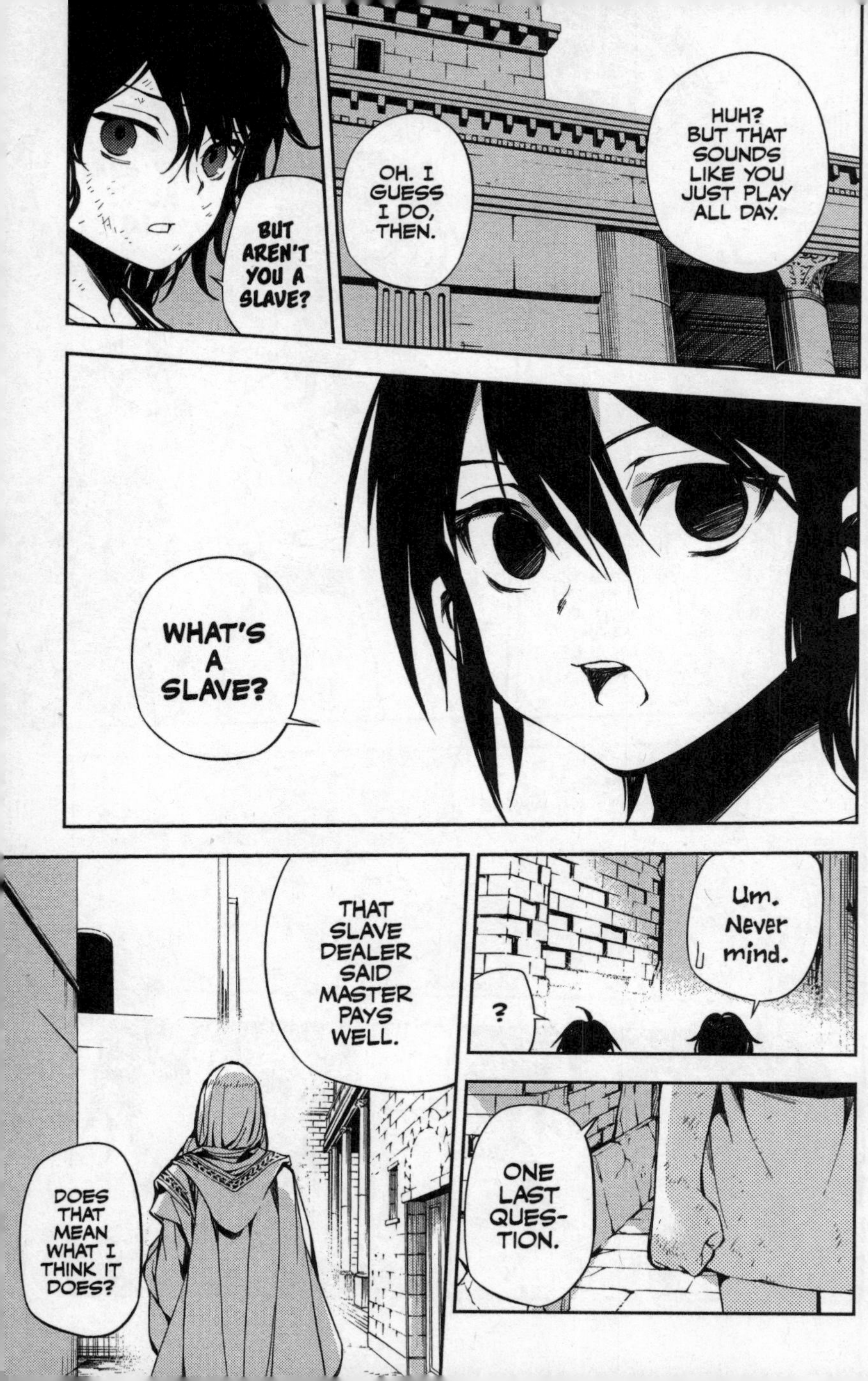
HUH? BUT THAT SOUNDS LIKE YOU JUST PLAY ALL DAY.
OH. I GUESS I DO, THEN.
BUT AREN'T YOU A SLAVE?
WHAT'S A SLAVE?
Um. Never mind.
?
ONE LAST QUES-TION.
THAT SLAVE DEALER SAID MASTER PAYS WELL.
DOES THAT MEAN WHAT I THINK IT DOES?

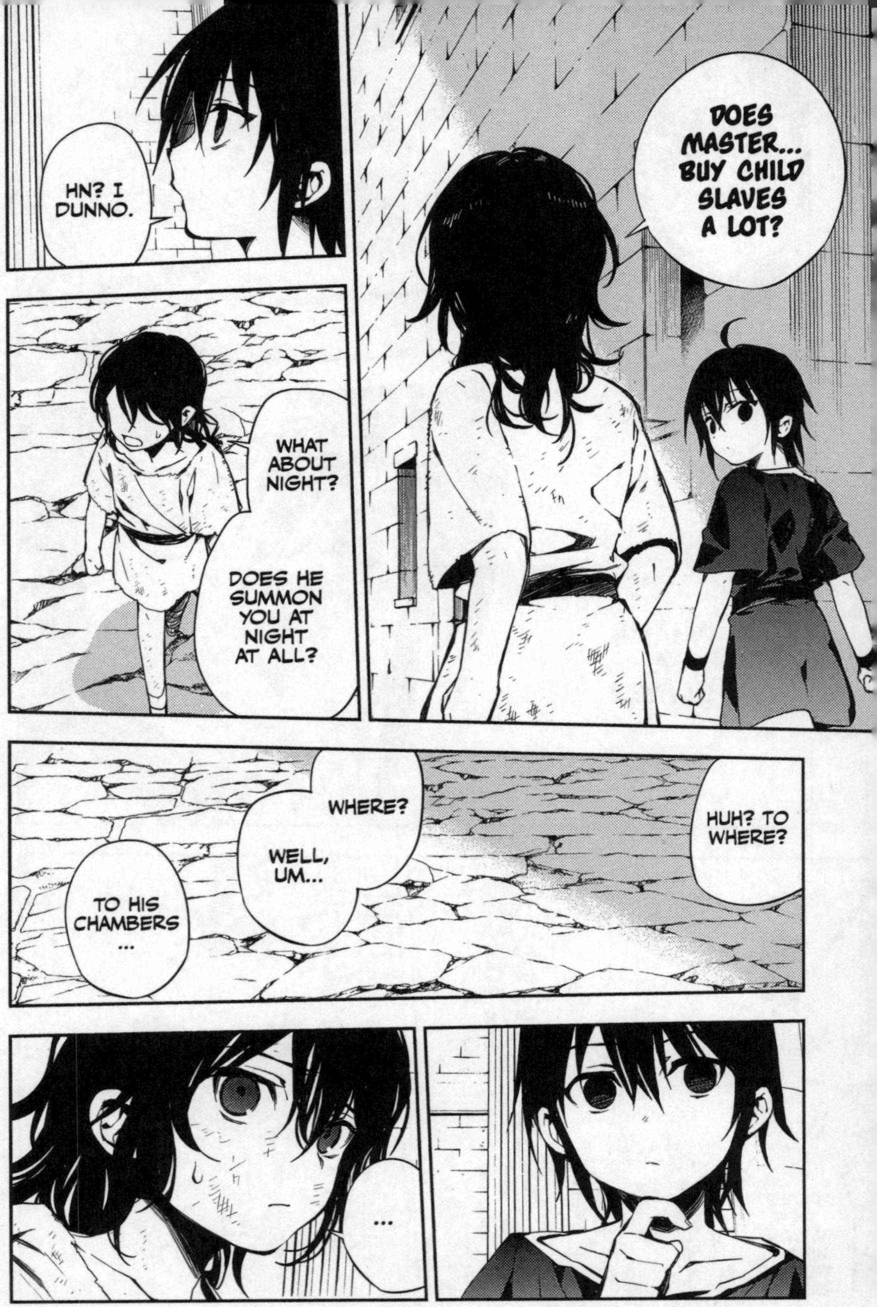
DOES MASTER... BUY CHILD SLAVES A LOT?
HN? I DUNNO.
WHAT ABOUT NIGHT?
DOES HE SUMMON YOU AT NIGHT AT ALL?
HUH? TO WHERE?
WHERE?
WELL, UM...
TO HIS CHAMBERS ...
...

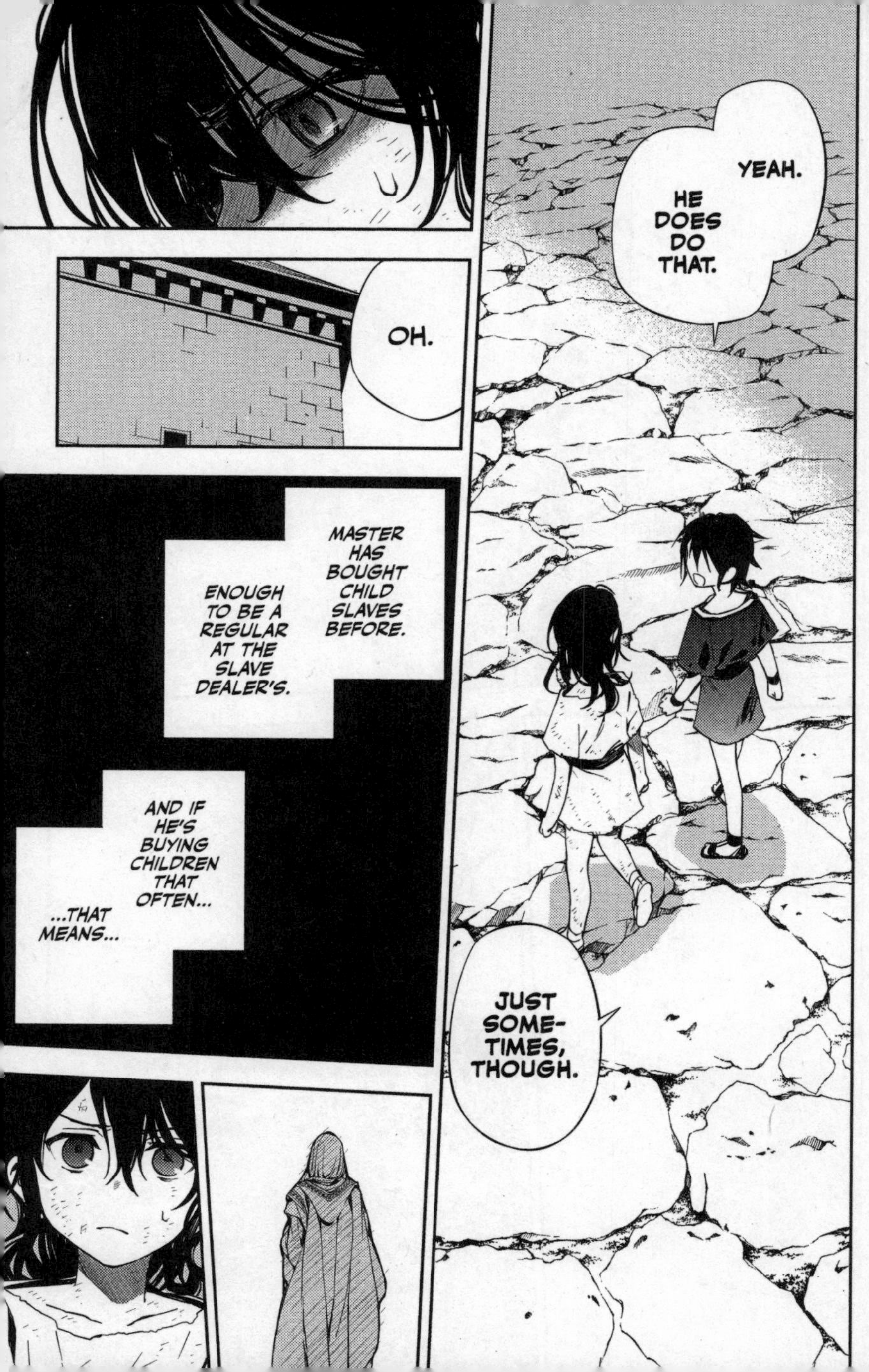
YEAH.
HE DOES DO THAT.
JUST SOMETIMES, THOUGH.
OH.
MASTER HAS BOUGHT CHILD SLAVES BEFORE.
ENOUGH TO BE A REGULAR AT THE SLAVE DEALER'S.
AND IF HE'S BUYING CHILDREN THAT OFTEN...
...THAT MEANS...

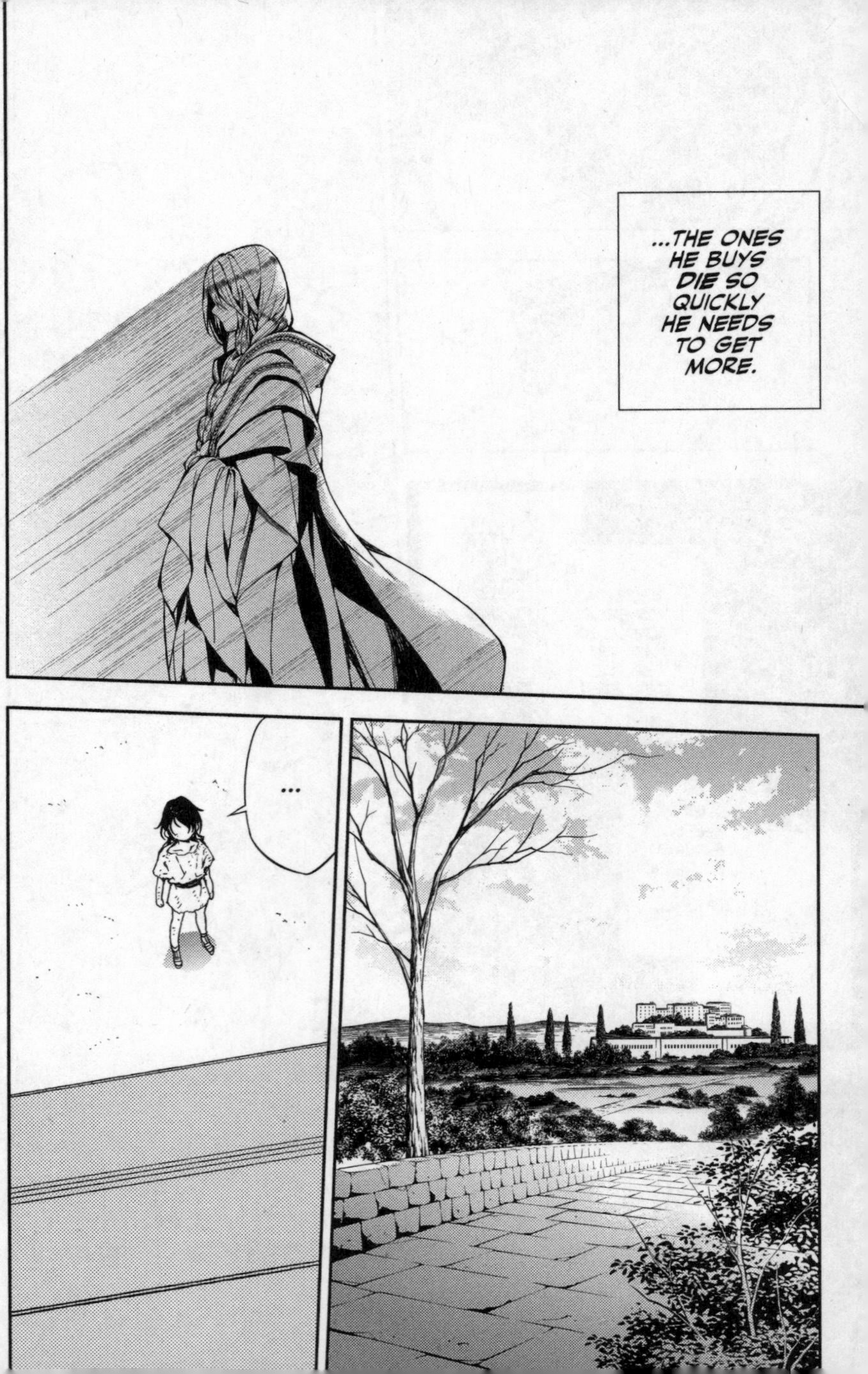
...THE ONES HE BUYS DIE SO QUICKLY HE NEEDS TO GET MORE.
...

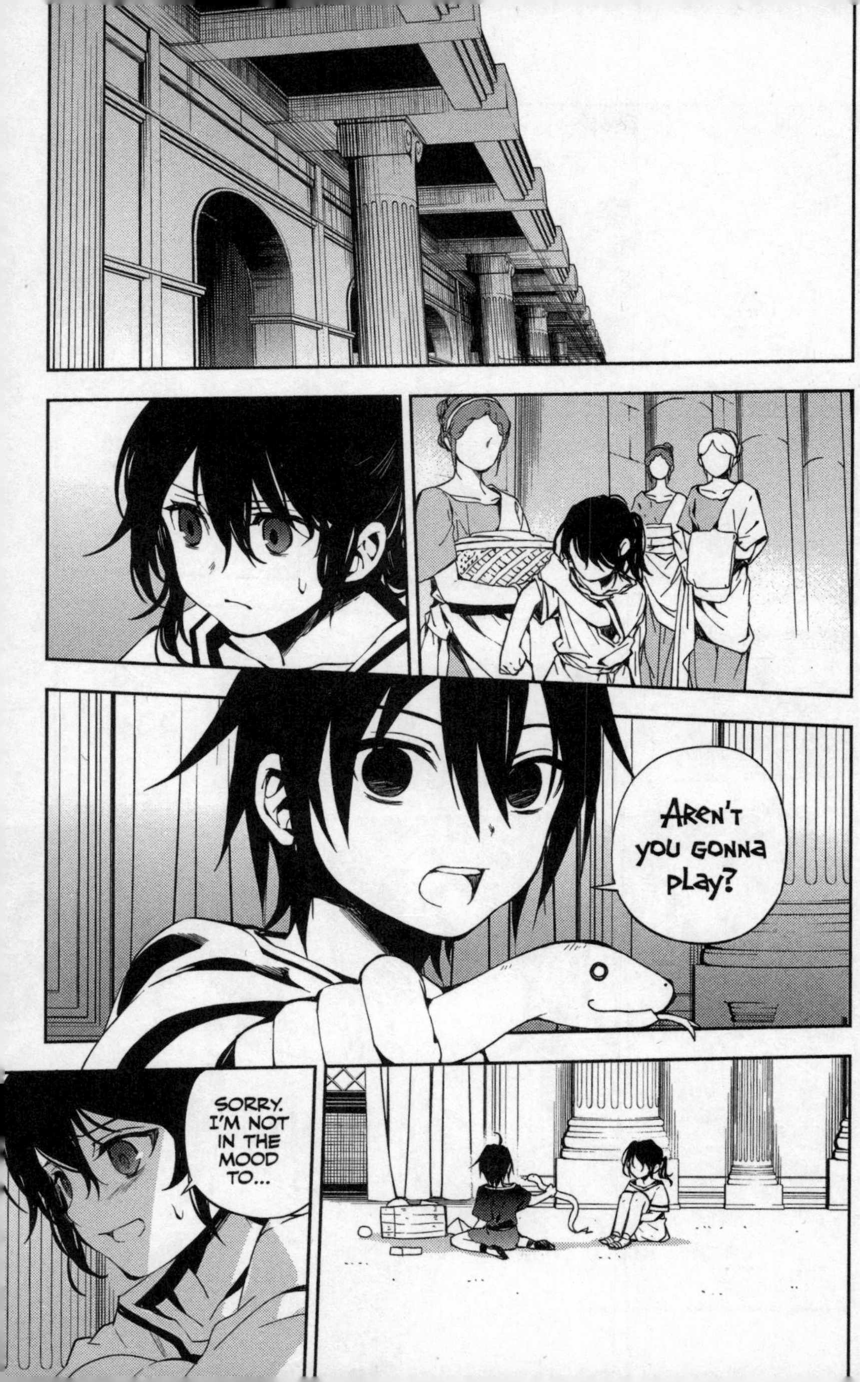
Aren't you gonna play?
SORRY. I'M NOT IN THE MOOD TO...

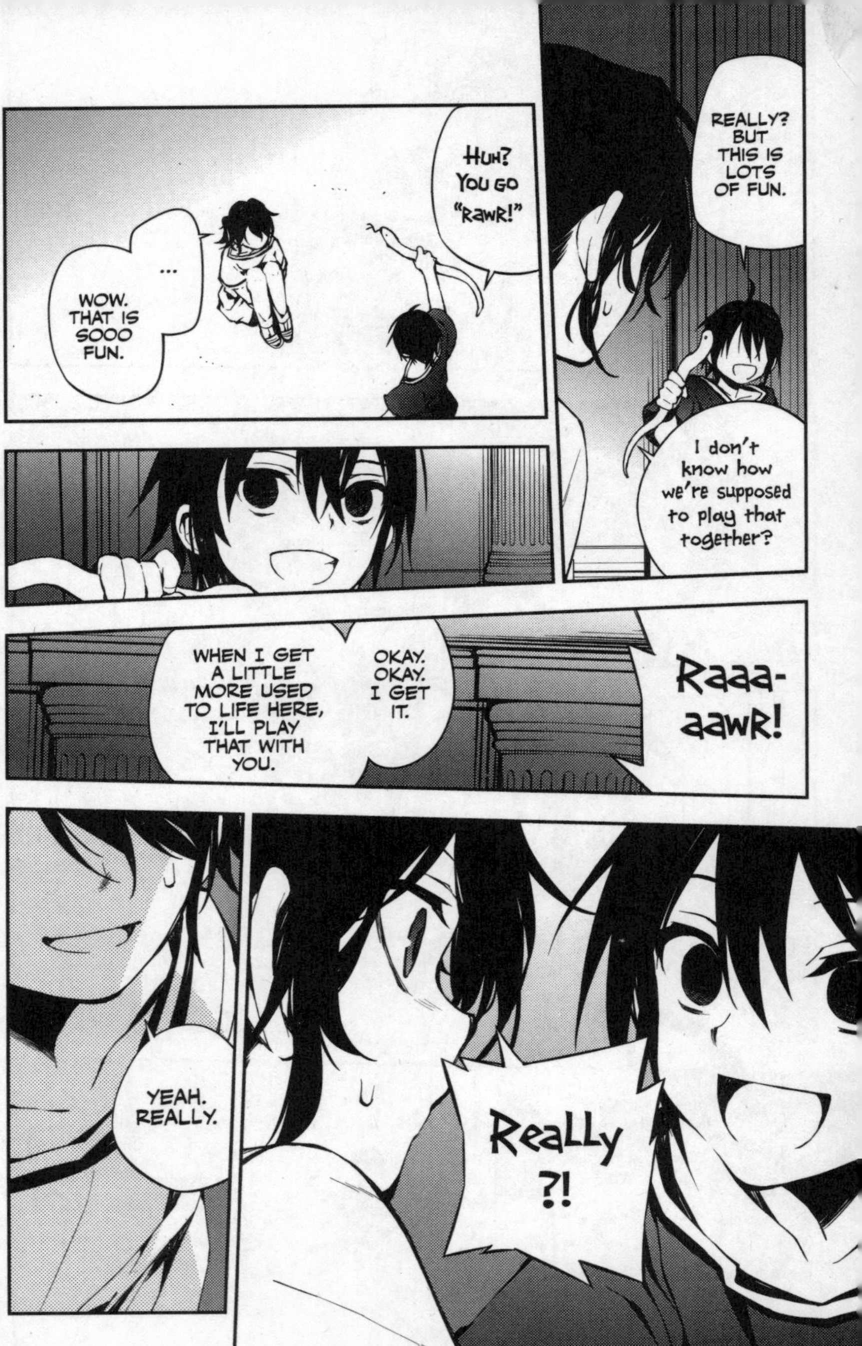
REALLY? BUT THIS IS LOTS OF FUN.
I don't know how we're supposed to play that together?
HUH? YOU GO "RAWR!"
...
WOW. THAT IS SOOO FUN.
Raaa-aawR!
OKAY. OKAY. I GET IT.
WHEN I GET A LITTLE MORE USED TO LIFE HERE, I'LL PLAY THAT WITH YOU.
Really?!
YEAH. REALLY.

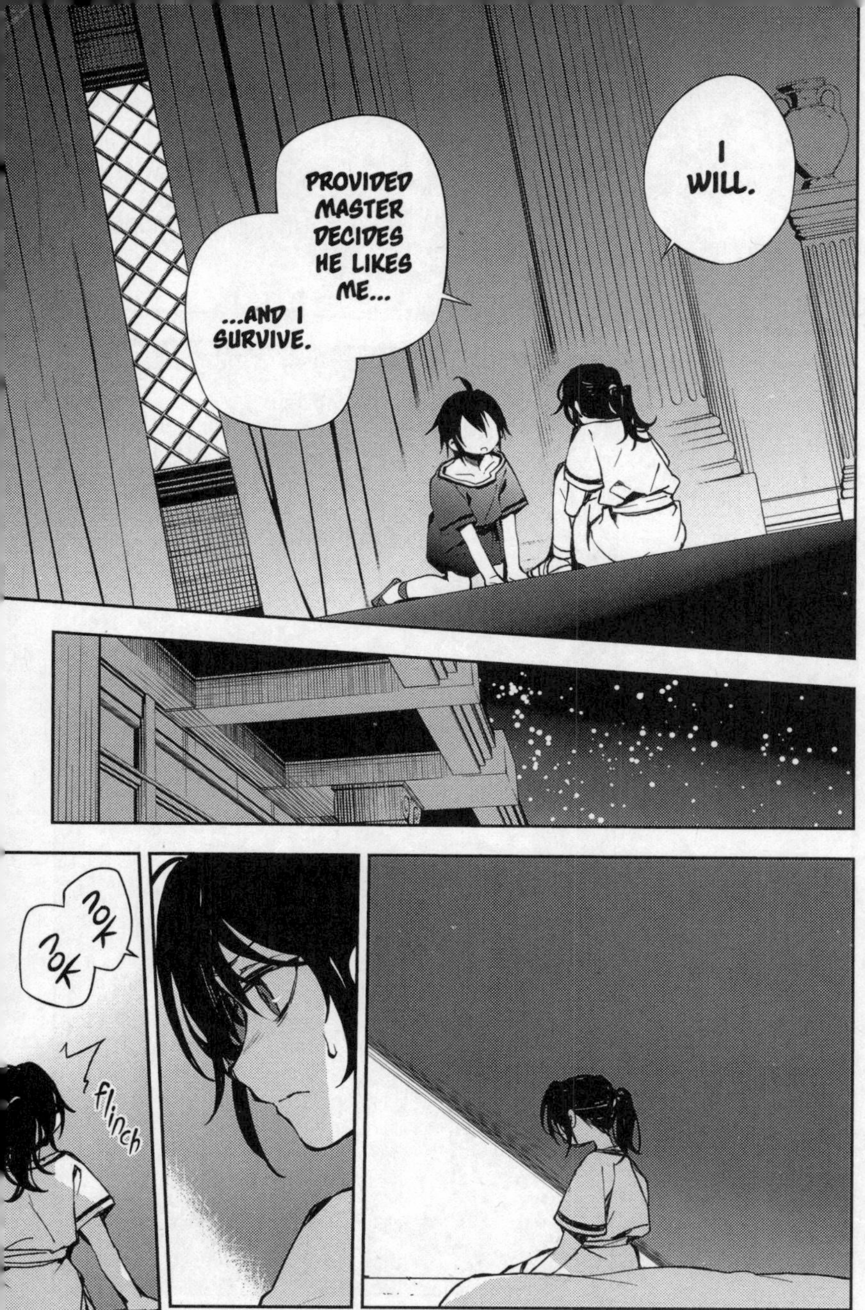
I WILL.
PROVIDED MASTER DECIDES HE LIKES ME...
...AND I SURVIVE.
nok nok
flinch

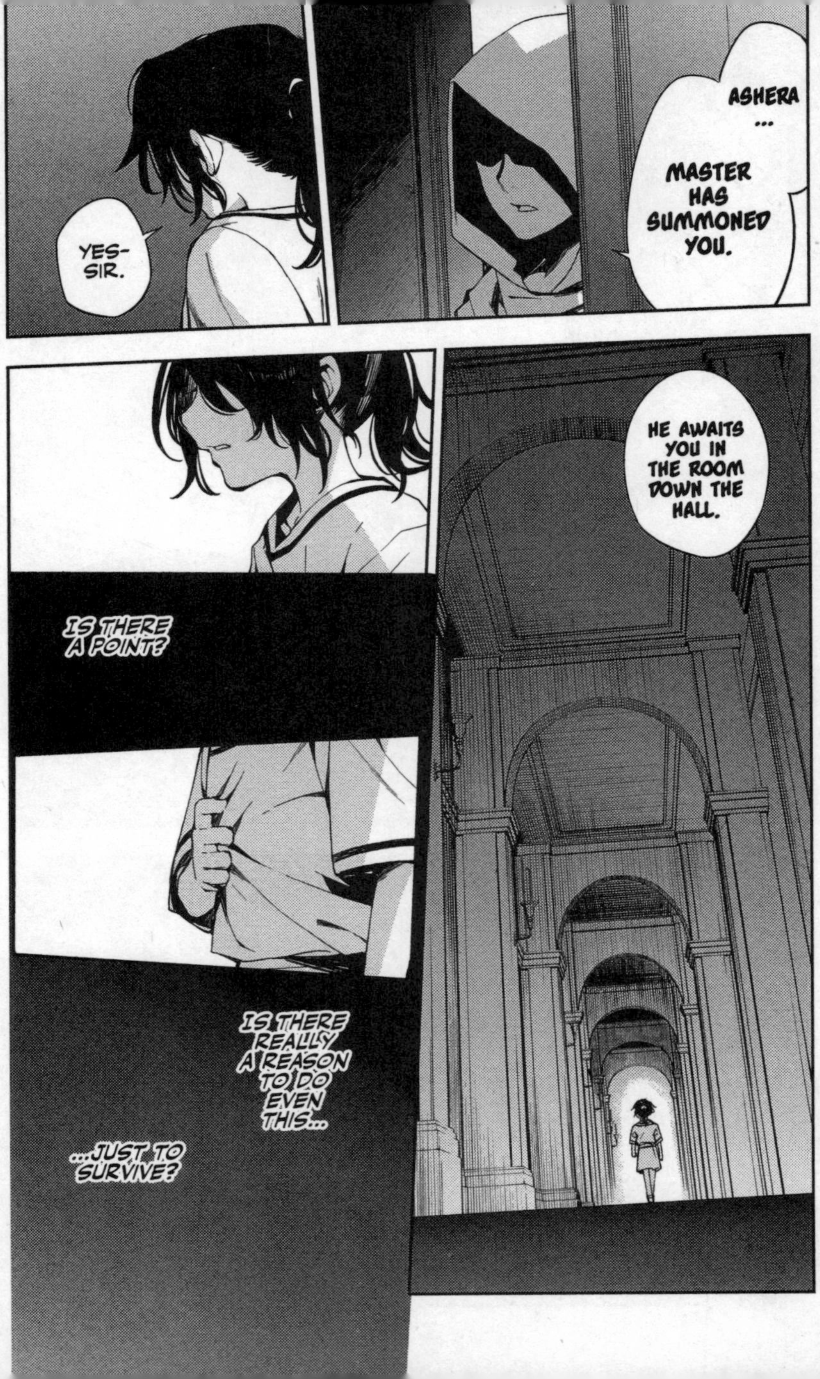
ASHERA ...
MASTER HAS SUMMONED YOU.
YES-SIR.
HE AWAITS YOU IN THE ROOM DOWN THE HALL.
IS THERE A POINT?
IS THERE REALLY A REASON TO DO EVEN THIS...
...JUST TO SURVIVE?

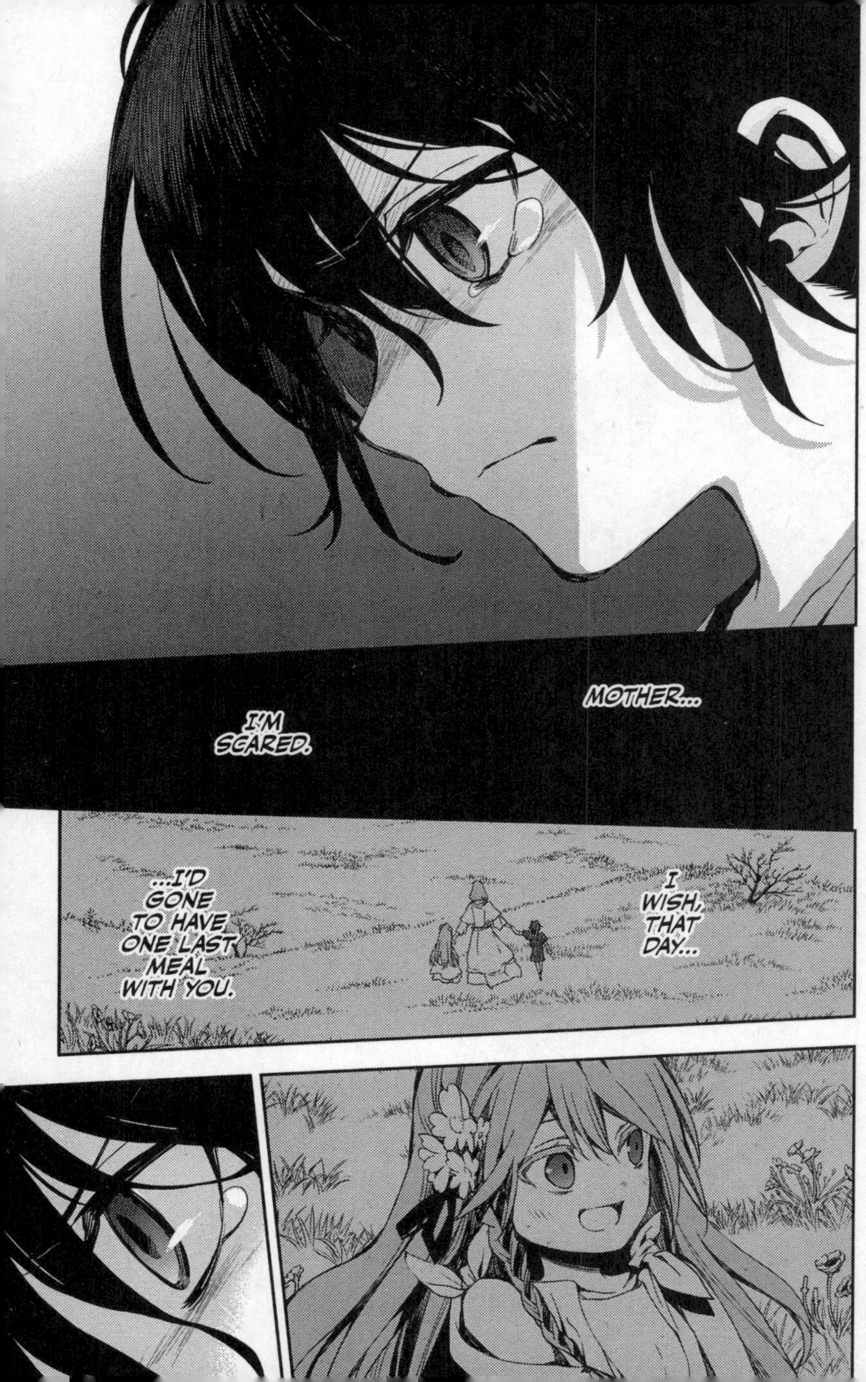
MOTHER...
I'M SCARED.
I WISH, THAT DAY...
...I'D GONE TO HAVE ONE LAST MEAL WITH YOU.

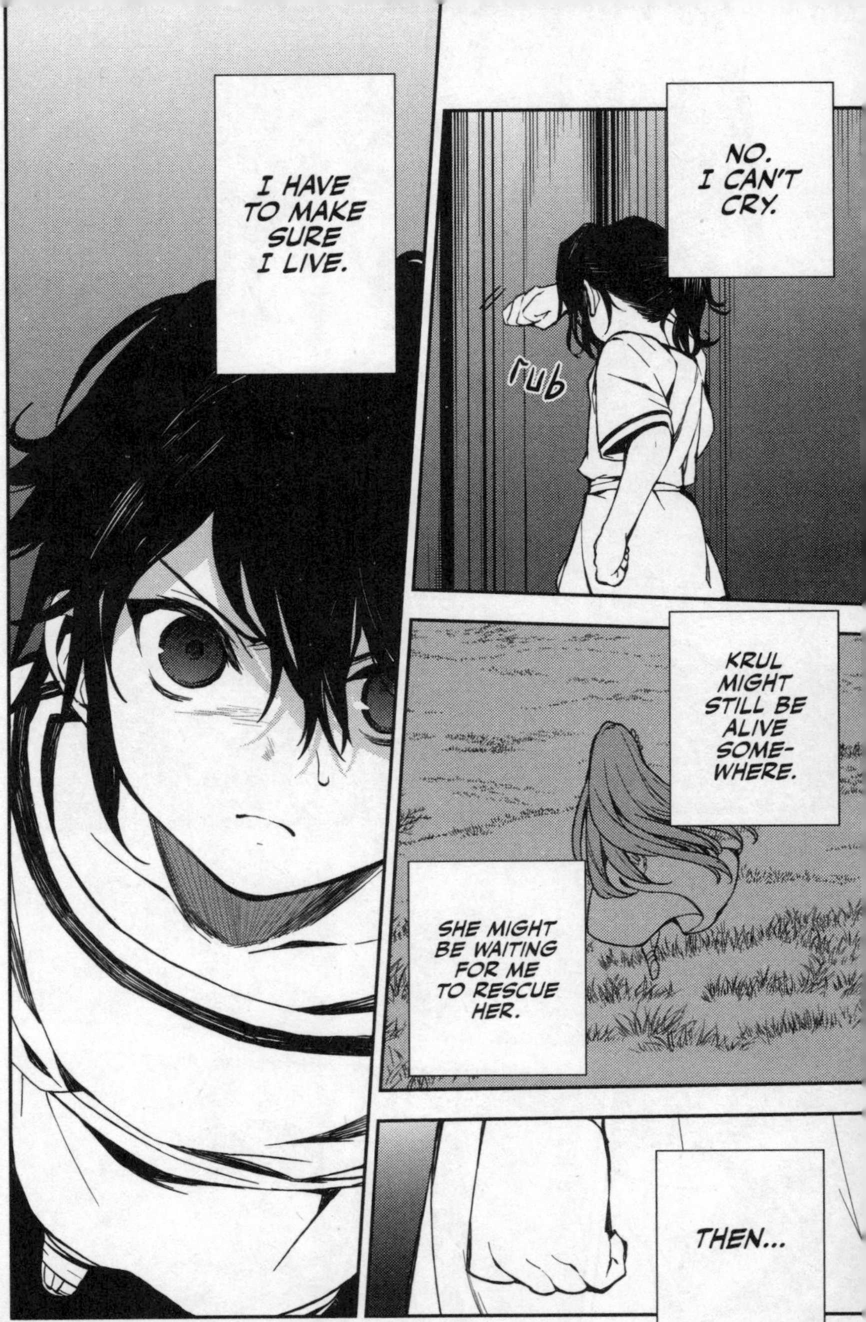
NO. I CAN'T CRY.
rub
KRUL MIGHT STILL BE ALIVE SOME-WHERE.
SHE MIGHT BE WAITING FOR ME TO RESCUE HER.
THEN...
I HAVE TO MAKE SURE I LIVE.

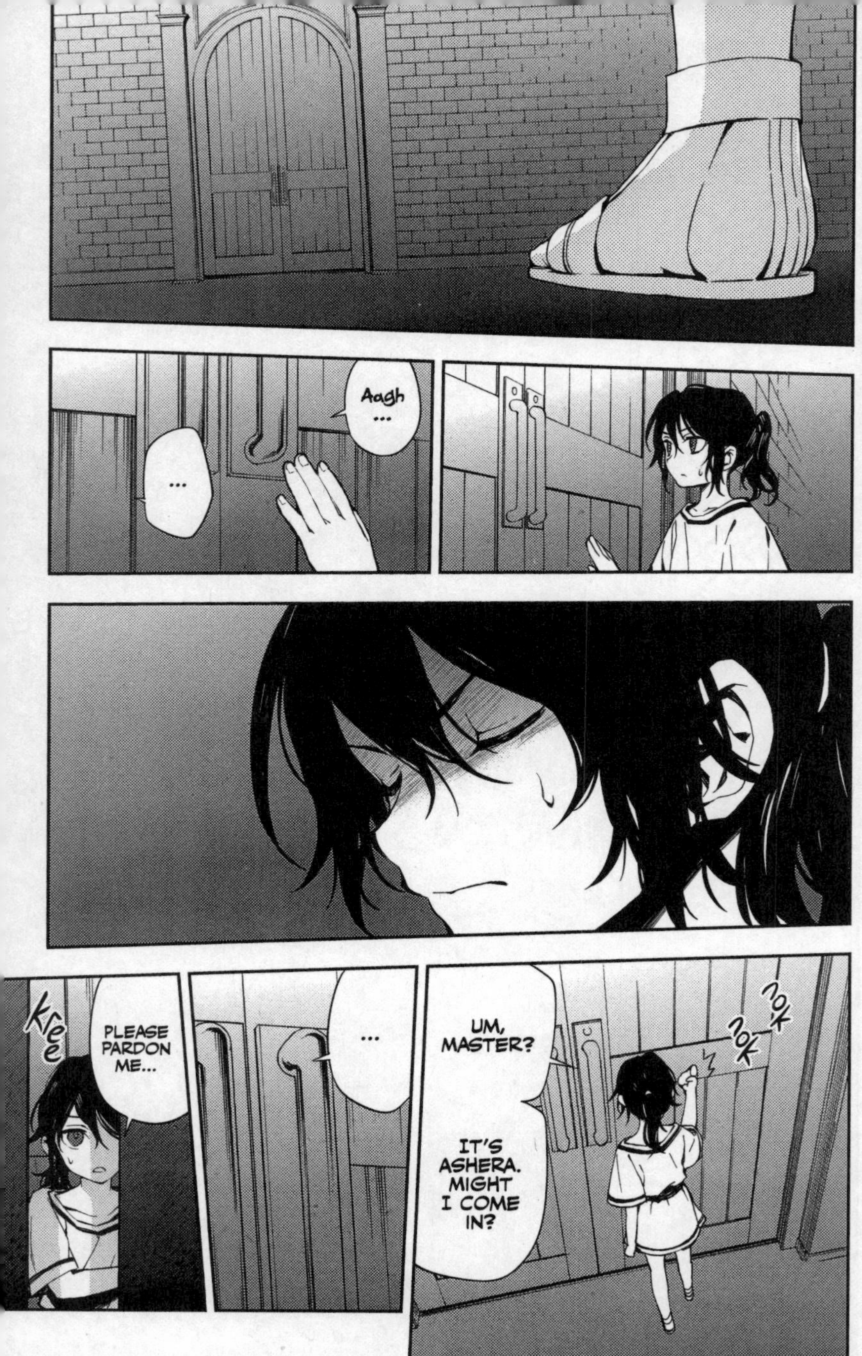
Aagh ...
...
nok
nok
UM, MASTER?
IT'S ASHERA. MIGHT I COME IN?
...
PLEASE PARDON ME...
kree

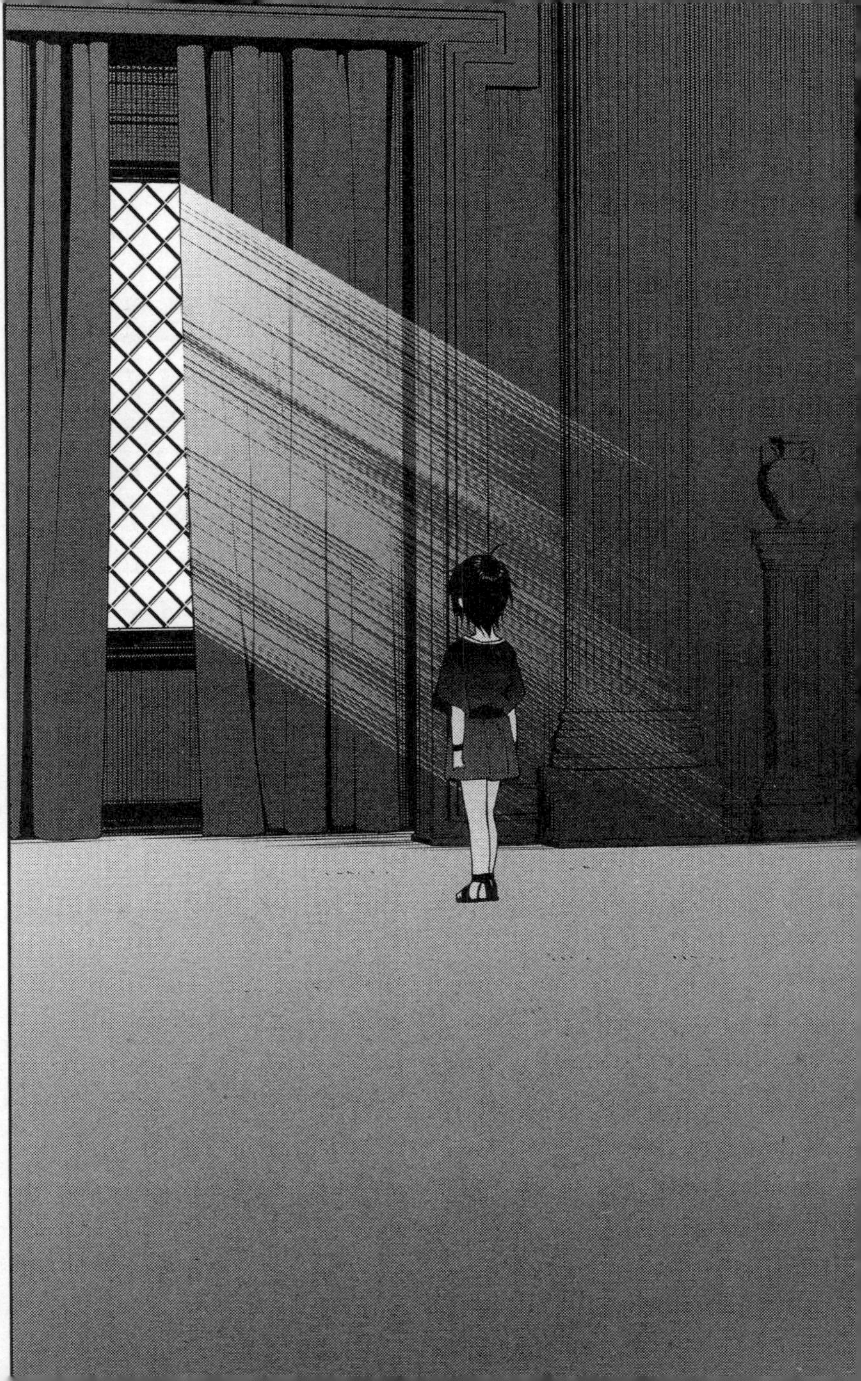

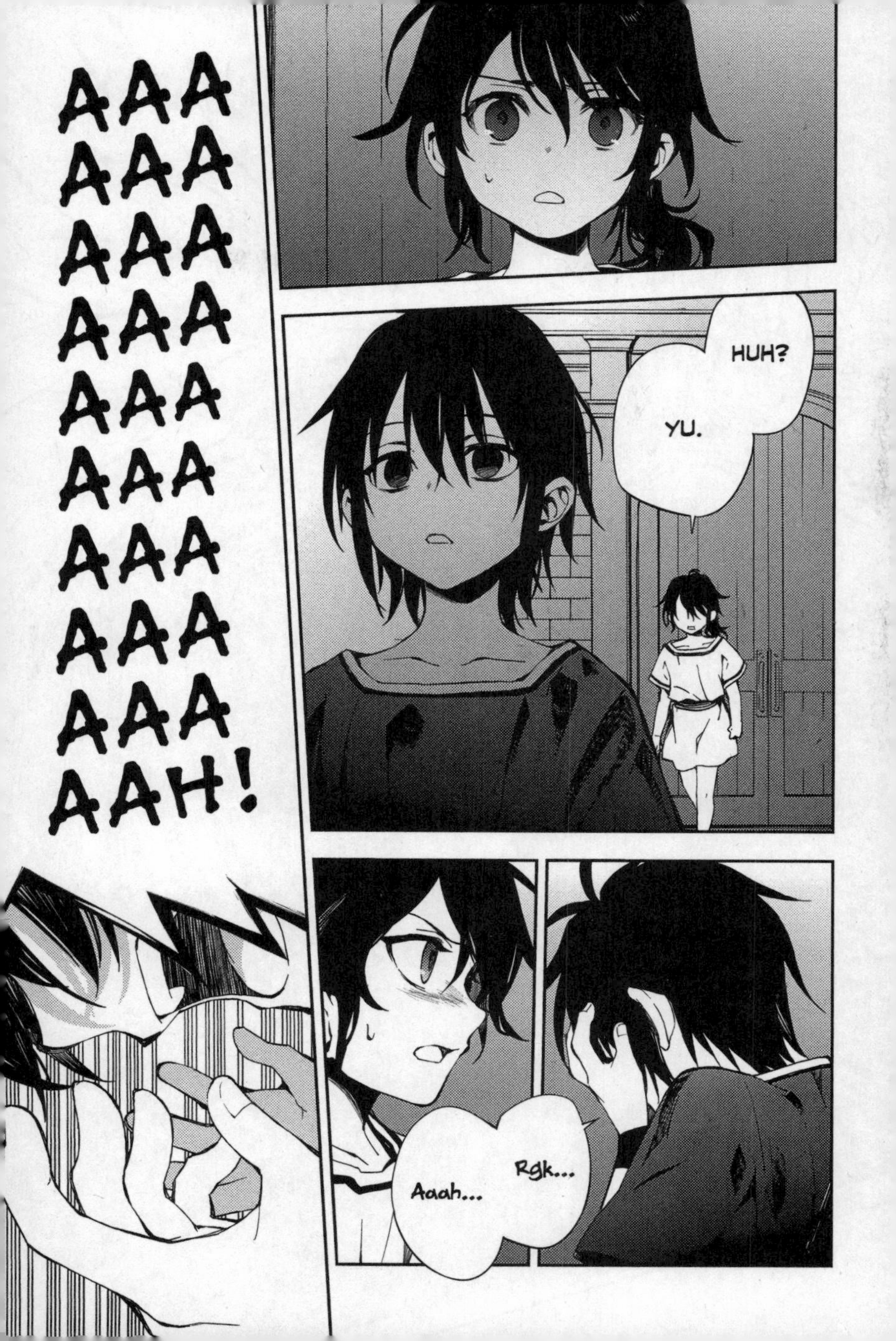
HUH?
YU.
AAAAAAAAAAAAAAAAAAAAAAAAAAAAAAH!
Rgk...
Aaah...

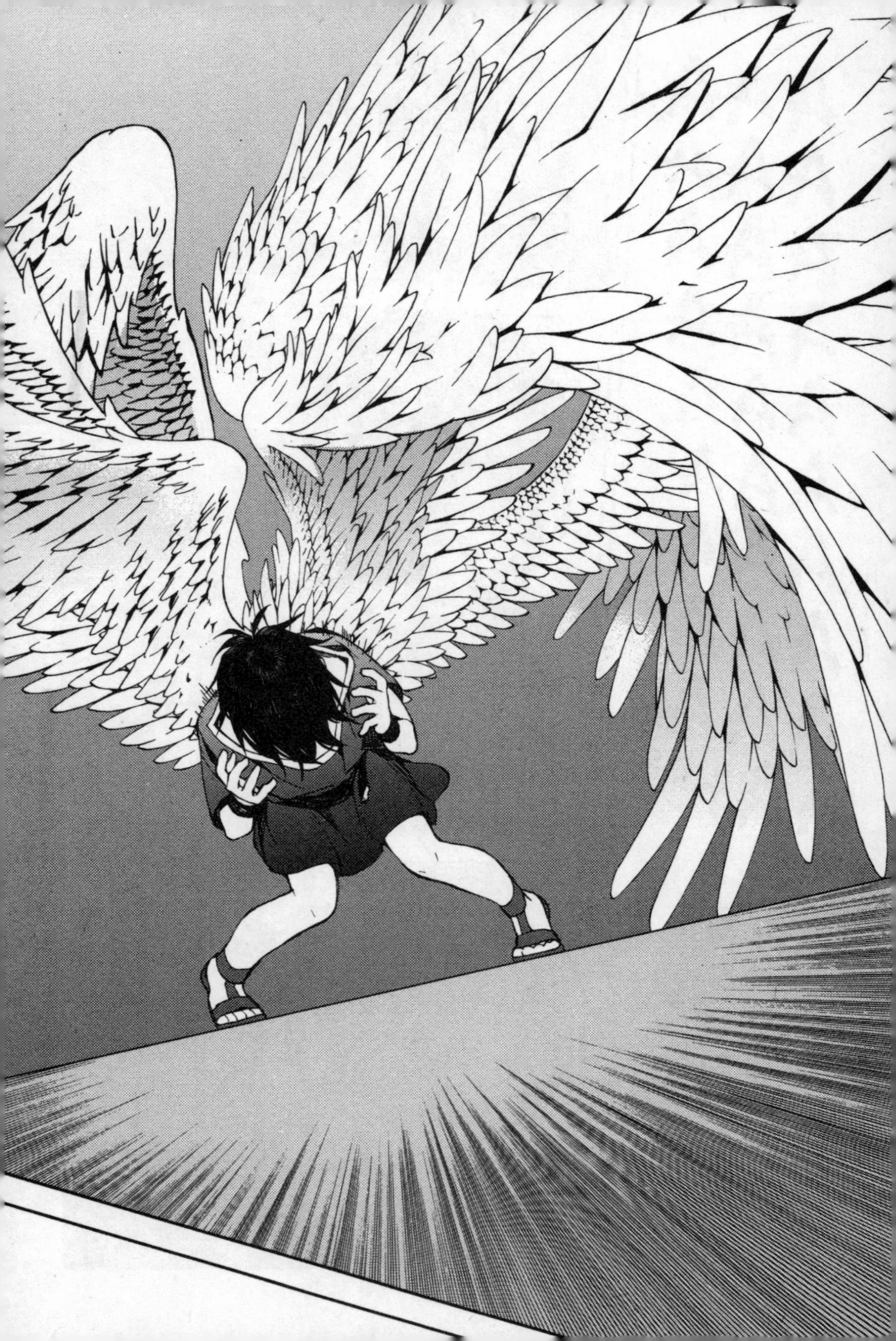

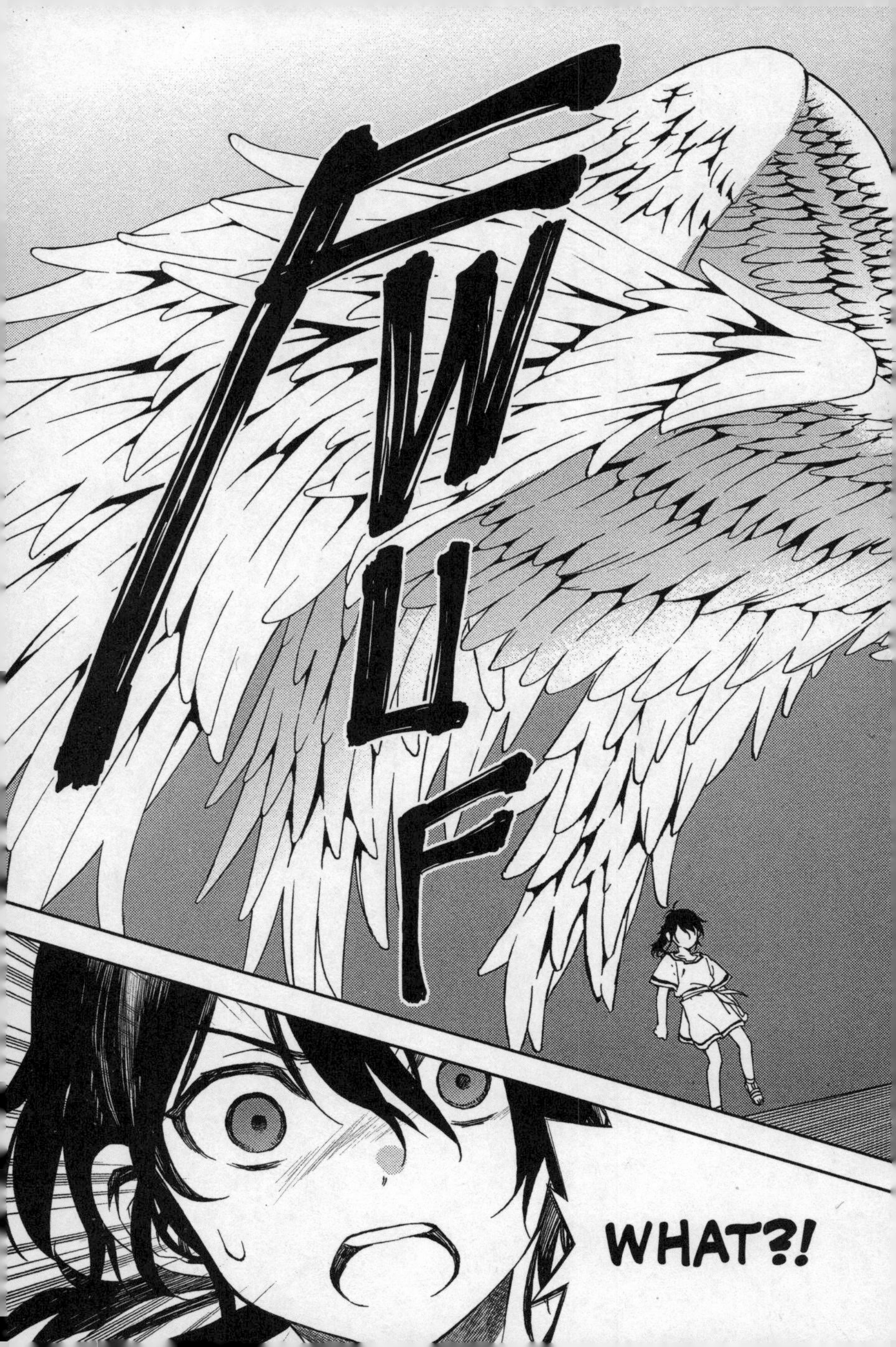
FWUF
WHAT?!

Seraph of the End
—VAMPIRE REIGN—

CHAPTER 79 Eternal Hell

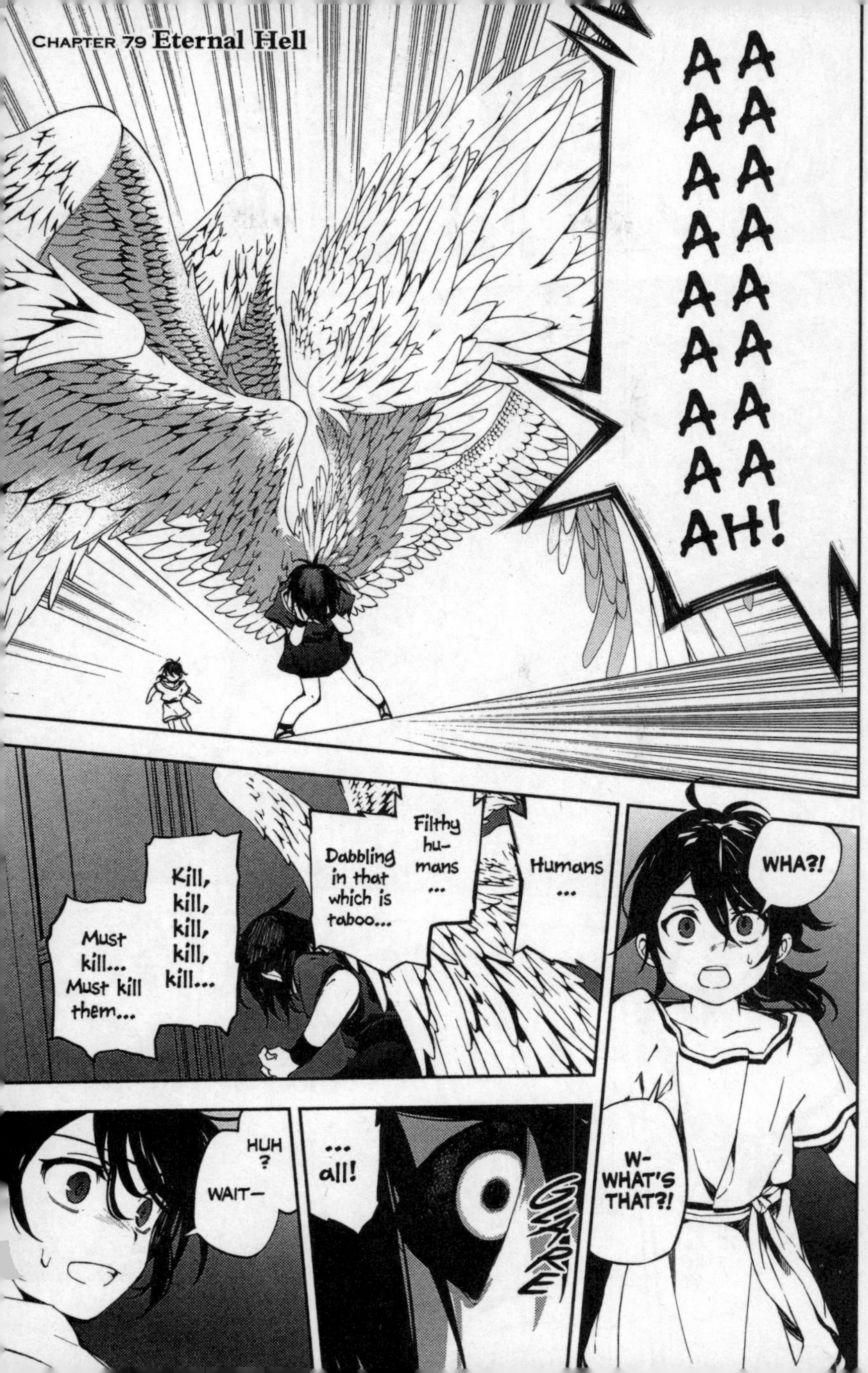
AAAAAAAAAAAAAAAAAH!
WHA?!
W-WHAT'S THAT?!
Humans...
Filthy humans...
Dabbling in that which is taboo...
Kill, kill, kill, kill, kill...
Must kill... Must kill them...
...all!
GLARE
HUH?
WAIT—

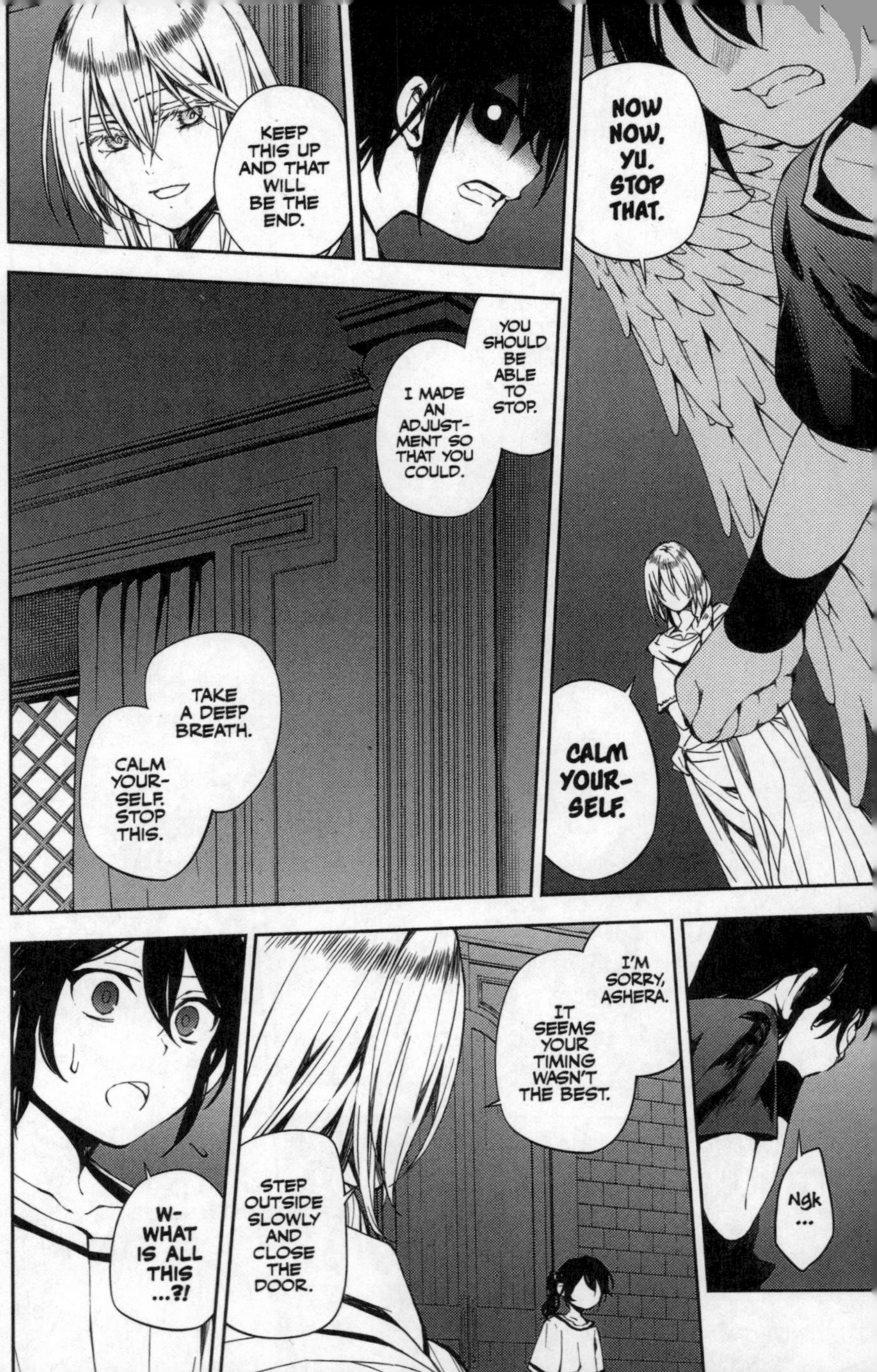
NOW NOW, YU. STOP THAT.
CALM YOURSELF.
KEEP THIS UP AND THAT WILL BE THE END.
YOU SHOULD BE ABLE TO STOP.
I MADE AN ADJUSTMENT SO THAT YOU COULD.
TAKE A DEEP BREATH.
CALM YOURSELF. STOP THIS.
Ngk ...
I'M SORRY, ASHERA.
IT SEEMS YOUR TIMING WASN'T THE BEST.
STEP OUTSIDE SLOWLY AND CLOSE THE DOOR.
W-WHAT IS ALL THIS ...?!

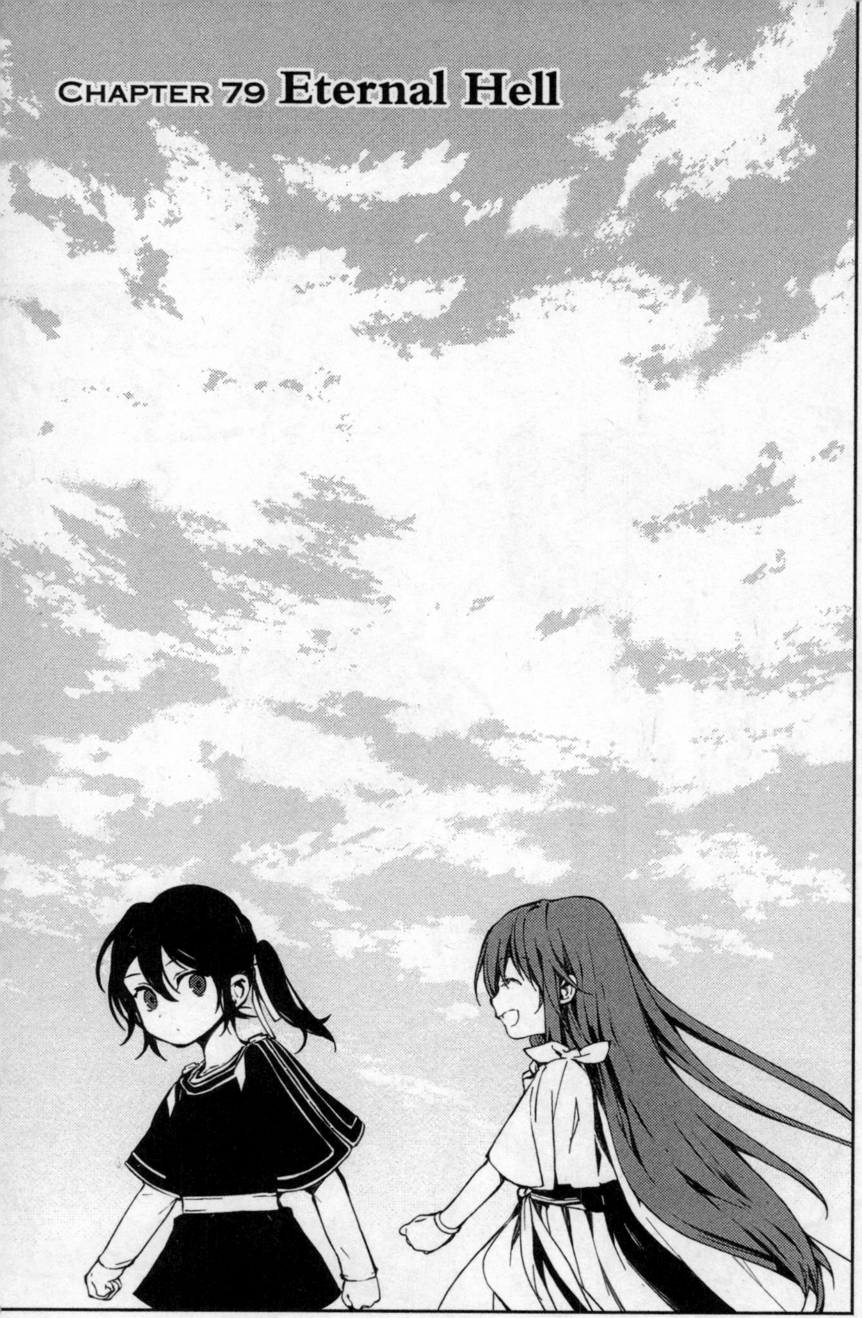
CHAPTER 79 Eternal Hell

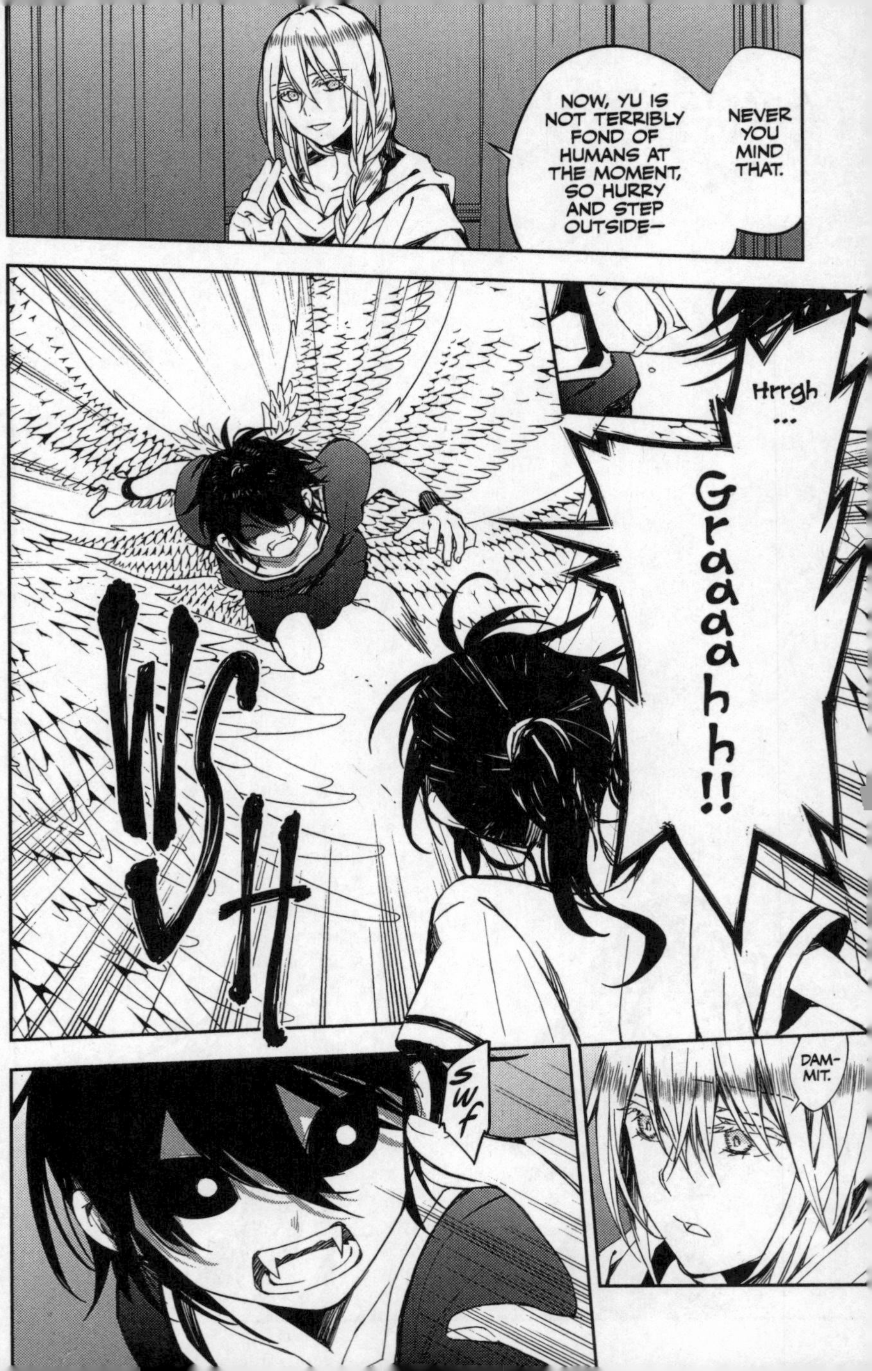
NEVER YOU MIND THAT.
NOW, YU IS NOT TERRIBLY FOND OF HUMANS AT THE MOMENT, SO HURRY AND STEP OUTSIDE—
Hrrgh ...
Graaaahh!!
WSH
DAM-MIT.
SWF

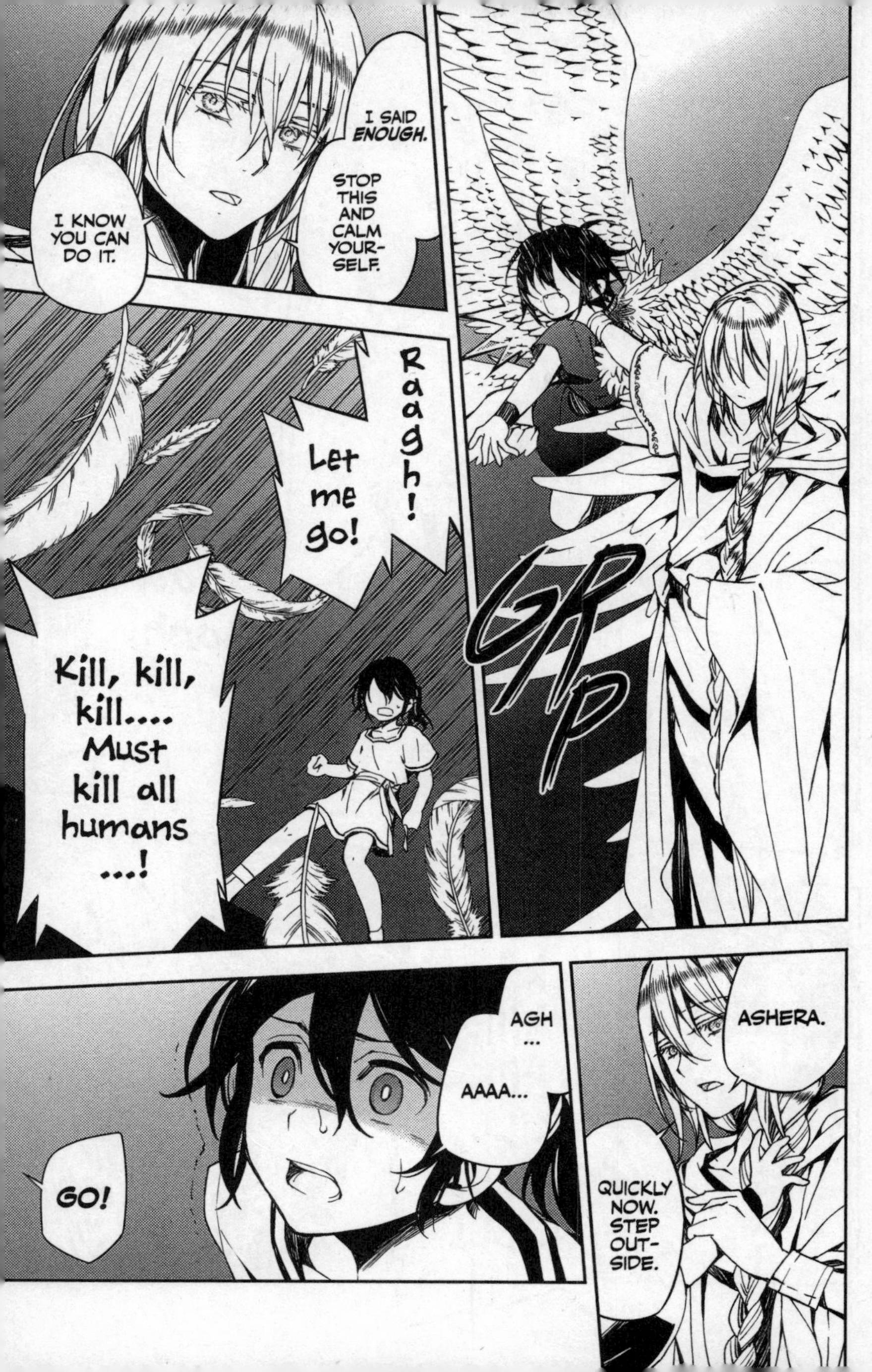
GRP
I SAID ENOUGH.
STOP THIS AND CALM YOURSELF.
I KNOW YOU CAN DO IT.
Raagh!
Let me go!
Kill, kill, kill.... Must kill all humans ...!
ASHERA.
QUICKLY NOW. STEP OUTSIDE.
AGH ...
AAAA...
GO!

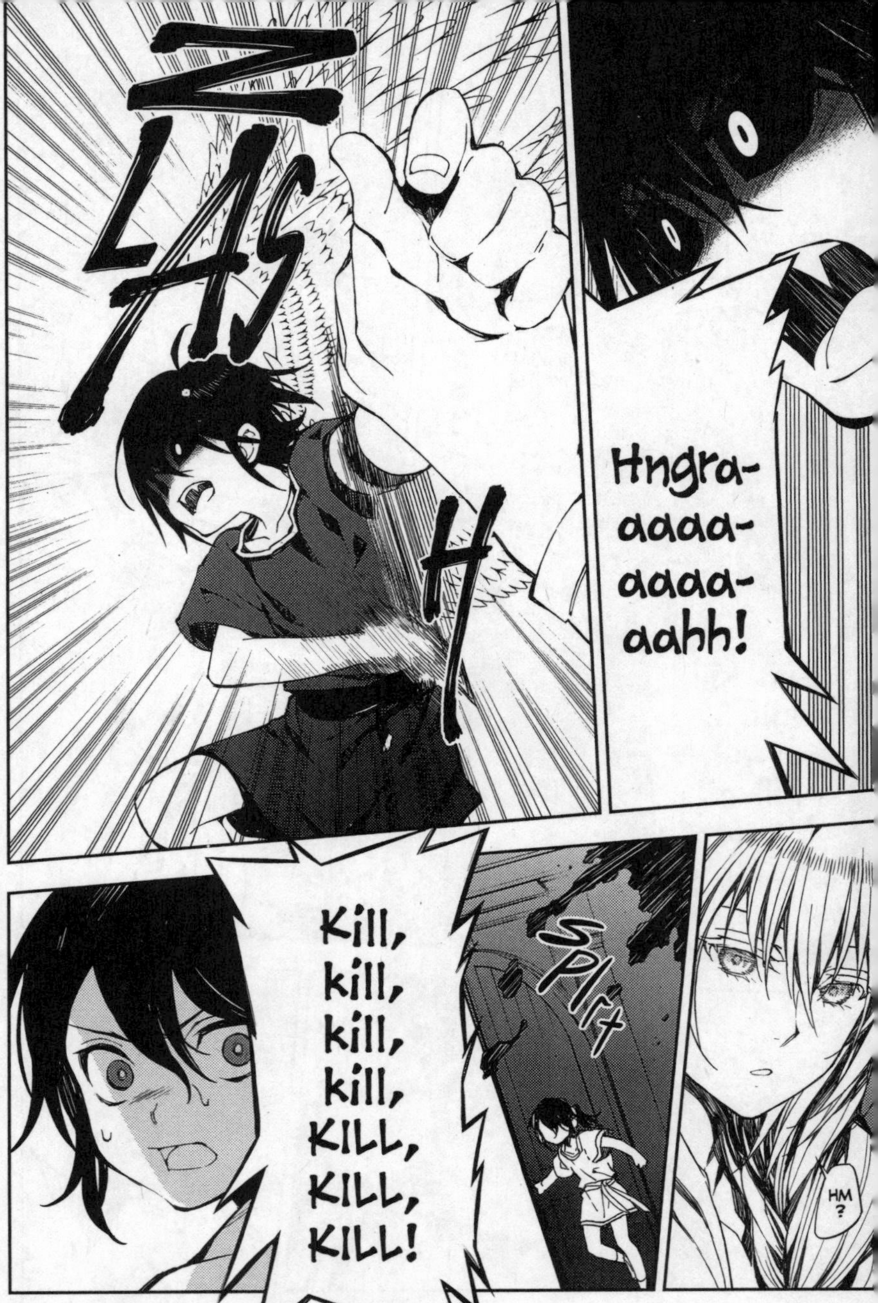
Hngra-aaaa-aaaa-aahh!
ZASH
HM?
Splrt
Kill, kill, kill, kill, KILL, KILL, KILL!

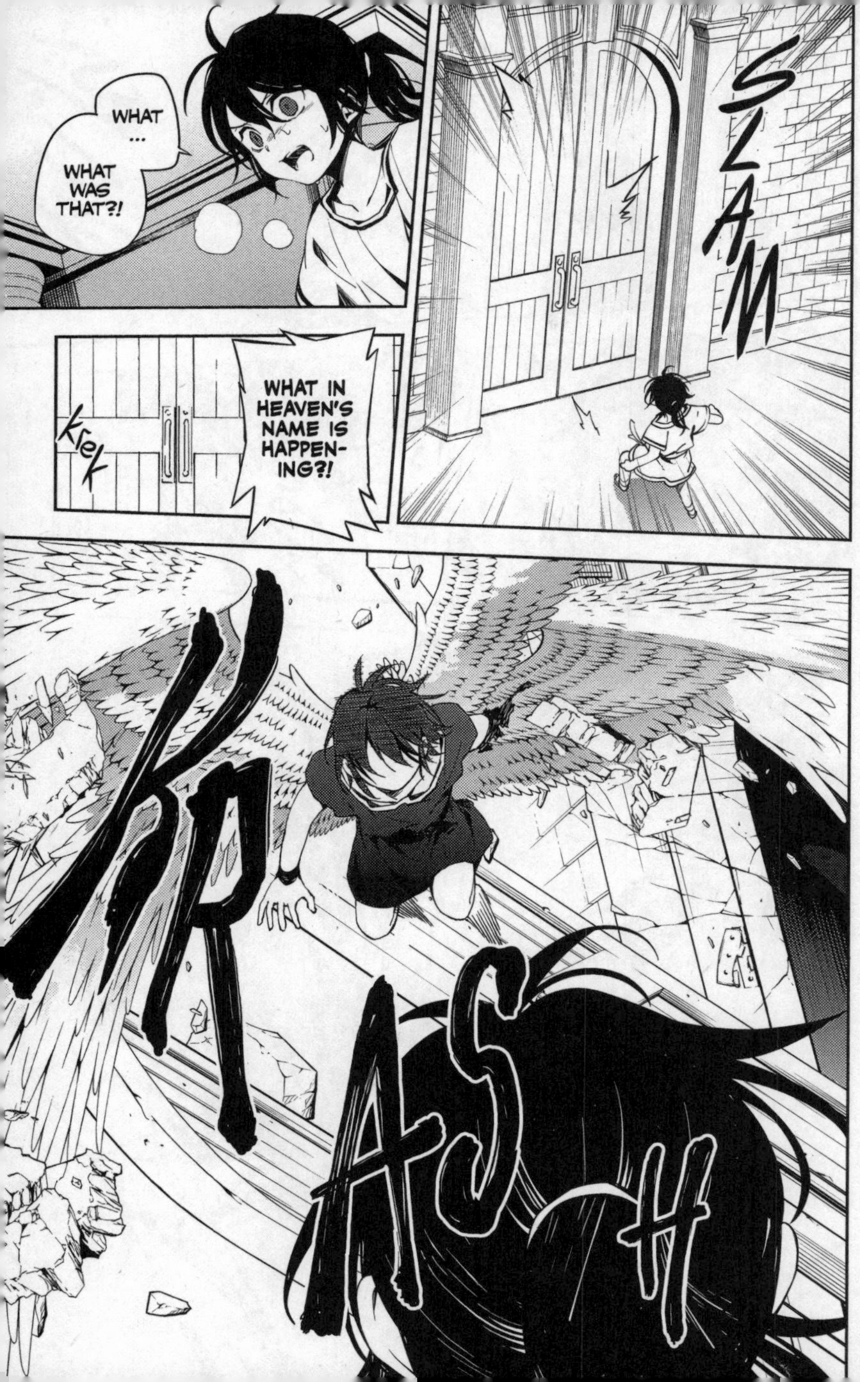
SLAM
WHAT ... WHAT WAS THAT?!
WHAT IN HEAVEN'S NAME IS HAPPEN-ING?!
krek
KRASH

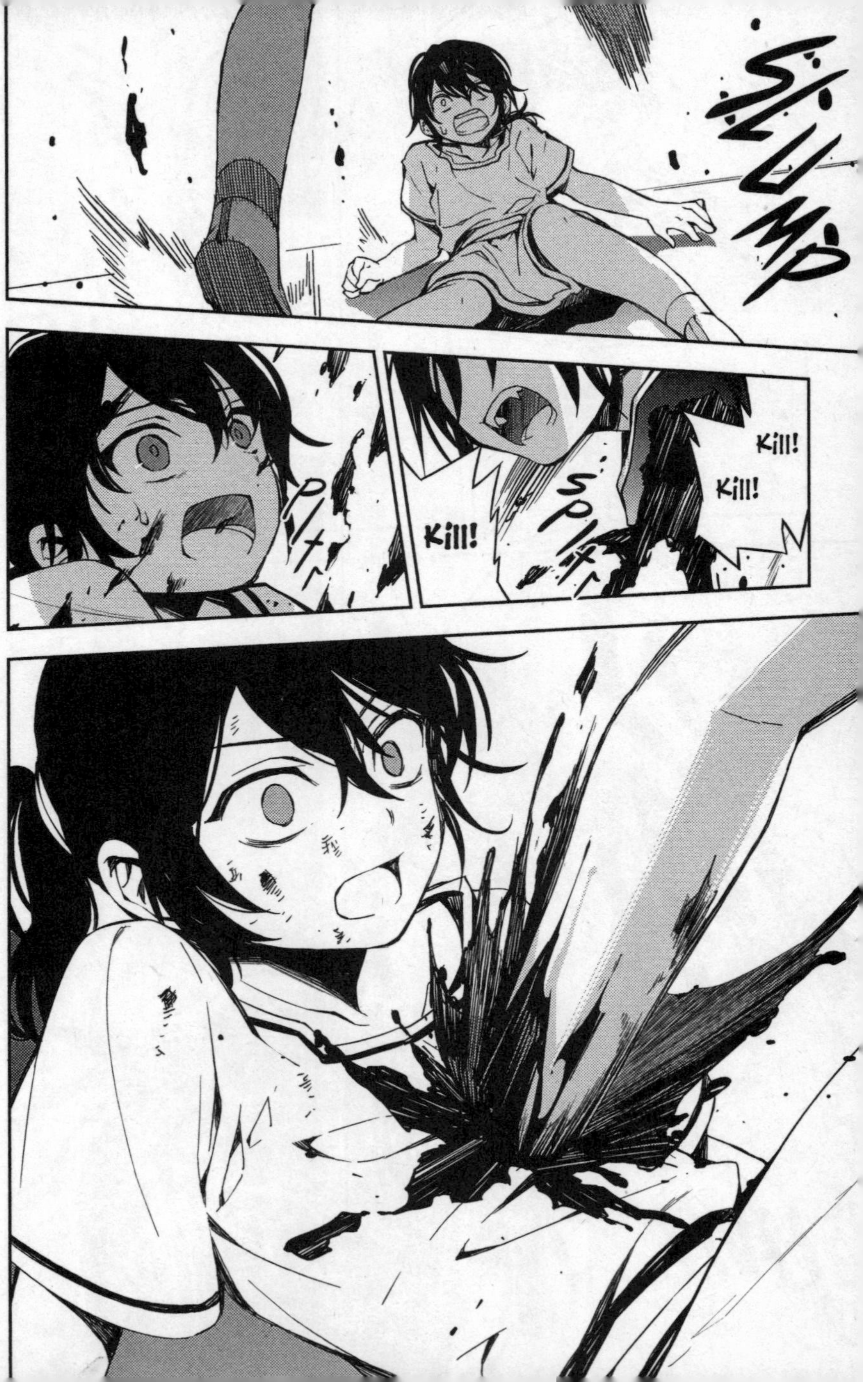
SLUMP
Kill!
Kill!
Split
Kill!
Plit

AND THAT...
...WAS THE MOMENT I DIED.
IT ENDED ALL TOO QUICKLY.
Aaaaaaaaaaaaaaa!
TMP

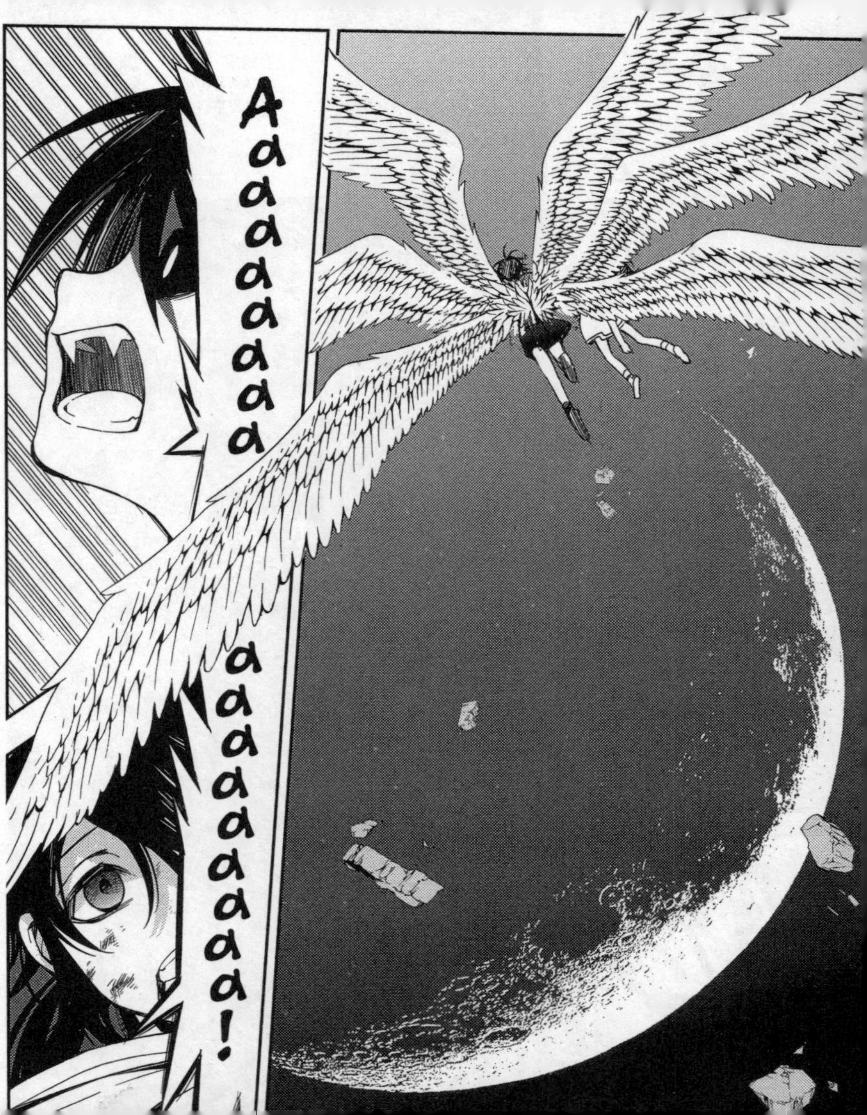
Aaaaaaaaaa
aaaaaaaaaaa!

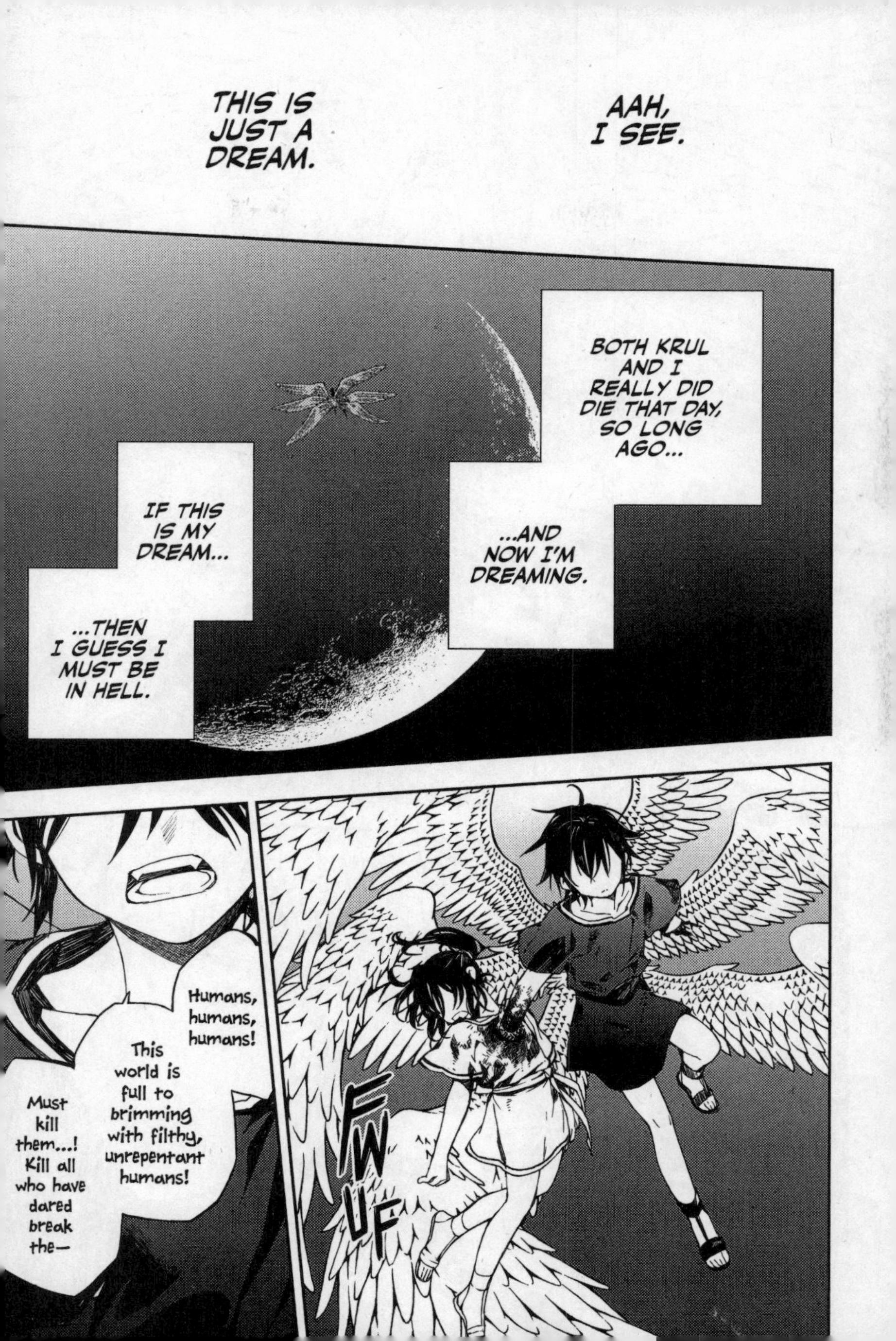
AAH, I SEE.
THIS IS JUST A DREAM.
BOTH KRUL AND I REALLY DID DIE THAT DAY, SO LONG AGO...
...AND NOW I'M DREAMING.
IF THIS IS MY DREAM...
...THEN I GUESS I MUST BE IN HELL.
FWUF
Humans, humans, humans!
This world is full to brimming with filthy, unrepentant humans!
Must kill them...! Kill all who have dared break the—

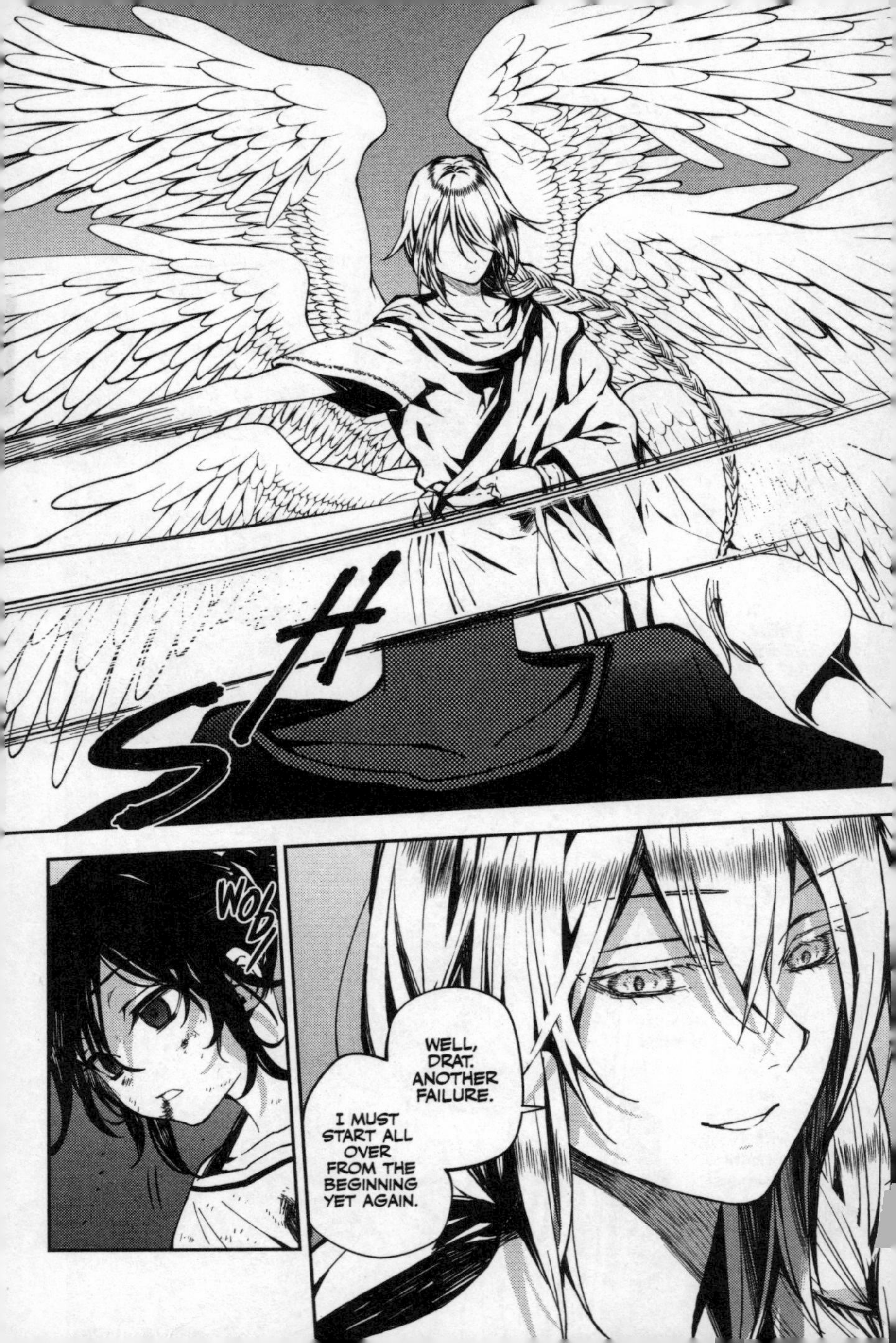
SH
WELL, DRAT. ANOTHER FAILURE.
I MUST START ALL OVER FROM THE BEGINNING YET AGAIN.
WOBL

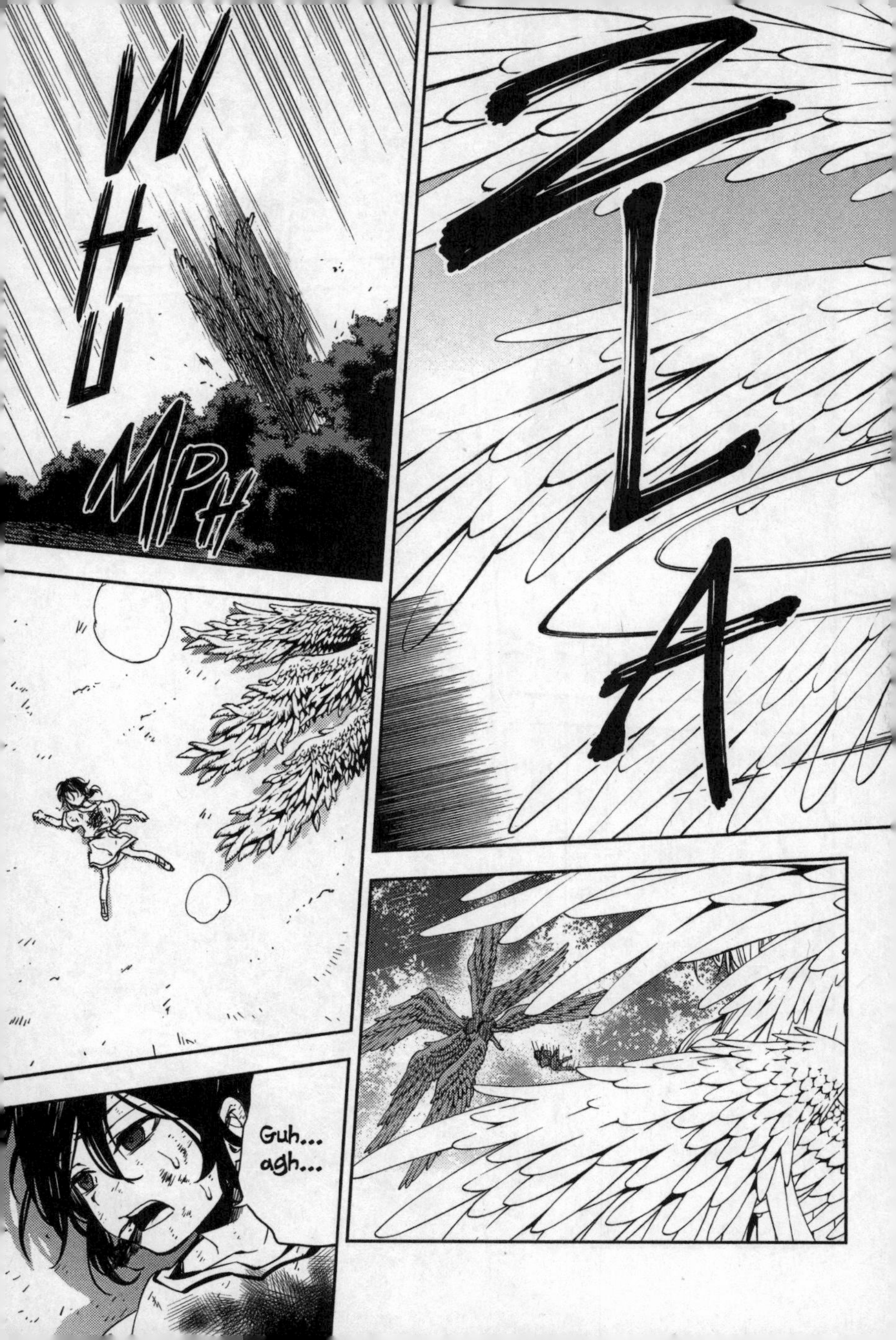
ZLA
WHUMPH
Guh... agh...

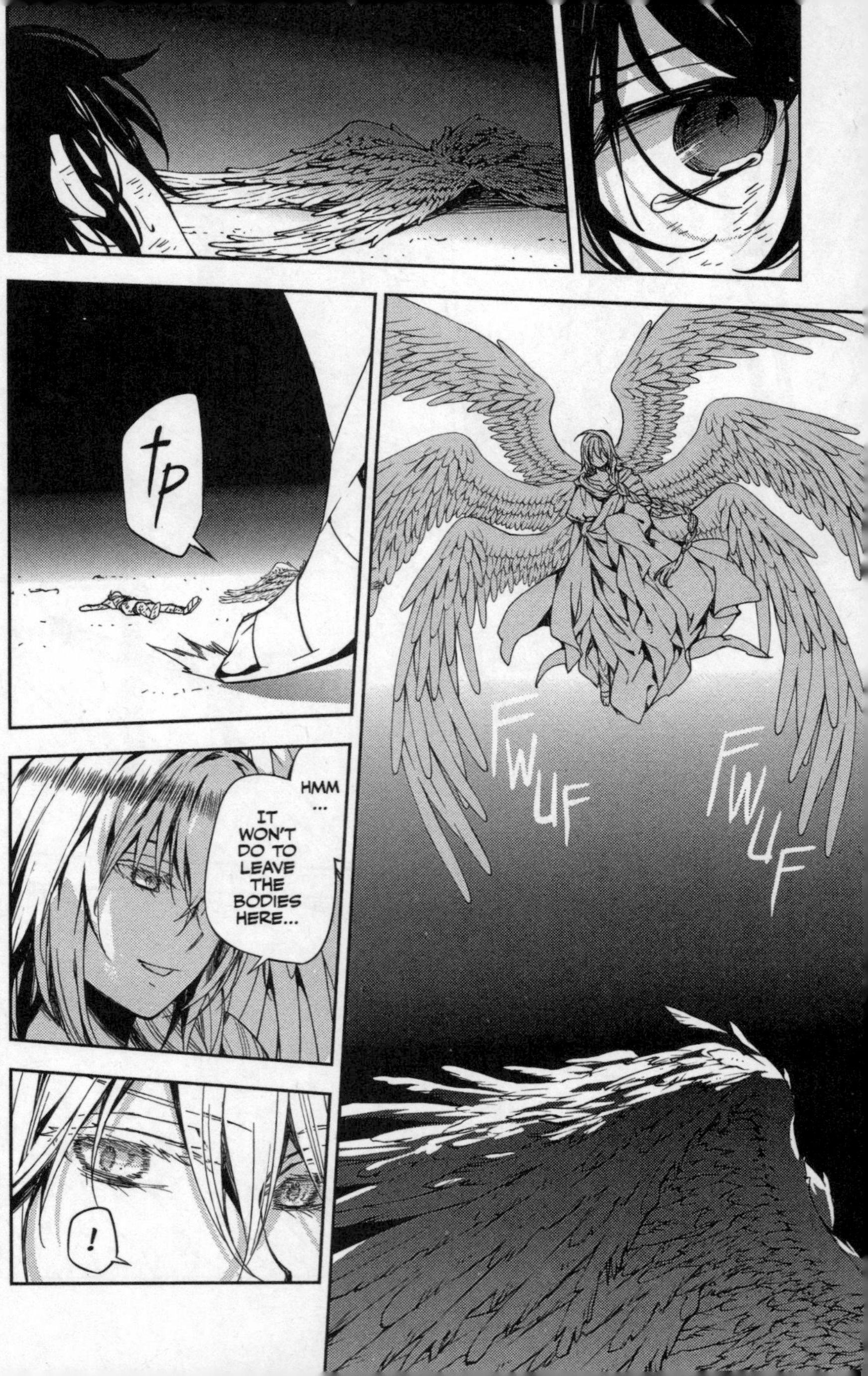
FWUF
FWUF
tp
HMM...
IT WON'T DO TO LEAVE THE BODIES HERE...
!

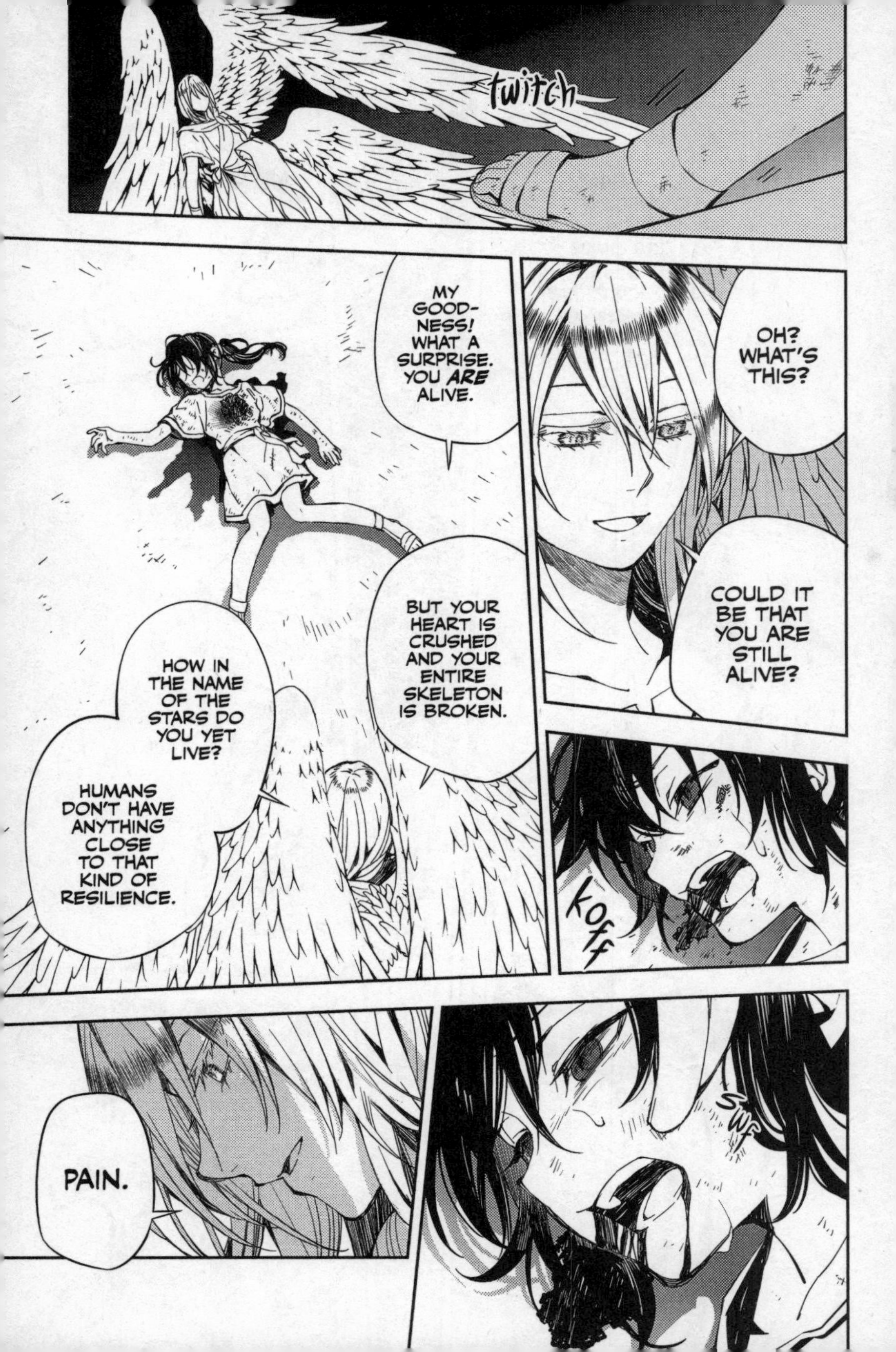

twitch
OH? WHAT'S THIS?
COULD IT BE THAT YOU ARE STILL ALIVE?
koff
MY GOODNESS! WHAT A SURPRISE. YOU *ARE* ALIVE.
BUT YOUR HEART IS CRUSHED AND YOUR ENTIRE SKELETON IS BROKEN.
HOW IN THE NAME OF THE STARS DO YOU YET LIVE?
HUMANS DON'T HAVE ANYTHING CLOSE TO THAT KIND OF RESILIENCE.
PAIN.

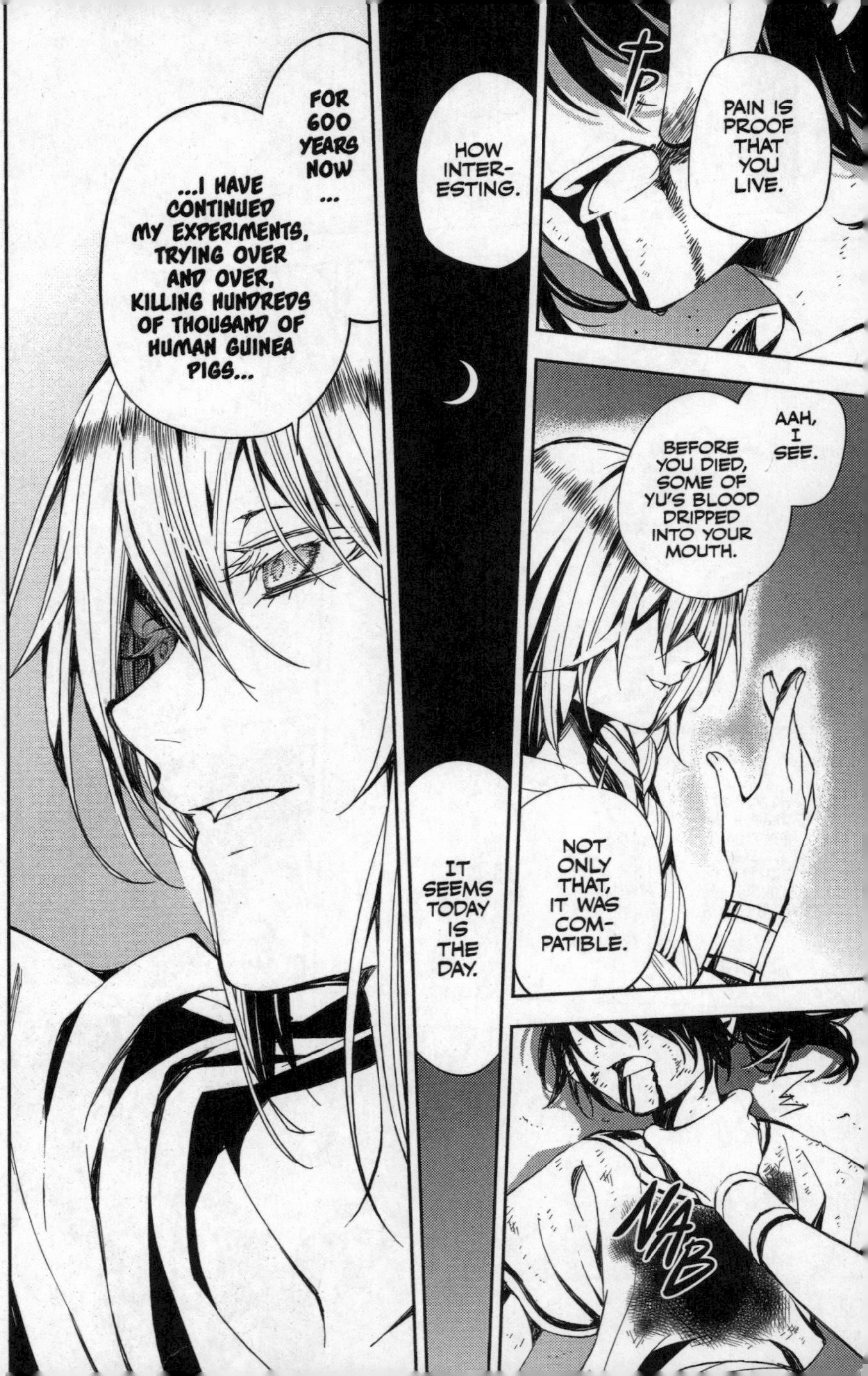
PAIN IS PROOF THAT YOU LIVE.
HOW INTERESTING.
AAH, I SEE.
BEFORE YOU DIED, SOME OF YU'S BLOOD DRIPPED INTO YOUR MOUTH.
NOT ONLY THAT, IT WAS COMPATIBLE.
NAB
FOR 600 YEARS NOW...
...I HAVE CONTINUED MY EXPERIMENTS, TRYING OVER AND OVER, KILLING HUNDREDS OF THOUSAND OF HUMAN GUINEA PIGS...
IT SEEMS TODAY IS THE DAY.

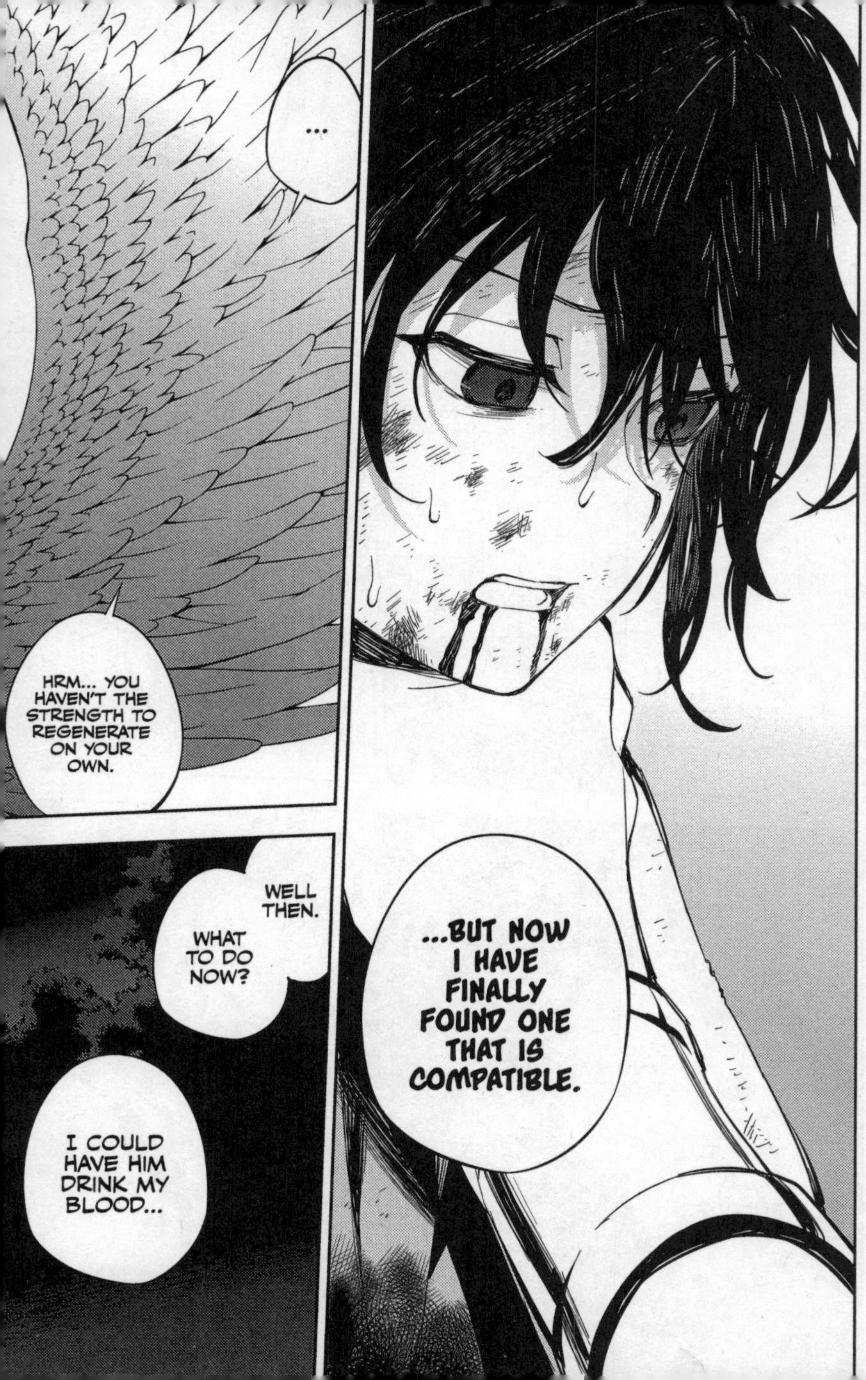
...BUT NOW I HAVE FINALLY FOUND ONE THAT IS COMPATIBLE.
...
HRM... YOU HAVEN'T THE STRENGTH TO REGENERATE ON YOUR OWN.
WELL THEN.
WHAT TO DO NOW?
I COULD HAVE HIM DRINK MY BLOOD...

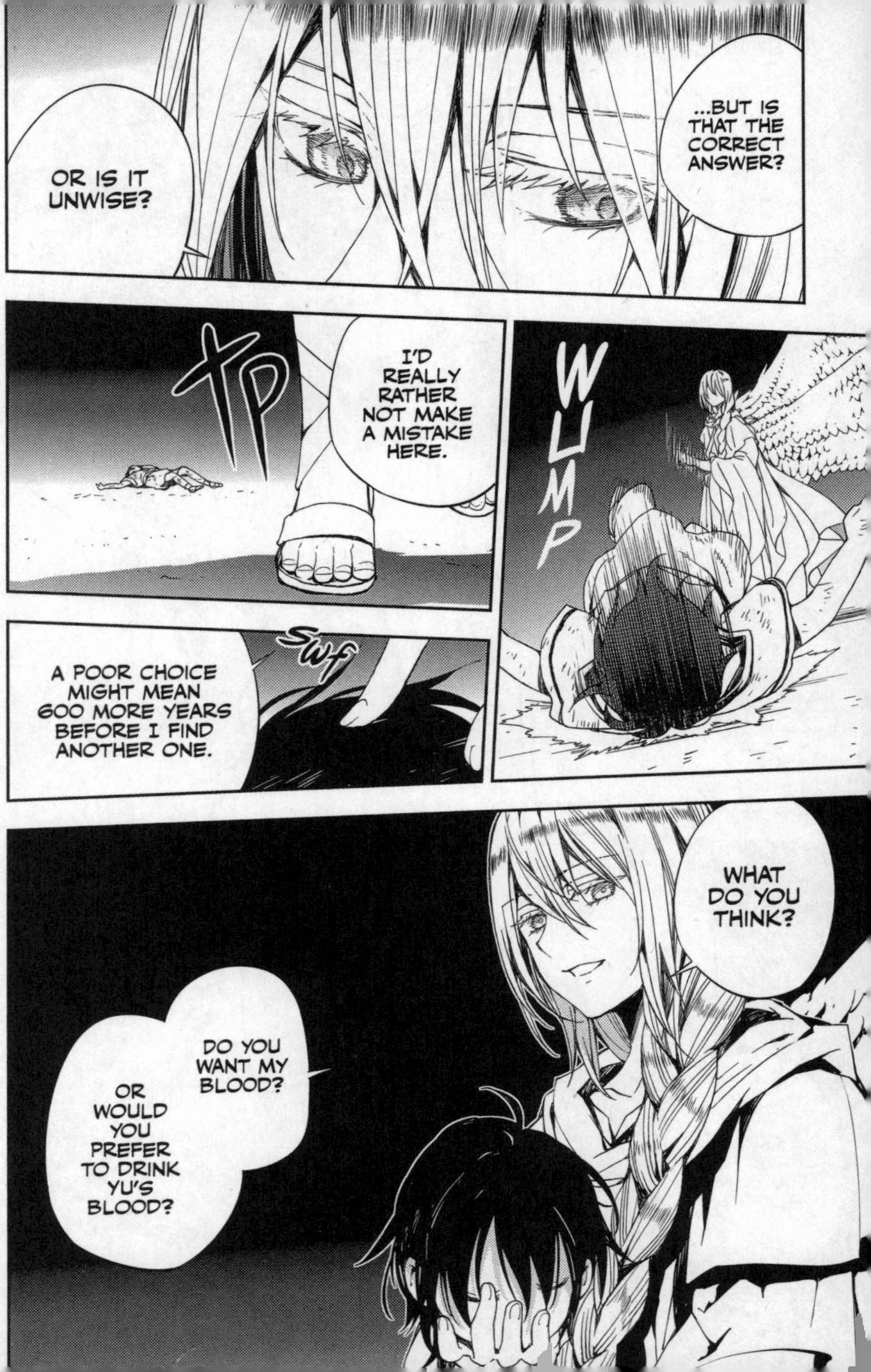
...BUT IS THAT THE CORRECT ANSWER?
OR IS IT UNWISE?
WUMP
TP
I'D REALLY RATHER NOT MAKE A MISTAKE HERE.
SWF
A POOR CHOICE MIGHT MEAN 600 MORE YEARS BEFORE I FIND ANOTHER ONE.
WHAT DO YOU THINK?
DO YOU WANT MY BLOOD?
OR WOULD YOU PREFER TO DRINK YU'S BLOOD?

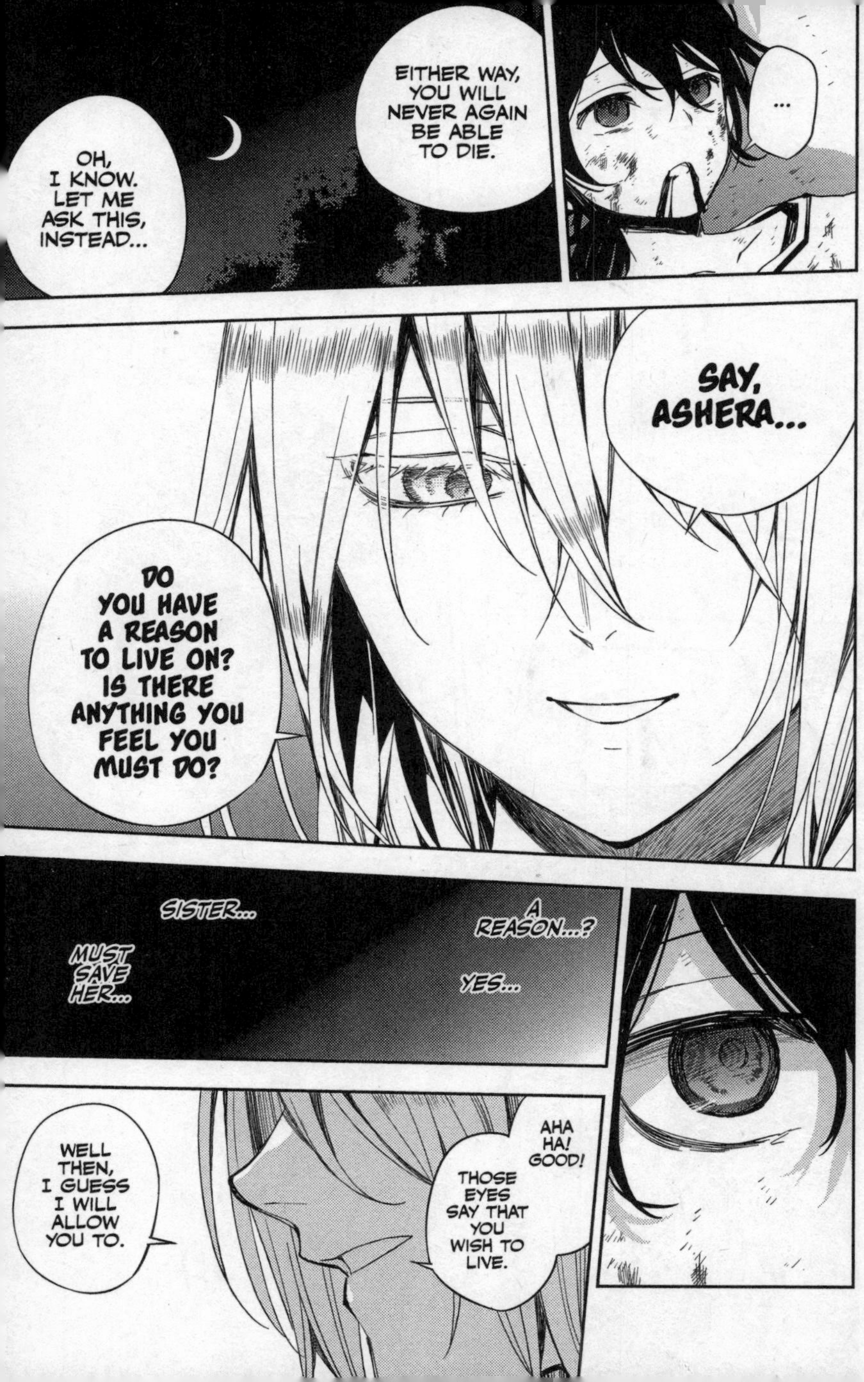
...
EITHER WAY, YOU WILL NEVER AGAIN BE ABLE TO DIE.
OH, I KNOW. LET ME ASK THIS, INSTEAD...
SAY, ASHERA...
DO YOU HAVE A REASON TO LIVE ON? IS THERE ANYTHING YOU FEEL YOU MUST DO?
A REASON...?
YES...
SISTER...
MUST SAVE HER...
AHA HA! GOOD!
THOSE EYES SAY THAT YOU WISH TO LIVE.
WELL THEN, I GUESS I WILL ALLOW YOU TO.

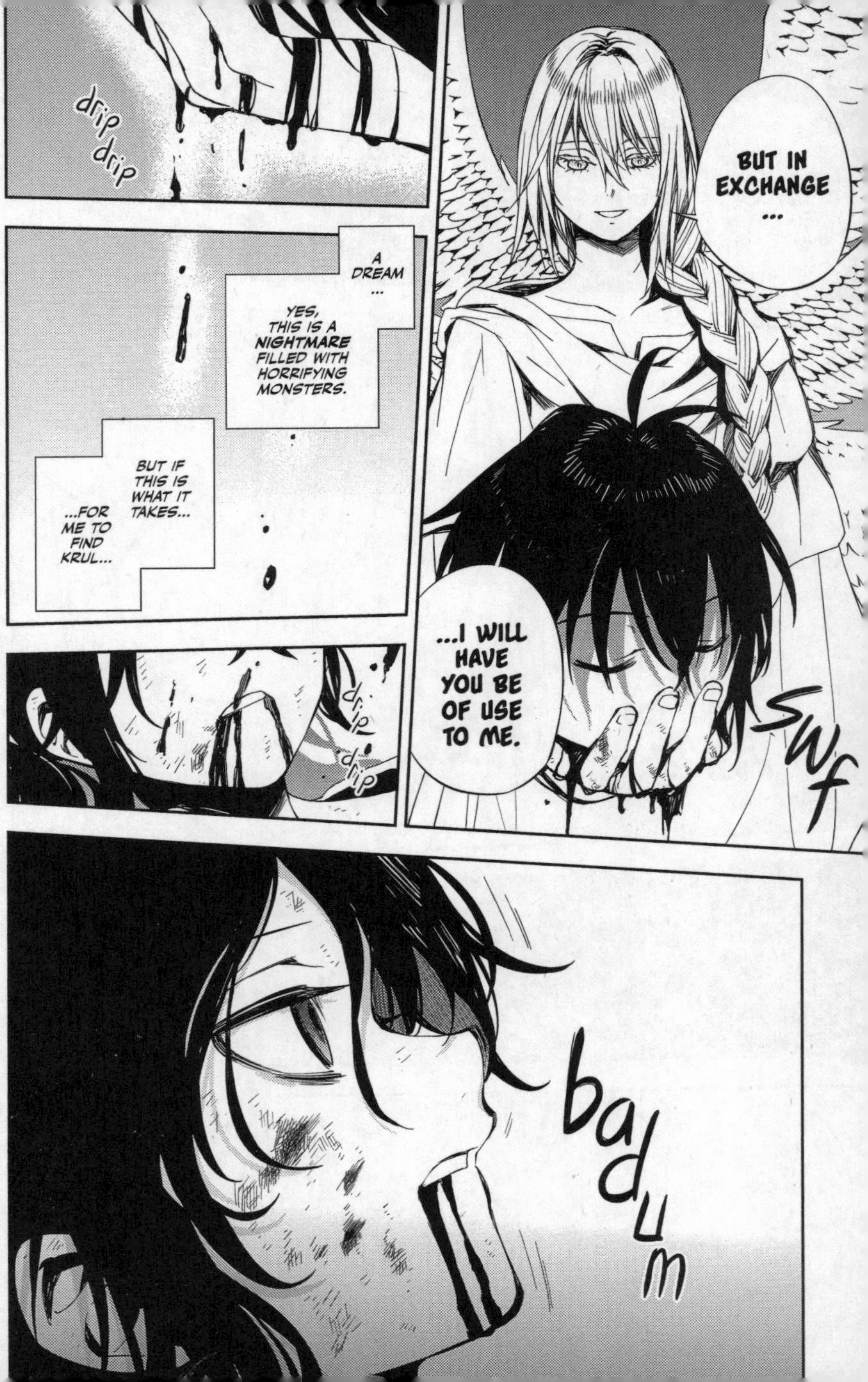
BUT IN EXCHANGE ...
...I WILL HAVE YOU BE OF USE TO ME.
SWF
drip drip
A DREAM ...
YES, THIS IS A NIGHTMARE FILLED WITH HORRIFYING MONSTERS.
BUT IF THIS IS WHAT IT TAKES...
...FOR ME TO FIND KRUL...
drip drip
badum

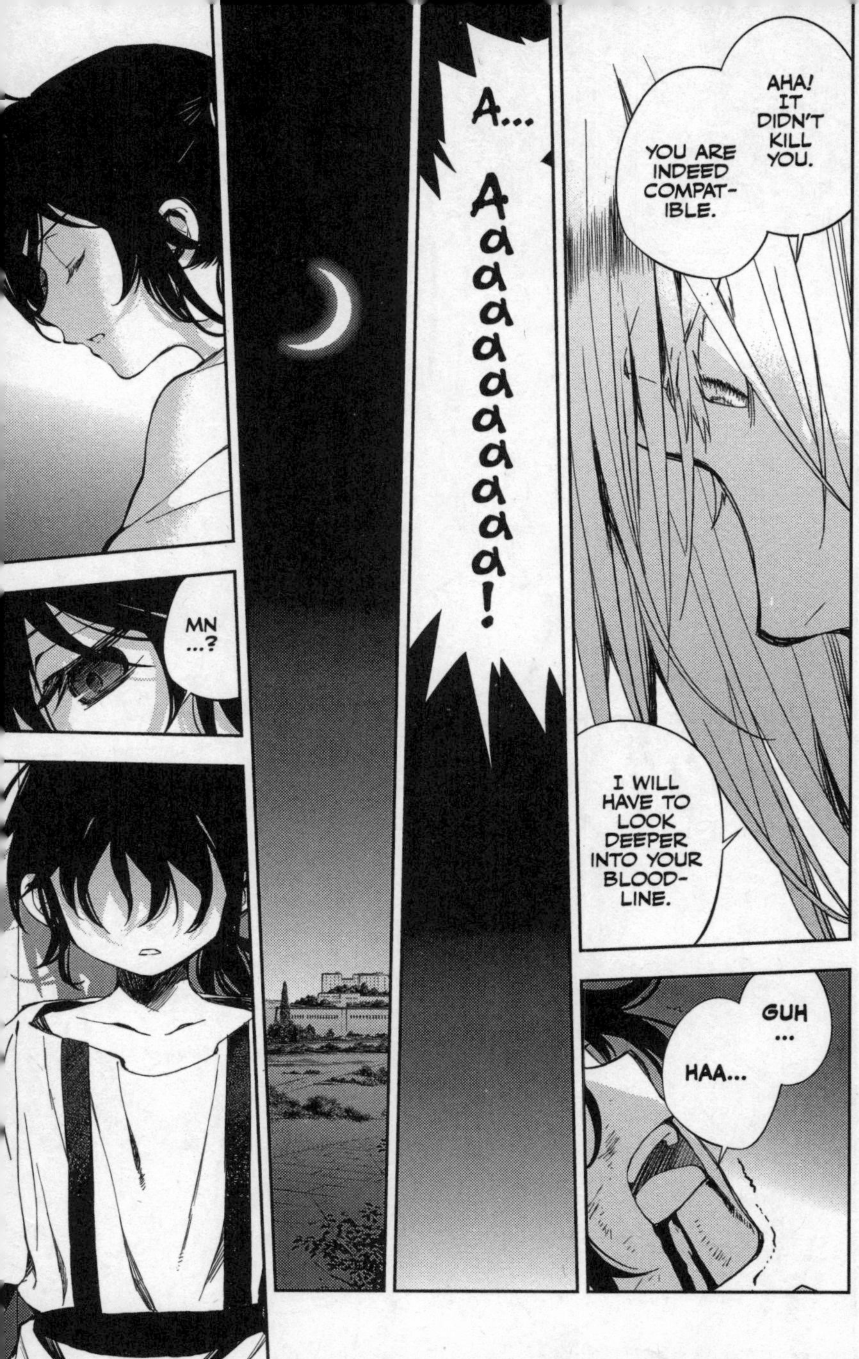
AHA! IT DIDN'T KILL YOU.
YOU ARE INDEED COMPAT-IBLE.
I WILL HAVE TO LOOK DEEPER INTO YOUR BLOOD-LINE.
GUH ... HAA...
A... Aaaaaaaaaaa!
MN ...?

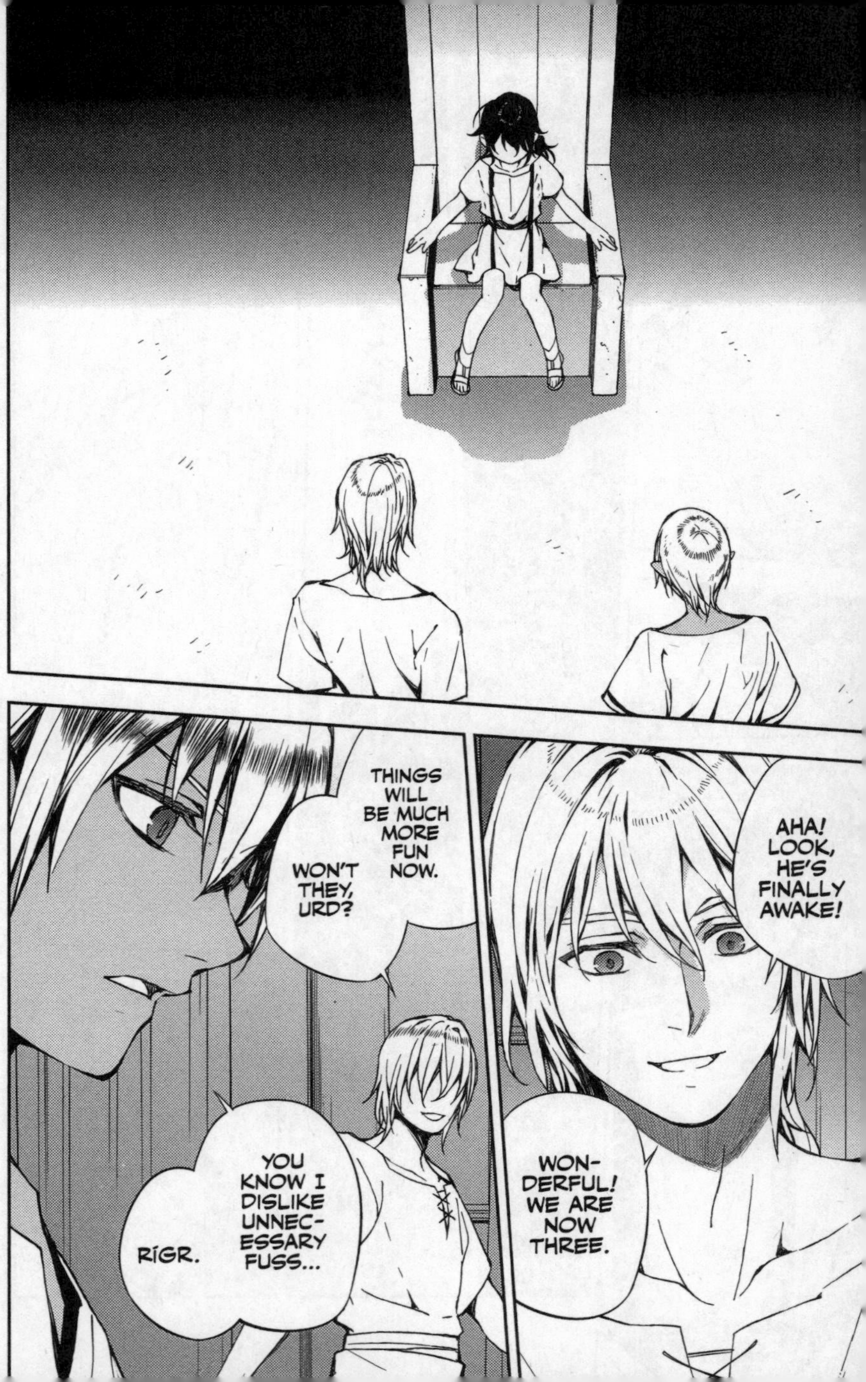
AHA! LOOK, HE'S FINALLY AWAKE!
WONDERFUL! WE ARE NOW THREE.
THINGS WILL BE MUCH MORE FUN NOW.
WON'T THEY, URD?
YOU KNOW I DISLIKE UNNECESSARY FUSS...
RÍGR.

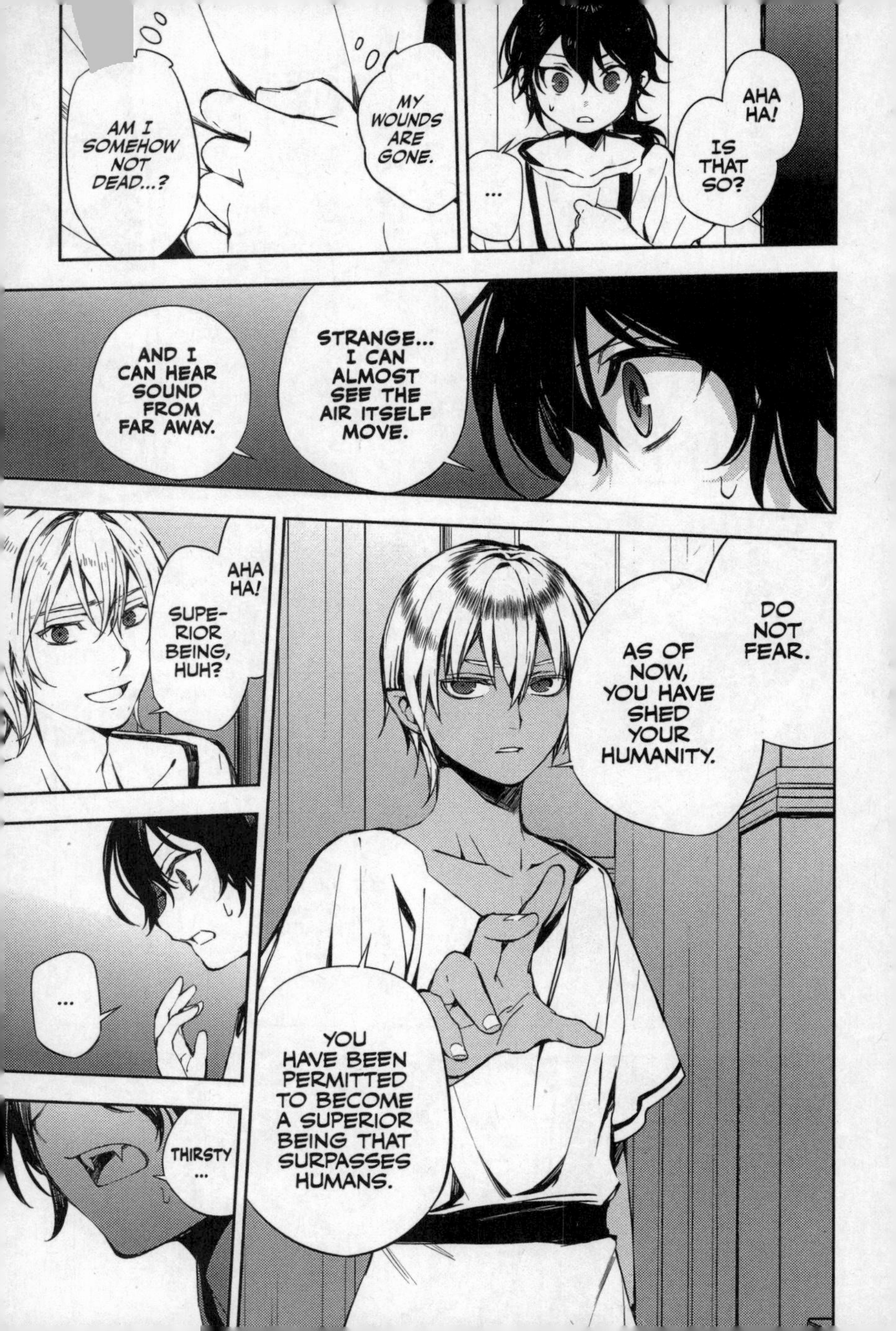
AHA HA! IS THAT SO?
...
MY WOUNDS ARE GONE.
AM I SOMEHOW NOT DEAD...?
STRANGE... I CAN ALMOST SEE THE AIR ITSELF MOVE.
AND I CAN HEAR SOUND FROM FAR AWAY.
DO NOT FEAR.
AS OF NOW, YOU HAVE SHED YOUR HUMANITY.
YOU HAVE BEEN PERMITTED TO BECOME A SUPERIOR BEING THAT SURPASSES HUMANS.
AHA HA! SUPERIOR BEING, HUH?
...
THIRSTY...

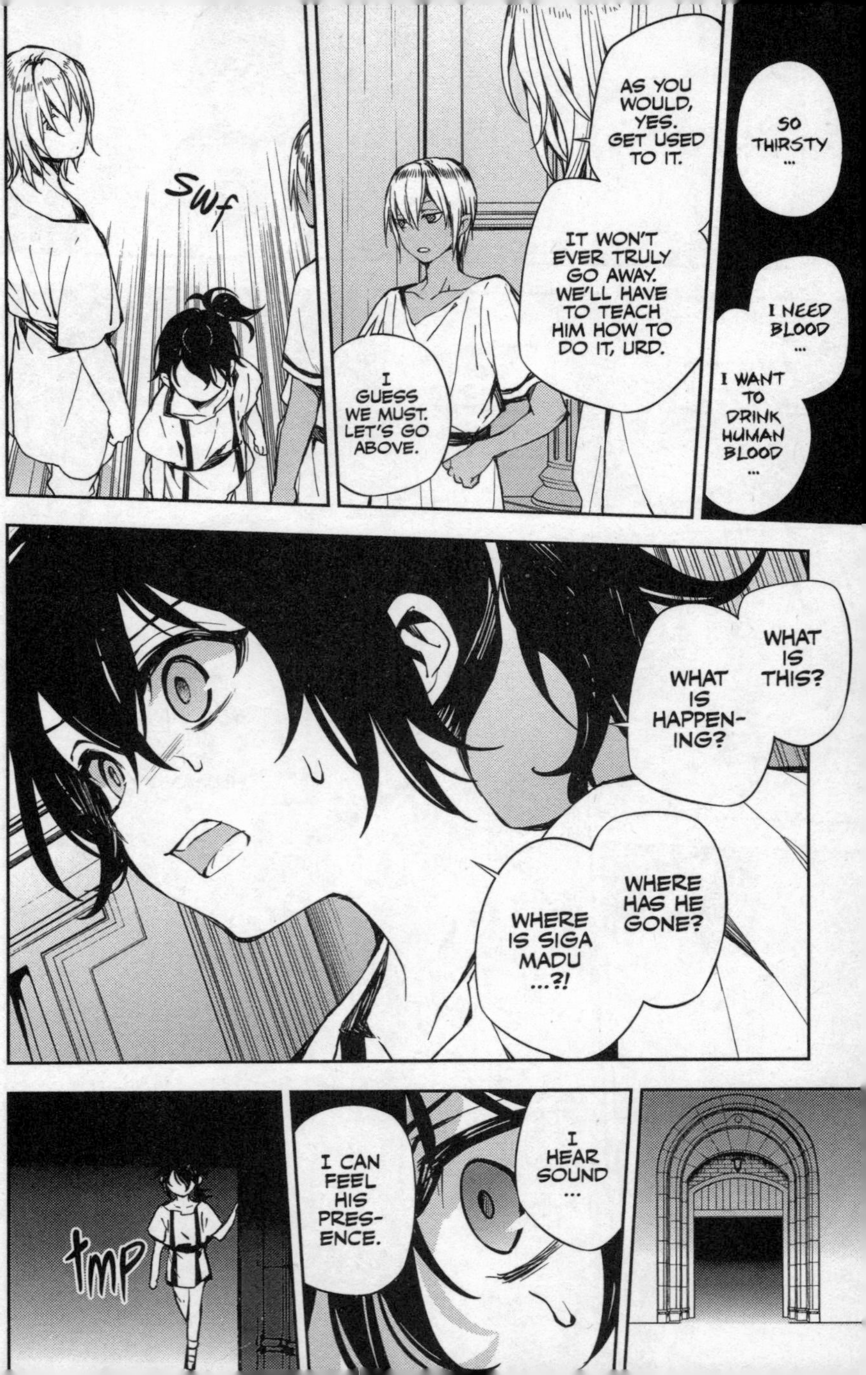
SO THIRSTY ...
I NEED BLOOD ...
I WANT TO DRINK HUMAN BLOOD ...
AS YOU WOULD, YES. GET USED TO IT.
IT WON'T EVER TRULY GO AWAY. WE'LL HAVE TO TEACH HIM HOW TO DO IT, URD.
I GUESS WE MUST. LET'S GO ABOVE.
SWF
WHAT IS THIS?
WHAT IS HAPPENING?
WHERE HAS HE GONE?
WHERE IS SIGA MADU ...?!
I HEAR SOUND ...
I CAN FEEL HIS PRESENCE.
TMP

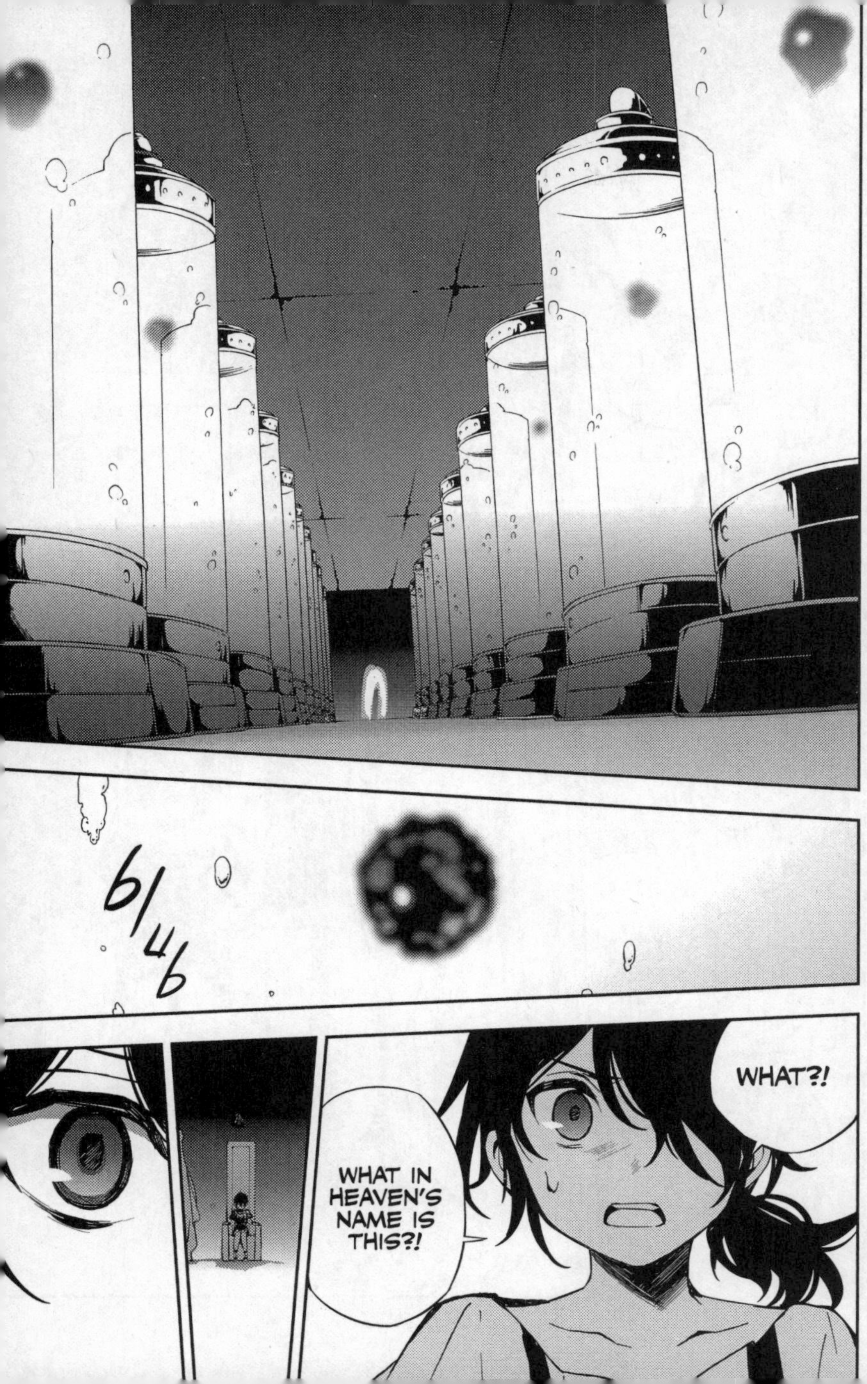
blub
WHAT?!
WHAT IN HEAVEN'S NAME IS THIS?!

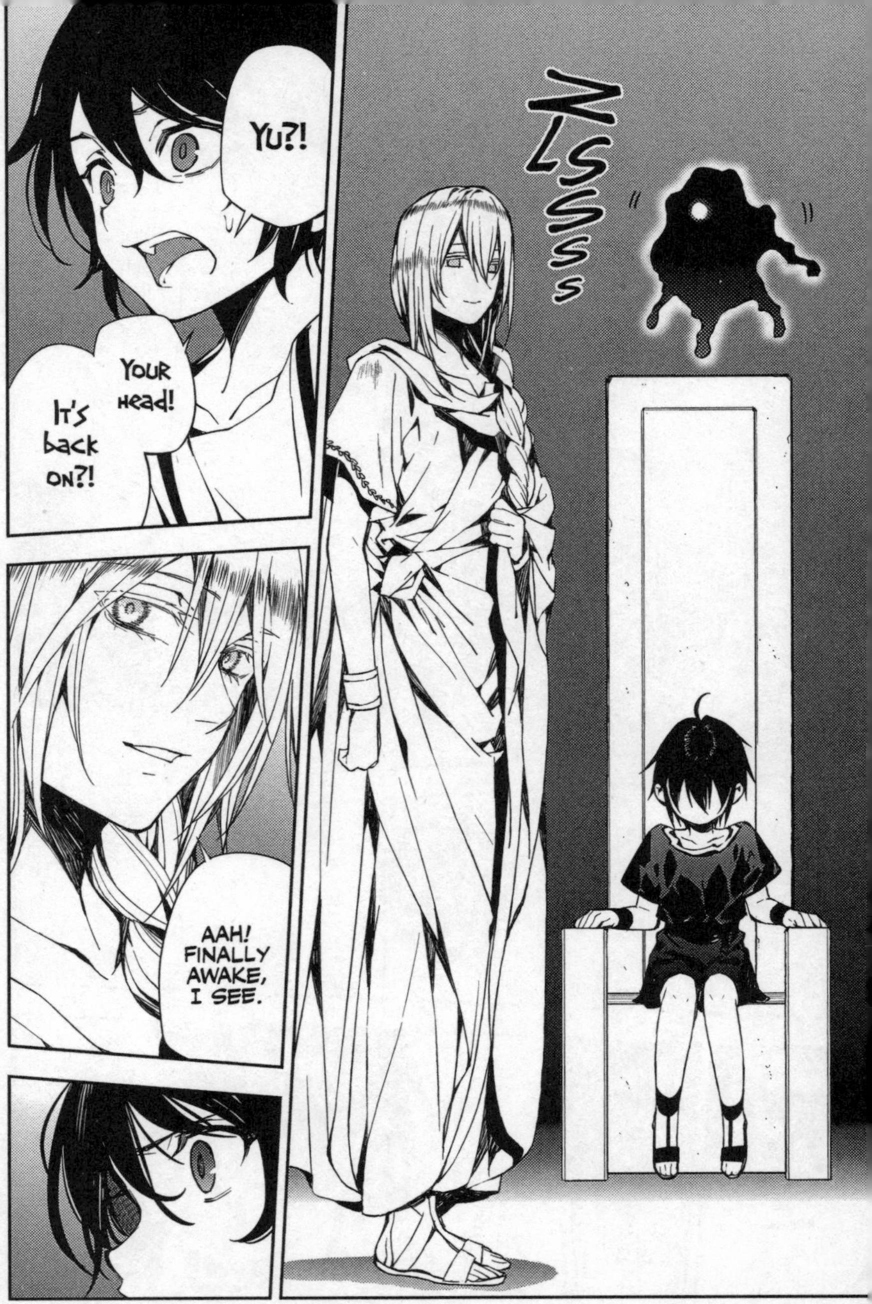
ZSSSSS
YU?!
YOUR HEAD!
IT'S BACK ON?!
AAH! FINALLY AWAKE, I SEE.

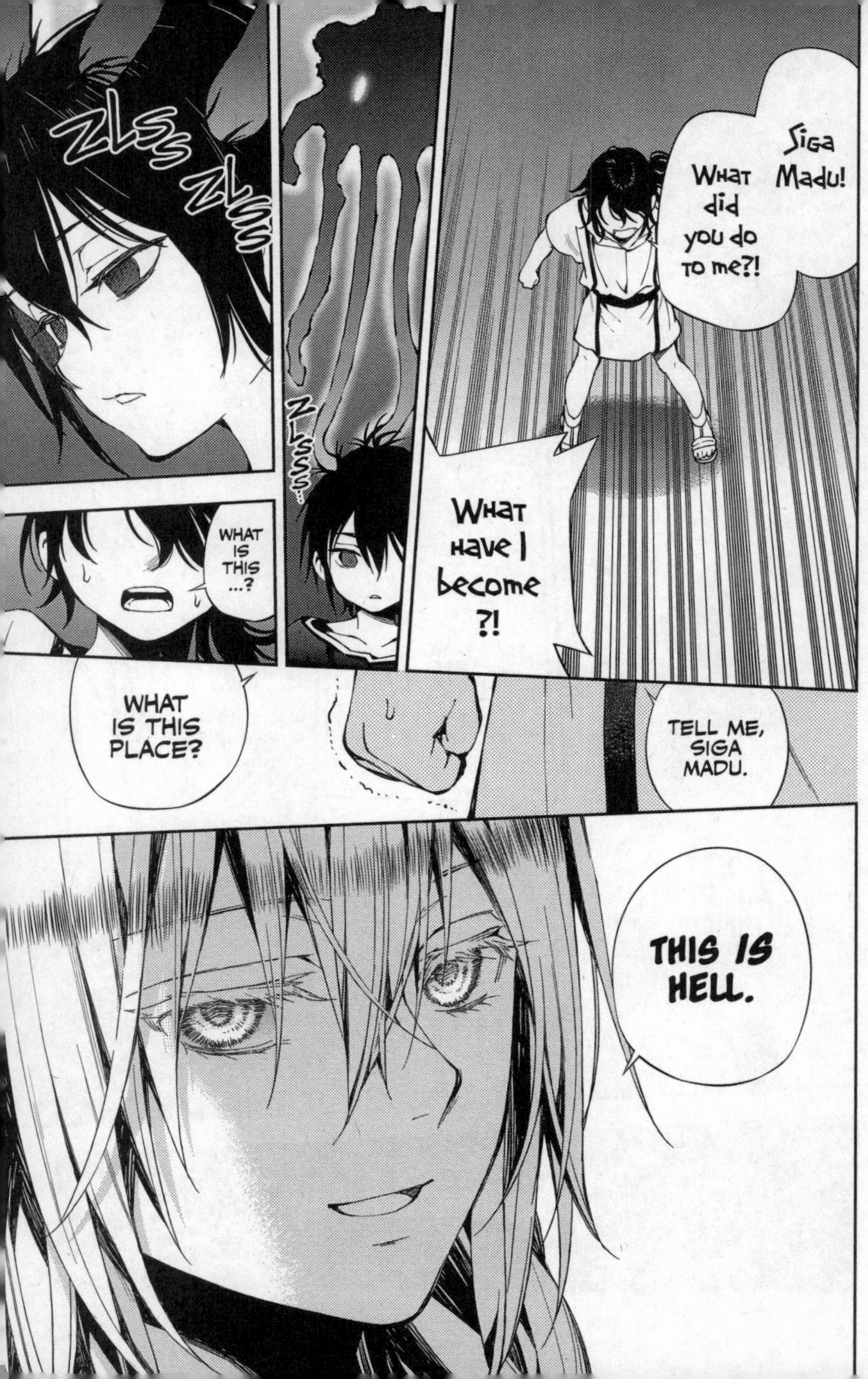
Siga Madu!
What did you do to me?!
What have I become?!
ZLSSS...
ZLSS ZLSS
WHAT IS THIS ...?
TELL ME, SIGA MADU.
WHAT IS THIS PLACE?
THIS IS HELL.

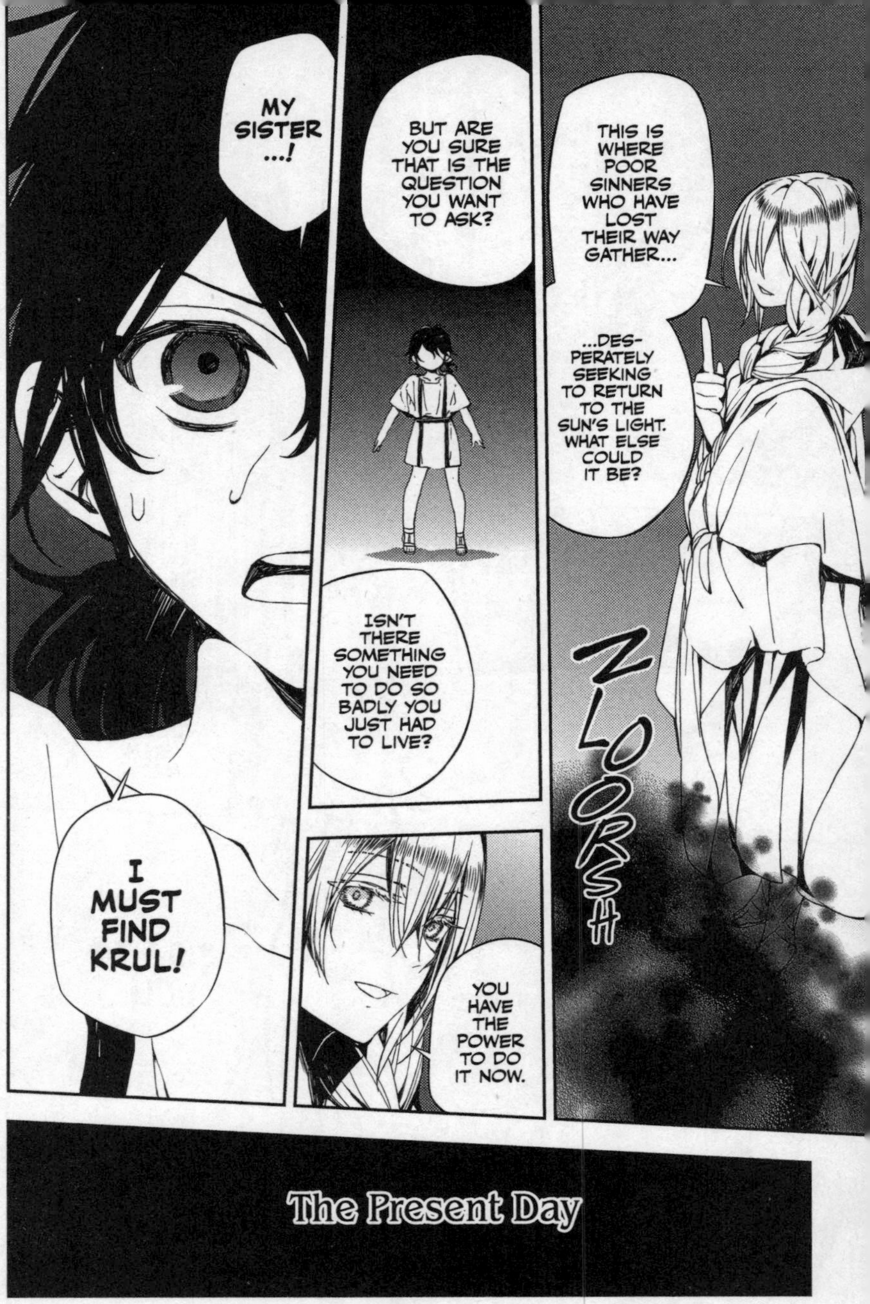
THIS IS WHERE POOR SINNERS WHO HAVE LOST THEIR WAY GATHER...
...DES-PERATELY SEEKING TO RETURN TO THE SUN'S LIGHT. WHAT ELSE COULD IT BE?
ZLOORSH
BUT ARE YOU SURE THAT IS THE QUESTION YOU WANT TO ASK?
ISN'T THERE SOMETHING YOU NEED TO DO SO BADLY YOU JUST HAD TO LIVE?
YOU HAVE THE POWER TO DO IT NOW.
MY SISTER ...!
I MUST FIND KRUL!
The Present Day

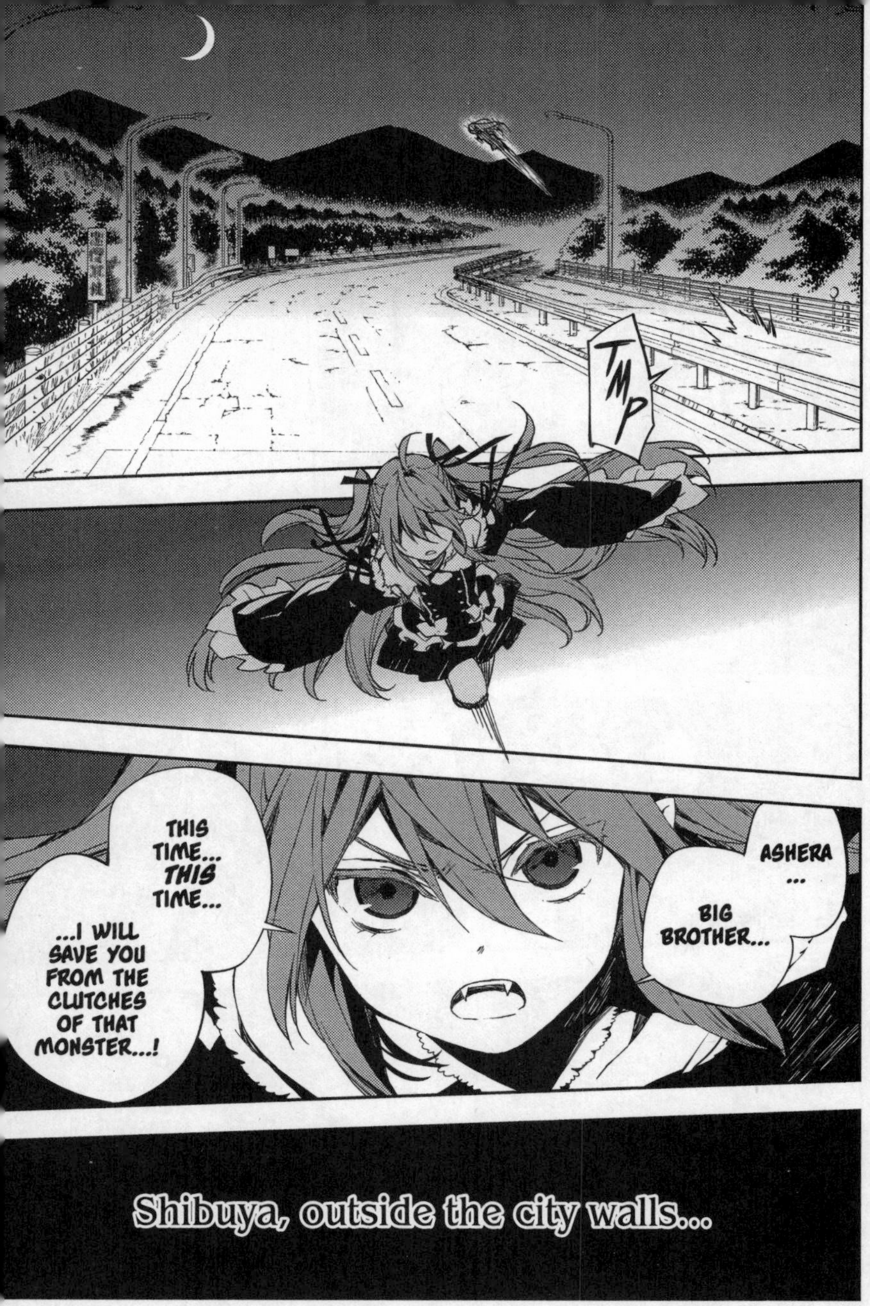
TMP
ASHERA... BIG BROTHER...
THIS TIME... THIS TIME...
...I WILL SAVE YOU FROM THE CLUTCHES OF THAT MONSTER...!
Shibuya, outside the city walls...

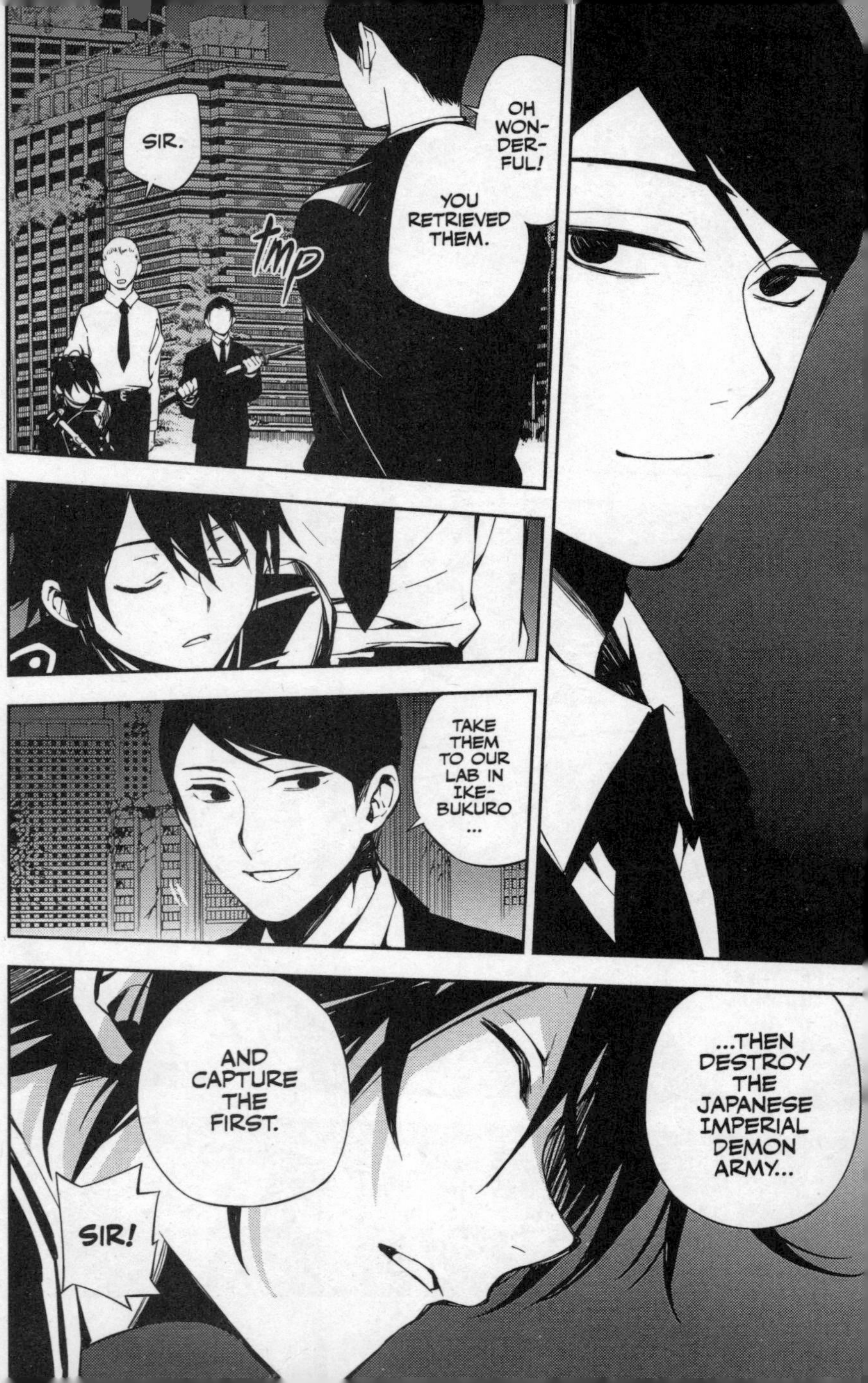
OH WONDERFUL!
YOU RETRIEVED THEM.
tmp
SIR.
TAKE THEM TO OUR LAB IN IKEBUKURO ...
...THEN DESTROY THE JAPANESE IMPERIAL DEMON ARMY...
AND CAPTURE THE FIRST.
SIR!

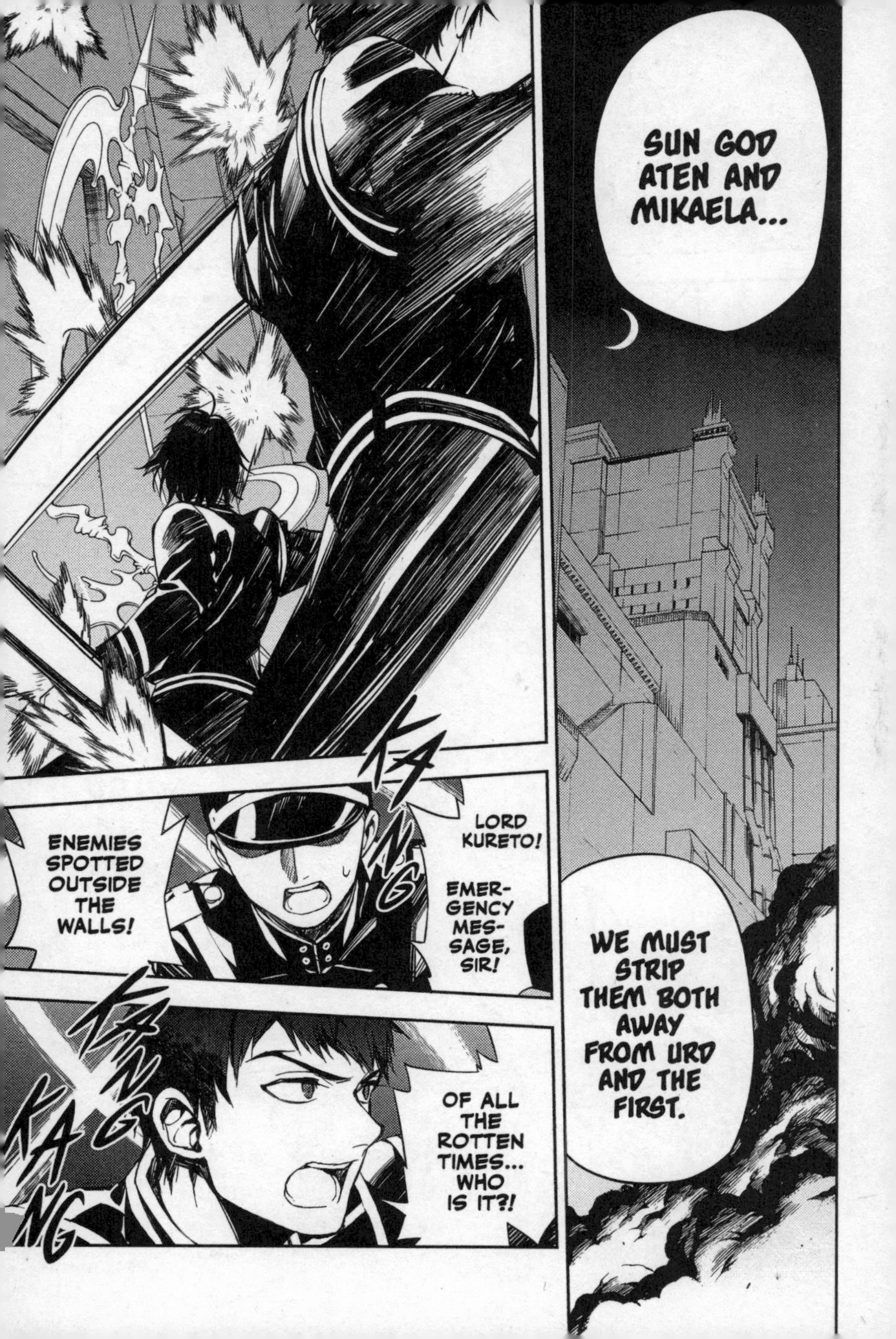
SUN GOD ATEN AND MIKAELA...
WE MUST STRIP THEM BOTH AWAY FROM URD AND THE FIRST.
KANG
LORD KURETO!
EMERGENCY MESSAGE, SIR!
ENEMIES SPOTTED OUTSIDE THE WALLS!
KANG
KANG
OF ALL THE ROTTEN TIMES... WHO IS IT?!

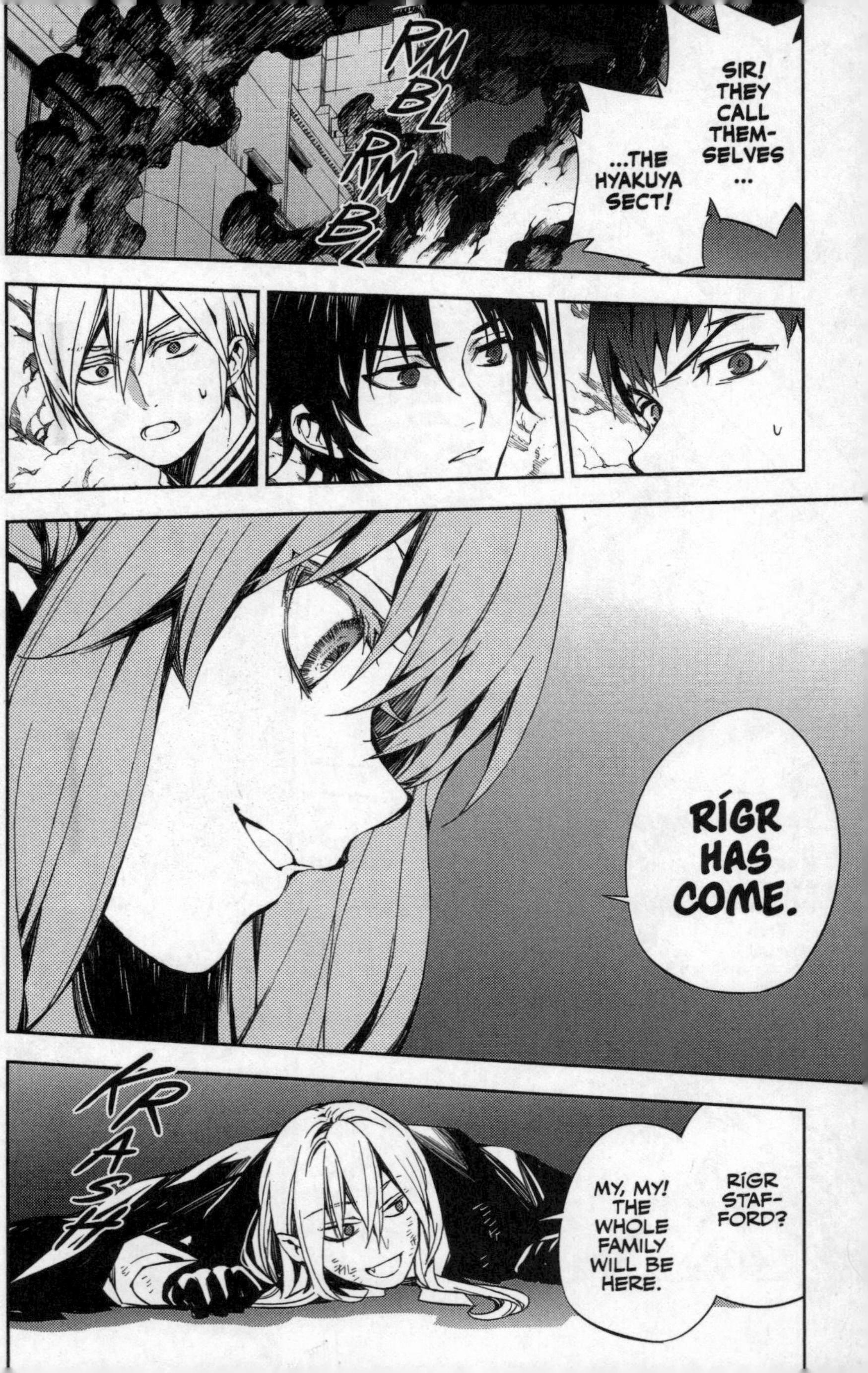
SIR! THEY CALL THEM-SELVES ...
...THE HYAKUYA SECT!
RMBL RMBL
RÍGR HAS COME.
RÍGR STAF-FORD?
MY, MY! THE WHOLE FAMILY WILL BE HERE.
KRASH

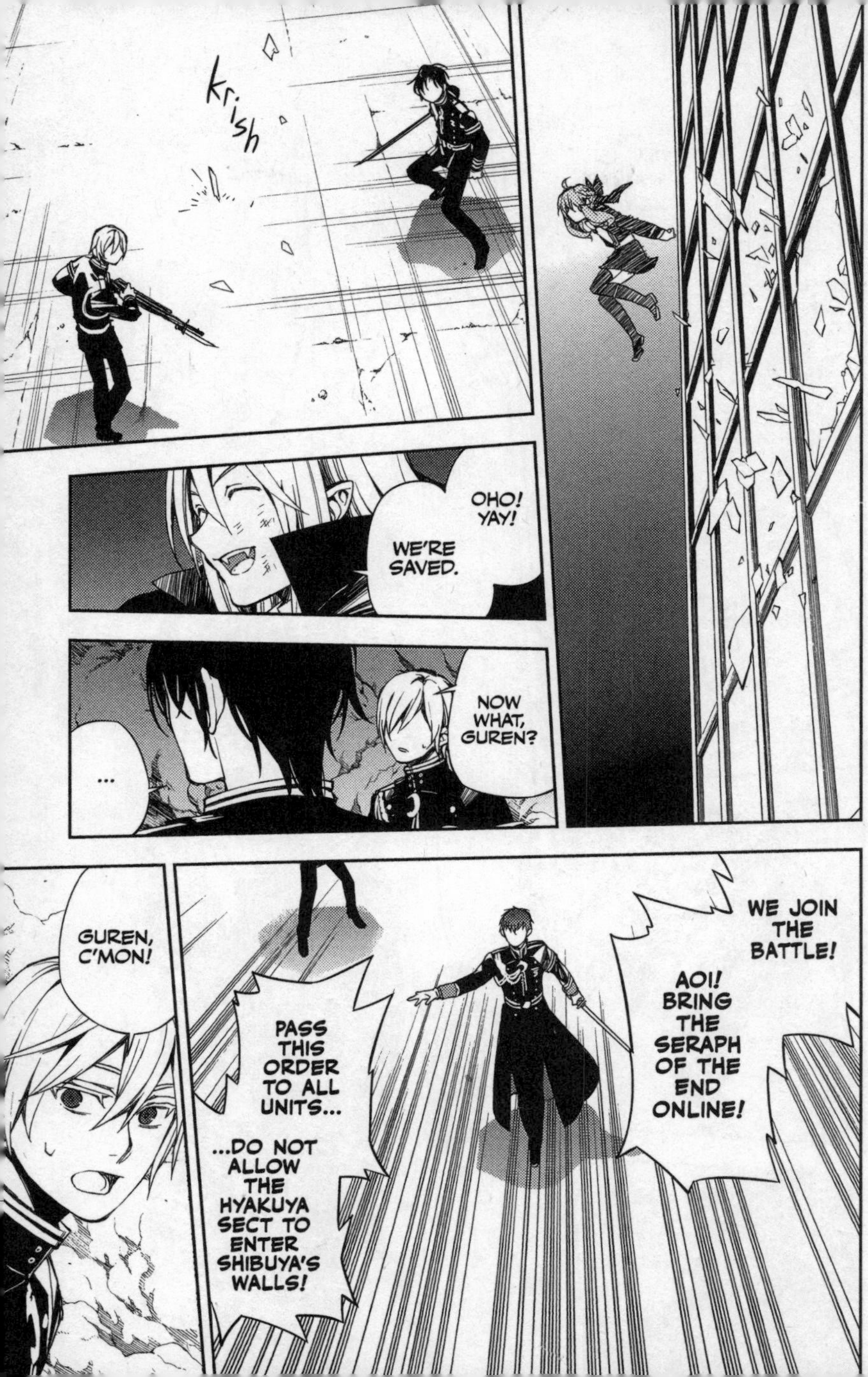
krish
OHO! YAY!
WE'RE SAVED.
NOW WHAT, GUREN?
...
WE JOIN THE BATTLE!
AOI! BRING THE SERAPH OF THE END ONLINE!
PASS THIS ORDER TO ALL UNITS...
...DO NOT ALLOW THE HYAKUYA SECT TO ENTER SHIBUYA'S WALLS!
GUREN, C'MON!

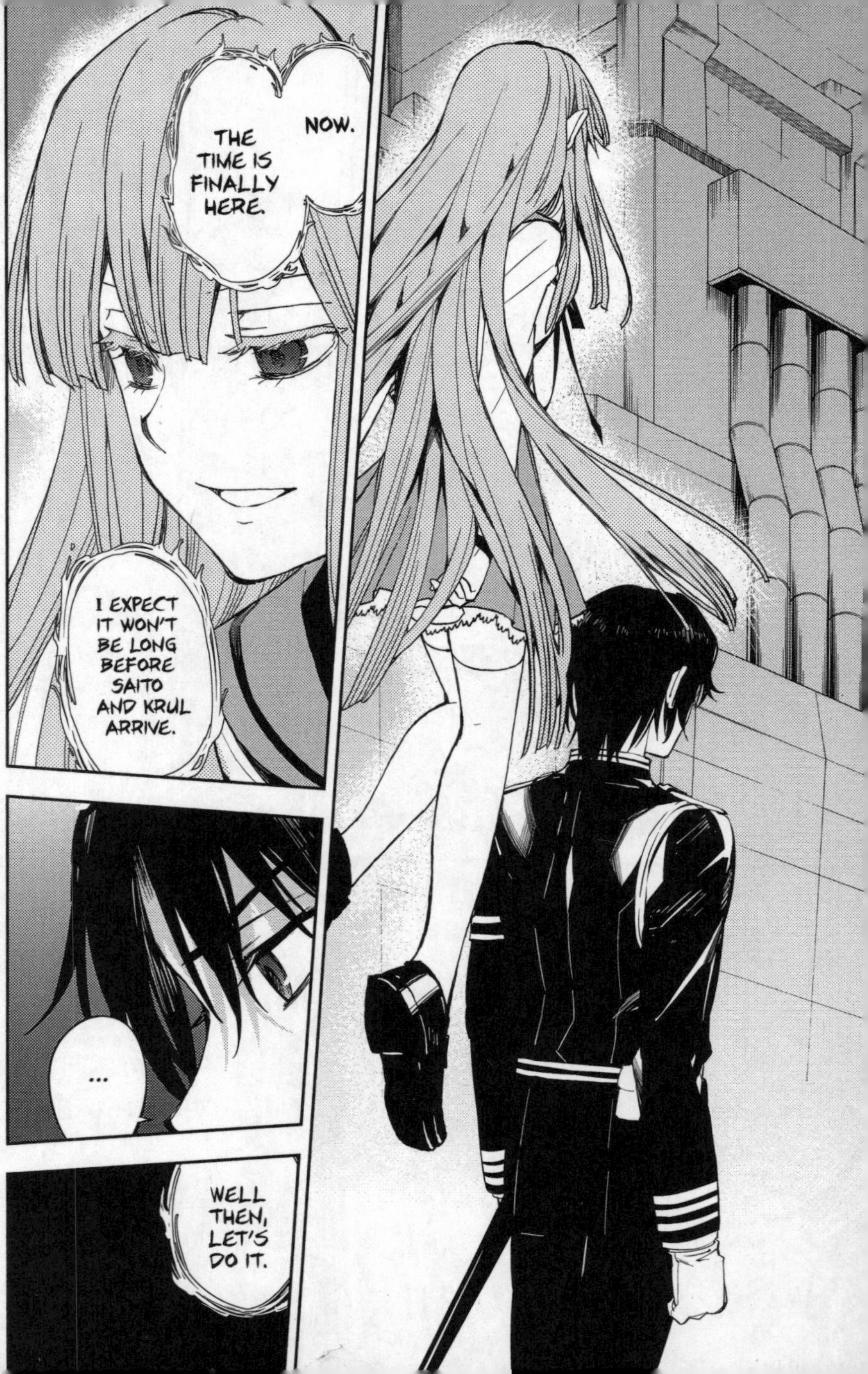
NOW.
THE TIME IS FINALLY HERE.
I EXPECT IT WON'T BE LONG BEFORE SAITO AND KRUL ARRIVE.
...
WELL THEN, LET'S DO IT.

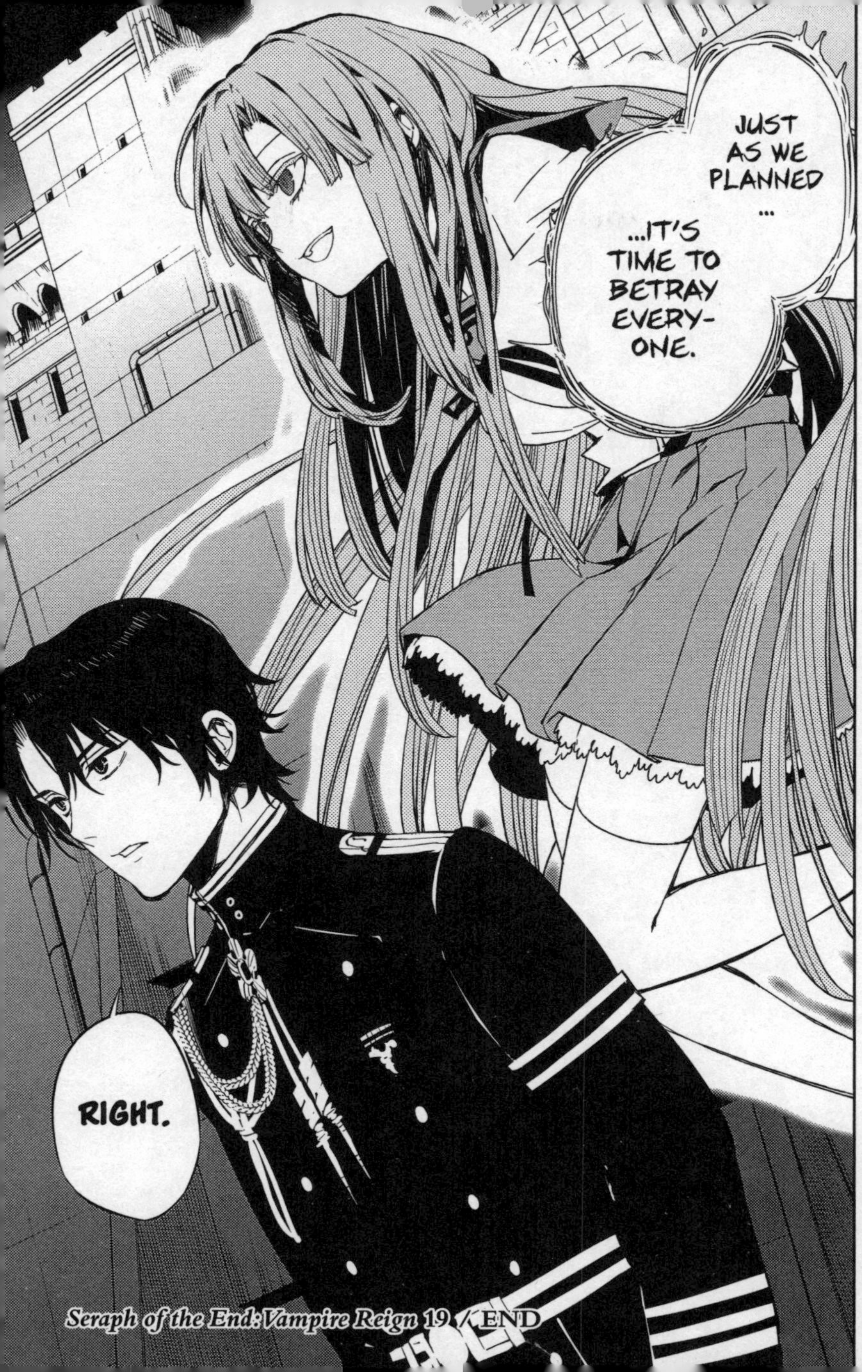
JUST AS WE PLANNED ...
...IT'S TIME TO BETRAY EVERY-ONE.
RIGHT.

Seraph of the End: Vampire Reign 19 / END

Seraph of the End

VAMPIRE REIGN

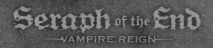

AFTERWORD

HELLO. I'M TAKAYA KAGAMI, THE WRITER OF THIS SERIES. SO
MUCH HAS BEEN HAPPENING LATELY THAT I FIND MYSELF LOOK-
ING BACK AND REFLECTING ON THINGS A LOT. ESPECIALLY LIFE
AND DEATH. NOT ONLY DOES WRITING *SERAPH OF THE END* MAKE
ME THINK ABOUT IT ALL THE TIME, I DO A LOT OF READING UP
ON HISTORY AND RELIGION, WHICH DEAL WITH THE SUBJECT
OFTEN AS WELL. I FIND IT TO BE A FASCINATING LESSON ON LIFE.

WITH THIS VOLUME THE OVERALL SCOPE OF EVENTS IS
REVEALED TO THE READER. EVEN WHILE WRITING THE NEWEST
CHAPTERS, I'M STILL DOING ALL THE STUDYING I CAN. PARTICU-
LARLY OF HISTORY. THE HIGHER RANK THE VAMPIRE PROGENITOR,
THE MORE HISTORY THEY'VE LIVED THROUGH, SO IT CAN GET
REALLY INTENSIVE. I READ HISTORY BOOKS. I WATCH HISTORY
MOVIES. I WATCH HISTORY VIDEOS ON MY PHONE WHILE I'M
SOAKING IN THE TUB. I TAKE WEB COURSES ON THE ERAS I'M
INTERESTED IN WHILE READING HISTORY REFERENCE MATERIALS.
I SHOUT TO THE SKY "HOW MANY ERAS DO I HAVE TO STUDY"
WHILE STUDYING HARDER THAN MOST COLLEGE HISTORY
MAJORS. (LOL)

ALL THAT ASIDE, LOTS OF THINGS HAVE BEEN GOING ON. JUST
LIKE THE GREAT JOYS AND TRAGEDIES ACROSS THE WORLD
ARE GENERALLY CONNECTED TO LIFE AND DEATH, SO IT HAS
BEEN FOR THE *SERAPH* TEAM. THERE HAVE BEEN EVENTS BOTH
OF JOY AND OF SORROW. BUT, I THINK TO MYSELF LOOKING
BACK AT HISTORY, THAT'S LIFE.

YU AND HIS FREINDS. GUREN AND HIS FRIENDS. THE VAMPIRES.
EVERYONE IS TRYING THEIR BEST TO LIVE, AND IT'S JUST GOING
TO GET MORE EXCITING FROM HERE. I HOPE YOU WILL ALL STICK
AROUND TO CHEER THEM ON.

RIGHT NOW, AS I'M WORKING ON THIS VERY AFTERWORD, I ALSO HAPPEN TO BE WORKING ON A SCRIPT FOR *SERAPH OF THE END: GUREN ICHINOSE: CATASTROPHE AT 16*—WHICH IS TYPICALLY PUBLISHED BY KODANSHA—THAT WILL MAKE AN APPEARANCE IN SHUEISHA'S MANGA ANTHOLOGY *JUMP SQ.* I EXPECT THERE WILL ALSO BE A CHARACTER POPULARITY POLL, TOO. WILL YOU ALL VOTE?

THINGS ARE GOING TO KEEP ESCALATING AND ESCALATING IN *SERAPH OF THE END* FROM HERE ON OUT. I HOPE YOU WILL ALL STICK AROUND TO THE END!

—TAKAYA KAGAMI

A brilliant sketch of Yuichiro by the author!

TAKAYA KAGAMI is a prolific light novelist whose works include the action and fantasy series *The Legend of the Legendary Heroes*, which has been adapted into manga, anime and a video game. His previous series, *A Dark Rabbit Has Seven Lives*, also spawned a manga and anime series.

66 Every year with summer comes the powerful urge to get out and ride a bicycle. By the time I work up the desire to buy one, it's already fall. Then winter arrives and I get over the whole thing. I have to wonder if it'll happen again this year too. 99

YAMATO YAMAMOTO, born 1983, is an artist and illustrator whose works include the *Kure-nai* manga and the light novels *Kure-nai*, *9S -Nine S-* and *Denpa Teki na Kanojo*. Both *Denpa Teki na Kanojo* and *Kure-nai* have been adapted into anime.

66 Shinoa has been turned into a vampire! What's going to happen next? Volume 19 dives deep into Yu and Ashera's history too. 99

DAISUKE FURUYA previously assisted Yamato Yamamoto with storyboards for *Kure-nai*.

Seraph of the End

—VAMPIRE REIGN—

VOLUME 19
SHONEN JUMP MANGA EDITION

STORY BY **TAKAYA KAGAMI**
ART BY **YAMATO YAMAMOTO**
STORYBOARDS BY **DAISUKE FURUYA**

TRANSLATION **Adrienne Beck**
TOUCH-UP ART & LETTERING **Sabrina Heep**
DESIGN **Shawn Carrico**
EDITOR **Marlene First**

OWARI NO SERAPH © 2012 by Takaya Kagami,
Yamato Yamamoto, Daisuke Furuya
All rights reserved. First published in Japan in 2012 by SHUEISHA Inc., Tokyo.
English translation rights arranged by SHUEISHA Inc.

The stories, characters and incidents mentioned in this
publication are entirely fictional.

Printed in the U.S.A.

Published by VIZ Media, LLC
P.O. Box 77010
San Francisco, CA 94107

10 9 8 7 6 5 4 3 2 1
First printing, July 2020

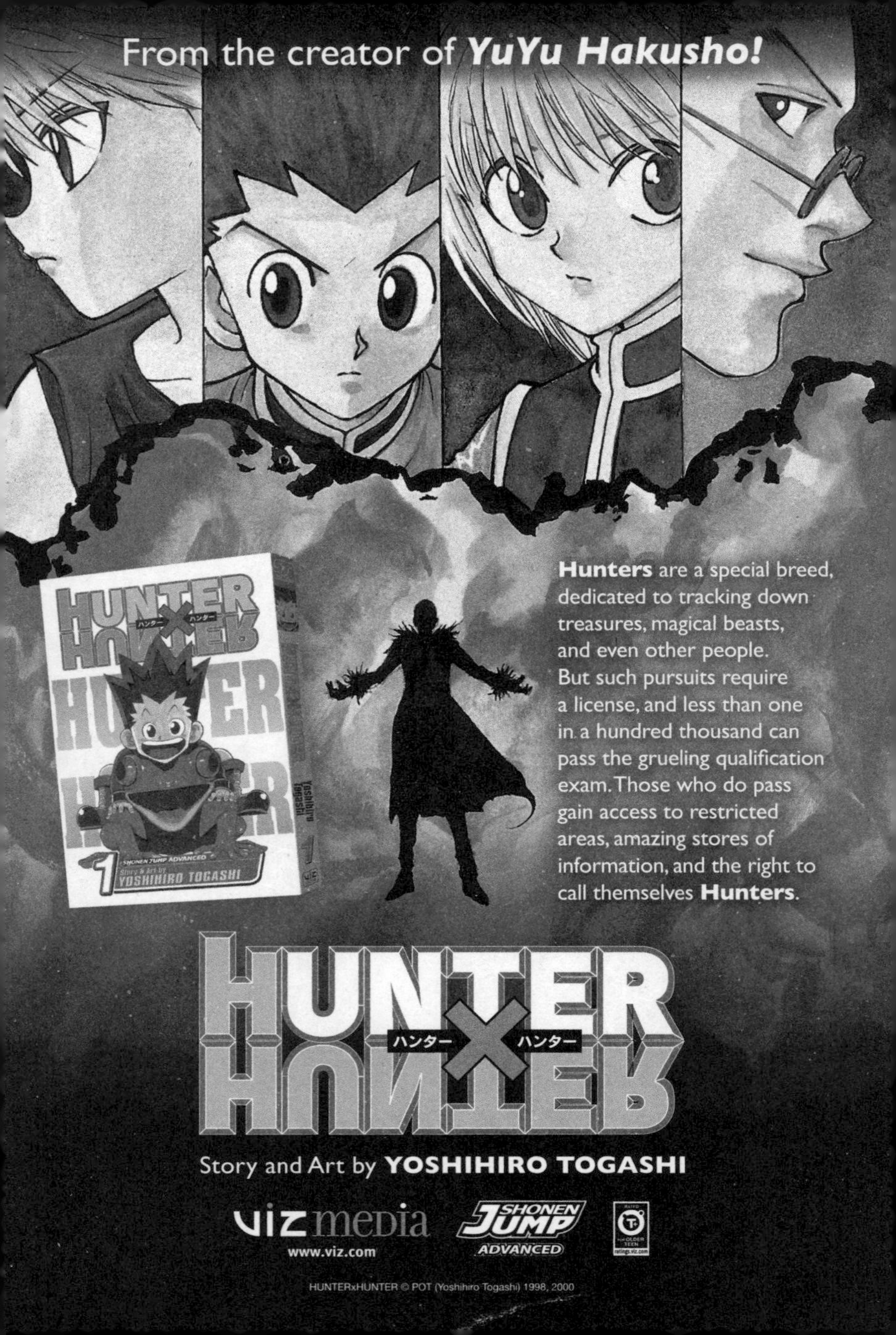
From the creator of *YuYu Hakusho!*
Hunters are a special breed, dedicated to tracking down treasures, magical beasts, and even other people. But such pursuits require a license, and less than one in a hundred thousand can pass the grueling qualification exam. Those who do pass gain access to restricted areas, amazing stores of information, and the right to call themselves **Hunters**.
HUNTER ハンター × ハンター HUNTER
Story and Art by YOSHIHIRO TOGASHI
viz media
www.viz.com
SHONEN JUMP ADVANCED
HUNTERxHUNTER © POT (Yoshihiro Togashi) 1998, 2000

Black ✦ Clover

STORY & ART BY YŪKI TABATA

Asta is a young boy who dreams of becoming the greatest mage in the kingdom. Only one problem—he can't use any magic! Luckily for Asta, he receives the incredibly rare five-leaf clover grimoire that gives him the power of anti-magic. Can someone who can't use magic really become the Wizard King? One thing's for sure—Asta will never give up!

YOU'RE READING THE WRONG WAY!

SERAPH OF THE END reads from right to left, starting in the upper-right corner. Japanese is read from right to left, meaning that action, sound effects, and word-balloon order are completely reversed from English order.

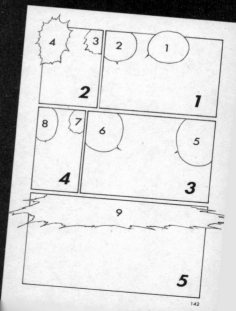